British Intelligence & Covert Action

British Intelligence and Covert Action

Africa, Middle East and Europe since 1945

Jonathan Bloch &
Patrick Fitzgerald

with an introduction by PHILIP AGEE

BRANDON

First published in Ireland 1983
Brandon Book Publishers Ltd
Dingle, Co. Kerry

Reprinted 1984

Cover design: Brendan Foreman
Typesetting: Leaders Phototypesetting, Swords, Ireland
Printed by Mount Salus Press, Dublin 4

Introduction

Among the many files I've acquired over the years is one I call 'Security Services – Britain.' The other day I took this folder from its cabinet in order to file recent newspaper and magazine cuttings on Geoffrey Prime, Hugh Hambleton and other darlings of London's 1982 spy-trial season. Once again I smiled with inner amusement. The file contained almost nothing on British secret operations. Rather, it was full of reports and cuttings about Soviet penetrations of British services, particularly its foreign intelligence agency known as MI6. It seemed that hardly a day had passed since World War II when the Russians did not have members of the British services reporting on those services' supposedly secret operations.

I was amused not because the Soviets had been able constantly to obtain Britain's most closely guarded secrets – and by extension many of America's as well. Rather, I felt satisfied that justice, however poetic, was being done. The British security establishment was getting its fair reward for all the years of cruel, nasty and downright dirty operations to protect its perceived interests, most often economic in nature, as the fabled Empire coughed, sputtered and tumbled into the grave.

I also recalled how, in the CIA in the 1960s, we used to howl with contempt on reading the shallow, sometimes pitiful, British reports that passed for 'intelligence' on Latin America. And, of course, knowing that Britain's security services were in part responsible for my having become something of an international pin ball in the late 1970s – what with various expulsions that began in Britain – their continuing tribulations gave sweet satisfaction.

No thoughtful reader, though, should expect satisfaction or amusement from this book. It is a tale of terror, murder, bribery, cheating, lying and torture, which have been practised in varying combinations from Malaya in the early 1950s to Ireland in the 1980s. In between, as colony after colony became independent, the British security services were there trying to install local regimes that would protect the interests of British companies, often in tandem with the CIA under the banner of the 'crusade against communism.'

When it comes to British imperialism, and its post-World War II partnership with the United States, I profess no even-handedness. My earliest political memory must be my mother's indelible hatred of British repression in Ireland – among Irish-Americans she was no exception. Yet years later I was in dire need to use that most hallowed of British institutions, the British Museum, for research on my memoirs of CIA operations.

Many times in the ten years since arriving in Britain to carry out my research I have wondered why British governments, both Tory and Labour, had allowed me to continue, finish and publish what until then was an unthinkable revelation of the CIA's secret operations and agents – a work the Agency itself would describe in its secret house journal, *Studies in Intelligence*, as a 'severe body blow.' I still don't have the answer.

There was, of course, intimidation by teams of people following me around London streets, as had occurred in Paris, but still I could work. Then just as I had finished the book in mid-1974 the smears began. Sensational stories originating with unidentified 'government sources' in the US and repeated throughout the world alleged falsely that I had already 'told all' to the KGB. Such stories, planted no doubt by the CIA and its allies, have continued without respite to this very day – sometimes consisting of reruns purporting to be new revelations. As the accuracy of what I have written and said over the years can't be challenged, their only recourse has been continual slander. To be sure, it was not unexpected.

Yet by early 1975, when the book came out, there was still no way to explain why British authorities had failed to prevent my use of British research facilities and a British publisher. No less mysterious was the seeming acquiescence in Britain to my continuous travels in and out of the country for lectures, political rallies, press conferences, film and television projects – all dedicated to focusing sharp attention on the CIA's presence and activities throughout Western Europe, Canada and Latin America.

But in September 1976 came an invitation from the Jamaican Commission for Human Rights. I accepted, and began to study the many allegations then current that the CIA was behind a campaign of terrorism and propaganda to turn people against the social-democratic government of Michael Manley which faced elections in a few months' time. Then in Jamaica I learned in much more detail the many ways in which the government was being undermined.

At public rallies in Kingston and Montego Bay, and in media interviews, I agreed with the charges of CIA destabilisation, recognising that they couldn't be proved outright, but showing parallels with similar operations from the period when I was in the Agency. By then everyone had also studied the Senate's report on CIA operations against the Allende government, and the Chilean pattern was easily discernible in Jamaica.

Although I concentrated on blaming the CIA and the American government, inside I was convinced that no major political action of that nature would have been undertaken without the approval, and probably the participation, of the British. After all, special rules apply for CIA operations in Commonwealth countries, as had already been exposed in the British press regarding the CIA's operations to overthrow the Cheddi Jagan government in Guyana in the early 1960s. But I avoided mentioning British participation because I didn't want to jeopardise my residence there.

It didn't work. In mid-November, some seven weeks after my return from Jamaica, the Cambridge police brought around a letter from the Home Office advising that Merlyn Rees, the Home Secretary, had decided to deport me 'in the interests of national security.' The law did not require him to give any reasons, but the letter went on to allege that I had 'maintained regular contacts harmful to the security of the United Kingdom with foreign intelligence officers, [that I] had been and continued to be involved in disseminating information harmful to the security of the United Kingdom, [and that I] had aided and counselled others in obtaining information for publication which could be harmful to the security of the United Kingdom.' These gratuitous allegations received wide media coverage, continuing the CIA's own themes of two years' running that I had sinister connections with the Soviets and Cubans. Indeed, Rees's charges provoked a brouhaha of allegations along similar lines in the press, the House of Commons and elsewhere that continued right up to my expulsion from Britain in June the following year.

From the moment Rees's letter arrived I was certain that the real reason behind the deportation was the spoiler role I had played against efforts by the CIA and British intelligence, probably MI6, to subvert the Manley government. (He and his party won a landslide victory in the December 1976 elections.) And I was just as certain that the decision had come from the Prime Minister, James Callaghan, as a result of American political pressure. My case, in other words, had gone up the ladder from the service-to-service concern that until then had failed to prevent my writing and other activities – at least in Britain. There could be no doubt either that the three vague charges were concocted to make me look like a 'communist agent.' And the marvellous thing about it was that I would have no legal appeal, no evidence would have to surface – the vague accusations were enough, and the press would run with them. Indeed they did. It was very well planned. The US government, as expected, denied any participation in the decision to deport me: it was a strictly internal British matter.

In order to defend myself, I presented a detailed history of my life since arrival in Britain in 1972. To it I attached the details of every trip I had made outside the country, lists of every rally I had spoken at, copies of every article I had written and my first book as well, copies of every printed interview I could find, and press cuttings of various sorts. All of this I presented to a sham 'review panel' that I privately called the "three wise monkeys," challenging anyone to find anything I had or said or written respecting British intelligence or security matters. Nobody did, but that didn't work either.

To my defenders in the House of Commons, who insisted that I be given some concrete charge that I could defend, Rees replied that going any further than the original general accusations could endanger the sources of the information that he had received from his 'security services.' He also told the House of Commons that the decision to deport me had been his alone. According to *Hansard* (3 May 1977) Rees said: 'It was taken neither at the behest nor after consultation with the Government of the United States or its agencies, including the CIA.' During the same debate, in answer to a question as to whether he regarded my work in exposing the CIA as harmful to the security of the United Kingdom, Rees replied: 'No, I am not concerned about the CIA either in the provision of information or anything else. My job is to protect not the United States of America but this country.'

It didn't matter that I had never worked in the joint CIA-British operations and had never known anything about British security matters. As my lawyer said, I was like Alice in Wonderland. But the operation was effective, I must admit. For over a year I had great difficulty resetting in Europe. Other expulsions followed, from France, Holland and West Germany, with disruptions of work and much personal stress. Each of those countries made reference to the Rees charges by way of justification. Only Italy was different. Though I was denied entry two times at Rome airport, the immigration police afterwards told my lawyer that they couldn't understand what had happened since there was no order barring me from that country.

Much of what I have written above about my deportation from Britain is fairly well known already, but I've gone back over it for a reason. Recently, through a lawsuit I brought in Washington under the Freedom of Information Act (FOIA), I have received some clues suggesting that Merlyn Rees may have misled the House of Commons in May 1977. Either that, or he really didn't know what was behind the deportation decision, if the decision was taken by Callaghan, the Prime Minister, and simply given to Rees to execute – although I find this possibility rather remote.

The Federal Court upheld the CIA's refusal to give me more than a handful of the documents on the grounds that, since they contained the most intimate details of my daily life, I would be able to identify their sources. In a long and twisting argument justifying their refusal even to give dates of the thousands of documents, they all but admitted that they had bugged the places I lived, tapped my telephones and read my mail. But I did receive copies of much of the voluminous reporting by State Department officers in the Kingston Embassy before, during, and after my 1976 trip. My every movement, it seems, was under scrutiny. The documents include verbatim transcriptions of radio and television interviews under headings like: 'Media Blitz on Agee Continues' and 'Agee Visit: Media Event of the Year.' The very volume of embassy reporting (apart from the CIA's reporting which must have been just as massive) suggested grave concern over the impact my trip had on US activities there. One classified embassy cable included the statement: 'Latest information is that Agee is leaving Saturday. (Thank God).'

The documents that really count, though, are ones that were withheld 'for security reasons', but that were described in indices. The State Department document index shows that on Thursday, 30 September 1976, the week I returned from Jamaica, the Department in Washington transmitted 'to the Secretary of State in London', i.e., Henry Kissinger, the seven-page text of the memorandum discussing me and Jamaica that had been written for Kissinger by an Assistant Secretary of State. Justification for refusal to give me the document reads: 'The memorandum to the Secretary contains information and comments on Jamaican internal political affairs which, if disclosed, could impair US relations with the Jamaican government and thus cause at least identifiable damage to US foreign relations with Jamaica.'

On Saturday, 9 October 1976, the Department in Washington transmitted a six-page cable 'to Embassy London for the Secretary of State.' This cable, classified secret, had originated in the embassy in Kingston on 25 September and also discussed me and Jamaica. Justification for refusal to give me the document is similar to the other cable for Kissinger in London: 'The document contains information and candid embassy comments on the Jamaican internal political situation and leadership which, if disclosed, could impair relations . . .'

I didn't remember Kissinger making a trip to London shortly before the deportation letter arrived, so I checked the *New York Times* for the dates when the cables were sent to the embassy in London for him. There was not a word of Kissinger travelling to London on either weekend. On September 30 he was at the United Nations in New York, but he dropped completely out of the news for the next five days

– presumably when he was in London. Similarly, he met with the Chinese Foreign Minister in New York on 8 October, but then he dropped out of the news for five days again. The *Times* of London index shows no Kissinger trip to London either on those dates.

The relaying of cables to London for Kissinger strongly suggests to me that he was taking up my Jamaica trip with high British officials and that the British decision to proceed with deportation was the result. But why were the two trips not announced? Most likely, I would say, in order to avoid any connection with the deportation action that would soon follow. Kissinger's intervention would have to be hidden. If what the FOIA materials suggest is true, Rees's remarks to the House of Commons that his decision was 'neither at the behest of nor after consultation with the Government of the United States' seem a trifle misleading.

Other entries in the State Department index suggest co-ordination between the two governments that they both denied. On 6 November, just over a week before Rees's deportation greetings, the US Embassy in London sent a cable, classified secret, to Washington reporting 'information given in confidence to an official of the US Embassy in London by a British government official.' This cable 'also concerns intelligence sources and methods' – the common term in the FOIA materials for CIA activities. I did not receive a copy of the cable because 'disclosure would be likely to cause serious damage to US foreign relations with the United Kingdom.' Most likely, this cable informed the Department that British intelligence had informed the CIA's London Station of details on how the deportation notice would be given to me – and that the CIA was reporting to its headquarters through its own channels.

There can be no doubt that the Americans were informed because a European Bureau internal memorandum dated five days later, and also classified secret, had attached to it 'Contingency Press Guidance concerning Mr Agee.' That was 11 November, just four days before Rees wrote his letter to me. The State Department refused to give me the memorandum and the Contingency Press Guidance. According to the index: 'The Guidance was not used by the State Department Spokesman, so far as can now be determined, and was presumably withdrawn for security reasons.' The Guidance and the memorandum also 'report communications with the British Embassy' in Washington. 'Disclosure of such foreign government information could cause serious damage to US foreign relations with the United Kingdom.'

Of course, without the documents themselves the FOIA materials only suggest that Rees misled the House of Commons; for Ministers of the Crown to be less than frank with members of Parliament is hardly rare. Nevertheless, my original suspicions that the American hand was behind the deportation, and that the destabilisation in Jamaica included the British, are reinforced. Why else would Kissinger need documents in London on my activities in Jamaica? And why would his trips to London be secret if not to avoid 'cause-effect' appearances when the deportation decision hit the front pages a few weeks later?

Having thus been on the receiving end of American and British dirty tricks – not unprovoked, I hasten to admit – the appearance of this book gives me enormous satisfaction. The authors have brought together an excellent historical survey of secret British operations in the Far East, Middle and Near East, Africa and Europe over the past thirty years. Their sources are well-documented and extremely broad. Without doubt this book is a significant contribution to the understanding of Britain's role in the aborted century of 'Pax Americana.'

On the marble wall of the grand foyer of the CIA's headquarters in Virginia, the Agency motto is etched in bold: 'Ye Shall Know the Truth and the Truth Shall Make You Free.' We should take that excerpt from the Gospel of John and apply it in our own efforts to discover how governments secretly promote the interests of elite and powerful groupings at great human cost. For me there is no greater evidence of the hypocrisy and sham behind 'liberal' preachings than the details of covert interventions.

This book should be read by all those who in the 1980s must defend the struggle against nuclear weapons from efforts by secret services to penetrate, divide and discredit the peace movement. You can be sure the British will be there, and the cases outlined in this book will contribute to that defense.

Philip Agee
Hamburg
December 1982

Acknowledgements

Since work began on this book, many people have provided infor-
mation, suggestions, encouragement, access to libraries and other
facilities. We would particularly like to thank David Beresford, Celena
Bledowska, Jim Chrystie, David Clark, Barry Cohen, Sue Cockerell,
Counter Information Services, Suzanne Cronje, Patricia Fitzsimons,
Richard Fletcher, Roger Faligot, David Henderson, Ian Henshall, Pete
Jordan, Mark Leopold, Andrew Nichol, Steve Peak, Brian Quinn,
Richard Rathbone, Dan Re'em, Carmen Saez, Toby Shelley, Elaine
Unterhalter, Ruth Weiss and Andrew Weir. We owe a special thanks to
Russell Southwood who assisted with some of the original research and
to Philip Agee who kindly agreed to write an introduction.

Jonathan Bloch

Patrick Fitzgerald

December 1982

Contents

Chapter 1
Intelligence and Covert Action

These opening sentences are written in the aftermath of a British military victory in one of the most absurd and futile wars ever fought, even using the often spurious criteria by which large-scale military actions are justified. Leaving aside the economics of the campaign, the unfortunate inhabitants of the Falklands/Malvinas, whose freedom was purported to be the underlying issue, fell foul of a government sufficiently racist to deny them full British citizenship – in case the occupants of Hong Kong asked for the same. The declared principle on which the war was fought is by no means immutable: the 1,300 population of Diego Garcia, supplanted to make way for new American military facilities, will testify as much.

Numerous instant books and some more considered works will illustrate in varying degrees of accuracy and sanguinariness, how and why the war was fought, and it is not our intention to join them. However, the immediate cause of the Falklands/Malvinas crisis serves as an effective example with which to introduce a central theme. The sending of the 'task force' to the South Atlantic ocean was precipitated by the failure of the British government to predict the Argentinian invasion of the islands. Their error was most surprising in view of the detailed information available to them on the movements of Argentinian forces. This was obtained from intercepted communications, American reconnaissance satellites or aircraft under various liaison agreements and should have been accurate to within several hours. In addition, the British foreign intelligence service MI6, had a single officer in Latin America, fortuitously based in Buenos Aires with two military intelligence attaches. About a fortnight before the invasion, they had furnished Whitehall with a long summary of the Argentinian military plans.

All governments feel the need to be informed of real or imaginary threats to themselves and their territorial and economic interests. Beyond that, they ask for information on weaknesses which can be exploited in pursuit of the same. In the domain of foreign policy, which is our main concern, their opponents are other governments; and their requirements cannot be fulfilled in the normal course of diplomatic reporting. Intelligence agencies exist to fill the gap. The nature of their targets is such that they frequently need to use clandestine methods, which distinguishes their activities from other forms of information-gathering. Once all the relevant material has been collected, it will probably require processing – decoding or translation, for example – followed by analysis in comparison with other material. The conclusions are released to the interested quarters – Ministry or Cabinet committee – which for an intelligence agency is more than a mere formality. At this stage it may be able to manipulate decision-making by the content, timing and veracity of its reports, depending on its relations with the political regime.

Government requirements of its intelligence system fall into two categories. Standing requirements are the permanent brief: Argentinian government attitudes towards the Falklands/Malvinas or the balance of political forces in the Middle East. Ad hoc requirements may arise within the context of a standing requirement (information on the Polish organisation Solidarity as part of the task of crisis monitoring) or in isolation (details of Icelandic shipping movements during the 'Cod War').

Classification of intelligence targets is difficult as the borderlines break down between political, economic and defence matters, and between internal and external affairs. The classes are roughly distinguished by scale and time-span. Strategic intelligence is generally conducted on a national or regional basis, concerned with, to take two examples, estimates of the strength of political opposition in a particular country or obtaining the specifications of a new weapon system. It is essentially long-term – individual projects may take several decades – but nuclear arsenals and the development of mobile assault forces have led to short-term strategic intelligence-gathering as well. Operational intelligence, by contrast, deals with 'real-time', that is immediate and highly probable developments: an assassination plot, for instance.

Clandestine collection methods divide into those involving intelligence officers and their agents in traditional espionage, and technical processes such as satellite or aerial reconnaissance and signals intelligence.

Technical methods have, since the Second World War, provided the greater proportion of unprocessed intelligence, nowadays probably between 80 per cent and 90 per cent. This is reflected in the size of the agencies working in this area, as will become clear in the description of the British intelligence apparatus. There are several advantages in technical collection which account in part for its growth: the relative safety of the operators compared to intelligence personnel on the ground, and the fact that the information is invariably accurate and contemporary. Communications, in addition, are usually the most vulnerable part of any active system and become more critical as a system increases in sophistication. Signals intelligence, which deals with the interception of radio and electronic traffic, thus acquires proportionally greater importance.

While the role of individual collection is less in volume terms, it continues to be the only way of obtaining certain kinds of information beyond the reach of satellites and electronic monitoring devices. Changes in a government policy, say, or tensions within ruling circles can often only be determined with the use of agents.

The mounting complexity of the intelligence environment, manifested in the rising volume of all types of communications and greater interdependency among nation states, is causing problems for intelligence services. The most serious is overkill. Material gathered through technical methods requires long, intricate processing before any conclusions can be drawn. Despite the growing use of computers, this is a time and labour-consuming buiness. In the case of signals, much is encoded, and the codes difficult or impossible to break. A steadily growing bank of both interpreted and uninterpreted receipts must be available for comparison with new signals. Analytical methods, particularly those involving the assembly of different species of raw material, rely even more on human skills which have yet to be imparted to computer systems. Developments at both these stages have failed to keep pace with those in collection techniques. The position is exacerbated by the concentration of resources in collection, to the detriment of processing and analysis. Former CIA director William Colby pinpointed the source of this latter problem in asking that planners should provide

> assurance that substantive consumer needs (rather than momentum of technological achievement and opportunity) is the driving force of investment in our expensive technical collection systems.[1]

Overkill is reached where the quantity of incoming material exceeds the capacity which analysts can cope with, causing a breakdown through their inability to make evaluations. The Pike Committee of the US House of Representatives, noting the intelligence system's failure to predict the 1973 Middle East War, delivered a terse indictment of overkill in the National Security Agency, the American signals intelligence department:

> intercepts of Egyptian-Syrian war preparations were so voluminous – hundreds of reports each week – that few analysts had time to digest more than a small portion. Costly intercepts had

scant impact on intelligence estimates.[2]

Overkill is likely to be more common among the superpowers than with the medium-size British intelligence system, but the consequences in either case are incalculable. To avoid overkill, some expansion of the intelligence complex will prove necessary independent of any emergent crises, shifts in the geo-political landscape or other problems unless governments accept a reduction in the range of issues on which they can be supplied with intelligence; an unlikely development. Colby notes that

> the business of intelligence may well require increases in budgetary terms if only to maintain today's capabilities at current resource levels.[3]

Similarly an expansion of the British intelligence apparatus can be expected after a period of contraction caused by decolonisation, particularly the removal of colonial security obligations.

The other major problem for intelligence systems is rooted in preconceived judgements which hamper their ability to assess new information properly. At the onset of the Yom Kippur war in October 1973, the Israelis were totally unprepared for simultaneous Egyptian and Syrian attacks. Despite complete information on the strength and development of Arab military units, Israeli intelligence was convinced that, after their defeat in 1967, the Arab states would never launch an attack unless they could amass superior forces. This they had not done, and therefore no invasion was expected.

It is not clear at this stage whether British intelligence suffered from either of these problems over the Falklands/Malvinas crisis. Military action was only one of several options open to the government to pressure for an Argentinian withdrawal: persuasion through diplomacy, economic sanctions and certain forms of covert action were other possible responses. In most cases, including the South Atlantic conflict, some combination of these is employed. Richard Bissell, formerly the CIA's Deputy Director, Plans, listed eight categories of covert operation:[4]

  i)   political advice and counsel
  ii)   subsidies to an individual
  iii) financial support and 'technical assistance' to political parties
  iv)   support of private organisations, including labour unions, business firms, co-operatives etc.
  v)   covert propaganda
  vi)   'private' training of individuals and exchange of persons
  vii) economic operations
  viii) paramilitary or political action operations

Essentially, covert action entails intervention or manipulation in support of a government's foreign policy in a manner which disguises its involvement. Clear advantages exist over those forms of overt response mentioned above; effective covert action does not carry any political cost. The major drawback is the risk of exposure, which can cause immense damage, and hence operational secrecy is paramount, even at the expense of successful execution.

Responsibility for covert action has almost always lain with the intelligence services, excepting cases involving paramilitary action. Of the categories listed by Bissell, covert propaganda and political action operations are the most common, and in both these and the remainder the requisite techniques are often merely extensions of the normal processes of espionage – the recruitment of agents, establishment of 'front' organisations for channeling money, and so on. The information and technical requirements for covert action will to a large extent derive from the intelligence system anyway, and given this close relation between intelligence and covert action, it seems appropriate that both functions should be performed by the same agency as far as possible. The assembly of a separate organisation to conduct covert operations would, in the view of Stansfield Turner, Director of Central Intelligence in the Carter regime,

> be costly and perhaps dangerous. You would end up constructing an organisation, with people overseas, just for covert action, whereas today we get dual service out of people. If there were a separate bureaucracy with good people in it, they would end up promoting covert action – not maliciously, but because they would be energetic. We should be ready to do what we're asked to do, but not be out drumming up business.[5]

The difficulties experienced by the CIA throughout the early and mid-seventies were in no small part due to splits between its intelligence and covert action functions. Marks and Marchetti write that

> it is one of the contradictions of the intelligence profession, as practiced by the CIA, that the views of its substantive experts – its analysts – do not carry much weight with the clandestine operators engaged in covert action. The operators usually decide which operations to undertake without consulting the analysts ... To ensure against contact with the analysts, and to reduce interference by high-level staff members ... the operators resort to tight operational security ... and to bureaucratic deceptions when developing or seeking approval of a covert action operation.[6]

In describing covert action as a response to real or imagined threats, it is important to clarify their nature. As far as the West is concerned they are not confined to military or economic attacks on a static system, because the viability of Western economies depends on the continual pursuit and development of new markets. A hindrance to the Western economic thrust – nationalisation of foreign assets by a Third World government, for example – can also be construed as a threat. Thus, the range of threats to Western governments, as they see it, is larger than those which could be portrayed as directly aggressive. This necessitates an aggressive foreign policy, of which covert action is an integral part.

Indeed, integral to American foreign policy to the extent that the Reagan administration has introduced

> a new method of influence: the open threat of 'destabilization'. In statements about Nicaragua and Cuba, for example, U.S. officials have made public threats of secret reprisals if those countries fail to change policies – even internal ones – of which the White House disapproves ... coercive diplomacy of this sort is a 'use' of covert action in the same way as a threat to shoot someone is a use of a gun. But it is a new use, which elevates destabilization from a sanction applied when others will not work to a commonplace tool of U.S. diplomacy.[7]

Richard Helms, CIA chief between 1965 and 1972, appears to have no doubt that covert action is a key component of foreign policy. In 1979, he attempted to justify it, arguing that

> Those who believe that it's immoral to do these things will tell you, even when we've had a success, that it was wrong. Looked at in that perspective, almost everything done in a foreign field is wrong because it's influencing events which theoretically should be influenced by other people. But history shows that world powers adopting that attitude have not survived very long.[8]

The use of almost exclusively American sources throughout this introduction highlights a particular problem with the United Kingdom. With a few exceptions, stimulated entirely by the political left, no open debate has taken place over the role of the British intelligence system beyond the existence or otherwise of various enumerated 'men', and brief, tentative explorations of the issues of accountability and control in the wake of the inevitable 'scandal' following the exposure of each.

One of the immediate conclusions from the examination of British covert operations in this book will be that the British government has shown no reluctance to use offensive clandestine methods in pursuit of foreign policy objectives, and a number of factors are likely to militate in favour of increasing use. The strong linkage of the British and American intelligence establishments, to be described in Chapter 2 is the most powerful, as covert action becomes a more acceptable option to American policymakers. Continuing US government sensitivity to certain types of operation, following the exposures of the last decade or so, leads to CIA requests to allies for assistance in launching covert action programmes which it is unable to squeeze through the oversight process. (There are indications that this constraint is declining in importance, however.) Additionally, the inevitable growth of the intelligence apparatus to avoid the danger of overkill will strengthen its influence within the foreign policy establishment and increase the tendency to look for 'intelligence' solutions. Significantly, the intelligence agencies were specifically excluded from recent staffing and budgetary restrictions first imposed on the Civil Service by the Conservative government in 1979. The persistent strife in Northern Ireland and the possibility of serious disorder in Britain as the economy worsens are, however, likely to divert intelligence resources away from covert operations overseas. Nevertheless, the critical importance of foreign trade to any recovery requires due attention and possible action to guarantee sources of raw material and markets.

We will return to these arguments in Chapter 5. The remainder of this chapter is concerned with the structure of the British intelligence and covert action system.

The British Intelligence Apparatus

Four agencies control intelligence-gathering in the United Kingdom. The largest in both establishment and output is the Government Communications Headquarters (GCHQ), which is responsible for the collection, processing and analysis of all signals intelligence. GCHQ grew out of the Government Code and Cypher School, the wartime code-breaking department located at Bletchley Park, Buckinghamshire. Over 6,000 staff worked throughout the war on the German and Italian communications cyphers. Among the first computers ever built were those of the Colossus series which were used to decode messages based on the Enigma, Lorenz and Geheimschreiber machines. The ULTRA operation, which broke the Enigma code completely, was particularly successful. Churchill is understood to have run the North Africa war virtually single-handed on ULTRA intercepts. The Lorenz code was also routinely cracked, although success with Geheimschreiber was limited.

GCHQ was first sited at Eastcote in north-west London soon after the war, but in 1953 began the move to its current location in two complexes near Cheltenham. The first, on Oakley Priors Road, houses the administrative centre and computer facilities; the second, at Benhall Park, consists mainly of laboratories and workshops, and also the vitally important National Security Agency (NSA) liaison office. The NSA is the American counterpart of GCHQ, and the 1947 signals intelligence pact which underpins co-operative work between these two and other Western signals agencies is a central feature of the

Anglo-American intelligence alliance. Chapter 2 describes this in greater detail.

Eastcote was still in use in 1975 – scientific recruits were stationed there while construction work at Benhall was completed –but was later handed over to the Joint Speech Research Unit, a department closely related to GCHQ, whose work includes development of computer recognition of the spoken word for automatic telephone tapping. The computer division is based on two loosely coupled IBM systems, with an electricity requirement of a medium-sized town. Bletchley Park is now GCHQ's central training centre; British Telecom and the Diplomatic Service also use it for wireless training.

GCHQ and the NSA are the world market leaders in the sophistication and scope of their code-breaking and interception equipment, a position both are determined to maintain. The two countries prohibit the export of cryptographic equipment unless the manufacturer hands over complete plans, making it difficult for Third World countries to obtain codes which cannot be broken. Britain's cracking of the Enigma code during the Second World War was not revealed for 30 years because electronic versions of the cypher were being sold to the Third World by European firms, providing easy targets to the British and American codebreakers.

GCHQ is operated jointly by the Ministry of Defence and the Foreign and Commonwealth Office (FCO). The director, Brian Tovey, is a deputy secretary in the FCO – only the permanent secretary, the departmental chief, ranks above him. Immediately below him are half a dozen superintending directors, with the rank of assistant secretary, who supervise GCHQ's four directorates: Organisation and Establishment, Sigint Plans and two operational directorates. Of these latter, Sigint Operations and Requirements is by far the larger, processing and analysing intercepts from a network of monitoring stations in both the United Kingdom and overseas. While the full number of foreign stations is not known, some have been identified, among them those in Cyprus, Gibraltar, Turkey, five in West Germany, Oman, and facilities run with the NSA in the Ascension Islands and with the Australian Defence Signals Division personnel from military signals units, usually army or air force, and civilians from the Composite Signals Organisation. All military communications monitoring has been controlled by GCHQ since 1963, following a secret Whitehall struggle in which it emerged as victor. Some of the easier, low-level work is done at the point of interception and the results relayed back to Cheltenham along with unprocessed material. All messages are subjected to a procedure known as a traffic analysis, which seeks to isolate the source of each message and the identity of the radio operator, and to make further deductions based on other characteristics of individual messages and their positions within a communications framework – detecting a military build-up, for example. Many of these communications are encoded, in which case copies of the intercepts are also sent to GCHQ's Division H which handles cryptanalysis (code-breaking). The fourth directorate is labelled Communications Security: its tasks are precisely to ensure that the work of foreign sigint agencies who take an interest in British communications is made as difficult as possible. Its methods range from cryptography (encoding and encyphering) to technologically advanced radio systems which change frequency many times per second. GCHQ technicians have developed 'spurt' radio devices which enable a large body of information to be broadcast very rapidly: they are a standard piece of Special Air Service equipment and also in use with M16, who receive substantial communications support from GCHQ. The NSA brief for communications security also includes listening to the messages of American allies to check that the correct security procedures are being employed, which serves as a pretext for intercepting them on a routine basis.[9] GCHQ does the same.[10] The number of people involved in British sigint runs into tens of thousands. 8,000 work at GCHQ Cheltenham alone. The cost of the whole exercise cannot be far short of £500 million per annum.

We will return to GCHQ again briefly in Chapter 5. The agency is not engaged to any significant degree in covert operations, other than perhaps disinformation through false messages, and hence is not of central interest. Nonetheless, as the major British intelligence producer, it has an important secondary role in supplying information for use in the planning and execution of covert operations and in providing secure communications for the main covert action departments.

Almost all of GCHQ's work is illegal under international law. The agency does not monitor conventional radio stations, but this is not to say that these are ignored. The BBC monitoring service at Caversham Park near Reading is one of the world's largest organisations following radio broadcasts, and it provides a valuable service for intelligence analysts and propagandists.

The BBC began its monitoring operations in 1933, after a government request for details of anti-British broadcasts to Arab nations by Italian stations. Government funding for a more systematic monitoring service was provided during the Second World War, under the control of Political Warfare Executive, which supervised British propaganda programmes. Throughout the war the monitoring unit produced daily transcripts of broadcasts around the world for use by the government and the BBC.

After the war the unit was maintained and expanded. It continued to be officially sponsored by the Foreign Office and financed by a grant in aid from the Treasury. According to the official BBC handbook, the function of the monitoring service is 'to listen to and report on the contents of broadcasts by foreign radio stations'. A special listening section logs changing programme patterns, frequencies and language of foreign radio stations. Of the 400-odd staff at Caversham, about 120 are engaged in monitoring. Each day, they listen in to some 400 news bulletins, commentaries, and press reviews from 34 countries. The main commitment has always been directed to broadcasts from the Warsaw Pact countries, although close attention is paid to critical Third World areas. Prior to the Iranian revolution and the Soviet intervention in Afghanistan, Caversham employed four monitors adept in the languages spoken there: Farsi, Dari, and Pashto. The number then grew to 12, and Iran achieved equal status with the Soviet Union as the only country whose broadcasts were monitored 24 hours a day.

The monitoring service has two main departments: the Reception department listens to the programmes and transcribes them; the News and Publications department edits material which is then sent to subscribers. These include foreign governments, news agencies and newspapers, universities, and commercial organisations, as well as most British government departments. The Ministry of Defence and the Foreign and Commonwealth Office have direct teleprinter links with Caversham, as does the BBC's news and current affairs department. Daily printed summaries are prepared on the USSR, Eastern Europe, the Far East, Middle East, Africa and Latin America. This service is able to produce up to 100,000 words daily. Weekly economic reports are compiled on the USSR, Far East, and Eastern Europe. Because not all the broadcasts the BBC desires to monitor can be heard in the UK, a number of ouposts have been established overseas, which file translated and edited copy back to Caversham Park by teleprinter. There is a monitoring unit in Nairobi responsible for monitoring broadcasts in East Africa and Central Africa. This unit was strengthened by flying out extra workers in the late 1970s to step up the monitoring of broadcasts in Angola and Mozambique. A BBC monitor was also stationed in Lilongwe, Malawi, to listen to broadcasts from Rhodesia and Zambia.

After World War II the BBC monitoring service and its American equivalent, the FBIS (Foreign Broadcasting Information Service) agreed to divide up the task of world-wide monitoring between them since the cost to each would be half that of either of them setting up such an operation on its own. As a result the BBC unit came to concentrate its monitoring activities in Europe and the USSR, while the FBIS took responsibility for China and the Far East. All information was shared between them. A more recent division assigned monitoring in East

Europe, North and East Africa to the BBC, and work on the Far East, Middle East, West Africa and Latin America to the FBIS. The FBIS and the BBC together with their respective governments consult constantly over whom they should be listening to, and their activities are carefully co-ordinated. The system is flexible enough to enable coverage to be extended, at a moment's notice, to almost any part of the world where events like a coup or a war create a special or temporary interest.

The BBC is proud of this American connection. Its 1977 handbook cited this as 'the most important factor enabling reports on broadcasts from remoter parts of the world to be compiled'. However what the BBC does not make public is that the FBIS is run by the CIA as part of its overt intelligence-gathering activities. While the BBC turns over all its raw monitoring reports to the FBIS station in Caversham Park, the FBIS does not quite reciprocate. It only provides the BBC with finished – i.e. edited – monitoring reports. The relevance of FBIS material may also be open to question. At one time, the organisation was in the absurd position of monitoring and distributing the texts of programmes originating from clandestine CIA stations in Taiwan broadcasting to the Chinese mainland.[11]

Monitoring is one way by which propaganda can be adapted to its audience. During the early years of Rhodesia's UDI the BBC was running a propaganda radio station against the Smith regime from Francistown, Botswana. A group of monitors stationed there listened to Radio Salisbury and adjusted the BBC broadcasts accordingly.

The editorial policy of the Reading publication is to select certain items, and highlight them by writing short introductions on the cover. Its editorial judgement usually reflects the orthodox values of the Foreign Office Peking and Kremlin watchers. These values are especially strong in the news since the Foreign Office is both a major user of the monitoring service and its principal source of funds. The role of the BBC monitoring service has clear significance for the present government: despite its morbid search for economies, it has specifically ordered that no cuts should be made in the service's budget. For its part, the BBC is content in the knowledge that on occasions such as the Hills affair* the Foreign Secretary's most up-to-date information came from the BBC's monitoring of Radio Uganda. The BBC is also proud of the edge it has over other stations in obtaining scoops from its monitoring prowess. Examples are the coups in Somalia (October 1969), Uganda (January 1971), and the attempted coup in Sudan, also in 1971. However, as is described elsewhere, it is not always true that the British Government is unaware of what is taking place.

* When a British businessman was held in custody by Idi Amin in Uganda.

Of all the structural reforms forced upon the British intelligence agencies since the war, the most radical have been directed against the military. The intermingling of the roles of the three armed services, as well as the increasing overlap with civilian agencies, forced defence and intelligence chiefs to reconsider the traditional system of an intelligence unit for each service. The sheer quantity of intelligence material arriving on the desks of Whitehall planners, much of it duplicated between different agencies, provided a further motivation to seek a more efficient structure for the military intelligence apparatus.

The first co-ordinating unit was set up in 1946, named the Joint Intelligence Bureau, and under the directorship of Kenneth Strong. The Bureau proved influential and reasonably successful despite its small size, and was taken as the model for the extensive reorganisation of military intelligence which took place in 1964. The newly-created Defence Intelligence Staff (DIS) took control of the majority of intelligence activity in the domain of the Ministry of Defence: the intelligence departments of the army, navy and air force and most of the Ministry of Defence's own security departments. The three services, however, were still more or less independent. The final phase took place during Denis Healey's period as Minister of Defence. The intelligence directorates for the individual services were abolished and a completely unified command structure was introduced, the senior posts of which rotate between the three services. The present head of DIS (Director General of Intelligence) is Vice-Admiral Sir Roy Halliday; his deputy, Lieutenant-General Sir James Glover, holds the position of Deputy Chief of the Defence Staff (Intelligence). Beneath them are five main departments, listed here with their current directors:

Service Intelligence	Air Vice-Marshal W.J. Herrington
Management and Support of Intelligence	Rear-Admiral J.K. Robertson
Logistics	D.E. Chamberlain
Scientific and Technical Intelligence	N.H. Hughes
Economic Intelligence	W.C. Rudkin

The first two named posts are the more important, and, as can be seen, DIS contains a mixture of military and civilian staff in over ninety individual departments.[12] Senior staff work at the Ministry of Defence building in Whitehall. Intelligence evaluation and report compilation is performed at the former site of the Metropole Hotel in Northumberland Avenue, London.

The Ministry of Defence keeps two security departments, those dealing with physical security and contract work, outside DIS control. All other security and intelligence tasks, including the screening of MOD personnel and their relatives, are the responsibility of DIS.

Wherever British forces are, DIS staff will be as well. DIS supplies the military attaches to overseas missions – about 150 acknowledged defence attaches are stationed at 65 missions – who collect and assess information on the capabilities of the host country's forces, exchange notes with allied missions or governments, and promote arms sales. In countries ruled by the military, where the military is influential in political life, or if a military coup is likely, the attache acquires a significant political role, since obtaining information may be easier for him than for an intelligence officer working under civilian or diplomatic cover.

Most DIS work is devoted to the forces of the Warsaw Pact countries. Their strength, weapon efficiency and details of their fixed installations are monitored. The Economic Intelligence department doggedly pursues the task of estimating Soviet defence expenditure. The activities of the Soviets and their allies in the Third World are carefully observed and reported. For all military intelligence recruits (not just the army), the 'internal threat' is stressed as well as that alleged from the Soviet bloc. Beneath the central DIS command, military intelligence divides along service lines. The army's Intelligence Corps has headquarters at a barracks in Ashford, Kent named after Gerald Templer, sometime Chief of the Imperial General Staff who ran the successful counter-insurgency war against the Malayan communists. The centre runs four training courses: air photographic interpretation, operational intelligence, security and interrogation, and is used by other British intelligence services as well as foreign visitors. One of these, Pedro Cardoso, became chief of staff in the Portuguese army in 1978 after a period in charge of organising a new intelligence service. Not all are satisfied with British methods: a group of visiting Brazilian army officers found the interrogation techniques too slow by their own robust standards.

The Intelligence Corps liaises with local security forces during overseas campaigns. Two officers and a number of sergeant interrogators are still available for posting at short notice to the remaining British colonies.

Naval and air force intelligence units concentrate more on signals and surveillance. Using its remaining foreign shore bases and specially equipped vessels, the navy monitors sea traffic and maritime communications. The two services work closely together on submarine tracking – RAF planes now use a device for detecting small magnetic variations and a EMI-made unit containing an infra-red scanner able to resolve 0.5°C differences in water temperature. The unit also possesses high altitude, low altitude and oblique cameras able to film beyond the aircraft's available air space. The undeveloped film is processed at the Joint Air Reconnaissance Intelligence Centre at Huntingdon, a combined services unit which is dominated by the RAF although the deputy director and around 15 per cent of the staff are army personnel. JARIC's customers include the civilian intelligence agencies as well as the three services, and the centre is believed to handle some film retrieved from American reconnaissance satellites.

Britain has no such satellites of its own. A military communications satellite, Skynet 2A, was launched in 1974 but failed to reach its determined geo-stationary orbit 22,500 miles above the Seychelles. A back-up, Skynet 2B, replaced it. Shortly afterwards British defence communications were integrated into the NATO system. However, reports at the end of 1981 describe plans for new, independent communications satellites for the armed forces, Skynet 4A and 4B.

Military intelligence personnel are not extensively used in covert action. Undercover offensive operations are more suited to the Special Air Service regiments. Propaganda in support of military campaigns is handled by psychological operations or 'psyops' units. Psyops are particularly important in counter-guerilla operations where they have two aims, firstly gaining the confidence and co-operation of the civilian population to assist military operations by precluding civilian support for the guerillas and ensuring a steady flow of information. Secondly, to lower the morale of insurgents, encouraging surrender and defection.

Planning a campaign involves an examination of the prospective audience to discover vulnerabilities, and deciding the type of propaganda most likely to influence them. This could be through posters, leaflet drops, the planting of articles in newspapers or even writing letters to editors. Co-ordination between the military and relevant political agencies is essential for success: the British model suggests a joint committee composed of a representative from the army intelligence corps, psyops and public relations staff, and delegates from the information services and police Special Branch.[13]

By 1971, the British army had a psychological warfare section of 30 people. Psyops staff were at three overseas headquarters and one unit was based at the Ministry of Defence. That year, counter-insurgency theorist Frank Kitson, in his book *Low Intensity Operations*, bemoaned the pitiful size of the British psyops complement compared to those of other armies: 'Undoubtedly the British are "bringing up the rear" in this important aspect of contemporary war'.[14]

Psyops training is undertaken at the Joint Warfare Establishment, which is housed at the National Defence College in Latimer. It moved to this site from Old Sarum near Salisbury at the end of 1978. The establishment distinguishes two types of course. One is for staff officers and the other for unit officers who will have to plan and work in psyops. The staff officer's course includes lectures on communist propaganda practice, the urban guerilla, modern advertising techniques and experience from recent psychological operations. The unit officer's course also includes propaganda and community relations and the role of a unit within the overall psyops plan.

In 1976, the Ministry of Defence confirmed that in the previous three years, 1,858 army officers and 262 senior civil servants had been trained to use psychological techniques for internal security purposes. The civil servants were drawn from the Northern Ireland Office, Home Office and Foreign Office, although a week after the details became clear the Home Secretary, Merlyn Rees, denied that any of his staff had been to Old Sarum, and also that any police officers had received psyops instruction.[15] Apart from the course, British commissioned officers are also seconded for training to the United States Army Special Warfare School at Fort Bragg and instructors from the Joint Warfare Establishment make lecture visits to Commonwealth countries. The establishment has two instructors in psychological operations on its staff in Section 7: Lieutenant-Colonel J.E. Pell and Squadron Leader A.H. Graveley.

Although the combat psywar units may be small in terms of number, the British army expects their influence to be quite extensive. The basic unit is designed to be independent, with one officer (a major or captain) and twelve other ranks, plus any necessary civilians. These units are equipped with vans and landrovers to carry loudspeakers, tape recorders and cinema projectors. Each has a photographic capability and limited facilities for producing pamphlets of simple design.

With psyops, the armed forces and the defence establishment have acquired or rapidly will acquire the ability to launch political campaigns in pursuit of military objectives entirely independently, that is without reference to the political regime. In a paper entitled 'Public Opinion and the Armed Services', Brigadier C.P.R. Palmer contended that Britain's ability to defend itself may depend more on public opinion as influenced by the media than its strength in terms of soldiers and military hardware. NATO hesitation over deployment of the enhanced radiation weapon, the so-called 'neutron bomb', was a result of public pressure on NATO governments with a subsidiary role played by Soviet-bloc propaganda, Palmer suggests.[16] Psyops, suitably employed, would by implication have overcome this difficulty. The military's conception of what constitutes self-defence is not necessarily shared either by other sectors of government or the population at large, but more effective and widespread use of psyops will enable them to prevail politically more often. A government's main defence against such a campaign is its security service; in Britain, MI5.

MI5 was established in 1909 to perform counter-intelligence in the United Kingdom, the possessions and colonial territories. Definitions of counter-intelligence vary, but MI5's main tasks are guarding against the activities of foreign intelligence services in Britain and monitoring home-grown dissident political groups. In Northern Ireland, where no less than five different intelligence agencies are working, the MI5 team is required to obtain information of assassination plots, mainland bombing plans and infiltration of the Royal Ulster Constabulary and the Ulster Defence Regiment by loyalist paramilitaries. Between four and five thousand staff work at the agency's headquarters in London and in a network of regional offices throughout the country and in the remaining colonies. Also,

> the security services of Britain, the United States, Canada, Australia and New Zealand are closely bound together by a series of secret co-operative agreements. Techniques, methods and security intelligence are widely exchanged, principally through high-ranking liaison officers attached to each capital.[17]

During the colonial period in those territories for which the service was directly responsible, regional offices were established under a Director of Intelligence in major capitals such as Nairobi, Singapore, Kingston, Lusaka and Kuala Lumpur. It was the responsibility of the Director of Intelligence and his staff to maintain a close liaison with military intelligence in his area, and with police and other security services. MI5 personnel would advise the Governor and local police particularly on external threats. In 1950 MI5 and the Special Branch also began to offer courses for colonial Special Branch officers. From 1956–62, the crucial period of decolonisation, MI5 seconded Security Intelligence Advisors to the Colonial Office to advise the Colonial Secretary.

The British were happy to make their experience of counter-intelligence available to their allies. In the late 1940s, Sir Percy Sillitoe, head of MI5, visited a number of Dominions including Canada and Australia. He claims in his autobiography that the Australian Security and Intelligence Organisation was established as a result of his visit. Also around this time, MI5 was engaged in its last major operation in the Middle East, combating Zionist guerilla groups fighting for an independent Jewish state and attempting to block the massive illegal immigration by Jews from Europe.

The legacy of MI5's influence in former British colonies can be seen subsequently in the structure of their intelligence systems. The established committee framework survived decolonisation and became the source of intelligence for the new rulers. In Ghana, for example, President Nkrumah chaired the Central Intelligence Committee, taking reports from the head of the Special Branch and from regional committees. The latter contained representatives from the Ministries of Labour and the Interior as well as the army and local Special Branch. Even after independence, key intelligence positions were often held by expatriates, some seconded from MI5. They can be precarious jobs, as Douglas Mott, the MI5 advisor to President Mancham of the Seychelles, discovered when he was forced to leave the islands after the 1978 revolution.

MI5 has rarely engaged in covert operations overseas. The last known occasion was in British Guiana during 1963 and 1964. The agency collaborated with a CIA plan to undermine the left-wing administration of Cheddi Jagan. Provoking a series of strikes and splits in the ruling party, the CIA and MI5 managed to cause the collapse of the Jagan government. In working with the Americans, the Director-General of MI5, Sir Roger Hollis, was acting on specific instructions from Prime Minister Harold Macmillan and Colonial Secretary Duncan Sandys.

The remainder of this section is devoted to the two organisations chiefly responsible for covert action. MI6 collects foreign intelligence using human sources and conducts secret political operations while the Special Air Services are the army's paramilitary and counter-insurgency force, although their chain of command lies outside the formal army structure.

Recent academic work on the history of British intelligence tends to disrupt any notion of introducing MI6 and its pseudo-mythical chief with 'In the beginning, there was C'. MI6 evolved from an assortment of spying organisations set up rather haphazardly by the Foreign Office, Colonial Office and India Office, which were formally constituted in the Secret Service Bureau in 1909. The Bureau's home department became MI5, and the foreign department, MI6. Initially, however, it was entitled MI1c.

In the ten years after the end of the First World War, MI1c was dominated by an anti-Soviet obsession, and poured agents and money into Russia in support of the White armies. Ultimately, this proved useless, but the Bolshevik victory was not the only setback from this period. The influence of radical politics in British universities was such that MI6 refused to recruit graduates, with the result that the intellectual standard of its officers was relatively poor. Low-grade information from the field plagued the service until the outbreak of the Second World War. Nevertheless, MI6 control of the codebreakers at the Government Code and Cipher School forestalled excessive damage to its reputation. The school consistently broke Russian diplomatic cyphers for ten years after the revolution, and was only stopped when the government announced – incredibly, for the fourth time – that it had been reading them. At this point, the Soviets decided to change their codes.

In the thirties, MI1c was renamed the Secret Intelligence Service (SIS), a name still used by some commentators and also by MI6 staff.

Around this time, it successfully developed high-altitude (then, over 8,000 feet) photography techniques and formed its Photo-Reconnaissance Unit, which was passed to the control of the Air Ministry in 1939 and later evolved into JARIC. Unfortunately, with a major war just under way, ground operations were in serious difficulty. The Nazi secret service, under Walter Schellenberg, had discovered SIS's European headquarters, at the offices of the Continental Trading Corporation in Amsterdam. From close surveillance of the building, the Nazis managed to identify a large proportion of the resident SIS staff, and build up a picture of almost the entire range of SIS European operations. Networks in Austria, and Czechoslovakia, as well as Holland were immediately wiped out on the annexation of each of these countries by the German army. The increase in intelligence requirements caused by the war and the destruction of its European network forced SIS to go recruiting on a large scale. On this occasion it showed none of its former reluctance to employ graduates, although they were vetted for Nazi or Communist leanings. Some mistakes were made, however, because of the urgency of the situation and a number of Soviet agents slipped through, among them Kim Philby. Gradually SIS re-established itself and towards the end of the war produced some very valuable information on the German rocket and heavy water programmes. At the same time it had garnered considerable credit from the ULTRA code-breaking operation, and ended the war with its prestige fully restored, ignorant of the troubles that lay ahead.

In 1944, anticipating political conflict following the likely defeat of the Axis powers, Britain's intelligence chiefs decided to set up a new section to embark on long-term penetration of the Soviet security apparatus. The first chief of Section Nine was Kim Philby, which made its task rather difficult. Over the next fifteen years Philby, George Blake, one of MI6's best field officers, Charles Zbytek, who worked for a MI6-controlled Czech anti-communist group and possibly others played havoc with MI6 operations against the Soviet Union and the new communist countries of Eastern Europe. MI6 agents parachuted into Albania to galvanise a coup against the fledgling regime of

Enver Hoxha were captured on landing. Networks of minority groups, favoured by the co-operating British and American intelligence agencies for stirring up dissent inside Russia, vanished without trace. MI6 contacts in Czechoslovakia and Hungary were rounded up en masse and jailed and executed.

Among its successes against the Soviet Union, the best known is MI6's recruitment of the GRU* colonel Oleg Penkovsky, who supplied over 5,000 secret documents over a period of 16 months prior to the Cuban missile crisis. The documents provided detailed descriptions of Soviet defence policy and weapon systems and Penkovsky himself was able to give briefings on the Kremlin's foreign policy aims at secret meetings with British and American intelligence officers in the West.

The main group used by MI6 for operations inside the Soviet Union until the end of the 1960s was the People's Labour Alliance (NTS) founded in 1930 in Belgrade by social democratic Russian emigres who sought the overthrow of the communist regime from within and its replacement with a parliamentary democracy. The NTS actively supported the Nazis before and during the 1941 invasion of Russia but became disillusioned and most of its leaders were eventually executed or imprisoned. At the end of the war the remaining leaders were released and the organisation reconstructed with Allied help.

NTS headquarters, according to Louis Hagen writing in 1968,[18] was at that time in Paris with an 'operational centre' in Frankfurt-am-Main. Organised roughly like an intelligence service, it adopted a cellular structure within the Soviet Union and contained a special section able to move in and out of the country which liaised with the cells. It also ran 'Radio Free Russia' and a training school in Bad Homburg. Members came to Britain for advanced espionage instruction from MI6 staff.

In general, the Soviets' large and effective internal security apparatus makes operations immensely difficult if not impossible, and Western intelligence services rely heavily on defections. A similar problem is present, though to a lesser degree, in other Warsaw Pact countries. Inevitably, the East-West conflict is used by both as a pretext for intervention in the Third World. With reference to Africa and the Middle East, we will examine the legitimacy of this claim from the British perspective in later chapters.

MI6 headquarters is Century House, a 20 storey office block in the Lambeth district of London. From here, a number of regional 'desks' communicate with the field officers and analyse material sent in with the help of an extensive filing system, known as the registry. The

* Glavnoye Razvedyvatelnoye Upravleniye, Chief Intelligence Directorate of the Soviet General Staff.

desks are, like those in the Foreign Office, organised geographically and grouped into six sections: United Kingdom, Europe, Soviet Bloc, Middle East and Far East. With only one station in Latin America, that continent is probably covered by one of the other regional sections, although the South Atlantic conflict may have prompted some reorganisation. Other divisions deal with administration, training, counterintelligence and security. The production and requirements departments, previously separate, have now been combined into a single division. There is also a large technical department, described as 'Special Support', staffed by locksmiths, video and audio technicians. All of these are supervised by the director of MI6 – as distinct from the chief, who heads the agency. The director is charged with the day-to-day running of MI6. The chief overlooks the MI6 departments handling relations and liaison with the rest of the Whitehall machinery (these are outside the director's control) and bears the ultimate responsibility for the agency's activities. The current chief is Colin Figures,[19] a career intelligence officer with a typical record of overseas service: first with the German Control Commission and later in Amman, Warsaw and Vienna.

The operational base for any given country is known as the 'station', used for planning, information storage and communications. It is usually inside an embassy, but may be at the offices of a front company, or the back-room of a delicatessen. Nor need it be in the same country as that against which it is targeted: the Soviet station, for example, is in Rome (there is a station in Moscow, but it does not undertake operations). MI6's London station is entrusted with recruiting agents from inside Britain and monitoring foreign diplomats and officials of interest to MI6. The London station is at 60 Vauxhall Bridge Road, SWI. For training, MI6 has three known establishments: an office block at 296-302 Borough High Street, a few minutes walk from Century House; Fort Monkton near Gosport for 'escape and evasion', sabotage, demolition, and other outdoor pursuits; meanwhile surveillance and interrogation (and resistance to it) are taught at the Intelligence Corps headquarters in Ashford. The Special Air Services also use Fort Monkton, which is run by MI5. For stations inside embassies, intelligence officers need to pose as diplomats. This is often the easiest method of entering a country and provides the advantages of access to embassy facilities, diplomatic immunity, and natural opportunities to meet important locals. The quantity of official diplomatic duties can easily be minimised to guarantee the officer ample time to pursue his intelligence work. This type of cover is known as 'light', as it is not particularly difficult for any counterintelligence department to determine which embassy staff are genuine diplomats.

Occasionally they give themselves away. An MI6 'diplomat' was assigned to accompany Moise Tshombe during the Congo crisis to and from his rendezvous with the UN negotiators. The closeness of the 'diplomat' to Tshombe aroused considerable suspicion, for on occasion he appeared to be supplying Tshombe with political advice and verbal support. The British Council also provides useful light cover: we know of one example where an MI6 officer obtained a job teaching English to a French-speaking African president, a position of immense potential intelligence value.

Some kinds of intelligence activity cannot be performed from light cover positions. In these circumstances the 'diplomats' must be supplemented by other officers under deep cover, who live as ordinary legitimate private citizens with backgrounds that should withstand thorough investigation. Deep cover officers are normally used for a specific project, unlike their light cover colleagues who are assigned to provide continual intelligence background – which may be little more than gossip – and operate the station and existing agent networks. They rely on the station for communications, guidance and administrative support. Considerable care is taken in preparing authentic covers, as the deep cover officer is relatively inefficient in terms of volume production, usually because of the need to maintain a full-time job. The value of deep cover lies in the sources to which that cover should be able to give access. Deep covers are not, on the whole, at all flexible. Often their very existence is dependent on the establishment of a persistent routine. In some countries there is an MI6 'resident', a long-term expatriate, who is able to organise cover and perhaps control agents. Field officers themselves rarely spend more than fifteen years abroad.

The most common types of deep cover are commercial and press. Frank Snepp, a CIA field officer in Vietnam in the seventies, described how he knew

> from first-hand experience that the British were using journalists as field operatives or that journalists were British field operatives ... certain MI6 men were operating under deep cover as journalists and we were using them to plant stories favourable to American interests in certain publications that we couldn't reach the same way.[20] *Hugo Young and Mark Lawson for starters*

In this quotation, Snepp touched on a point which requires particular emphasis. There is an important distinction between intelligence officers who pose as journalists (that is, use journalistic cover) and working journalists who are recruited by an intelligence service as agents, either on contract for a fixed spell or pro rata.

The editor of 'one of Britain's most distinguished journals' believes that over half its foreign correspondents are on the MI6 payroll.[21] The

Foreign Editor of another paper, the *Daily Telegraph* gave an MI6 link-man journalistic credentials,[22] and both the *Economist* and the *Observer* employed Kim Philby. More recently, a 'former' MI6 man tried to join the *Sunday Times*, causing an internal row which made it impossible for him to be employed. With journalistic contacts a certain amount of give and take occurs – the co-operative journalist is provided with intelligence information to help with or on which to base stories. ❙MI6 holds a dossier on many journalists noting their professional abilities, personalities and recommendations on what circumstances they should be used under. ❙

Similarly, businessmen and women who travel to, or have contacts in, sensitive areas can be recruited. Greville Wynne, who carried microfilmed documents from Penkovsky (see p.33) out of the Soviet Union, was a salesman busily hunting contracts in Eastern Europe. He had worked for MI5 during the Second World War as a contract agent under guidance from an MI5 case officer. In 1955 this same man, who had since moved to MI6, approached Wynne again and asked him to be a courier, which he agreed to. People with intelligence experience such as Wynne can also be asked to control agents and provide cover. Of course, if anything goes wrong, they will be disowned. But MI6 does not always get its own way. An economic consultancy firm used to working with Third World countries gave a job to an old Cambridge friend of one of the partners. Their new recruit said he had previously worked for the War Office and had useful contacts there. As one partner told it:

> . . . pushed hard for the Congo account, as he called it. He wanted us to do PR for Cyril Adoula (at that time Prime Minister of newly independent Congo). He wanted us to set up a separate company and he said he had a man waiting in Hong Kong, who'd already had his jabs, ready to go out and work for us. It was obvious we were being pushed into something. We were only being offered £10,000 by Adoula for the job, which wasn't enough. . . ., however, said that his contacts in the Foreign Office had offered to make it up with another £10,000. We would have been compromised so we refused.[23]

After this fiasco, this same consultancy was approached again just before the Biafran civil war:

> . . . had sent back atrocity pictures from Enugu through the High Commissioner's diplomatic bag. Shortly afterwards we were visited by a man from Foreign Office intelligence. He proposed that we make notes on the people around Ojukwu (the Biafran leader). He asked questions like 'Was there a man with insurance agencies?' He wanted to know how many abattoirs the Biafrans had and how much meat was in them.

> Not long afterwards we met with a guy at the Great Eastern hotel. He didn't seem very knowledgable. He asked after the last ship out of Port Harcourt carrying groundnut oil before the war broke out. I fed him lots of information which he diligently scribbled down. It all came out of Lloyds intelligence service. We met again with someone else but the relationship terminated during the war because we were on different sides.[24]

Tourism, despite its non-professional nature, is not immune from the interest of the intelligence agencies. In his widely-reported 1971 interview with the Soviet newspaper Izvestiya, Kim Philby described Operation Polygon, which was designed to get tourists into the 'forbidden zones' of the Prebaltic, Western Ukraine and the Urals, from which diplomatic personnel are barred. A further objective, he said, was the creation within the Soviet Union of 'political and ideological diversion', whatever that may be.[25]

Whether agents come from the indigenous population of the target country or from the ranks of British travellers, the golden rule for MI6 officers is to make them feel important, even if they cannot be paid much. MI6 may go to some lengths to guarantee this, if the potential dividends seem to justify it. In the early 1950s the service found a possible recruit in a moderately high position in an African government, but who refused to commit himself until he met its head, the mystical 'C':

> We had a number of ex-MI6 staff members – men in their 50's – who had retired on half service ... we chose one who was distinguished looking enough to be 'C', and we dressed him up for the part. We gave him a fine suit, an umbrella, and a bowler hat. He flew out and met the man. As far as that man knew, he had been personally recruited by 'C' and he was delighted.[26]

Finally, MI6 recruits professional criminals. The government formally admitted in 1973 that Kenneth and Keith Littlejohn were used to carry out bank robberies in the Irish Republic over a year period in order to discredit the Official IRA. Kenneth Littlejohn also claims that he was detailed to assassinate Sean Mac Stiofain, sometime Provisional chief of staff. Howard Marks, an Oxford graduate turned drug dealer was recruited to supply information on Provisional arms smuggling networks, in exchange for immunity from prosecution. Both schemes went awry when the Littlejohns were arrested by the Irish police and sentenced to long jail terms, and the British Customs and Excise caught up with Marks and pushed ahead with two embarrassing court cases.

MI6 staff themselves are drawn from the armed forces, universities, and the police, with a recent concentration on relatively young ex-service personnel. The droves of former members of Indian police forces who joined the intelligence agencies, particularly MI5, after independence have passed through or on. At the end of the sixties, MI6 underwent a massive purge, according to one report[27] 'on a scale that KGB leaders might hesitate to have implemented'. The Metropolitan Special Branch provided much of the new intake. Police officers are also seconded to MI6 for criminal investigations in which the service has an interest. Of the universities, Oxford and Cambridge are still preferred, though everywhere the recruiting sergeants seem to be having difficulty persuading ambitious young graduates that a career in espionage is worthwhile. The groundwork was done, up until recently, by a 'talent-spotter', a tutor or supervisor with Whitehall contacts who would make the initial recruitment pitch which, if successful, would lead to a series of interviews.

In 1979, apparently on the suggestion of Prime Minister James Callaghan, graduate recruitment was formalised to use the Civil Service Commission and the university careers services. Students aspiring to careers in foreign affairs are told of other appointments which 'occasionally arise in addition to those covered by the diplomatic service'. Preliminary interviews are now done by Foreign Office or military staff, with subsequent discussions at 3 Carlton Gardens, behind London's Pall Mall, in offices described as occupied by 'Co-ordinating Staff, FCO'. Those holding leftish views are not disregarded, as some are believed to have a better understanding of political violence. The difficulty in finding recruits has been put down to a change in attitude towards the secret services. Although pay rates are only slightly higher than those in the diplomatic service, field officers have almost unlimited expense accounts. The only additional benefit is retirement on full pension at 55. But as Chapman Pincher points out: 'Few people leave MI6 completely'.[28] Shortly before official retirement, employees are asked if their houses can be used as mail drops. To counter the dearth of recruits, the pass mark in the Civil Service examination has been set below that for the diplomatic corps.

Estimating the size of MI6 is difficult. The number of officers who work in the field is somewhere between 300 and 500, half of whom are overseas at any given time. About 600 staff work at Century House, under the watchful eyes of the feared security sub-section. The total seems to be between one thousand and fifteen hundred. The overseas stations – some thirty of them in the Third World – are usually staffed by two people, a man and a woman secretary (about 40 field officers are women). John Stockwell, who led the CIA's Angola task force in the mid-seventies, estimates that between 20 and 25 MI6 officers work in Africa. One station in Buenos Aires covers the whole of Latin America, and the British rely largely on CIA reports in this region.

Most contemporary MI6 operations involve working with the CIA which means that liaison with the Americans is of the utmost importance to MI6. Given the close co-operation in matters of defence and foreign policy this is no great surprise. In Chapter 2 we describe intelligence collaboration in the broader context of Anglo-American relations. In operational terms, the partnership is described thus:

> The Britain station is almost identical with that of the CIA except perhaps that it is smaller, better covered and better integrated into the embassy to which it is assigned. Also it is poorer, its budget normally being about a third of the budget of its American counterpart. For this reason, it is in most parts of the world a primary duty of the British station chief to use his superior prestige and cunning to persuade his CIA colleague to join with him in joint Anglo-American operations for which he supplies the brains and the CIA colleague supplies the funds.[29]

The author fails to elaborate on the reasons for the 'superior prestige and cunning', but if it exists, the respective training procedures may provide the answer. Americans tend to specialise in one particular aspect of field intelligence work: electronics, encoding, recruitment or whatever. Because of their service's smaller size, on the other hand, MI6 officers need a broader knowledge of 'tradecraft' and are generally able to apply all the necessary techniques satisfactorily. Also

> He's probably much better trained in languages ... able to move from one area of the world to another with relative ease and with a great deal of background knowledge ... (he knows) how to track ... use invisible inks ... the Minox camera ... generally a great deal more about firearms.[30]

The service as a whole is now said to be strong on political analysis, particularly the Middle East, and individual profiles. A senior West German intelligence official recalled that it achieved 'notable accuracy in the case of Krushchev'.[31] CIA officers also point to MI6's long-standing emphasis on commercial affairs, but it is difficult to estimate how accurate or useful it is in this area.

MI6 covert action operations are organised by a distinct department within the organisation, although some of the regular field intelligence officers are undoubtedly used to execute them. Philby[32] describes a 'Special Political Action' section set up in the mid-fifties with the various tasks of organising coups, secret radio stations and propaganda campaigns, wrecking international conferences and influencing elections. Miles Copeland[33] confirms the existence of a separate 'political action' department.

The current agency policy on assassinations is unknown. Maurice Oldfield is supposed to have circulated an internal memorandum stating that such practices are not tolerated, following the claims by MI6 agent Kenneth Littlejohn that he was detailed to kill several leading Irish republicans. Certainly MI6 has arranged assassinations in the past. More recently, an officer working on the Czechoslovak desk was apparently killed following the defection of a Czech intelligence officer to the CIA who revealed him as a double-agent.

Covert operations of a military nature, or with a significant military component are not carried out by MI6, but by the Special Air Services (SAS), three army regiments with a unique and inherently political function beyond that of the British armed forces as a whole.

Stephen Harper's description of them as 'the military arm of Britain's Secret Intelligence Service'[34] is misleading as it implies a subordinate relationship which does not in fact exist, although Harper's indication of the closeness of the two services is broadly accurate. Tony Geraghty's recent work on the SAS suggests that force is used 'sparingly, as a precise cutting tool for political policy'.[35]

The first SAS regiment was founded in 1941 by Lieutenant Colonel David Stirling, then a subaltern in the Scottish Guards. Its purpose was to carry out sabotage and reconnaissance missions behind the enemy lines and it was first active in North Africa in November 1941. During the subsequent years of World War II it undertook further operations in most combat areas. A Special Boat Section commanded by Capt. G.B. Courtney had been formed a year before Stirling's unit, and used similar techniques. Towards the end of the war it was expanded and eventually assimilated into No. 2 SAS, headed by David Stirling's brother, William.

The wartime SAS was made up of squadrons which included Rhodesians, Australians, French and Belgians. In 1945 when the British SAS was (temporarily) disbanded, the soldiers of other nationalities maintained their SAS identity, including the regimental emblem of a winged dagger with the motto 'Who Dares Wins'. The War Office was, on reflection, loath to desert the concept of a SAS unit within the British Army and in 1947 the British SAS reformed as a territorial and volunteer unit, the 21st SAS (Artists). A regular (full-time paid soldiers) regiment was created in 1952, the 22nd SAS. This was formed from a unit of Malayan scouts created two years earlier which had been using some of the techniques developed by the wartime SAS against the jungle insurgents of the Malayan Communist Party. Britain was aware that, with the break-up of her Empire, she was in sore need of trained and expert low-profile counter-insurgency troops. In 1952, 22 SAS left Malaya and returned to Britain. It was posted first to

Malvern, Worcestershire but in 1960 moved to its present site at Hereford. In 1959 a second territorial regiment of SAS was formed, 23 SAS (TAVR – Territorial Army Volunteer Reserve) to give practice in 'escape and evasion' techniques. 23 was modelled on a wartime department known as MI9, whose task was to assist Allied airmen who had crashed behind enemy lines, although by the end of the war it had turned into an anti-communist espionage organisation. Thus there are today three SAS regiments. Although the size and structure of the SAS regiments is classified secret, several publications have made educated guesses. The *Daily Telegraph* in 1975 estimated that the three SAS regiments comprised 1,500 men, and *Time Out* suggested in 1978 that the regular regiment 22 SAS had 850 – 900 men serving with it. A restricted MOD guide to the SAS obtained by the *Leveller* showed that the regimental headquarters was responsible through the Colonel Commandant (commanding officer) General Sir Robert Ford to the Director of SAS, at present Peter de la Billière. This is an important feature of the SAS. No other army regiments appear to need a director as well as a commanding officer. 22 SAS is made up of a number of operational squadrons, each one consisting of 72 men and six officers. They are further divided into five troops, viz. the amphibious troop, the air troop, the surveillance troop, the mountaineering troop, and the specialised signals troop. The troops generally comprise 15 men and one officer, although the signals troop usually has additional men seconded from the Royal Corps of Signals. These troops typically operate as four-man teams including specialists in signals, medicine, demolition and languages. To avoid a patrol being put out of action through the death of one member there are cross-specialisations. In addition, SAS has a research centre evaluating new equipment (colloquially known as 'the Kremlin'), an intelligence wing, and a training wing. The training wing is in turn split into an initial training cell, a counter-revolutionary warfare cell, and a Northern Ireland cell – the most recent addition to the regiment. Communications are provided by 63 (SAS) and 264 (SAS) signals regiments, based in Southampton and Bournemouth respectively. The territorial element in the SAS is completed by 'R' Squadron, a reservist standby group of ex-22 Regt. members. Members of the SAS have their own equipment and arms and each is allowed 'within reason' to choose his own personal weapons. They are known to favour armalite rifles and high-velocity machine pistols for close quarters work.

Unlike other territorials, 21 SAS and 23 SAS are integrated closely with the structure of the regular regiment and are commanded by regular officers. 21's headquarters are a block in the Duke of York's Barracks in Chelsea, London (also the regimental headquarters) and squadrons are based at TAVR centres in Dulwich, Hitchin (Herts.)

and Cosham, near Portsmouth. 23 squadrons are established in Leeds, Invergowrie (near Dundee), Port Glasgow and Prudhoe, near Newcastle. Their headquarters are in south Birmingham. 'R' Squadron is split between the HQ's of the 21 and 23 regiments.

The SAS describe their duties as 'basically long range reconnaissance and offensive operations 'behind the line' in war: in peace it adapts to the varied requirements of the time as does any other regiment in the army'. Rather more detail on SAS activities is provided in the regiment's recruitment literature. According to a recent recruitment advertisement: 'Long range reconnaissance and sabotage is what SAS is all about'. The recruitment handbook boasts of 'operating in small patrols in enemy held territory, feeding back information on the enemy to the British and Allied HQ'. The most detailed outline of SAS duties is to be found in the British Army's own handbook *Land Operations Manual Vol. III. Counter Revolutionary Operations*. It states:

> SAS squadrons are particularly suited, trained and equipped for counter-revolutionary operations. Small parties may be infiltrated or dropped by parachute, including free fall, to avoid long approach through enemy dominated areas, in order to carry out any of the following tasks:
> a) the collection of information on the location and movement of insurgent forces
> b) the ambush and harassment of insurgents
> c) infiltration of sabotage, assassination and demolition parties into insurgent held areas
> d) border surveillance
> e) limited community relations
> f) liaison with and organisation, training and control of friendly guerilla forces operating against the common enemy.

SAS thus has definite roles in any conflict. They are not intended to be cannonfodder for generals but rather to pursue specific objectives for which they have the special training, weaponry and back-up.

Grooming the SAS squadrons entails a rigid selection process and a gruelling training programme designed to test 'independence, stamina, has to prove himself as an individual'. Towards the end, potential recruits are subjected to endurance tests which involve long journeys over mountainous country heavily loaded. Those selected go through a 14 week period of continuation training with seven weeks general training, three weeks combat survival, and four weeks special parachute training. Instruction is even provided in the use of herbs and fungi. After this they are accepted into the regiment for a year's probation, during which time they are taught jungle warfare, demolition work, medical aid and signalling as well as skiing, medicine, mountaineering, radio communications, underwater swimming and languages.

The SAS is for young Army personnel or civilians willing to suspend their identity and advancement for three or more years. The average age of recruits is 27, though the territorial regiments are open to any male between the ages of 18 and 32. Recruits for 22 SAS come only from the armed forces, and of these about one third are volunteers from the paratroopers. 22 SAS recruits parade with their local squadron after a security clearance while being tested. If they pass, they become a band one SAS trooper, equivalent to a private. In all three regiments, soldiers serve an initial three year tour of duty which can be renewed. After their service, members of 22 SAS return to their original regiments. Although on joining SAS they are stripped of rank, their promotion continues once they return to their original regiment.

The strenuous training programme and extreme physical fitness demanded in SAS work are made much of by those who seek to build up the mystique of the SAS regiments. They similarly vaunt the intelligence of SAS soldiers, needed to absorb and apply the vast range of crafts. Especially after the resolution of the Iranian embassy siege in London in 1980, the SAS were easily presentable as a breed of contemporary super-heroes.

The SAS themselves must feel ambivalent towards this kind of publicity, for they are well aware that they do not exist to assist the army's recruitment propaganda or for boosting national morale in times of recession. Since World War II they have been involved in 32 theatres of war, usually in countries who do not want the troops' presence to be known. At the end of 1976, an anonymous SAS troop commander stated that 'all our squadrons are now committed in various places in the world'.[36] Equally the British government has no wish to have the foreign activities of its elite counter-insurgency force publicised, as deniability is often the only, often flimsy, defence against charges of warmongering, imperialism, interference and so on. Exposure can also precipitate escalation, as other powers lend or increase military support to their chosen side.

These political structures affect both the struggles in which the SAS are used and their methods. They have never fought on the insurgent side, but always in support of an established regime. In the field they work as closely as possible with indigenous forces, even trying to pass themselves off as such on occasion. SAS squads disguised as locals were deployed in Kenya and Cyprus to carry out reconnaissance or undertake terror raids. With the Marine Commandos in Borneo in the mid-sixties they established small groups of irregulars, the Border Scouts, composed mainly of Iban tribesmen from Sarawak. These groups were each led by two SAS men in disguise. So successful were the SAS that overall command of British land troops in Borneo was placed in their hands. They also fought in Vietnam where they were attached to Australian and New Zealand SAS squads despite declared British government policy that no British troops would be involved in the Vietnam war. Some were seconded to Fort Bragg, home of the United States special forces, and then inducted into the US army.

The formation, training and equipment of guerilla groups is a long-standing SAS tactic, as a former SAS commander in Oman explains:

> The SAS have much experience of dealing with irregular forces, from the Senoi Praak of the Malayan emergency in the 1950s through to the Border Scouts of the Confrontation with Indonesia ... the average regular officer or soldier finds dealing with irregulars a frustrating experience because they are anathema to all his military upbringing.[37]

Obviously close co-operation is required between MI6 and the SAS before and during overseas campaigns and SAS squadrons receive briefings from MI6 before departure. Both MI6 and MI5 are keen to recruit former SAS officers once they have left the army.

A less dramatic though equally important part of SAS foreign work is the training of security forces. Anti-guerilla and anti-hijack instruction has been provided for American and European units as well as those from Indonesia, Thailand, Pakistan and numerous African states. The Shah of Iran's Special Forces were SAS-trained and SAS men were entrusted with the protection of a monitoring station on the Irani-Soviet border directed aginst the Soviet Union. Four of them were captured by Fedayeen guerillas in 1972 and executed. A SAS detail was supposed to have assisted in the abortive mission to rescue hostages from the American embassy in Tehran, but pulled out when they discovered that the helicopters provided were for marine rather than desert use. The SAS said that the craft would fill up with sand and crash, which is exactly what happened. American forces, and also Koreans, were trained by the SAS at the British Jungle Warfare School, then situated in Malaysia, for action in Vietnam. (The School is now in Belize.) Members of Third World paramilitary police corps raised to deal with internal unrest have benefited from SAS instruction and experience; Ben Gethi, the commander of the Kenyan General Service Unit, was in Aden with the SAS.[38]

Within the United Kingdom the SAS have been extensively deployed in Northern Ireland, mainly in border observation, interception and ambushing of Provisional IRA units. In 1977 160 SAS men were operating in the province and a senior SAS officer was attending all major army and security force briefings. Some of their work is similar to that of other British army regiments, whose uniforms the SAS wear when not in plain clothes. However, the army says the SAS are better at these tasks because of their special training. Persistent reports of SAS assassinations are invariably dismissed because they emanate from republican sources, but they have undoubtedly had a bad affect on army efforts to ingratiate itself with the catholic population. Simultaneously their justifiable reputation for ruthlessness – one former British soldier who worked with them in the Middle East described them as 'the coolest and most frightening body of professional killers I have ever seen'[39] – is believed by the army to be a powerful and useful weapon as a deterrent to some forms of IRA activity. Since Harold Wilson broke with precedent by announcing publicly that the SAS were being sent to Northern Ireland in 1975 (itself misleading as they had been there since 1969) politicians have continually played the SAS 'card', couched in terms of increasing undercover operations, both in attempts to frighten the IRA and placate Protestant paramilitaries.

In Britain, SAS members work on 'special detail' with the police Special Branch in all major cities[40] and during the 1979 election campaign were used as bodyguards and stewards at political meetings. They are also used to protect British VIPs in dangerous areas of the world. The same year 21 SAS advertised for 'young, fit men' to undertake 'part-time, secret work of national importance within the United Kingdom',[41] possibly in connection with the same.

Outside the SAS there is limited scope for the use of such nefarious talents as its members acquire. Many used to join the Rhodesian SAS, originally 'C' Squadron of the British wartime regiment.

It fought with 22 SAS in Malaya where Lt. General Peter Walls, who commanded the Rhodesian Army until 1980, and Major Ron Daly, who headed the Selous Scouts, had SAS training.

Connections between the Rhodesian SAS and the British regiments remained close. The 21 SAS regimental newspaper *Mars and Minerva* stated in 1978 that 'The Rhodesian SAS is still affiliated 13 years after UDI to our own'. In 1961 the first parachute instructors for the Rhodesian SAS were trained at Abingdon, and in 1962 the British and Rhodesian SAS had a joint training programme in Aden. During the UDI period of the war with the Patriotic Front, ex-SAS men serving in the Rhodesian army made frequent recruiting trips to Britain where they visited the Hereford barracks and were given a cordial welcome. The Selous Scouts osprey insignia hangs on the wall of the palud-R-Inn Club in the SAS Hereford barracks as a mark of appreciation.

Around 50 former British SAS were in the 350 strong Rhodesian regiment at the time of independence. The unit was to have played a key role – securing important urban installations – in a possible army coup envisaged by a British officer during the transition period to majority rule.[42] But it was not to be: almost immediately after taking office, Prime Minister Robert Mugabe formally dissolved the regiment. By the time he did so, however, most of its members had travelled to South Africa, where the regiment has been incorporated into the army, virtually intact, as a 'reconnaissance unit'.

'At arms length' – Mercenaries and the role of private enterprise

Other restless ex-SAS men join one of a plethora of security firms which provide bodyguards, training units and mercenaries. The mercenary business is often misinterpreted as a purely commercial exercise, albeit rather seedy. In fact it is subject to relatively tight political scrutiny and operations which run counter to official foreign policy are blocked. Some initiatives are discreetly promoted by Whitehall because, in the event of some mishap, they are completely deniable. Mercenaries are preferred if the British government wishes to support an insurgency, for it is sensitive to allegations of subversion and careful to preserve its international reputation. It is also reluctant to provide fighting troops for allied governments under military threat, and resorts to the device of providing 'loan service personnel', serving members of the British armed forces seconded to foreign countries. These are in effect government-sponsored mercenaries, as they are not supplied free of charge, even though it might be hidden within an aid package. Occasionally British soldiers are sent directly: they are normally SAS units and disguised as training teams. The number currently on secondment is about 750, with the largest contingents in Oman, Zimbabwe, Brunei and Kuwait.

Closely related is the supply of training teams proper, and again both government and private enterprise are involved, with the demarcation dependent on political and financial factors. As Bissell pointed out (see p. 18), military and security training constitutes a form of covert action, because it represents an attempt to enhance the stability of a favoured regime in the same way as covert funding to a political party is designed to increase its electoral chances (if undiscovered). As a valuable by-product, it also provides useful cover for intelligence-gathering.

Beyond these two classes are a further group sometimes described as 'white-collar mercenaries', technicians and maintenance staff who arrive in the Third World from developed countries to look after the menagerie of high-technology hardware with which modern wars are fought. Nowadays they are as sought after as their traditional fighting counterparts.

The central political question is the precise nature of relations between government's covert agencies and the private companies that operate in the same area. The best established of these companies are those employing former SAS personnel, which appeared shortly after the beginning of the civil war in North Yemen. Leading the way, not surprisingly, was SAS founder David Stirling.

After he resigned as president of the Capricorn Africa Society (see chapter 2) in 1959, Colonel Stirling's career took a new course. He stopped perpetually flying from one conference to another and took stock of what he was doing. He decided to go into the business of selling television programmes and expertise overseas. Besides the need for a steadier source of income, he felt motivated by the need to try and spread the Capricorn ideas of multiracialism through television broadcasting, especially through the interest he acquired in a network in southern Africa. One of his first successes was to win a TV contract in Mauritius to supply programmes to the local network. A few years later, in 1966, he became one of the major backers for a new television network in Kenya.

At about the same time as the TV network was set up in Kenya, Stirling was asked by the Kenyan government to negotiate with the British government a scheme for training Kenya's special forces, including the paramilitary General Service Unit. He got this job because of his friendship with Bruce McKenzie, a leading white politician in post-independence Kenya and an old friend of Stirling's from Capricorn days. Stirling wrote a paper on the training of Kenyan forces which later formed the basis for their training by the SAS.

A year later he set up a company called Watchguard on the island of Guernsey, a haven safe from the demanding detail required by British company law. To sell its services, Watchguard produced a tasteful emerald green-bound brochure which gave details of some of its services.

a) Military Survey and Advice

Watchguard carries out surveys and gives advice ... Some countries have employed Watchguard specifically for surveys

b) Head of State Security

This includes the training of Close Escort units of bodyguard teams for Heads of State and other key officers of Government ... This is the company's speciality.

c) Special Forces

The training of forces to combat insurgency and guerilla warfare.

But as Stirling explained in an interview given in 1979, the company was blessed with complete government approval:

> The organisation was designed to tackle really important military objectives which couldn't be tackled officially because of questions in the House of Commons. The British government wanted a reliable organisation without any direct identification. They wanted bodyguards trained for rulers they wanted to see survive.[43]

Stirling has, with this statement, unambiguously confirmed that private enterprise is used by government to broaden its range of covert action options beyond those which it has with its own agencies, which are occasionally hamstrung by the vagaries of parliamentary democracy. It should be added that the government is glad to see skills, imparted at some expense to itself, in continuing use and in support of its foreign policy.

Kenya would have been Watchguard's first contract but it was decided that a SAS detachment would be used instead. So Watchguard's first contract was actually won in Zambia with Kenneth Kaunda whom Stirling had met in the course of his work for Capricorn. It was hired to provide instructors to train a special force to guard President Kaunda. The training team was headed by Malcolm Macgillivray, son of the former chairperson of the Kenya Council of State (another Capricorn contact of Stirling's). Many of its recruits were former SAS soldiers.

Watchguard made several efforts to get a contract to train the bodyguard for President Banda of Malawi. He failed because the expatriate head of Malawi security believed that better training was offered by the Americans, Israelis and South Koreans. Stirling's other publicly known contract in Africa was in Sierra Leone to protect President Siaka Stevens:

> This was done by Watchguard originally but was taken over by Malcolm Macgillivray. I did it on request from HMG. I didn't like the regime there ... so I left after it was set up. Macgillivray was there for two to three years.

Other Watchguard contracts were mainly with rulers in the Gulf states. It is difficult to determine the precise nature of Stirling's relationship with the government. Every so often, in a personal capacity, he has worked with MI6: the best example is mercenary recruitment for the mid-sixties guerilla war against the Egyptian-backed North Yemeni government. Watchguard was centrally involved in the so-called 'Hilton Operation' of 1970, aimed against the fledgling regime of Colonel Qathafi in Libya. Stirling was approached by a South African named Steve Reynolds with a proposal for a coup, for which the trigger was to be the release of imprisoned royalist supporters from Tripoli jail – known as the Hilton. Last minute intervention from the Foreign Office obliged Stirling to drop out because the Americans felt that Qathafi would be fairly easy to control.

Watchguard, which was known in mercenary circles as 'Plan-A-War', closed down in 1976. Stirling moved onto other pet projects, such as Truemid*, but by this time numerous other firms had moved into the market.

Eight of these companies featured in a list distributed to SAS territorial and reserve units informing them that 'service in the Regiment was incompatible' with work undertaken for these firms.[44] The list was a convenient blind for it gave 'proof' of official displeasure while in no way actively stopping the harnessing of SAS skills by mercenary recruiters. Five former SAS men feature prominently in KMS Ltd, a firm specialising in this kind of recruitment, both for mercenary forces and bodyguards: Brigadier Mike Wingate Gray, sometime defence attache in Paris; Colonel James Johnson, an insurance broker and former commander of 21 SAS; Majors Russell West and David Walker, and finally Major Andrew Nightingale from SAS Group Intelligence who was Lord Carver's bodyguard in Rhodesia during Callaghan's diplomatic initiative. SAS Group Intelligence is believed to be the primary link between the regiment and the private firms.[45] KMS had a useful contact in Detective Chief Inspector Ray Tucker, one of the Special Branch's Arab specialists: 'the man you first meet from the SB if you're organising mercenary activities', according to the mercenary recruiter John Banks. Apparently all KMS recruits are from the SAS; assignments include fighting with the Sultan of Oman and augmenting embassy protection in a few sensitive areas: a recent case was the British High Commission in Kampala after Amin's overthrow.[46] A week after *Time Out* exposed KMS, the firm was thrown out of its Earls Court offices for violation of council planning regulations. They moved to the offices of their sister firm Saladin Security at 13 Sloane Street, SWI, close to SAS regimental headquarters. Saladin and another firm staffed by ex-SAS members, Control Risks, are the market leaders in the specialist insurance field of kidnap and ransom protection. Kidnapping as a political fundraising exercise, or lucrative crime became widespread in the 1970s, and 'K and R' is now described by one American insurance company as 'the most dynamic insurance product of the immediate future'.

Two other noteworthy firms in the somewhat incestuous world of the '24 SAS', as this end of the private security industry is sometimes dubbed, are Thor Security Systems, established in 1976, and J. Donne Holdings. The first managing director of Thor was Major Anthony Hill, who at the time of the firm's establishment was still serving in the

* the Movement for True Industrial Democracy, a right-wing trade-union pressure group

who wrote "inside access" books about the SAS. Uclogising them

Royal Ordnance Corps. He was obliged to give up the directorship, albeit temporarily, when this potentially conflicting interest was discovered.[47] Russell West took over from him until May 1978 when Hill resumed control of the company. Thor Security System's last filed accounts, submitted shortly after Hill's return, describe him as 'Army Officer (retired)'. Since then, in April 1980, Hill has established Thor Security Consultants. J. Donne was, until its closure in October 1981, run by a former Intelligence Corps officer, Major Frederick Mace, with two ex-SAS men, Barry Wynne and H. M. Harclerode, as chief executive and training director respectively. They have had overseas contracts in Kuwait, Oman, Kenya, Nigeria, Botswana, India and Libya, where they trained Colonel Quathafi's bodyguard. Thor and J. Donne are unusual in supplying hardware as well as personnel, including radar, sonic sensors, night vision equipment, infra-red sensors and hydraulic road blocks.

These firms and another, less impressively connected group, led by John Banks – who provided the British mercenary corps for the Angolan civil war – are the mainstays of the British mercenary circuit. The demand and opportunities for work are both high.

MI6 takes a strong interest in the private security and mercenary companies, for it is in part its job to ensure that their activities lie within policy limits. And MI6 too calls upon private enterprise to carry out sensitive intelligence and covert action tasks. Early in 1980, the *New Statesman* described the example of Diversified Corporate Services, a firm staffed almost entirely by former MI6 and Intelligence Corps officers. Formed in 1970 by Colonel Alan Pemberton, an ex-Guards officer with no intelligence experience, it made the unique move in 1973 of demonstrating some of its electronic equipment to the *Observer*, to the consternation of the government agencies who arrange contacts for it.

It was never hired directly – always through an intermediary – but reported straight to MI6, and occasionally MI5, on completion of an assignment. At their behest, and with full government approval,

> DCS trained intelligence agents for Oman, Nigeria and other countries. Secret missions were carried out in Oman, Iran, Sudan and elsewhere in Africa and the Middle East. Training schools were set up in Enfield and in Wandsworth.[48]

According to unconfirmed reports, at least one American firm also works for MI6. Intertel describes itself as the 'top private security and intelligence' company in the United States. About half its staff are former FBI agents. Its head, Robert 'The Needle' Peloquin, admits that Intertel works for both the British and American governments.

Of the British firms supplying defence technicians to foreign governments, the largest is Airwork Ltd, a subsidiary of the British and Commonwealth Shipping Company. Airwork specialises in air-craft maintenance and pilot training but its activities have expanded over its fifty-four year history to cover many areas of defence procurement and maintenance. Its operations are typified by close alignment and co-operation with official foreign and defence policies. As 90 per cent of its work is sub-contracted from the Ministry of Defence, this is not wholly surprising. During the Second World War its extensive facilities were put at the disposal of the government, cementing a relationship which began with the training of RAF pilots several years before (and which continues to this day): between 1936 and 1954 the company trained some 35,000 air crew. Airwork has contracts for the maintenance of Royal Navy aircraft at Yeovilton and the administration of a number of military airfields. In 1950, the company acquired the distinction of being hired by the Air Ministry to provide the first Royal Auxiliary Air Force transport squadron. It is also responsible for the operation and maintenance of Britain's principal tracking station. 3,000 specialists, mostly ex-service, are employed by Airwork. Many of them are in the Third World, particularly the Middle East, where Airwork has its largest contracts. The company has branch offices in Oman and the United Arab Emirates.

Airwork moved into Africa and the Middle East after 1945, helping in oil exploration and setting up national airlines, of which it has established eight in all. Its planes were used to transport British troops to colonial trouble spots in West Africa and Malaya. As early as 1949, press reports had begun to comment on the strangeness of Airwork's anonymous charter flights and use of different names and uniforms.

Airwork has been particularly useful in countries wary that orthodox defence aid might be construed as neo-colonialist. It is able to provide a complete airfield with logistical support, including communication and radar units, aircraft, missile systems, computers and ground vehicles. It is able to train local staff to operate and maintain all the equipment, and provides English language tuition. Most important, Airwork advises on and assists in the purchase of defence systems, which gives it a substantial role in the formulation of national defence policies. Recently, it has become heavily involved in recruiting mercenaries to serve in the Sultan of Oman's rapidly growing navy and air force, as well as senior officers for the army. This operation has increased in scale since 1977 when the RAF, which had provided the country's only effective air defence, left its bases. The part played by private enterprise in the British covert action programme is highly significant, especially since decolonisation and the economic contraction, both of which emerged as inevitable during the late 1950s and early 1960s. The manner in which private contracts in this field are obtained and executed is clearly aimed at obscuring the distinction between commercial activity and government-inspired foreign policy initiatives. There seems little doubt that the firms described above function with Foreign Office and MI6 approval, but some questions remain over the control, and indeed the understanding, of their political masters. It is easy to speak, as we ourselves have done, of government in a monolithic sense. Yet, we find once again that its mechanisms are designed to hide the relations between the political regime and civil service departments. In the absence of enlightenment from either quarter, there is little choice other than to apportion general responsibility evenly. With the last part of this chapter, some attempt is made to resolve this problem.

Ministers, ministries and the intelligence establishment

Accountability is a vogue word in state-watching circles, and nowhere more so than among investigators of the British intelligence establishment. The swaddlings of official secrecy obscure the workings of even the ordinary civil service, so there is inevitably constant speculation rather than hard information about the control to which the covert agencies are subject. This depends on factors both inherent in intelligence systems everywhere and unique to Britain.

Under the British scheme of control, the ministers in each department are supposed to be in charge of their respective intelligence agencies: the Home Secretary for MI5, the Defence Secretary for DIS, while MI6 and GCHQ are supposed to work under the Foreign Secretary. This division of responsibilities is largely nominal since the Prime Minister usually takes a strong direct interest in intelligence and may, as Harold Wilson did with George Wigg, appoint a minister specifically to oversee the intelligence complex. Thatcher is understood to have given a similar task to Cranley Onslow, a junior minister at the Foreign Office.[49] The directors of the above four have immediate access to the Prime Minister under exceptional circumstances; it is believed that the director of the SAS also has this facility.

The intelligence reports which arrive on ministers' desks do not come, as a rule, direct from the producing agencies. The task of collating and analysing reports from different agencies belongs to the Joint Intelligence Committee (JIC) and two departments of the Cabinet Office Secretariat which work under it. (The Secretariat as a whole is responsible for servicing the Cabinet and its committees.) One of these, the Assessments Staff, provides long-term estimates while the other, known as Current Intelligence Group, takes a more immediate perspective. Both of these are headed by a Cabinet Office deputy secretary. The JIC itself, which passes the final reports, is composed of the heads of the four intelligence agencies, the chair and deputy chair of the Assessments Staff, the head of the Permanent Under-

Secretary's Department in the FCO (which specialises in intelligen matters), and the Co-ordinator of Intelligence and Security (see below). JIC is chaired by a FCO deputy secretary, currently Patrick Wright.[50] Economic intelligence is dealt with by a separate committee, led by a deputy secretary from the Treasury.

JIC and its economic counterpart are the final links in the chain of intelligence production. Neither of them direct or supervise the work of the intelligence agencies. The authority for this rests with a permanent secretaries' steering group and in particular the Co-ordinator of Intelligence and Security, at present Anthony Duff.[51] The group, formally entitled the Permanent Secretaries Committee on Intelligence Services, controls the intelligence budget and approves collection priorities. After consultation with selected ministers, it also approves major covert operations. The senior civil servants from the Cabinet Office, the FCO, the Home Office, the Ministry of Defence, and the Department of Trade and Industry sit on the group along with Duff and the Chief of the Defence Staff.

Covert action, which has greater attendant political risks than pure intelligence-gathering, requires closer scrutiny. Although the initiative may come from elsewhere, foreign operations are planned in MI6's requirements division. On completion, they are submitted to the agency's FCO adviser, who consults with the relevant FCO regional departments. if a plan is acceptable, it is returned to MI6 for clearance by the chief, who will need to agree the format with the FCO and if necessary, the JIC.

The maze of committees and liaison procedures has the effect of obscuring the way in which intelligence and covert action policies are formulated. This in turn inhibits meaningful discussion of foreign policy as a whole outside the select band of cognoscenti with access to the shrine of official secrets. Their privilege is defended by resort to the icon of 'national security', a concept somewhat comparable to the 'rule of law' in its treatment as absolute and immutable. Yet it is even more transparently subject to interpretation according to the values of those assigned to guard it. In simple terms, for 'national security' read 'status quo'. Foreign policy at this level depends on consensus, which by and large survives changes in government: it has not shown the fluctuations in ideological approach which have marked the domestic scene. Were it to do so, however, the consensus would disintegrate with serious consequences. The most likely trigger would be the rise to power of a strongly socialist government. It is accepted by all intelligence commentators that Anglo-American intelligence co-operation, detailed in Chapter 2, would be an immediate casualty; and, further, that British intelligence would do a great deal to defend it.

It is difficult to estimate what would happen, but some experiences from the second Wilson administration (1974–6) give useful pointers. After his resignation, Wilson wrote an autobiography, *The Governance of Britain*, containing the notorious one page chapter on security and intelligence with no useful information in it whatsoever. For some reason, he then began leaking his suspicions that MI5 had been conspiring to undermine his administration, although the evidence is not conclusive and Wilson's description of the circumstances variable. One concrete example, however, comes from Northern Ireland, which has been the subject of bitter disputes within Whitehall and between MI5 and MI6.

While Merlyn Rees was Secretary of State for the province, MI5 found him more reluctant than his predecessors to sign internment orders, and both he and Wilson had spoken of phasing out internment, a notion to which MI5 objected strongly. A crucial figure in Rees' calculations was the percentage of released internees who were returning to paramilitary activity. The figure was supplied by MI5, who adopted the simple ruse of fabricating their estimate (over half, against a true figure of under a quarter) in support of their stance.[52]

If an account given to the *Irish Times* by a former intelligence officer can be believed, politicians are viewed with remarkable disdain:

> Sometimes we told the Secretary of State we knew things that really we didn't: sometimes we pretended not to know things, that we did. From an int. point of view, politicians can be manipulated quite easily. There's no audit system for int.; it's watertight.

Subsequently, the same officer developed this theme with some force:

> Be clear on one point above all else. The intelligence world is not answerable to Secretaries of State. It is accountable to nobody – not the Prime Minister, not Parliament, not the courts.
>
> An intelligence department decides what information politicians should be given and they're rarely, if ever, given the full facts.[53]

Often the withholding of information is justified by intelligence agencies on the grounds of operational security. MI6 showed a marked reluctance to supply the 1974–9 Labour government with complete reports from Southern Africa as they believed that a number of ministers were sympathetic to nationalist movements in the region, possibly jeopardising the position of their agents.

There is little a government can do in the face of cynical and devious intelligence officers. Cutting the budget is a possible remedy to their excesses; but effective ministerial control of the budget is suspect. The money officially designated to intelligence is known as the 'Secret Vote', and is presented to Parliament as a lump sum in the annual Treasury cash limits. These are debated as a whole, and as a result of the minute proportion that the 'Secret Vote' represents, intelligence expenditure fails to generate much interest. The figure for the financial year 1981/2 was £62,000,000, and is well short of the true figure. As mentioned earlier, GCHQ probably costs around £300m. per annum while MI5 and MI6 together consume perhaps half again. A 1979 report in the Financial Times suggested that the cost of the entire British intelligence effort may be as much as ten per cent of defence expenditure, which for 1981/2 is fixed to a cash limit of £11,535 million.[54] The balance between the 'Secret Vote' and the true cost is made up out of the budgets of the FCO, Home Office and the Ministry of Defence:

> it has been Whitehall's practice to conceal the true size of the Government's intelligence and counter-intelligence operations by putting its secret budgets under several headings which, in total, exceed the sum admitted to by the Treasury

since 1946, says the *Times*.[55]

The other sanction available to the political regime is the ability to appoint and dismiss service directors. This has been used on at least one occasion since the war, following a visit to Britain by Soviet president Nikita Krushchev in 1956. MI6 sent a retired naval frogman, Commander Lionel Crabbe, to examine the hull of the cruiser *Ordzhonikidze* on which Krushchev had arrived. Crabbe, who had a weak heart and a drink problem, made two dives beneath the ship. He never returned from the second. The Russians, who had discovered that their vessel was under investigation, complained bitterly. The Prime Minister, Anthony Eden, furiously demanded to know who had cleared the operation. It transpired that although some Foreign Office staff were aware of the plan, it had not been discussed at the requisite level. The director-general of MI6, Sir John Sinclair, was dismissed as a result.

The effectiveness of this power depends on service discipline. Intelligence is a closed profession dominated by a rigid structure of norms and mores – imbued from the first weeks of training, during induction – with 'national security' at the apex. These must consistently be able to provide the stimuli and morale boosts which, unlike in other occupations, cannot be sought externally. GCHQ staff in Cheltenham, for example, are actively discouraged from socialising outside their workplace. The 'need to know' principle, which limits the information available to any one officer to the minimum necessary for a given task, frustrates intelligence staffers already threatened by lack of job security: a mishandled operation or defection can lead to a wave of expulsions. In the words of an American congressional committee

> In some respects, the intelligence profession resembles monastic

life with some of the disciplines and personal sacrifices reminiscent of mediaeval orders. Intelligence work is a life of service, but one in which the norms of American national life are sometimes distressingly distorted.[56]

It is hardly surprising if intelligence personnel suffer acutely from, in David Leigh's phrase, 'sociological tunnel-vision'.[57] But it is also true that the clubby camaraderie of intelligence professionals – christian names are in common use around Century House – tends to promote a fairly high level of discipline. Whitehall's efforts to keep the intelligence establishment under control by appointing outsiders to head the agencies may prove counter-productive.

It is in the field, especially overseas, that the temptations to cut corners and break rules are most often felt. A recent *New Statesman/ Daily Mirror* investigation[58] into the GCHQ station in Hong Kong revealed extensive corruption and malpractice, while the MI6 of the mid-1950s and the late 1960s often showed scant regard for the requirements of policy-makers. At the same time, the experience of American congressional inquiries into alleged CIA abuses should be borne in mind. On the whole, these found that, where political chicanery was proven, the CIA was responding to executive demands.

'Need-to-know', despite occasional violations through the 'old boy network', restricts the opportunities to indulge in policy-making to senior agency level, although career intelligence officers are manifestly ill-equipped to do it. Studies of executive power in Britain have illustrated the difficulties of isolating precise responsibility for the emergence of individual policies. To do so while taking covert agencies into account is no easier.

The control of the intelligence complex itself bobbles uneasily in the misty region between Cabinet and mandarins. Its nebulous character is a handicap to effective and genuine parliamentary rule. As far as foreign affairs are concerned this probably makes little difference since they rarely generate much interest. Besides, the foreign policy consensus, even with significant intervention from Parliament, is unlikely to shift in the foreseeable future.

Notes

1.   *Perspectives for Intelligence 1976-81* CIA classified document published in *Covert Action Information Bulletin*, No. 6 (October 1979) p.24
2.   *CIA: The Pike Report*, (1977) p.143
3.   *Perspectives for Intelligence*, p.21
4.   V. Marchetti and J. Marks *The CIA and the Cult of Intelligence* (1974) p.41
5.   *Time* (6 February 1978)
6.   Marchetti and Marks *The CIA and Cult of Intelligence* p.39
7.   *First Principles* Vol. 7 No. 3 (January 1982) p.1

8.   *Observer* (16 December 1979)
9.   *Ramparts* (August 1972)
10.   *New Statesman* article (2 February 1979)
11.   Marchetti and Marks *The CIA and the Cult of Intelligence* p.139
12.   Tony Bunyan *The Political Police in Britain* (1977) p.189
13.   Classified documents from the Joint Warfare Establishment published in *Irish Times* 1976
14.   F. Kitson *Low Intensity Operations* (1971) p.189
15.   *House of Commons Hansard* (4 November 1976)
16.   *Sunday Times* (22 October 1978)
17.   *New Statesman* (16 October 1981)
18.   L. Hagen *Secret War for Europe* (1968) chapter 7
19.   *Sunday Times* (7 November 1982); *Diplomatic Service List*
20.   1981 interview on *Panorama* BBC Television (23 February 1981)
21.   *Washington Post* (22 February 1975)
22.   David Smiley *Arabian Assignment* (1975) p.118
23.   Private interview
24.   *Ibid*
25.   *Izvestiya* (2 October 1971)
26.   *Christian Science Monitor* (29 September 1980)
27.   *Magill* (June 1979)
28.   Chapman Pincher *Inside Story* (1978) p.7
29.   Miles Copeland *The Real Spy World* (1978) p.93
30.   Frank Snepp, interview on *The Profession of Intelligence* part 5 BBC Radio 4 (30 August 1981)
31.   Reinhard Gehlen *The Gehlen Memoirs* (1972) p.250
32.   *Izvestiya* (2 October 1971)
33.   M. Copeland *The Real Spy World* p.73
34.   Stephen Harper *Last Sunset: What Happened in Aden* (1978) p.47
35.   Tony Geraghty *Who Dares Wins: A History of The Special Air Service 1950 – 80* (1980) p.7
36.   *Guardian* (11 December 1976)
37.   A. S. Jeapes *SAS: Operation Oman* (1980) p.230
38.   *Sunday Times* (10 August 1978)
39.   P. S. Allfree *Warlords of Oman* (1967) p.114
40.   *Guardian* (5 May 1981)
41.   *Daily Telegraph* (11 February 1981)
42.   *Leveller* No. 32 (November 1979)
43.   Private interview
44.   Tony Geraghty *Who Dares Wins* p.104
45.   *Time Out* (21 July 1978)
46.   *Observer* (20 April 1980)
47.   *Sunday Times* (17 July 1977)
48.   *New Statesman* (22 February 1980)
49.   *Sunday Express* (18 July 1982)
50.   *Guardian* (2 November 1982)
51.   *Times* (30 January 1983)
52.   *Irish Times* (24 April 1980)
53.   *Irish Times* (24 April 1980)
54.   *Financial Times* (17 November 1979)
55.   *Times* (22 August 1980)
56.   US Congress *Senate Select Committee to study Governmental Operations with respect to Intelligence Activities* (1976) book 1 p.7

57.   David Leigh *Frontiers of Secrecy* (1980) p. 185
58.   *New Statesman* (16 May 1980, 23 May 1980)

Chapter 2
Decolonisation and the Cold War

The Post-war political environment

> If we did not fulfil our world-wide mission Britain would sink
> to the level of a second-class power and become either a
> European Soviet state or a penurious outpost of American
> pluto-democracy, or a German *Gau*, as the forces might
> dictate.[1]

This was approximately the analysis of the Foreign Office in 1942
of future trends in Britain's most important foreign relations. The
possibility of coming under German domination was seen as slight;
given the recent entry of the United States into the war, an eventual
Allied victory was felt to be little more than a matter of time. While
some, mainly younger, Foreign Office staff foresaw inevitable global
domination by America and the Soviet Union, senior officials found
the prospect of a series of agreements among major powers laying the
foundation of a new world order both realistic and attractive. A
four-power plan with the participation of the so-called 'Big Three' –
Britain, the Soviet Union and The United States – plus France became
a primary objective, under which each would be the dominant nation
and guiding influence in a carefully delineated region. From the
British point of view, agreement with the Soviet Union was essential
to moderate the United States, which appeared to be developing a *Pax
Americana*.

Britain's wartime Prime Minister, Winston Churchill, was con-
tent with a three-power plan to the exclusion of the French of whom he
had always held a low opinion. Both he and the Soviet leader, Josef
Stalin, entertained the idea of complementary spheres of influence in
Europe. At a meeting in Moscow in October 1944, the two sat down
and negotiated over their respective degrees of influence in various
European states; 50/50 in Yugoslavia, 75 per cent to the Soviets in
Bulgaria. President Roosevelt and the Americans had other ideas.
Emerging from their inter-war isolation into a strategic alliance with
the United Kingdom of remarkable cohesion with full co-operation at

every level in almost every area of mutual concern, the Americans began to realise that whatever the outcome of the war, they would end up in a position of immense power. The role of supervising the world's free trade system, for so long a function performed by the British, was soon to be passed to them, and they planned accordingly, determining that

> in order for the United States economy to prosper without internal changes, without any redistribution of income or power or modification of structures ... the minimum area strategically necessary ... included the entire Western hemisphere, the former British empire which they were in the process of dismantling, and the Far East.[2]

In other words, at least this area would have to be open to American trade penetration, development and exploitation to guarantee continuing domestic economic growth.

Ultimately the American view prevailed, mainly because the exhausted British were unable to acquire urgently needed military and economic aid from anywhere except the United States. The notion of an accommodating treaty with the Soviet Union was rapidly discarded following the completion of the division of Europe; obvious ideological differences and mistrust of Soviet intentions proved insurmountable obstacles. An independent, Gaullist-type foreign policy received little consideration. The British were shocked and annoyed, having unequivocally aligned with the Americans, when the Lend-Lease scheme for economic assistance was abruptly terminated shortly after the end of the war. Rapid development of plans for American troop withdrawal from Europe, on grounds of cost, was also causing concern given the uncertainty about Soviet policy. Despite the election of a Labour government in July 1945, the new Foreign Secretary, Ernest Bevin, differed little in his perception of Soviet policy from his opponents on the Conservative benches. Indeed, a desperate need for economic support drove the British to adopt a policy of persuading the Americans to remain engaged in Europe. The new Truman administration was more receptive to arguments of Soviet expansionist tendencies and sensed potential instability in Europe, with a real chance of communists taking control in France and Italy. A large communist bloc encompassing most of Europe would present a very real threat to the United States vision of an international capitalist trading system designed to service its own economy. Crudely, American military and financial support to non-communist Europe was adjudged to be worth the price in those terms.

The financial aspect was enshrined in the Marshall Plan, under which more than $12,000 million of subsidies, loans and conditional aid was provided to nations outside direct Soviet influence, with

Britain receiving nearly a quarter. It was widely assumed in Britain that the money would be sufficient to reconstruct the economy and once again assert its independence although in a close military and political relationship with the United States. For Attlee's government there was the additional advantage that opposition from Labour's left wing to alignment with America subsided once the plan was announced: the plan was popular in the country, and they realised that an attack on it might cost them political ground. At the beginning of 1948, over two years after the withdrawal of Lend-Lease had triggered a major financial collapse, the first of the money began to arrive. In July, the bombers returned, ostensibly as a temporary measure during the Berlin airlift. They have never since left, and subsequently the entire range of American air force hardware crept into the country: fighters, reconnaissance planes and aerial refuelling craft, while weapons stores and command and communications bases, some controlled by the US Navy, sprouted on the ground. Most of the agreements under which these facilities were provided were classified and remain so, but it seems that the majority were signed in 1947, as were some of the intelligence co-operation pacts.

The Marshall Plan also signalled the initiation of a long-term American foreign policy campaign: the formation of a European political and economic union of which, it was hoped, Britain would become a member. The British were not keen on the idea, feeling that although political control of the empire was loosening, it would still provide a resource base through which the economy could be regenerated once war damage was repaired. It seems they failed to realise that the United States was actively seeking the dissolution of the empire, not so much out of a liberal morality but in pursuit of their goal of a free world trade system. The main problem in American eyes was the imperial preference scheme, devised by the British and established at the 1932 Ottawa Conference. Import duties were considered a legitimate device but that system's discrimination against third parties was deemed unacceptable. In March 1942, a commercial adviser to the State Department vowed that

> never again would the great American nation allow the British and the Dutch to dictate the prices at which it could buy its tin and its rubber.[3]

British and American officials held talks throughout the second half of the war on the future of the colonies, but failed to reach agreement.

For many years after the war, the economic growth in Britain fostered by the Marshall Plan led British policy makers to concentrate their attentions on overseas matters, ignoring the major structural flaws in the economy – inadequate investment, obsolete machinery and archaic transport systems. Their persistence in maintaining an overvalued parity for sterling, the supreme symbol of British economic potency, caused a constant haemorraging of reserves. Defence co-operation prospered with the formation in 1949 of the North Atlantic Treaty Organisation (NATO), which gave Britain a significant role in organising European defences as the Soviet Union was increasingly portrayed in the West as a savage and aggressive regime. Britain could find a world role, it seemed, in a category of its own; as a minor superpower, somewhat behind the US and the Soviet Union but well ahead of the rest. Richard Crossman, later a minister in several Labour cabinets, wrote in 1952 of the search for

> a balance of world power and in that balance the restraining influence of a Communist China on Russia may be as vital as that of a socialist Britain on the USA.[4]

The history of the immediate post-war period shows that in no sense did Britain act as a 'restraining influence', particularly during the 1945–51 Labour administration, during which 12,000 British troops were despatched to fight in the Korean war and the Foreign Office established its Information Research Department, a cold war propaganda instrument of enormous size and scope. (see pp.90-100).

In the same period the army fought Zionist guerillas in Palestine and Chinese-backed communists in Malaya (pp.71-4). The Indian question, the only major point of difference between Bevin and his Conservative opponents, was resolved in 1947 with the granting of independence. Britain was seen as having acted wisely over the issue, despite subsequent wars between India and Pakistan, which had been split off and established as a separate nation on independence.

Many political historians refer to a 'time-lag' between changes in the international political environment and changes in government policies required to meet them. The return of Winston Churchill to Downing Street in 1951 heralded an effort at time-reversal. Churchill was preoccupied to the point of obsession with re-establishing the United Kingdom as the European superpower, a project he justified in terms of Britain's membership of each of what he called the 'Three Circles': the empire and Commonwealth, the English-speaking nations, and Europe. This overblown idea was taken extremely seriously:

> the concept became a major foundation of Britain's foreign policy to the point of the government instructing diplomatic missions to use it in their publicity. It was a pronouncedly egocentric conception, the effect of which can be likened to that of geographical projections ... by the sheer method of presentation, the country becomes the centre of the earth.[5]

Policy towards Europe was vague and uncertain, however. Churchill, as had Attlee before him, refused to join in the Schuman plan to extend Franco-German co-operation in coal and steel production to other products and other countries. American aid became profoundly biased in favour of continental Western Europe as they sought to build up the West German economy and develop its defence policy within the NATO framework. British pressure on the United States to withdraw support was futile. A more positive development of relations with other European countries would, with the benefit of hindsight, have been a better option for governments of the period than attempting to maintain a global role based around a sprawling, heterogenous and disintegrating imperial system in the face of opposition from the world's two most powerful nations.

The British nuclear weapons programme, which was founded in wartime co-operation with the Americans, was held up by the McMahon Act, which prohibited disclosure of atomic information by the United States to any foreign country. The British felt their world standing would be much enhanced by exploding a nuclear device before the Soviet Union. Repeated and desperate efforts to overturn the act and persuade the Americans to provide materials and test facilities failed. The Russians tested their first weapon very much sooner than had been expected, dealing a further blow to British prestige in the process. This development, which, it may be argued, reduced Britain's central strategic role in US defence policy, simultaneously reinforced their common perception of the alleged Soviet threat which was the basis of the renewed 'special relationship'.

While the British thought the relationship useful in affecting US policies, the decision-making process for the latter was already sufficiently complex from its numerous internal inputs, and as the above examples show, the Americans were not inclined to change their policies to suit the British. Although they gave more frequent and careful consideration to British representations than to those from elsewhere, they were not as preoccupied with the cherished British ideal.

To execute their global plan, the Americans needed a large intelligence system. British and American intelligence had worked together during the war in all types of operation, and the war against communism, which had been briefly supplanted by a war against fascism, gave substantial common ground for close co-operation to continue despite their governments' differing objectives. Furthermore, the Americans were relatively new to some intelligence techniques and were prepared to accept British tutelage, while the British were happy to have an additional source of finance for some of their projects. The foundations were laid in the form of a series of intelligence-sharing agreements, the first of which were the signals intelligence pacts signed by Britain and the United States during 1947 to co-ordinate the two countries' programmes for the world-wide interception of military, diplomatic and commercial traffic. The wartime exchange of broken Japanese military codes from the Americans and the British Enigma intercepts provided the technical and administrative format which was easily adapted to peacetime. Three other nations, Canada, Australia and New Zealand, joined soon afterwards as junior partners, sharing identification and labelling procedures and security arrangements. Most important, though, is the global division under the pact which assigns an area of responsibility to each country; these arrangements are subject to continuous review to allow for changes as international conditions dictate.

Within this intelligence multinational the UK/USA link is the central axis. The author of a recent book on the American National Security Agency (NSA) states that

> the relationship between NSA and GCHQ is stronger than any between the NSA and any other American intelligence agency.[6]

The NSA was set up in 1952 under a classified directive from the National Security Council, and like GCHQ it soon took control of military signals operations. Within two years it had concluded joint policies and objectives with its British counterpart. The NSA is now a very much larger organisation and in no sense is the relationship even. GCHQ passes all its intercepts to the Americans, but in return receives only selected ready-processed material and some raw intercepts for analysis using those of its computers more advanced than those available to the NSA. Some financial support is given to GCHQ by the NSA to help run British monitoring posts.

At present GCHQ's monitoring brief includes the African continent. Its station at Francistown in Botswana was used to pick up signals from guerillas operating in neighbouring Zimbabwe as well as those of the South African government. Through its NSA link, GCHQ obtained intercepts from crucial meetings of the Zimbabwean Patriotic Front leaders held during the 1979 conference of non-aligned nations in Havana. Mrs Thatcher particularly thanked President Carter for this information on her visit to Washington in late 1979.[7]

During the Vietnam war the monitoring station at Little Sai Wan in Hong Kong provided the Americans with intelligence up until 1975, long after Harold Wilson had – publicly, at least – expressed his government's opposition to the war. The NSA co-ordinated all signals intelligence in South – East Asia, and Little Sai Wan was linked to this operation. Its intercepts of North Vietnamese military traffic were used by the American military command to target bombing strikes over North Vietnam. Together with NSA stations in Thailand and the Philippines, it also monitored North Vietnamese surface-to-air missile sites, enabling warnings to be relayed to bomber crews in mid-flight, allowing them to choose the safest air corridors to their targets. Diplomatic intercepts by GCHQ were also helpful to the US during the build-up to the 1972 Paris peace conference. President Nixon and Dr. Henry Kissinger, then National Security Adviser, attached great importance to the mood of the North Vietnamese and the Hong Kong station's information, which suggested Hanoi was far from capitulation, led to the decision by Nixon and Kissinger to 'bomb the North Vietnamese to the conference table'.[8]

The co-operation between GCHQ and NSA extends to monitoring their domestic opponents and European allies. Two NSA stations in Britain, at Menwith Hill in Yorkshire and Morwenstow in Cornwall are able to tap telephone and telex traffic to and from Britain and the continent, and across the Atlantic. At the time of Morwenstow's construction, resistance to it from the British government was overcome by GCHQ director Leonard Hooper, who argued its importance to the NSA, appealing to the special relationship in justification. By calling upon its ally, either agency is able to evade domestic legal constraints on communications interception. The NSA also routinely intercepts British government communications.

The alliance has proved to be the most resilient of the Anglo-American intelligence agreements to political ruptures between the two countries. The passive nature of the work and the absence of the major problems of policy clashes and, until very recently, penetration that have affected other agencies are the main reasons. The Suez invasion of 1956 was the only known occasion on which relations broke down, amid accusations in Parliament that the Americans were intercepting and decyphering British military and diplomatic messages.

A smaller, looser intelligence combine is made up of the foreign intelligence services from Britain, America, Canada and Australia. Both the CIA and the Australian Secret Intelligence Service (ASIS) were established with British assistance, the CIA in 1947 and ASIS a year later. ASIS in particular remains very close to MI6, having received some 50,000 reports from the British over the years in exchange for 12,000 of their own. Australian intelligence officers are still trained in Britain free of charge. ASIS officers continue to refer to MI6 headquarters as 'Head Office'.

The CIA outgrew this stage long ago, but in its infancy was eager to be as close to the British as possible. One account suggests that 'liaison reporting from other countries accounted for some seventy per cent of the raw information reports to CIA in its early years,'[9] and it can be assumed that the British were by far the largest contributors. Co-ordination on covert operations between MI6 and the CIA began in earnest soon after the establishment of the Information Research Department. The Americans watched IRD at work with a mixture of admiration and curiosity, showing particular interest in the joint IRD / MI6 propaganda campaign against the Malayan communists. From 1948, the CIA instituted similar campaigns modelled on and complementary to those of the British, giving special priority to Eastern Europe. Both the British and American governments sought to prevent communist governments taking control in post-war Europe: assets acquired from the war, like the NTS, were dusted down and sent back to work. In Greece, MI6 handed over to the CIA a clandestine support operation aimed against the Greek communist party.[10] Another, better known project, involved parachuting agents into Albania to link up with the resistance movement fighting the new communist government of Enver Hoxha. Its failure has been generally attributed to the presence of Kim Philby, then senior MI6 liaison officer in Washington, on the planning committee but it is now accepted within the CIA that the scheme was far too ambitious and assumed a scale of resistance which was, in fact, grossly overestimated. After almost a decade of efforts to catalyse uprisings in the Soviet bloc, the two agencies more or less gave up, although they later organised and trained the Norwegian E-grupper* for sabotage and guerilla raids inside the Soviet Union.

There were few quarrels over collaboration in Europe. The Middle East was a very different matter: declassified documents in the United States highlight a sharp clash over American proposals for broad Western military and intelligence co-operation in the event of war in the region. In particular, they suggested that the Supreme Allied Commander, Middle East should operate under the direction of a steering committee 'probably including French and Turkish members, in which event', MI6's Sir John Sinclair told the Americans during a 1950 visit to Washington, 'there are implications on which the British Secret Service is not prepared to commit itself.'[11] The British asked for, and got, a separate arrangement with the Americans in this area. Almost immediately the 'war planning' division of MI6 (since abolished) began work on covert action plans for execution during war.

The Suez crisis, which produced a rift across the entire range of political and defence links, also damaged MI6 – CIA relations, but not as severely as the exposures of Philby and George Blake. MI6's professional competence was seriously in doubt, and their clearance for CIA reports fell to an all-time low. The British offer of an equal share in running GRU colonel Oleg Penkovsky may be an indication of the lengths to which they were prepared to go to reingratiate themselves with 'the cousins'. The CIA accepted, with costs split equally, but typically made repeated attempts to remove him from British control,

* E-groups, after the Norwegian intelligence service, Etterretningstjenesten

thwarted only by Penkovsky's resolute anglophilia. Such attempts are commonplace among allied intelligence organisations, although among Western agencies there is no formal mechanism. The Soviet KGB reserves the right to assume control of any agent recruited by another Eastern bloc service, each of which has a KGB officer as one of its deputy chiefs.

MI6 and the CIA run a joint defection programme, which in September 1976 led to the arrival in Japan of a Red Air Force pilot flying a MiG-25 'Foxbat' aircraft. An MI6 agent made the initial advance after surveillance of the pilot indicated discontent caused by slow promotion and marital disharmony.[12] Similarly, they co-operate in monitoring nuclear developments, both in the Soviet Union and among prospective members of the nuclear club such as Israel, South Africa and Pakistan. Strangely, military intelligence, given the Western preoccupation with the Soviet forces and consequent community of interest, appears less well co-ordinated. In 1980, at the prompting of the American Defence Intelligence Agency, various United States intelligence services spent some £9 million in pursuit of information on the gun calibres of new Soviet tanks, with no success. According to the same report,[13] details were eventually supplied on request by the British, who had obtained them along with photographs of the cockpits and technical manuals at the cost of £200. In general, good liaison arrangements are more important for smaller agencies such as MI6, for without these it is unable to obtain information on areas where the cost of maintaining stations is prohibitive: in the British case, parts of the Far East.

Latin America is recognised as more or less exclusively CIA territory: there is just one MI6 field officer for the region and minimal Soviet activity. In the Far East – apart from China, where MI6 have a good network – they rely on both the CIA and ASIS. The Hope Commission on Intelligence and Security, which reported to the Australian government in 1977, described the type of information MI6 was supplying in return:[14]

> Chinese central government directives as shown in provincial discussions and reactions. Egyptian government intentions. Political and economic reporting on India, Bangladesh and Pakistan, including Indo-Soviet relations.

General agreements not to operate in each other's territory or sphere of influence without prior arrangement were forged early in the life of the CIA, but the interpretation of both agencies seems to be that such agreements exist to be violated. Several ex-CIA officers say that infiltrating Western governments and intelligence services is standard American procedure.

There are about 70 American intelligence officers based in London, from the CIA and NSA. The NSA runs numerous listening posts in Britain, some of which were mentioned earlier. The CIA has a station in the embassy, mainly concerned with liaison, and possibly two other offices. One of these, in London, is understood to be the agency's Western Europe headquarters, which moved from Paris in the early 1970s. The other is outside London, and described as 'a training and planning base for subversive activities in Africa'.[15]

CIA intervention in British politics dates back to the end of the war. The Labour party was elected on a platform of extensive social reform at home and peaceful co-existence with the Soviet Union in Europe. The influential right-wing of the party, fearful of the spread of communist influence, sought to make the counter-struggle their top priority. Covert financing of international student and trade union movements began about this time. The right organised around the journal *Socialist Commentary*, originally set up by refugees from Hitler's Germany but reorganised in 1947 to adjust to the change in circumstances. *Socialist Commentary* became the most important mouthpiece for this faction, which under the new Labour leader Hugh Gaitskell grew in confidence and influence. In 1953, *Encounter*, a monthly journal aimed at European social democrats, was launched under the editorship of Irving Kristol, who had worked on one of the original American anti-communist publications, *New Leader*.* *Encounter* was a joint Anglo-American venture involving, on the British side, the Honorable C.M. "Monty" Woodhouse, a covert action veteran with experience in Greece and of the tricky negotiations with the CIA preceding Operation Ajax (p.111).[16] The magazine used many of the same staff and writers as *Socialist Commentary* and exchanged facilities. An article entitled 'Africa and Democracy', written by Rita Hinden, one of *Socialist Commentary's* cold war recruits, in the same journal was reprinted by *Encounter* in a series of pamphlets. *Encounter* was financed by the Congress for Cultural Freedom, a CIA front exposed in 1967. Both *Socialist Commentary* and particularly *Encounter* were important weapons for the right in the battles over defence, especially the issue of German rearmament, and nationalisation during Labour's long period of opposition.

While promoting and supporting their cold war position in the Labour party through these journals, the Americans took steps to undermine the opposition. On one occasion this took the form of a blatant threat. German rearmament was a central feature of US policy in Europe. Strong opposition in both France and Germany made the attitude of the British Labour party pivotal. *Citizen*, a left-wing paper supported by the party with a circulation of three-quarters of a million,

*The London correspondent of *New Leader* during the 1950s was Dennis Healey.

was decidedly against rearmament. Suddenly the assistant editor and a number of prominent journalists were fired after pressure on the board of Reynolds News, which owned the paper, from Labour party headquarters. Their replacements changed the line of the paper to promote the American plan. In fact, the origin of the manoeuvre was Washington. Via the London embassy, it was explained to Labour's leaders that if the party did not support rearmament – and *Citizen's* role here was seen as critical – then support for the party would be prejudiced and the prospect of a Labour government jeopardised.

The role of British intelligence in these affairs, *Encounter* apart, is unclear. Certainly they did little if anything to prevent the American intervention. The routine surveillance of all embassies, including the American, would have revealed contact between Labour politicians and American officials. Indeed, British intelligence has exchanged information on British subjects for other material.

The congressional enquiries into the CIA during the mid-1970s caused a great deal of concern in Britain. The congressional committees' practice of issuing sub-poenas to obtain agency documents led some British officials to withhold source details in the liaison reports which would only be provided 'on loan' to prevent scrutiny by the committees. Furthermore, the view developed in Britain that the CIA's integrity was compromised by the exposures of CIA practice in books by former officers, particularly Philip Agee (*Inside the Company*) and Victor Marchetti (*The CIA and the Cult of Intelligence*). The *Times*[17] noted that these developments were compounded by personality clashes, although these were not as pronounced as those between officials at the Foreign Office and US State Department.

Around the same time, there were frequent rumours of MI6 displeasure at CIA operations in Britain about which they had not been kept informed. MI6 found they had not been forewarned of certain CIA surveillance operations in Britain during the mid-1970s, and in retaliation confirmed to a group of left-wing Labour MPs that a list of ten CIA officers working in London, which Agee had supplied, was accurate.

The South Atlantic briefly illuminated Anglo-American intelligence co-operation, and almost all impressions gave good reports of it. It would be premature to estimate the consequences of Geoffrey Prime's exposure as a Soviet agent at GCHQ, but there have been reports pre-dating it of serious disagreements in the Middle East, where the British have apparently been exploiting the CIA's lack of manoeuvrability arising from the Reagan administraion's untrammelled support for Israel.

The British have long been fearful of American moves towards more open government, not only because of the risk of exposure, but also the knock-on effect of stimulating pressure for similar legislation in the United Kingdom, and campaigns against the Official Secrets and contempt laws, D-Notices and the rest of the censoring paraphernalia. Much recent work on British intelligence has derived from documents released under the US Freedom of Information Act, which led to pressure from London for its restriction. Ironically, the most powerful lobby for the act before its passage in 1974 was from the business community, worried by the growing powers of central government.

With regard to Europe, intelligence co-operation has up until recently been a low priority for the British. Given the tendency of successive post-war governments to conduct EEC relations purely in terms of Anglo-French relations, and the disdain and suspicion with which British intelligence view their French equivalents, this is not wholly surprising. Once Britain joined the EEC, changes inevitably occurred. Some sections of the British establishment, particularly the Foreign Office, have always held the prospect of political co-operation within Europe to be as important as the original and better-known economic arrangements. The European Convention on Terrorism, ratified by the EEC nations in December 1979, provides a legal basis for the exchange of information and techniques between member police forces and intelligence agencies. British intelligence representatives sit on the fourteen-member* Kilowatt Group, which is concerned with Arab guerilla activity. Clearly, some co-ordination in Europe at field level was felt necessary after the shooting by German police of Iain Macleod, a British intelligence officer infiltrating the Baader-Meinhof group in search of possible IRA links. Special Air Service teams have been training special forces in several European countries, including Italy where they have worked with the police and the paramilitary Carabinieri against the Brigate Rosse.

There are also agreements between Britain and some European countries on the exchange of signals intelligence, but on a much reduced scale to those enshrined in the original Sigint pact provisions. These arrangements, made by the so-called WASP (White Anglo-Saxon Protestant) countries at the end of the 1940s, continue to dominate British intelligence liaison. The rationale at the time was clear: Britain was assigned to be America's senior lieutenant in executing the US plan for a new world order. Although this process was long ago completed, the British intelligence establishment has not responded to subsequent shifts in the international environment which have, albeit slowly, redefined the priorities and perspectives of other

* Belgium, Canada, Denmark, France, Ireland, Israel, Italy, Luxembourg, Netherlands, Norway, Sweden, Switzerland, United Kingdom and West Germany.

government departments. The net benefits of the WASP pacts, if any, are most unlikely to outweigh the fundamental inconsistency between intelligence liaison policy geared towards the United States and orthodox diplomatic and trading policy, which looks first and foremost to Europe. The pacts also provide another mechanism through which the American state and its British collaborators can constrain and manipulate political innovation in the United Kingdom.

Colonial Security and Decolonisation

The post-war crusade against communist takeover of British colonies began in Malaya, whose vast mineral wealth – particularly tin, rubber and iron – had lured substantial British investment into the peninsula along with colonisation. The Japanese demand for iron ore, essential to the reconstruction of their war-damaged economy, was entirely satisfied from Malayan deposits. To the south, the island of Singapore housed the headquarters of all British forces east of Suez.

All of this was under threat from the guerillas of the Chinese-backed Malayan Communist Party (MCP), who began an armed campaign against the British authorities in June 1948, which the British referred to as 'The Emergency'. The defeat of the MCP is cited as the outstanding success of British counter-insurgency theory: the result was due not only to the undermining of the insurgents' political base by portraying them as Chinese immigrant agitators, but also to the introduction of political reforms; and to the existence of an effective intelligence apparatus. Singapore and Malaya were covered by the Malayan Security Service (MSS), set up two years previously and based in Singapore. In the year preceding the crisis, MSS began an investigation of the MCP almost from scratch. Its work was hampered by the reluctance of the police CID, who held all the available information, to pass it on.

Despite its difficulties, the MSS accurately predicted an MCP-led insurrection. The decisive evidence came from monitored discussions at a Soviet-sponsored conference of Asian communists held in Delhi. The MSS was, however, unable to persuade the government of the validity of their information. When fighting did break out, MSS was blamed for the authorities' ill-preparedness, and disbanded. Its role was assumed by the Special Branch, then a section within the CID.

The director of operations, Lieutenant-Colonel Briggs, sought to strengthen and expand the Branch, and Sir Hugh Jenkins was brought over from India to supervise the changes. Bad relations with the police hierarchy made progress difficult for Jenkins, and he resigned after a year. Briggs, suffering from poor health, departed soon afterwards. His replacement was a former director of military intelligence, General Gerald Templer, whose experience in this job had taught him a cardinal rule of anti-guerilla operations:

>The Emergency will be won by our intelligence system – our Special Branch.[18]

The deputy director of MI5, Jack Morton, was seconded to reorganise the Special Branch. His chief recommendation was that it should be split off from the CID. Templer gave it top priority in recruitment and funds, and a Malayan Police officer, Guy Madoc, became the head of the new department.

Meanwhile, the propaganda campaign against the communists was stepped up, using military psyops units on the ground backed by a broader programme run from Singapore by MI6 and the Foreign Office Information Research Department. A study instigated by the Army Operational Research Establishment was conducted by the psychologist F. H. Lakin. He interviewed 430 captured guerillas, and found that about one-third believed in communism; of the remainder, over two-thirds were largely attracted by promises of better material conditions while fighting. This rather unlikely conclusion indicated to Lakin that this group – 47 per cent of the total – should be the main target of psyops.[19] Hugh Carleton-Greene, later Director-General of the BBC, was brought in to revamp the Government Emergency Information Service. Greene laid down a set of tasks for the Information Services, which included the following:

1)   to raise the morale of the civil population and to encourage confidence in the government and resistance to the communists with a view to increasing the flow of information reaching the police.

2)   To attack morale of the members of the guerilla groups and their supporters and to drive a wedge between the leaders and the rank and file with a view to encouraging defection and undermining the determination of the communists to continue the struggle.

3)   To create an awareness of the values of the democratic way of life which was threatened by international communism.

Greene doubled the number of cinema projectors and speakers for showing governmental propaganda, installed 500 radio sets in villages and appointed a Controller of Emergency Broadcasting. Together with the management of Radio Malaya, the Controller was able to increase the output of anti-communist radio programmes in accordance with the planning of the Director of Operations. To encourage defectors, rewards for surrendering were increased by 30 per cent, large amounts of money were made available to the Special Branch to encourage informers and leaflets seeking to undermine guerilla morale were issued by the million.

Contacts inside the communist cells were rare, for they operated too far inside the jungle. The only readily accessible sources of information were the civilian staff, the Min Yuen, a large number of whom had been 'turned', recruited by the Special Branch as agents-in-place.

The Special Branch used a standard procedure for 'turning': once a target had been identified, they set about compiling evidence of his or her complicity in illegal activities. In due course the future agent was arrested and confronted with the details assembled by the Branch. Little additional pressure was ever required to achieve a successful 'turning'. The most useful information for the Branch was the location of supply and exchange points, message drops, food and ammunition dumps; the sources of supplies and funds and the identity of leaders. One of the most successful tactics initiated by the Branch was the rigorous searching of people leaving villages on the outskirts of the jungle. Frequent discoveries of food, which was to be smuggled out to the guerillas, hampered their effectiveness. Tricks such as stuffing rice inside a bicycle frame were usually discovered. As guerillas grew more desperate, they started to come out of the jungle in search of food. All too often they found that a village apparently rich in provisions was no more than a trap arranged by the Special Branch. In fact most ordinary villagers had been driven out of their homes and relocated in population centres under what the colonial authorities described as the 'strategic hamlets' scheme.

The Branch was fortunate to have within its ranks one of the most able practitioners of 'turning': Evan Davies, at one time Churchill's bodyguard, was engaged in counter-insurgency work during most of the Emergency, but his most successful operation took place during its latter stages. Davies was especially sent for to deal with a particularly troublesome guerilla leader, Goh Peng Tun. Goh commanded the group which held the region of Johore in south-west Malaya, and all previous efforts to wrest it from his control had failed. Davies managed to recruit one of Goh's most trusted men, known as Raven. Raven supplied the location of Goh's retreat, deep in the jungle, and in a low-level aircraft attack the camp was destroyed. Goh was killed during the raid. Davies returned to England, where he worked on MI5's Africa desk.

Malaya was also the first testing-ground for the post-war Special Air Service. M Squadron of 21 SAS had been sent east in 1950 to participate in the Korean War, but when their prospective role was assumed by the American Green Berets, the regiment was diverted to Malaya, where they were placed under the command of Mike Calvert who led the Malayan Scouts. Initially they were used to assist the Field Police Force in jungle edge patrols and guarding jungle forts. As the war progressed, the SAS became an important intelligence-gathering unit, particularly in the Temengor region of Northern Malaya. They spent four years in the area, leaving in 1957. The regiment also became famous for a practice known as tree-jumping. A unit would parachute into a jungle area and hope that the canopies would catch in the trees, enabling the soldiers to lower themselves safely to the ground. Tree-jumping was discontinued when it was discovered that at least one serious injury occurred on every occasion. The SAS were officially withdrawn from Malaya in 1959, shortly before the war came to an effective end. An estimated 500 guerillas under the British-trained veteran Chin Peng crossed the jungle border into Thailand and went into hiding. Ever since they have emerged periodically to launch attacks up and down the peninsula. A SAS detachment remained in the country after 1959, and according to the *Far East Economic Review*,[20] the Malaysian government asked them to leave in 1971. Military sources maintain that they were still fighting on the Thai border in the summer of 1973. They add that under the auspices of the Joint Border Committee, they have operated on both sides of the border, where as well as Malayan communists, the Pattani United Liberation Organisation, a moslem separatist movement, has also been active. British soldiers in Cyprus claimed to have seen dead SAS men on a plane refuelling in Cyprus en route to Britain from Penang, in Western Malaysia. In 1975 the Defence Secretary equivocated in reply to questions in the Commons as to whether the SAS was still serving in Malaysia.

Victory for the British in Malaya afforded them considerable prestige. A 'British school' of counter-insurgency theory developed, based on a number of simple tenets: first, the importance of a loyal and competent civil service; second, simplicity and co-ordination of organisation to facilitate rapid and decisive action; finally, as Templer continued to point out, an efficient and dedicated intelligence apparatus. A number of additional factors, while important, were recognised as being unique to Malaya. Eager to try out their theories again, the British experts, headed by Sir Robert Thompson* later went to Vietnam under the title of the British Advisory Mission. Although influential, the British proposals were not adopted in full which, they would argue, contributed to the Americans' ultimate defeat.

Africa presented a larger and more awkward problem. It was not a straight fight against communism for the British and they could not present it as such. Years of colonial occupation had spawned nationalist movements to which the colonial authorities ultimately had no counter. As explained, the Americans had no interest in supporting

---

* Sir Robert Thompson was head of the Mission until 1965. Subsequently he visited Vietnam a number of times before being appointed as a special consultant by President Nixon. In 1978 he was invited to Rhodesia by the Rhodesian Promotion Council, an organisation sponsored by the Smith regime. His arrival was heralded as that of a counter-insurgency specialist – what he told his hosts on this occasion is unfortunately not known.

the imperial system and the British would have had to decolonise sooner or later. The strategy was to cede power to local rulers with a strong political base, sympathetic to Britain and the West and immune from the persuasions of 'militant' nationalism or communism. The British government hoped to persuade the new rulers to keep expatriate Colonial Service officials in the administration. They had a figure of 20,000 in mind for the whole of Africa, who would be carefully vetted by MI5 beforehand. The appointment of suitable Africans to management positions within British companies operating in the continent and the control of economic aid was expected to guide African industry in the direction best suited to British interests, while it would appear that African governments were developing industries themselves. The colonial security and intelligence authorities established a number of organisations to oversee the transition.

Education was an essential precursor, and constituted a major hurdle. The colonial philosophy was underpinned by the notion that educating Africans would cause more problems than it solved; besides, Africans were assumed to be naturally inferior. The British authorities decided to establish universities and colleges with carefully chosen teaching staff to train Africans in administrative and managerial skills, and in the process convince them of the necessity of co-operating with the white colonialists. Thus it became a race against time for the British to produce a suitable breed of leaders before being overwhelmed by nationalist fervour.

In the central and eastern parts of the continent, the presence of large numbers of hard-line white settlers, determined to defend their privileged status was a serious complicating factor for the government; they were basically sympathetic to the settlers and unwilling to displease them, not least because of domestic public opinion.

An example of the dilemma is to be found in Harold Macmillan's memoirs, where he recalls advice from an unidentified colonial governor to the effect that although his African ministers would not be ready for a dozen years or so, failure to grant independence would necessitate suppressing political unrest and putting nationalist leaders behind bars. Under such circumstances, 'training' could not continue, and the investment required to ensure economic stability would not be forthcoming. Pre-empting and subverting the campaigns of nationalist groups was essential to avoid direct confrontation and gain time. The responsibility for these tasks fell to the police Special Branches.

The majority of colonial police forces were modelled on the Royal Irish Constabulary (which policed Ireland prior to 1922) and organised as semi-military forces, trained in arms and capable of undertaking quasi-military operations. Advance warning of disturbances or precise information on the identity of troublemakers, supplied by the Special Branch, enabled comparatively small forces to contain local troubles. Special Branch surveillance was afforded to anyone who upset or threatened to upset the status quo. The list of targets included religious leaders and witch doctors, though in the post-war years the emphasis shifted to the emerging nationalist parties, and trade unions. Plain-clothes Branch officers took notes at meetings, watching closely for the merest hint of incitement to anything illegal. For those who stepped out of line, a whole battery of laws was available to the authorities which would provide suitable pretexts for arrest. Security and political activity in each colony were so closely tied together that while the Governor was being advised by his Special Branch to ban one group, he would often actively be encouraging another. And security operations extended beyond these more obvious targets. An ex-Special Branch officer in Nyasaland explained how their area of surveillance also included the church:

> Religion in Central Africa was an alternative to politics. It provided an alternative structure of ambition. In Malawi, we monitored the different religious sects as they emerged and kept an eye on the external organisations willing to support breakaway sects; especially the American ones. The main church in Malawi – the missionary Church of Scotland – took an independent stand and was considered 'progressive'. We kept a tight watching brief on them. They also controlled the leading university and were involved with many tribes so they were a useful place to pick-up information.[21]

The church, especially in Nyasaland, was deeply involved in the nationalist struggle. So many of their mission-trained 'boys' turned up in the forefront of nationalist activities that not to have supported them would have gained the church the contempt of their former pupils. But many church people genuinely believed in the cause of independence and often acted as a moderating force. Nevertheless, their sympathies, however mildly expressed, did not endear them to the Special Branch. Thus ex-colonial civil servant Sir Charles Jeffries: 'The task of counter-action (against subversives) is not made easier by the fact that the ill-disposed often use the well-meaning as their unconscious agents'.[22] Separating the 'ringleaders' from the 'well-meaning' was not a task which was to trouble the Special Branch. Both were watched and complaints were met with the common retort 'If you're not breaking the law, you've nothing to fear'.

Trade unions were also carefully watched. The cold war split in the international union movement between East and West was a matter for considerable concern:

> The division was between the American-backed International

Congress of Free Trade Unions (ICFTU) and the Russian-inspired World Federation of Trade Unions (WFTU). Both of these organisations offered trips and money to trade unionists. Special Branch monitoring was done to ensure that these blandishments were as free from conditions as the colonial governments would tolerate. It was also desirable to determine how the ICFTU and WFTU would determine union policy. Many unions were run solely on money from ICFTU and WFTU.[23]

Often as not, the American influence wielded through the ICFTU was as much of a nuisance to the colonial government as the Russian-backed WFTU. In competing for African support with the WFTU, it often had to support militant nationalism. This made its visiting representatives suspect in the eyes of the Special Branch who put them under close surveillance.

The range of intelligence targets was large enough for some of the work to be done outside the Special Branch. Every level of the colonial administration in the field submitted Political Intelligence Reports. Ordinary police officers were also asked to compile Special Branch reports. In Tanganyika, the standard of those submitted was so patchy that Police Headquarters sent out a secret circular giving instructions on how to prepare such a report. This contained useful advice like: 'It is essential you obtain from your agent or informer his sub-source'. And more obvious hints and tips:

> If it is a highly secret document (your agent has given you) and your agent does not appear to worry whether you keep it for half an hour or several days, it is possibly a false document which he himself has prepared, whereas if he shows great anxiety for its safe custody and he wishes to return it with the minimum delay, in all probability it is a true document.[24]

Even government employees, like hospital staff, were expected to help: as one colonial civil servant involved with security in Zanzibar remembered: 'If a militant nationalist was injured and had to go to hospital, the orderlies and his doctor would watch and take note of those who came to visit him'. Nationalist politicians would talk at length about their rivals' activities to government officials and their comments were duly noted in the weekly political intelligence reports, and subsequently in the Special Branch files. African doctors and teachers would often talk to Special Branch officers who they thought were ordinary police personnel and their intimate knowledge of the community was highly valued. Proper informers were actually paid for their information and for struggling party officials trying to make ends meet on a meagre salary, the temptation often proved too great. Information came cheaply as the African standard of living in most colonies was very low. The Kenyan Special Branch in Ngong District had £750 to disburse to informers and found it sufficient 'unless large rewards have to be given'. Most of the information given was little better than gossip and the skill of the Special Branch lay in assessing the credibility of its sources. A letter from an informer at the beginning of the Mau Mau revolt gives some idea of their quality and tone:

> . . . has stated openly that he is the 'big man' of the Mau Mau in this cell or at Kiawa. He has never boasted of being the oath administrator.[25]

This hearsay was then backed by circumstantial gossip the informant had picked up in the course of his work as a doctor. Informers were often paid just to loiter outside the local headquarters of the nationalist party and notice who was going in and coming out.

The paid informers were notoriously unreliable, often embroidering their stories to make them fetch a better price. An apocryphal tale was told by an ex-military intelligence officer, who explained how an informer was able to sell the same information to the Special Branch, military intelligence and the police. As all three reported the same developments they were presumed to be true, often with disastrous results. It was not until intelligence-gathering was co-ordinated that these anomalies began to show up.

The information gathered by the Special Branch in each colony was passed on to the Security Committee, which was given different names in different colonies but whose basic function was the same. Its responsibilities are given in a brief for the Intelligence Co-ordination Committee in Ghana (then the Gold Coast):

> (i)   To provide a means whereby information of Political and Security Intelligence interest can be exchanged between the Army, the Administration and the Police,
>
> (ii) To co-ordinate the Intelligence activities of the Army, the Administration and the police and often ensuring that proper and unduplicated channels of information . . . are maintained.
>
> (iii) To make recommendations upon the methods by which such information may be distributed.

The brief was given in 1949 when the Ghana Committee's structure was being overhauled in the wake of the trouble at the demonstrations of black Ghanaian war veterans. It was carefully laid out that each section was responsible for:

> It is proposed that Special Branch of the Police should collect all security intelligence (i.e. about any groups or individuals taking part in subversive activities or activities likely to endanger peace and good order) . . . that the political administration

collect only political intelligence unless asked to help the Special Branch collect security intelligence about specific matters; and that the Army should not itself collect security or political intelligence but should make its appreciation from the information supplied to the committee. Certain information would also be available from the periodic intelligence reports already being sent by the Commissioner of Labour to the District Commissioner and the Commissioner of Police.[26]

This information reached the committee from the Special Branch and the political administration in much the same way. Each sub-district officer would submit a political or security Intelligence Report. These reports would then be digested into a District Report, which in turn was collated into the Report presented to the Security Committee. Those serving on this committee usually included the Civil Secretary (the Governor's number one civil servant who chaired the committee), the Attorney-General, the Commissioner of Police and a Special Branch Officer from the Civil Secretary's Office responsible for all security paper work. The Committee would normally meet once a month to consider the various reports prepared for it. A former Civil Secretary described his work:

> We would sit swopping notes on who had said what and who was where (in nationalist politics). Often we'd argue about who's information was correct and what had really happened. Political and security considerations were very close. I would always be present at all political meetings between local organisations and the colonial administration and so saw both sides. At the end of the meeting we would try and reach a conclusion like 'On the Political Front – Current dangers to security are ... '. Then we'd list things like interference from Russia and China, note that Egypt's influence was waning. The Special Branch was the right hand of this committee.[27]

To maintain its security, the colonial administration had a whole battery of laws. If an individual was considered particularly troublesome, 'it didn't matter how you got him out of the way, the important thing was that he was taken out of circulation before he caused more trouble. You could arrest him for driving a bicycle without a light, anything'. Detailed notes were issued in one territory to police officers in a confidential circular. It consisted of a catechism of seven questions designed to answer doubts about when a nationalist speaker at a meeting could be arrested and what would be the best charge to use. A typical question – number five – gives the flavour:

> At a public meeting the speaker says that the chiefs are deceived by the Government so they help to prolong foreign rule.
> a) A charge would probably be under section 27 of the African

Chiefs Ordinance No. 27 of 1953 which carried a penalty of two years or a fine of 2,000 Kenyan shillings (£100) or both. I think it would be unlikely this is an offence against section 63B of Cap 16.

b) The words themselves must be proved and, if possible, it should be proved by surrounding circumstances, that a particular chief is being attacked.

c) A defence that the remark did not refer to any chief in the area where the Baraza* was held might show that the words were not calculated, i.e. likely to undermine or interfere with the authority of a chief.

Often the legal justification for an arrest would be very flimsy. In 1955 the colonial administration in Zambia decided to ban a magazine called *Africa and the Colonial World* sent by Fenner Brockway of the Movement for Colonial Freedom to the African National Congress. The administration had been particularly irked by a report used in the magazine, sent in by the Congress on disturbances in the Gwembe valley. Congress headquarters, however, continued to receive it by post, although arrangements were being made to ship all the issues to Southern Rhodesia where the magazine was still legal. Before this could happen, the police made a dawn raid on the home of Kenneth Kaunda, a leader of the African National Congress. Here, they produced a search warrant and asked to go to Congress headquarters. According to a police statement after the raid, 'red pamphlets' were discovered. At Kaunda's home, his wife Betty, worried that the police might be after other pamphlets, 'hid them in a large pot in the kitchen and covered them with an empty sack'. But police were watching the house, so when the officers returned with her husband, they went straight to the kitchen and checked the titles on a list of prohibited publications they carried. For possessing banned literature, Kaunda and Nkumbula (another important nationalist leader) were put in prison for two months with hard labour. The pamphlets were described by the magistrate as 'cheap, disreputable and scandalous', and: 'the identity of the political organisation to which they belong is immaterial'. The jail sentence was a decisive factor in weakening Harry Nkumbula's militancy.

The most useful piece of legislation for the intelligence-gatherers of the Special Branch was the Societies Ordinance in each territory. This required the formal registration of each branch of a society before it could be legally established. It gave the colonial governments the power to refuse or to withdraw the registration of societies for failure to meet the rigorous formal requirements of registrations. As each local party branch had to be registered, it provided a fairly accurate list

* local tribal gathering

of the political leadership of a nationalist party. The Special Branch would often send people as police officers to make enquiries to check information submitted. If the local secretary of a party changed, this gave them a good excuse to go in and 'chat with' the new person. For this reason, any move to ban a party was often strongly opposed by the Special Branch who found it harder to keep under surveillance an underground party. With the legal cover of the Societies Ordinance, the colonial governors were able to ban parties, both at a local and national level. In 1957, the Tanganyika Africa National Union was unable to operate in ten districts because of refusals to register branches and withdrawal of registration. In the 1959 Emergency in Zambia, the Governor was able to declare all branches of ZANC (Zambia African National Congress) illegal under section 21 (2) of the Societies Ordinance in that territory.

Another check on political activity which could easily reflect the wishes of the administration was the granting of permission for political meetings. Shortly before the complete ban of ZANC, it was refused permission to hold a meeting in Lusaka. In open opposition to this, Kenneth Kaunda announced the beginning of ZANC's defiance campaign.

Perhaps the most serious attempt to crush political influence using security methods was the colonial authorities' handling of the Jomo Kenyatta case in Kenya. Shortly after the beginning of the Mau Mau land revolt in Kenya, Kenyatta was arrested along with several other militant nationalists. After a controversial trial, he was given a prison sentence. The intention, according to a well-known British broadcaster in Kenya at the time, was to write Jomo Kenyatta out of history:

> The British decided to pretend that Kenyatta never existed. They tried to make him an 'unperson'. Every trace of him was eliminated. His house was burnt down and his land divided. When he had served his sentence he was detained in an inhospitable region, miles from anywhere. The British then worked on the basis that he no longer existed. His name was never mentioned in debates in the legislative council.[28]

As time went by this solution became unworkable. Kenyetta, like Makarios of Cyprus, was not forgotten but became a rallying figure for the country's nationalist forces.

While attempting to contain the nationalists, the British government was looking round for political formulae with some appeal to mainstream black sentiment. Domestic opinion and African suspicion of governmental initiatives constrained their options, so they used the tactic of giving discreet support to suitable political movements outside their direct auspices.

Already famous for his exploits as the 'Phantom Major' in the wartime Special Air Service, David Stirling finished the war with a considerable reputation. In 1949, he began to put it to use in promoting his new venture in Africa, the Capricorn Africa Society (CAS). Stirling's deep religious beliefs put him in touch with many christian intellectuals who supplied the theoretical basis for the Society's work. The zebra with its white, black and brown stripes was chosen as a symbol to illustrate its multiracial approach.

Stirling had gone to Africa at the end of the war influenced by the climate of optimism which asserted, among other things, that the continent was rich and there for the taking. On arrival, he was surprised to find little of the entrepreneurial drive he had been expecting. With his brother Bill he started a firm called Stirling-Astaldi, which built a large number of roads in Tanganyika. Most shocking of all, however, was the racism of his fellow white settlers: a born patrician, he believed that a person's status should be determined by their education and wealth, not by the colour of their skin. He began to dabble in politics, buying a small newsletter 'after a good day at the races'.

Stirling began to develop his political programme, beginning with a federation of Northern and Southern Rhodesia and Nyasaland as a good way of promoting investment, and subsequently expanding it towards a United States of Africa. The idea attracted much publicity when Capricorn was launched. An early *Daily Express* article on CAS provided a clear summary of Stirling's plans for the fight against his latest enemy, 'racial wretchedness':

> the plan is for a federal citizenship with three population groupings. For the predominantly African regions such as Uganda and Barotseland, there would be crown states guided by federal officials. In the mixed territories, such as Kenya and the Rhodesias, there would be open areas where non-Europeans would have restricted property ownership, but would be eligible for political rights by test of education. In the third group would be African development areas. The objective is the emergence of an African middle class and increasing self-administration.[29]

In short, whites would give up blatant discrimination in return for black acceptance of limited franchise. The Society's first public statement was the *Capricorn Declarations*, and today it seems very timid stuff: but in 1952, when it came out, Dr Malan was putting the finishing touches on apartheid for South Africa and in Kenya, the frustrated, landless Kikuyu exploded in rebellion. So it was small wonder that *The Capricorn Declarations* was hailed as 'a coherent alternative to Dr Malan's barren policy and the dangerous faith of racial strife', although Sir Philip Mitchell, a former governor of both Kenya and Uganda, described it as 'apartheid in sugar icing, but not the less apartheid for that'.[30]

From the start, the Capricorn African Society received backing from the Colonial Office and the Commonwealth Relations Office. On 8 February, 1952, Stirling met with representatives of both ministries and received detailed advice on how he should go about organising CAS in Africa. He also had a close personal relationship with Colonial Secretary Alan Lennox-Boyd, who exchanged many letters with him, giving political advice on CAS. Jonathan Lewis, one of CAS's London organisers, captured the spirit of the relationship:

> he always supported us. But he wouldn't touch anything contentious. I'm related to him through his wife, he certainly smiled on us.[31]

In July 1954 Rowland Hudson, Head of the African Studies Branch, approached Assistant Under-Secretary William Gorell-Barnes to ask whether he could help Capricorn:

> I should like to help by giving Oldham [the Christian intellectual behind many of CAS's ideas] any information which may help him, without divulging state secrets or getting myself involved in the Capricorn or other political activities. If you see no objection I will run down to Midhurst next week and spend the evening with Oldham who has been a good friend of Africa. I think it would be churlish to rebuff him.[32]

By September their relationship was sufficiently close that Hudson was making amendments to a memo Oldham had written called 'Foundations of a Multi-Racial Society'. The Colonial Office adopted a somewhat paternal view towards Capricorn, but nevertheless senior officials saw it as a useful counterweight to African nationalism:

> I do believe that if the objectives set out, with which I agree, are to be achieved they must be pursued quickly and vigorously because the demand for African self-government is bound to grow rapidly and there will be much communist and Asian propaganda to the effect that the conception of a multi-racial society is an imperialistic device to hold Africans from achieving self-government ... Capricorn must try to produce an emotional appeal to outbid that of African nationalism or communism.[33]

William Gorell-Barnes, Assistant Under-Secretary, remembered the help they were able to give to CAS:

> We used to see David Stirling from time to time. He was running on the multi-racial ticket and this was what we were talking about. We both wanted more participation and more expenditure on education. Political development was still fairly

slow but we were trying to get ministers to move in that direction. We were able to help in small ways. We addressed despatches to governors of territories about CAS. They (CAS) published a book called *New Hope in Africa* which we sent round to all governors. For instance, the Colonial Office let Evelyn Baring (Governor of Kenya) know if there was an African coming (back to Kenya) who was worth taking care of. We were trying to build up multi-racial communication.[34]

Most of Capricorn's money came from British and American sources: prestigious British companies including the merchant bankers Kleinwort Benson and the United Africa Company gave cheques: on the other side of the Atlantic, the Ford Foundation, Time-Life, the Rockefellers and the mining corporation Amax made contributions through the American Friends of the Capricorn Africa Society.

The society's main activity was the establishment of Citizenship Committees, which met regularly throughout five territories to discuss Capricorn ideas. These committees organised youth clubs, set up public debates and campaigned against petty racial discrimination. This was, as one CAS organiser observed, the 'tea-party phase of white liberalism in Africa'. These earnest drawing-room discussions failed to break down the racial divide. Musa Amaleembam, a black Kenyan 'moderate', thought it all ended when you said goodbye to your white host at the front door:

The acid test of social integration came after the meetings when Africans rode back to the African location on bicycles. Only few Europeans offered lifts and the Africans had to weather the darkness and rain at times.[35]

The sort of people it attracted were the cream of settler society. Professionals like lawyers, doctors and architects were all prominent as its most active members, although a considerable number of white farmers made up its rank and file. On the African side, its appeal varied from territory to territory. In Tanganyika and Nyasaland, where the African nationalist movement actively campaigned against it, the word 'capricornist' became synonymous with 'informer'. But in Southern Rhodesia and Kenya it attracted a whole generation of the black nationalist elite, many of whom are now prominent politicians.

The peak of Capricorn's political success was the Salima Convention in 1956. This was a large conference held at Salima on the shores of Lake Nyasa where Capricorn delegates from all the territories it covered thrashed out the basis of a Contract in which they solemnly pledged themselves to work for

a society free from discrimination rooted in racial prejudices and acknowledging our human unity under God and our unity in one loyalty to the crown.

Although it was not much noticed at the time, there was only a token delegation from Tanganyika because the Tanganyikan nationalist party, the Tanganyikan African National Union, had already fallen out with Stirling and actively campaigned against CAS. The same was true for Nyasaland. Stirling's critics claim that he was high-handed at the conference and railroaded the Contract through. For Stirling, it was the end of his almost manic involvement with CAS. He hoped he had got the organisation rolling and that from now on it would move under its own steam. Mentally and physically exhausted, he withdrew from the presidency.

After Salima, CAS faced a dilemma. It was not a political party but it wanted to have political impact. While Stirling had been president of CAS, he was unwilling to dirty his hands with grubby compromises. He wanted the pragmatic, white politicians to commit themselves to Capricorn ideals and wasn't pleased with the idea of working with them on any other basis. But the demand for a political role from CAS's followers was very strong. As Guy Hunter wrote to CAS in London, its followers were asking for 'a frank admission that Capricorn *is* political'. After Stirling resigned, it tried several times to enter electoral politics.

On its first attempt, which had actually taken place before the Salima Convention, it was beaten by the rival United Tanganyika Party set up by the Colonial Governor Edward Twining. The local branch of CAS, which changed its name to the Tanganyikan National Society, soon sank without trace when official support was switched from CAS to the new party. CAS was obliged to set up such parties, as it was forbidden by its constitution to indulge in politics. Two further efforts were made to obtain representation for Capricorn-backed groups. The Kenya party, established in 1957, pledged itself to 'work for self-government for the colony with allegiance to the British Crown'. The party's biggest catch was Ernest Vasey, a settler politician who had acquired something of a reputation for his work in the colonial Kenyan government. The party fared badly at the election, however, and Vasey decided to move to Zambia shortly afterwards. CAS was hardly more successful in Northern Rhodesia in 1959. It allied itself to Harry Franklin, an ambitious settler politician and Northern Rhodesian government minister, who put together the Constitution Party. This attracted a number of prominent Northern Rhodesian white liberals and a leading black trade unionist, Lawrence Katilungu. Almost immediately Katilungu came under fire from his union colleagues and resigned shortly afterwards. Franklin had, however, persuaded Harry Nkumbula, president of the main African nationalist organisation, the ANC, to fight the forthcoming election in alliance with the Constitution Party. He led Nkumbula to believe that the ANC would be recognised by the colonial Northern Rhodesian government if only he could rid the party of its extremist secondary leaders. This manoeuvre was headed off when one of the more militant ANC members found out that the alliance scheme that Nkumbula was proposing to his colleagues was identical to the version distributed to Constitution Party officials. The close relationship between Harry Nkumbula and Harry Franklin eventually split the ANC. The ill-fated Constitution Party lasted only six months.

The collapse of Capricorn's electoral projects forced it to devote the remainder of its life to adult education schemes, which had been in progress since Salima. Backed by Sir Philip Mitchell, it created Citizenship Colleges in Rhodesia and Kenya. These were aimed at training an African elite in the ideals of the Capricorn Society and were the most lasting of its activities. Both were eventually transformed into ordinary adult education colleges.

In the end, Capricorn failed because its members were too naive. They concentrated on attracting quality not quantity and were never able to pose an electoral challenge to either white supremacy or African nationalism. Among the white settlers, it was outflanked by new political parties like the New Kenya Group and the Northern Rhodesian Liberal Party, which were more pragmatic in their responses to the last stages of decolonisation. In political terms, a senior ex-Capricorn official told us, Stirling suffered from 'uncertain judgement'. By the beginning of the 1960s, Capricorn was left with just the London office and a decision was taken to transform it into a charity to provide hostels for African students coming to London.

While political repression and economic inequality persisted, it was almost inevitable that somewhere the decolonisation strategy would fail and precipitate a war between black Africans and colonial government. It is in some ways surprising that the British were only required to fight one major counter-insurgency war in Africa, against the Mau Mau rebels in Kenya.

Kenya's largest tribe is the Kikuyu. Under the post-war colonial government, they were unable to persuade the authorities to give them lands, as had been granted to other tribes, in their traditional tribal areas. The importance of this issue was reflected in the name by which many of the insurgents called their movement – the Land Freedom Army. By 1952 their frustration had grown to the point where there existed majority support within the tribe for armed opposition to the British regime.

Again the colonial government was largely unprepared for an uprising. There were strong Kikuyu organisations in both the countryside and the towns and Mau Mau groups were active in each. The police Special Branch, which was fairly small anyway, did not operate in African rural areas, which were policed by officials employed by the relevant regional administration. Intelligence reports from these two sources were sent to two different departments in central government without collation. The senior official responsible for law and order, who also doubled as Attorney-General, received most of the blame for this situation.

As in Malaya, an official from MI5 was despatched to reorganise the Kenyan security services. The chief of the British service, Sir Percy Sillitoe, visited Kenya twice, in November 1952 and April 1953. A plan was developed for the integration of all services. An intelligence adviser to the Governor, an MI5 official and staff were appointed and the Special Branch greatly expanded. For purely military (i.e. combat operational) intelligence, a military Senior Intelligence Staff Officer was established at General Headquarters.

The peacetime security committee had been designed to monitor political developments and occasionally undertake minor operations to control their course. There was no way it could be an executive committee to carry out a war, according to white settler politician Michael Blundell:

> I attended what we called the 'Sitrep Committee' (Situation Report) . . . A more unsuitable body than this committee to deal with an Emergency I could not imagine. Any officer who had the remotest connection with ops. attended. A report was made by the Commissioner of Police and others who might have been engaged in the day's ops. Discussions then took place, and the meeting would then break up with no concerted plan and, above all, no incisive direction to the various officers as to the actions and operations which they were to carry out.[36]

The apparent suddenness of the revolt had caught the whole colonial security apparatus in Kenya off-balance. The fact that the army had to be called in was a plain admission of failure and it was a good few months before any strategy to contain the revolt emerged. The Special Branch found that many of their informers were killed within days of the fighting breaking out and what sources they had left were more inclined to keep their mouths shut. With morale at an all-time low, the Kenyan Special Branch resented the attachment of Military Intelligence Officers (MIOs) from the Army's Intelligence Corps to their ranks. Seven or so of these officers were sent out in the course of fighting. One of the first two was Captain (now General) Frank Kitson. The Special Branch felt it knew the territory and was unable to see what the MIOs would be able to add. The feeling of resentment was mutual and the MIOs were also frustrated by the difficulty of getting their point of view across to the civil authorities.

They were fairly well versed in intelligence methods, most having served in a similar capacity in Trieste and Malaya.

The first attempt to sort out the differences between the various security departments was the Emergency Committee, but as Blundell explained in a letter to Kenyan Governor Evelyn Baring, 'the Emergency Committee has not worked as it was originally conceived'. He thought the Committee was not executive enough. A sense of powerlessness was beginning to creep through the colony and irate right-wing settlers were calling for blood. In those dark days for the colony's rulers, the Deputy Prosecutor was even rung up by a person who claimed to be the Mau Mau leader Deda Kimatti: the conversation lasted some 40 minutes, but the authorities were unable to locate the origin of the call. A note was made 'to examine the machinery for tracing the source of telephone calls'.

This confusion within the colonial administration lasted until March 1954 when the Emergency Committee was changed to the War Cabinet. This was a slimmed-down executive committee designed to guide a strategy for beating the Mau Mau rebels with a combination of politics and brute force. The Committee had only four members: the Governor, the Deputy Governor, the army's Commander-in-Chief and Michael Blundell, the most vocal spokesperson of the European community. The Cabinet was assisted by a Cabinet Secretary sent out from Britain whose task seems to have been to ensure a smooth flow of decision making and keep a weather-eye on the costs of the military operation. One military operation in the Highlands of the country had cost a staggering £10,000 for every dead Mau Mau. Also, the number of British troops in Kenya had risen from 1,485 before the Emergency to 7,109 on 31 August 1954.

To bring about co-ordination at all levels, a structure similar to that used in the Malayan Emergency was followed:

> In simple terms, it meant that at Province and District level, Joint Emergency Committees meeting regularly decided general policy: Joint Operational Committees planned the actual day-to-day operational programme; an executive officer common to both committees provided the per warrant link. In each case the committee consisted of the senior available representative of the army, the police and the administration, and in addition a suitable local civilian. Attached to the committees were intelligence and communications officers.[37]

The MIO's original brief was to relieve Special Branch police officers from the task of obtaining information about Mau Mau operational methods. At their disposal were some 40 Field Intelligence Assistants drawn from the Kenya Regiment and the Kenya Police Reserve. Their most important function though was controlling the 'pseudo-gangs', groups of ex-guerrillas who changed sides after capture. With their knowledge of Mau Mau practices they were able to penetrate deep into Mau Mau territory, and their relatively large numbers were crucial in the eventual defeat of the rebels. SAS officers working in pairs were also detailed to lead some of these units. Although attached to 'I Force' of the Kenya Regiment, 'pseudo-gang' operations were unofficial as the government felt that a number of policy side-issues existed which were too delicate and potentially embarrassing to be jeopardised by giving official approval. Only in 1955 was 'I Force' recognised as a legitimate unit by the army leadership.

The army was withdrawn at the end of 1956. The initial mess, which took two years to sort out, was largely caused by defects in its emergency capacity. HQ East Africa was not geared to active operations and there was no effective civil-military command structure. The Army Command Headquarters, based in Nairobi, which covered Kenya, Uganda, Tanganyika, Mauritius, Nyasaland and Northern Rhodesia, came under the War Office; while the Governor of Kenya took his orders from the Colonial Office. The Command was a sleepy outpost, more used to mounting ceremonial parades than counter-insurgency operations. All attention in the colonial security network was focused on the emergency in Malaya. After Mau Mau, East Africa was set up as a separate command to enable it to respond more quickly to local events. Finally, an emergency strike force was set up at Kahawa base in Kenya, with its own intelligence unit. This force, a battalion of lightly armed soldiers with jeeps, was trained as a rapid deployment force available to fly anywhere, including the Gulf. The base included an Operations Room staffed by intelligence officers who kept close watch on the flow of reports from all territories, ready to pick up an emergency at a moment's notice. Ironically, this base consisted largely of temporary units for most of its period of usage by the strike force. Large sums were spent on building a permanent base but this wasn't ready until after independence, by which time the political climate had changed and the new Kenyan government felt unable to offer such a facility to the British army. The force then moved back to Plymouth and was disbanded in 1965.

The end of the rebellion roughly coincided with the climax of the Suez crisis, which was the telling blow to residual British pretensions to a significant global role. Decolonisation accelerated, and responsibility for intelligence and covert action in the former colonies passed to MI6, while security was a task for the new governments. Some of them retained seconded MI5 officers as advisers. The British continued to show something of an imperial mentality towards their former colonies, tinkering and meddling with the fledgling adminisns in pursuit of the correct pro-Western balance. Colonial expatriates and former settlers who returned to Britain provided a valuable source of knowledge and experience for dealings with the new states. Britain and America slowly began to develop common policies for Africa, based on the threat of communist expansion into the strategic 'vacuum' created by British withdrawal and designed to maximise the potential for economic exploitation. Chapter 4 illustrates clandestine operations in post-colonial Africa.

Secret UK-Based Cold War Operations

Propaganda Exercises

While the influence of communist ideas among African nationalists was causing concern to the colonial authorities, it was no less of a problem for those sections of the British government who were attempting to shift public perception and international opinion from the menace of fascism to the menace of communism.

In 1947 Christopher Mayhew, a bright junior minister at the Foreign Office, sent a confidential memo to his boss, Ernest Bevin, proposing a secret 'propaganda counter-offensive against the Russians'.[38] To do this, he recommended setting up a new department to tackle the task. The idea was eagerly picked up by Prime Minister Clement Attlee who gave the go-ahead to launch the department. To conceal its existence from the public, the money to carry out its operations was obtained from Parliament on the 'secret vote'.

The new department – the Information Research Department – had two main purposes. It created 'grey' propaganda for overseas consumption, containing no direct lies, but factual material to which 'spin' could be added at will. This 'grey' propaganda was directed against communism, a catch-all label which included anything remotely left-wing or anti-imperialist. The IRD produced a hierarchy of regions as a guideline to the intensity of the propaganda to be directed at each. The primary targets were Western Europe, particularly France, Italy and Germany, and south-east Asia (in connection with the outbreak of the Malayan emergency). In the second category were India, Pakistan and the Middle East while the Soviet bloc, which was left largely to the Americans, took third place. These priorities reflect a distinct imperial bias in British covert action policy. The department's second area of interest was the moulding of domestic opinion in Britain. It used the anti-communist material created with government funds to aid right-wing social democrats within the Labour Party and the trade union movement.

Mayhew had been number two to Hugh Gaitskell during the war in the Ministry of Economic Warfare, and thus no stranger to political manipulation. From the start, he used IRD's resources in Britain itself to considerable effect. In March 1948, Mayhew told Fred Warner, the supervising under-secretary in charge of IRD:

> I have been running over in my mind the possibilities of organ
> ising a series of speaker's notes which we could supply on
> demand to ministers and friendly Labour MPs to help them in
> combatting communist-inspired opposition in the Labour Party
> and the trade union movement. At present, as you are well
> aware, we get a number of requests of this kind and deal with
> each one ad-hoc. [39]

Among the topics suggested were 'American Imperialism' (with
the inverted commas), the Colonies and a whole series on the Soviet
Union, covering its alleged expansionism, diplomatic intransigence
and low living standards of its citizens. Later in the year, Mayhew
reported to Bevin that he had made arrangements with Herbert Tracey,
publicity secretary of the Trade Union Congress, 'for the dissem-
ination inside the Labour Movement at home of anti-communist
propaganda which we are producing for overseas consumption'. [40]

In January of 1948, communists had taken control of Czechoslovakia, and the resulting influx of emigres to Britain proved fertile
recruiting ground for the IRD. No less than 22 briefing papers were
produced on various aspects of Stalinism that year. Mayhew wrote to
Bevin, giving details of IRD's progress: 'IRD material is at present
circulated to Information Officers at Overseas Missions ... I believe
that some impact has already been achieved by this propaganda'. [41]
These Information Officers often included full-time IRD personnel
under light cover who co-ordinated specific local campaigns.

The staff of the Department were a strange mixture. Emigres,
such as those from Czechoslovakia, featured prominently: many were
the flotsam of failed intelligence operations. Others were carefully
chosen writers and journalists whose specialist knowledge the department needed. It became a favourite resting place for MI6 people
washed up at the end of their careers. Secrecy was so endemic that it
was possible for someone to be recruited, as one ex-IRD worker told
us, with the idea that they were going to be doing research as the
department's title suggested. Relations with MI6 were close, particularly with section IX, which dealt with the Soviet Union. The IRD was
represented at liaison meetings in London between MI6 and the CIA
during most of its lifetime. The head of the IRD between 1953 and
1958, John Rennie, was later head of MI6.

In its prime, during the fifties, the IRD staff numbered between
three and four hundred – the Soviet section alone had more than sixty
people working in it. A twelve story office block in Millbank, River-
walk House, housed the IRD until its dismantling. The department
was divided into regional 'desks', with special sections dealing with
Economics and Arms Control. In each area, the department

maintained officers on the ground, usually undercover in embassies to look after its interests.

The information from IRD, which former senior officials of the department concede was heavily 'slanted', was circulated to a long list of journalists considered politically reliable by the department. They were asked not to reveal the source of their information when they used IRD's material. IRD's material fell into two categories described succinctly by Ralph Murray, the department's head in 1949:

> Category A is secret and confidential objective studies re. Soviet policies and machinations which are designed for high-level consumption by heads of states, Cabinet members, et cetera ... none of this material publishable or quotable for obvious reasons.

> Category B is less highly-classified information suitable for careful dissemination by staff of British missions to suitable contacts (eg. editors, professors, scientists, labour leaders et cetera) who can use it as factual background material in their general work without attribution. Success of category B operations depend upon the activity of British representatives in various countries.[42]

According to a British diplomat, Category A material was 'derived from diplomatic and intelligence sources. It is entirely distinct from that which might be utilized in the secret propaganda campaign'.[43] Category A material was also not used in the smear campaigns MI6 occasionally mounted against troublesome nationalist leaders. Colin Legum of the *Observer* recalls that:

> the favourite official line was to discredit any militant anti-colonial leader as a Communist. We were fed confidential reports from MI6 proving the Moscow links with all these colonial agitators.[44]

The Category B part of IRD's output was a group of regular publications with names like Background Briefing and Latin American Topics. There was also a special series on International Front Organisations and later a loose-leaf information file on the IRA.

Some briefings on very sensitive topics were so secret they didn't even have an imprint to show their origin. These often included information supplied to IRD from the intelligence services. MI6 would supply confidential information in red folders marked Top Secret. Great skill was needed to put this information into circulation without giving away its source.

To start a particular propaganda campaign, IRD would often call in a well-trusted journalist and brief him or her individually. Once the journalist had published their 'IRD exclusive', without even the usual 'official sources' attribution, IRD would then transmit the story as gospel all round the world to be picked up by local press in the Third World. The department was able to conclude deals with several British newspapers which gave it permission to reprint and distribute articles from them to foreign newspapers. These reprints acknowledged the original author but made no mention that the articles had initially been mailed to the papers by the British government. The staff of IRD were also able to arrange British government funds for foreign newspapers who were finding difficulty in paying the subscription rates to British news services.

IRD in addition hired some of its ex-personnel as 'freelance' journalists. Using their new role as cover, these 'freelancers' were able to place material in papers without the editor being aware of the source. And as the *Daily Express's* tame spy watcher, Chapman Pincher noted: 'Most journalists who worked freelance for IRD were paid – as were the staff of a well-known magazine'.[45]

In the early fifties the IRD was busily trying to persuade Arabs that communism was incompatible with the teachings of Islam, and working on a joint propaganda operation with MI5 and MI6 in Malaya. It made use of any literature which could be interpreted as anti-communist, including George Orwell's *Animal Farm* and *Darkness at Noon* by Arthur Koestler. Cartoons, one luridly titled *I was Mao's Lady Secretary*, were produced for placing in foreign magazines and newspapers.[46]

A typical IRD operation was its contribution to the worldwide 'Red Navy in the Indian Ocean' scare. In early 1974, Britain and America were worried about the Soviet naval build-up in the Indian Ocean after the Somalis had offered the Russians a naval base close to the Gulf. In March two articles inspired by private, verbal IRD briefings appeared. One was written by Brian Crozier in *The Times* and the other penned by David Floyd in the *Daily Telegraph*. Both concentrated heavily on the number of Soviet advisers in neighbouring countries and the fear that the Soviet naval force was about to be strengthened by the presence of the aircraft carrier Kiev. IRD produced its own briefing paper along similar lines for wider distribution in April:

> Soviet policy in the Indian Ocean area as elsewhere, seeks to enhance Soviet influence at the expense of western interests and to stop the spread of Chinese influence. It is assertive in the attempt to demonstrate the position of the Soviet Union as the superpower and to derive the political advantages.[47]

Much of the information – such as the siting and likely purpose of the installations at Berbera – was clearly provided by intelligence sources. Following this IRD briefing, an article on the subject appeared in the *Financial Times* by their East European correspondent.

As the *Leveller* magazine, who put together the detail of this operation, commented:

> The IRD material was part of an orchestrated western campaign – around the same time, the US State Department released photos of the naval facilities at Berbera, taken by spy satellites. By the time the campaign had run its course, it would have taken no little persistence, a great deal of courage and an encyclopedia of facts, to dispel the carefully created illusion that Somalia was a Soviet puppet.[48]

It was richly ironic that this 'Soviet puppet' actually kicked out all Russian military advisers in 1977 during its war with Ethiopia.

IRD was capable of maintaining a continuous flow of material on a particular region as well as arranging the publication of articles at a pertinent moment. The Cultural Revolution in China provides a useful illustration. Drawing on diplomatic communiques, transcripts of interviews with refugees in Hong Kong and broadcasts from radio stations (courtesy of the BBC's Monitoring Service), the department compiled a weekly news sheet, *China News Summary* (CNS), as well as the routine untitled sheets of foolscap. It was not averse to using Soviet reports on the situation, which would then be cited as 'reliable sources'. Anthony Ashworth, who acquired a reputation for intelligence work in Aden (in 1972 he was posted to Northern Ireland from Hong Kong) took charge of the operation. CNS was posted to all Hong Kong newspapers, most foreign journalists and some academics. Reuters and others quoted it extensively, often verbatim. The circulation of the unheaded foolscap sheet was far more restricted: typed on it was usually a brief account of some atrocity, again attributed to 'reliable sources'. CNS was less bloodthirsty, featuring such items as the public destruction of a radio set belonging to a family who had been listening to foreign broadcasts. The family was then 'purged'.[49] In a discussion of Sino-Soviet border clashes, however, the IRD, through CNS, excelled itself:

> Do the Chinese authorities really believe that the chances of the country's involvement in war are as great as they declare them to be, or are they deliberately creating a war psychosis to serve objectives they have been unable to obtain by other means, such as those of welding the people together after the fragmentation caused by the Cultural Revolution, and increasing production with the minimum possible outlay?[50]

IRD tactics frequently necessitated the repetition of the same 'doctored' story in order to ensure its credibility. IRD thus paid close attention to news agencies. After an abortive attempt to buy the *Observer's* Foreign News Service, it concluded a deal with them which gave IRD the right to distribute articles cheaply, or even free of charge, to the media of selected countries.[51] IRD even gave serious consideration to subsidising a well-known Commonwealth news agency through a loss-making period.

About the time IRD was set up, MI6 decided to reactivate a war-time news agency, Britanova, launched by the Special Operations Executive as part of the anti-Nazi propaganda effort. A number of changes were made in the board of directors of Britanova and the allied Arab News Agency, which began as its Middle East branch. Among the new directors were Alan Hare, son of Lord Listowel, who worked for the Foreign Office from 1947 to 1961 and is now chairman and chief executive of the *Financial Times*; Lord Gibson, later chairman of the holding company Pearson Longman which owns the *Financial Times* and Victor Cannon Brookes, a solicitor and controlling shareholder of one of IRD's publishing outlets, Ampersand Ltd. Adelaide Maturin, a career intelligence officer who moved from SOE to MI6 at the end of the war, was appointed secretary. Between 1948 and 1953, three news agencies were established: Near and Far East News (NAFEN), NAFEN (Asia) Ltd., and Arab News Agency (Cairo) Ltd. All these companies were run very closely together and subsequently spawned further agencies based in India, Pakistan and in Africa.

Richard Fletcher, whose UNESCO study of mass media uncovered many of the details of British cold war propaganda, makes particular mention of the Arab News Agency as 'one of the largest and most effective news organisations in the Middle East'. ANA operated

> the most comprehensive service in English and Arabic available ... it had branch offices in Damascus, Beirut, Baghdad, Jerusalem and Amman, and representatives in some 15 other cities, including Paris and New York. It was taken by nearly every Arab newspaper, as well as ... All-India Radio and the BBC.[52]

ANA played an important role in the propaganda offensive prior to the 1956 Suez crisis, and functioned as the centre of a British intelligence network in Egypt (see p. 122). The main key to ANA's success and that of the other agencies was that the massive subsidies directed by the IRD enabled it to undercut rivals by distributing very much cheaper and even free of charge on occasion. The subsidies appear to have extended to the directors' shareholdings: none of them are understood to have bought their own, and most believe that either the IRD or MI6 put up the money.

The UK-based agency Reuters was the main victim of ANA's cheap news. During both world wars, Reuters enjoyed large grants from the British government in exchange for distributing helpful stories, but after the Allied victory in 1945 the board of Reuters decided as a matter of principle to stop accepting them. By 1954

Reuters found it was virtually unable to operate in the Middle East, and was forced into either reaching an agreement with ANA or pulling out. The board opted for the former, and struck an agreement whereby ANA became Reuters' sole agent in the region. In 1963 the NAFEN group moved into new premises adjoining Reuters main London office in Fleet Street. However, in the same year a new general manager, Gerald Long, took over at Reuters. Long objected to the arrangement with ANA and began negotiations with IRD to bring it to an end; in the event this took six years since Reuters desperately needed the money, £28,000 per annum. The Britanova group disintegrated shortly after this agreement ended. Alan Hare resigned as director of International News Rights and Royalties (INRAR), set up in 1963, which had assumed Britanova's central operating role. Tom Little, an experienced Middle East journalist who for a time ran ANA, arranged for James Holburn to replace Hare. Holburn was unaware that 3,500 INRAR shares had been registered in his name and later said that he'd never bought them. The shuffling wasn't over, however. At the end of the 1960s, the stable started to distribute its material under the name World Feature Services, which was formally launched in 1971, by Cannon Brookes, along with another agency, Africa Feature Services (AFS). AFS had the rather unusual practice of not requiring newspapers to credit them as being the source of the material. This agencies do to identify their work to get payment for it. Former AFS employees have told us that a considerable amount of material was actually used by English-language papers in Africa. For most of its existence until its recent closure, the service sustained considerable losses, which were absorbed by its chief shareholder, Seventh Nominees. This was a nominee company controlled by Victor Cannon Brookes and the accountants closely connected with all these operations, Wilding and Hudson.

IRD also took an interest in books as a propaganda vehicle. A number of leading academics contributed to a series of short books published by the small Ampersand company, at the initiative of the IRD. Among these were Hugh Seton-Watson, Professor of Political Science at the London School of Economics and Michael Kaser, lecturer in economics at St. Anthony's College, Oxford. There is no evidence that any of them were aware of Ampersand's connection with IRD. Ampersand was set up just after the war by ex-wartime intelligence officer, Leslie Sheridan, and Victor Cannon Brookes. In 1953, these two were joined by another director, Stephen Watts, who also had wartime intelligence experience. He would discuss titles with the heads of IRD before commissioning them. He also told the *Observer* that British Information Officers would encourage publishers in the Third World countries to produce local editions 'by buying up obscure language rights on the cheap and passing them on for free in the country concerned.' The US Information Service also picked up language rights for Ampersand Books – in one case for 45 countries.

Meanwhile IRD was sponsoring the *Background Books* series (edited by Stephen Watts), first through Batchworth Press, then through Phoenix House until 1960 when Bodley Head became the publishers for the next decade. IRD's method was to use Ampersand to buy the *Background Books* from Bodley Head and, at the end of the year, to reimburse Ampersand for its outlay. Bodley Head's managing director, Max Reinhardt, disclaimed knowledge of any IRD link: 'Ours was an orthodox publishing arrangement with Stephen Watts. I naturally had no idea of Ampersand's connection with IRD or the Foreign Office.'[53]

One of the books on Africa was *Africa Between East and West*, written by John Dumoga, a Ghanaian who was among the continent's first black journalists and later joined Africa Features Service. His work was typical of IRD output:

> In Africa, as elsewhere, communism has presented itself as the only sincere ally of nationalism. Through propaganda, slogans, aid programmes, foreign policy pronouncements and smooth diplomacy, the Soviet and Chinese governments are desperately trying to penetrate the African continent by their identification with African leaders and by equating communism with nationalism, anti-colonialism and anti-neo-colonialism.[54]

> The GPP under Nkrumah was closely patterned on the communist model of a political party; it used communist methods of organisation – intimidation, blackmail, character assassination, deceit, rigged elections, single lists of election candidates, and every other trick from the communist book to win and retain power and finally imposed a merciless dictatorship on Ghanaians.[55]

Another Background Books author, undoubtedly better-known in Britain than Dumoga, was the current *Times* editor, Charles Douglas-Home, who wrote *The Arabs and Israel* for the series. He told us that 'It seems unlikely to have been funded by [the IRD] in view of the fact that I did the book more as a labour of love than for the money.'

The decline of IRD began in 1964 after the last wave of independence celebrations in Africa, and the department suffered the first of a series of cuts. In 1966 the Singapore office, which had played an important part in propaganda operations against the Malayan communists, was closed down. Two years later the Foreign Office Permanent Under-Secretary, Sir Denis Greenhill, pruned it more drastically. Even before that there had always been a strong lobby in the straightforward Information Department of the Foreign Office, which believed that IRD's work could easily be handled by them. In addition, Labour ministers were increasingly worrying about the right-wing complexion that IRD assumed. In 1974, Anthony Crosland, then Labour's Foreign Secretary, pruned the IRD list of journalists taking off some of the more right-wing journalists who had become a political liability. In classic civil service procedure, its end was slow in coming. Two years later, it was again reviewed. Sir Colin Crowe, a former High Commissioner in Canada, was brought out of retirement to look at its functions. He submitted the secret Crowe Report. Among his conclusions was a restatement of the Department's aims:

> IRD should retain a global capacity but [overseas] Regional Offices should be cut. Individual operations, publications and distribution lists should be kept under regular scrutiny.

> The Counter-Subversion Fund* should come under IRD control. The FCO Inspectorate should examine the possibility of reorganising Information Departments to produce a more co-ordinated and focused information/propaganda effort.

The staff of IRD was now down to 110, and its demise seemed imminent. The primary reason for the department's eventual closure was its relationship with the Institute for the Study of Conflict (ISC), a right-wing pressure group set up in 1970 by Brian Crozier, a journalist who had previously worked for Reuters, the *News Chronicle* and the *Economist Foreign Report* as editor. At the time, Crozier was also head of Forum World Features, a London-based news agency which emerged in 1965 from Forum Service, a small cultural features service started by the magazine *Encounter* (see p. 68). Forum World Features became a widely accepted source, particularly in the Third World, and at its peak was supplying over 250 newspapers worldwide. Forum received backing from the Central Intelligence Agency through Kern House Enterprises, a publishing firm run by a former US ambassador to Britain, John Whitney. In 1975 a team from the television programme *World in Action* uncovered a memorandum from CIA headquarters dated 1968: addressed to Richard Helms, then director, it described Forum as having

> provided the United States with a significant means to counter propaganda, and has become a respected feature service well on the way to a position of prestige in the journalism world.

Handwritten at the bottom was a note stating that Forum functioned 'with the knowledge and co-operation of British intelligence'.[56] Forum was suddenly closed down in 1975, shortly before its exposure.

Kern House supplied the funds for Crozier's project; Forum's

---

* A Foreign Office fund which is used, among other things, to finance some propaganda operations. It is still in existence.

library and some of its research staff were absorbed into ISC, and Forum then paid ISC £2,000 in order to use the library. The Kern House subsidy continued until at least the middle of 1972, by which time other sources of finance had materialised. Together with 2,000 odd subscriptions to ISC publications they make up ISC's budget of, as of 1976, over £30,000. British intelligence showed a positive attitude towards the new organisation, in fact

> in a letter to the international Herald Tribune, the well-known foreign correspondent Bernard Nossiter claimed that he had been told by a senior official of British intelligence that Crozier's institute was actually run by the British.[57]

Crozier has denied the existence of any connection between ISC and Forum, and also of any links with British or American intelligence. He himself has now left the organisation.

ISC's administrative director is Michael Goodwin, who previously worked for IRD's publishing instrument, Ampersand, while two ex-IRD staff, Lynn Price and Kenneth Benton, have been regular ISC writers. The institute's output comprises the monthly 'Conflict Studies', the 'Annual of Power and Conflict' and occasional 'Special Reports'. Most of the writers are journalists and ex-academics, with a sprinkling of emigres and academics, notably from the School of Oriental and African Studies in London and St. Anthony's College, Oxford. The emphasis is towards discussion of foreign affairs although five studies on Northern Ireland and a report on the influence of left-wing groupings in the British trade union movement have also been produced.

Files removed from the offices of research director Peter Janke in the summer of 1975 showed extensive contacts between ISC and the British police and military establishments.[58] In June 1972, Janke visited the Police College at Bramshill at the invitation of its then commandant, John Alderson, who later became Chief Constable of Devon and Cornwall and acquired a reputation as something of a liberal among senior police officers. Alderson wanted ISC to assist in developing a training programme on subversion and terrorism for the college. The initial meeting went well: Janke and others recommended by him have since lectured on numerous occasions at the college, and the police make use of an ISC 'Manual on Counter-Insurgency'. ISC has provided lecturers for several military establishments, including the National Defence College, where on other courses 'psyops' are taught. Outside Britain, the documents revealed Janke had had contacts with South African intelligence, who had supplied information on guerilla groups like FRELIMO. The detailed exposure of ISC contacts and methods had little impact on its publishing programme.

The present council – the institute's governing body – is like its predecessors composed entirely of luminaries from academia, diplomacy, and the military: former defence intelligence chief Sir Louis Le Bailly; counter-insurgency theorist Sir Robert Thompson; Sir Henry Tuzo, for two years Deputy Supreme Allied Commander of NATO forces in Europe and former GOC Northern Ireland; Sir Christopher Foxley-Norris, sometime member of the Chief of Staffs committee; ex-diplomat Sir Edward Peck and the academics Leonard Schapiro, Max Beloff, Paul Wilkinson, Samuel Finer, Lawrence Martin and George Seton-Watson. The calibre of its personnel, with intimate knowledge of the workings of the state, makes the ISC an influential part of the right-wing lobby.

The Information Research Department was finally put to sleep by David Owen at the end of April 1977, but this did not end the government's propaganda programme. A 'think tank', established after the submission of the Crowe report was sceptical of IRD's value but commented that its unattributable material had a role to play in creating 'helpful political attitudes' in the more influential Third World countries. Owen established a smaller, less secretive organisation known as the Overseas Information Department (OID), which assumed many of IRD's techniques, including sending briefing papers to selected lists of journalists. Many of IRD's key staff were transplanted into OID, including its head, Ray Whitney.* OID published two sets of papers: *Background Briefs*, with material on current topics prepared as guides for overseas missions, and *Foreign Policy Documents*, which tend to be much longer and designed mainly for internal Whitehall consumption. Both series are, in theory, publicly available, although the difficulty in obtaining them prompted criticism from the House of Commons Expenditure Committee's Sub Committee on External Affairs. The *Background Briefs*, three or four loose-leaf sheets stapled together, are marked at the bottom in italics with the words:

> This paper has been prepared for general briefing purposes. It is not and should not be construed or quoted as an expression of Government policy.

During 1981, the OID was absorbed into the FCO's Information Department, which has acquired, as a result, a new function of

> the provision of guidance and background briefing on matters of general concern affecting Government policy.[59]

Such anodyne phrases are the distinguishing mark of whichever department happens to be responsible for overseas propaganda. In a television interview on the first anniversary of her election, Mrs Thatcher called for 'a massive propaganda effort of a kind we have never mounted'[60] against the Soviet Union and communist influence.

* Now Conservative MP for High Wycombe.

Thirty years of experience guarantees the Foreign Office a central role in the campaign: smearing, distorting and lying in the spirit of the halcyon days of the 1950s. Christopher Mayhew, whose memo started the IRD, recently wrote to the *New Statesman* after an attack by the magazine on IRD-type operations:

> Instead of publishing renewed insults about us, should you not now give us some credit for telling the truth, in a good cause, at some political risk to ourselves?[61]

Behind this piece of brazen hyperbole seems to lie a confirmation of the adage that propagandists usually end up believing their own propaganda. But propaganda via mass media is not the only means of influence.

Intervention in the International Student Movement

The end of the Second World War brought a spirit of optimism to political movements across Europe. The nascent tensions among the allied powers were not widely recognised while a positive opportunity to rebuild the continent in an atmosphere of genuine international co-operation appeared to exist. National student and trade union organisations, always among the more outward-looking of movements seized the chance to extend their foreign contacts as their interests became internationalised. The associations formed as a result naturally came under scrutiny from governments in the emerging European power blocs who were quietly preparing the cold war. Their potential in terms of political influence was immediately recognised and the covert action departments set about taking control of them. Although the CIA's manipulation of the student movement is a notorious and fairly well-publicised story, it is pre-dated by similar British activity.

In 1947, like its trade union counterpart, the international student movement began to split. Those supporting the Soviet bloc-funded World Federation of Democratic Youth (WFDY) constituted the single most organised section, and there was no natural home for right-wing and social democratic student and youth organisations. To fill the gap, the National Council of Social Service in Britain decided to organise a conference out of which a complementary international student body could be launched.

British intelligence took a great deal of interest in student affairs, as one former activist, now a businessman, explained:

> When I was a student just after the war and wanted to see the world, I decided to go to Argentina for this Peronist conference. While I was there, I helped organise the British delegation ... the British embassy was very kind and helped by lending us their duplicator. Shortly afterwards, when I was back in England, I was called to meet a senior NUS official. This was followed by an approach at a party by a civil servant. Was I

interested in government work? How about an interview? It turned out they were interviewing for MI6. Later I was told that I wasn't accepted. But often I think now of how I could have become a spy.[62]

Meanwhile the Foreign Office circulated a memo to its overseas missions asking for an assessment – to be marked 'secret' – of who should be invited to join the new organisation. Africa was not included in this operation as it was the responsibility of the Colonial Office and not yet considered important. The Foreign Office's notes to the conference organisers made quite clear who they thought it expedient to invite:

> We are anxious that the Finns should be brought into association with the western democracies as much as possible, and therefore we shall be glad, if you can find some way to justify it, for Finland to be invited.[63]

Youth organisations were carefully judged on their strength and ability to combat communism. J.R. Roper wrote from the British Council in Uruguay:

> The Associacion Patriotica is at present very much anti-communist and is emitting propaganda to this effect.[64]

Armed with this information, the conference organisers began making up their budget for the event to be held in mid-1948. On their initial estimates, there was a short-fall of over £5,000 between income and expenditure. Luckily, through hefty government support, the figures looked more healthy when revised. Costs now were estimated at £12,000 and over three-quarters of these were covered by grants from various government departments. One of the largest items – £3,000 – was listed as 'Grant from Prime Minister's Fund (South African Aid to Britain)'. In a memo to George Haynes (later Sir George), head of the National Council of Social Service, his number two Violet Weston was able to report on this item: 'She (Miss Powell of the Foreign Office) also thinks it likely that an approach to the Prime Minister's Secretary would also produce an affirmative reply regarding the reference to the South African Aid to Britain Fund'. Whatever the source of these funds, it was certainly not South Africa. It is far more likely to have been money passed under the Secret Vote.

The product of the conference was the World Assembly of Youth (WAY), which started life with its headquarters in Paris. It received considerable help from the French government which, like the British, also provided covert funding to the WAY affiliate in its own country. In Britain a National Committee was elected whose initial membership was politically quite broad, including a number of socialists with no alignment to Moscow. However, it was not long before the right asserted itself and the student movement became an acceptable stamping ground for those wanting to make their name in preparation for parliamentary politics. Their views were almost entirely in tune with those of their Foreign Office advisers throughout the 1950s and 1960s while the National Committee remained in the hands of the right. The Foreign Office for its part knew what it wanted. At a meeting between the British National Committee of WAY and the Foreign Office, the Colonial Office and the Commonwealth Relations Office, Geoffrey McDermott of the Foreign Office raised the topic of hospitality for overseas students:

> This was an important activity and should be examined, since it was known that the Communist Party made a special attempt to influence all such visitors.[65]

WAY's value to the Foreign Office did not exempt it from financial problems, its president, Guthrie Moir, discovered in late 1952:

> I have just received a number of dire warnings from the Foreign Office that the very considerable grant aids to the activities of WAY, both international and national, may fall together under the Chancellor's axe in 1953 unless I can enlist some support at Cabinet level ... I have just succeeded in getting the first batch of dollar aid for WAY from the Foundation for Youth and Student Affairs [a CIA foundation] in New York.[66]

This threat to WAY's regular Foreign Office grant could not have come at a worse time. Moir was convinced that there was a real possibility of 'building up the World Assembly of Youth into a really useful anti-communist influence'[67] and the organisation was planning a major assembly of world delegates in Singapore. When the axe eventually fell, a swift lobbying campaign followed that attracted support from the highest quarters. The Foreign Office remained enthusiastic and blamed the meanness on the Treasury. MPs from all parties pleaded for the retention of WAY's grant. Labour backbencher Woodrow Wyatt, erstwhile recipient of IRD handouts and now a *Sunday Mirror* columnist, described WAY as

> an organisation which does extremely valuable propaganda for the free world without looking like a propaganda organisation.[68]

Indeed, so cleverly had its name been chosen that some of its delegates were once detained at London airport because Special Branch thought it was a communist front.

By April 1954, however, it had become clear that Whitehall had formulated a compromise, as a parliamentary reply to Tory MP John Hay showed:

> In the first place, it is for the British National Committee of the World Assembly of Youth to do a little more to make itself financially self-supporting. There are things it can do, and HMG

will do everything in their power to assist in those matters.[69]

This assistance included putting WAY in touch with major establishment figures. A Friends of WAY was launched and immediately attracted a solid list of patrons; the Prime Minister, Sir Anthony Eden, ex-Labour Prime Minister Clement Attlee (in whose period of office it had been set up), Viscount Chandos (ex-Colonial Secretary) and Lord Mountbatten's wife, Edwina. The matter became an issue of confidence for everyone concerned. Mr J.K. Thompson of the Colonial Office told Sam Page of WAY that the 'weak link must be in the Treasury'.[70] WAY was on the brink of organising a major political event and it was having to ask the Foreign Office to investigate the possible use of troop ships to get its delegates there. The event planned for Singapore was ambitious. WAY wanted to invite Africa's newest black President, Kwame Nkrumah of Ghana to address the Assembly. The attraction for Nkrumah would be the British government's willingness to pay his expenses for a tour of India at the same time.

The importance of the WAY event cannot be under-estimated. With Britain hard-pressed in neighbouring Malaya by communist guerillas and experiencing the first effective resistance by African nationalists in West Africa, what better way of seizing the initiative than by inviting the leader of Pan-Africanism to a 'free world' conference. And more sinister forces were at work, as Joseph Burkholder-Smith, ex-CIA station chief in Singapore at the time, attests in his book *Cold War Warrior*:

> As for the WAY meeting, 10 [the CIA division which handled front groups] had a certain amount of liaison already going with the British [MI6] in London, on all its operations in the world front field, and WAY in particular. They wanted ... to have British assistance in steering the meeting towards their ultimate objective of WAY's becoming a free world front group.
>
> On top of this, I0 wanted the Singapore station to direct operations with the student leaders they were trying to manipulate at the meeting.[71]

This keenness did not pass entirely unnoticed for as Sonia Richardson of the British National Committee wrote to Guthrie Moir in two separate letters:

> The Foreign Office are very wound up about it and have repeated the information that Washington is in touch with them and so on ... I don't understand entirely why the State Department and the Foreign Office are so keen or how they knew we were discussing it at all.[72]

The event did not turn out to be quite as promising for the British or American intelligence services as they hoped. Much hot air and pious sentiment was not what they were looking for. But WAY continued to find government favour and Foreign Office finance was soon resumed. It was, however, reduced to just under half of the organisation's yearly budget and the Friends of WAY were sent a letter of recommendation for their appeal in 1958 by Foreign Secretary, Selwyn Lloyd. Having solved its financial problems, WAY continued with much the same work it had been doing before for the government. It began to work through the Colonial Office to extend its influence in Africa, setting up National Committees in Kenya, Mauritius, Sierra Leone, Seychelles, and Uganda. This ministry regularly brought WAY events to the attention of the African colonial governments, arranged for WAY film shows and helped pay the travel expenses of the generally penniless African delegates. For instance, the local Colonial Governor in Sierra Leone agreed to cover 80 per cent of the expenses of the local Sierra Leone delegate and even helped to make the arrangements by government telegram. In Mauritius, the WAY committee was faced with the daunting task of reversing the flow of affiliations to the local communist-supported youth league, which was providing many more scholarships and trips abroad. Jean Delaitre, the deputy minister for Health and Labour and a WAY committee member, wrote to WAY headquarters asking for help. He feared the growth of communism before independence and asked WAY to assist 'the free youth movement of Mauritius'. The request to Paris was duly passed to the British National Committee where they arranged advice on the problem from the Department of Technical Co-operation[a CIA foundation].

This moderating role was often misunderstood by right-wing British traditionalists like Lord Colyton, who in 1963 complained that WAY was communist-inspired after an issue of WAY Review had carried articles on the liberation movements in Angola.

Bill McGowan, Secretary of the British National Committee of WAY, wrote to the Foreign Office desperately trying to be helpful:

> It is ... suggested that Mr Holden Roberto, President of UPA*
> and Prime Minister of the Angolan Government in Exile, is
> himself communist backed. This, I also gather, is not proved.
> It would be, therefore, very useful from our point of view if
> some positive proof is placed in our hands.[73]

Two years before, McGowan had been on to the Foreign Office for information about communist front organisations. Tom Barker replied from the Foreign Office recommending three pamphlets published by right-wing pressure groups, one of which was Industrial Research and Information Services. McGowan wanted one particular publication, however.

* Union of the Peoples of Angola

I had in mind a rather large book which Maurice Foley had at his office at the European Youth Campaign and which I seem to think I mentioned to you on one occasion when I met you there ... it was a confidential document which gave a full list of all front organisations ... you may rest assured ... that it would be well cared for.[74]

The book, *Facts about International Communist Front Organisations*, was produced by the Information Research Department, who contacted McGowan directly, sent him a copy and put him on the mailing list for the IRD monthly bulletin *International Organisations*. WAY were able to circulate unattributed IRD material on British foreign policy at their meetings.

Maurice Foley was one of a number of young social democrats who began their political careers in the cold war trojan horse of WAY. He was secretary of the British section of the European Youth Campaign from 1951-59, during which time EYC as a whole received over £1,300,000 of CIA money. The largest proportion of this came to the British affiliate. Foley was at least aware of allegations of CIA funding, since a public dispute in 1952 over American money led to the withdrawal of the Labour Party's youth organisation. In 1975 Tom Braden, an ex-CIA officer who served as head of its International Organisations division, confirmed that the agency had funded the European Movement, with which EYC was closely connected. Foley denied any knowledge of CIA involvement. He subsequently became a trustee of the Ariel Foundation along with two other WAY hopefuls: Charles Longbottom and Barney Hayhoe, the latter having been chairman of the British National Committee during the late 1950s and early 1960s.

The exposure in the late 1960s of CIA financial aid to WAY headquarters through a group of foundations precipitated WAY's downfall. The International Secretariat in Paris became increasingly discredited and the organisation's affiliations began to lapse. The British National Committee, which was renamed the British Youth Council, disaffiliated in 1977.

Notes

1.   Lord Gladwyn *The Memoirs of Lord Gladwyn* (1972) p.117
2.   Noam Chomsky, writing in the *Guardian* (15 June 1981)
3.   Summary of the Interim Report of the Special Committee on Relaxation of Trade Barriers (18 December 1943)
4.   Richard Crossman *New Fabian Essays* (1970) pp.31-2
5.   J. Frankel *British Foreign Policy 1945-73* (1975) p.157
6.   *Sunday Times* (14 March 1982)
7.   *New Statesman* (8 February 1980)
8.   *Observer* (22 June 1980)

9.   John Prados *The Soviet Estimate: US Intelligence and Russian Military Strength* (1982) p.57
10.   Quoted in Trevor Barnes *The Secret Cold War* article in *The Historical Journal* Volume 25 No.3 (September 1982)
11.   *Ibid*
12.   *Daily Telegraph* (11 May 1981)
13.   *Washington Post* (24 November 1981)
14.   Quoted in Richard Hall *The Secret State* (1978) p.132
15.   C.M. Woodhouse *Something Ventured* (1982) p.135
16.   *Time Out* (7 March 1975)
17.   *Times* (22 March 1975)
18.   Quoted in Harry Miller *Jungle War in Malaya: The Campaign against Communism* (1972) p.90
19.   F.H. Lakin *Psychological Warfare Research in Malaya 1952-5* UK Ministry of Defence Army Operational Research Establishment Paper given to 11th Annual US Army Human Factors Research and Development Conference (October 1965)
20.   *Far East Economic Review* (11 September 1971)
21.   Personal interview
22.   Sir Charles Jeffries *The Colonial Office* (1956) p.179
23.   Personal communication to the authors
24.   From papers in Rhodes House archives, Oxford
25.   Rhodes House papers
26.   From papers collected by Richard Rathbone
27.   Personal interview
28.   Personal interview
29.   *Daily Express* (29 June 1953)
30.   Diary of Sir Philip Mitchell (10 April 1952) quoted in Richard Frost *Race Against Time* (1978) p.249
31.   Personal interview
32.   Letter from Hudson to Gorell-Barnes (30 July 1954)
33.   Letter from Hudson to Oldham (23 September 1954)
34.   Private interview
35.   Quoted in Tabitha Kanogo *Politics of Collaboration or Domination: A Case Study of the Capricorn Africa Society* article in *Kenya Historical Review* Vol. 2 No. 2 (1974) p.134
36.   Sir Michael Blundell *So Rough A Wind* (1964) p.129
37.   Fred Majdalany *State of Emergency - The Full Story of Mau Mau* (1962) p.170
38.   From Mayhew papers, quoted in Richard Fletcher *The Free Flow of News* unpublished paper (August 1979)
39.   Mayhew papers
40.   Mayhew papers
41.   Mayhew papers
42.   Richard Fletcher *The Free Flow of News* unpublished paper (1979)
43.   Richard Fletcher *The Free Flow of News*
44.   *Observer* (24 January 1982)
45.   *Guardian* (27 December 1978)
46.   *Observer* (28 February 1982)
47.   Information Research Department *The Soviet Presence in the Indian Ocean* (1974)
48.   *Leveller* No. 13 (March 1978)

49.   *China News Summary* No.301 (18 December 1969)
50.   *China News Summary* No.279 (17 July 1969)
51.   *Observer* (29 January 1978)
52.   *Guardian* (18 December 1981)
53.   *Observer* (29 January 1978)
54.   John Dumoga *Africa Between East and West* (1969) p.114
55.   John Dumoga *Africa Between East and West* p.121
56.   Steve Weissman *CIA, Students of Conflict* article in *Embassy* magazine (August 1976) republished as *The CIA makes the News* in *Dirtywork: The CIA in Western Europe* (1978) pp.204-210
57.   Steve Weissman *The CIA makes the News*
58.   *Time Out* (5 September 1975)
59.   *Diplomatic Service List* (1982) p.8
60.   *Guardian* (6 May 1980)
61.   *New Statesman* (13 March 1981)
62.   Personal interview
63.   From material in the British Youth Council archives
64.   *Ibid.*
65.   *Ibid.*
66.   *Ibid.*
67.   *Ibid.*
68.   *Ibid.*
69.   'Parliamentary Reply' (p.143) *House of Commons Hansard* Volume 526, column 777-8
70.   British Youth Council archives (April 1964)
71.   Joseph Burkholder-Smith *Cold War Warrior* (1976) p.165
72.   British Youth Council archives
73.   *Ibid.*
74.   *Ibid.*

Chapter 3
Covert Operations in the Middle East 1950–80

The Middle East of the 1950s was the scene of some of the most aggressive and cavalier activity by MI6 during its seventy year history. Unlike Africa, some decolonisation had already taken place, but Britain retained considerable influence throughout the region. For many years before, she had skilfully exploited inter-Arab rivalries and after the dismantling of the Turkish Ottoman empire at the end of the First World War, held an imperial duopoly with the French stretching from Libya to Iran and from Syria to Aden. The establishment of Israel, which took up some four-fifths of Palestinian territory west of the Jordan river, was not a major blow to the British, despite the counter-insurgency campaign against Zionist groups; the Arab-Israeli conflict had not assumed the dominating status of today and the British prepared themselves to counter Arab nationalists and encroaching foreign competitors.

To the east of the Persian Gulf, Iran sported a British-style constitutional monarchy, with Mohammed Reza Shah Pahlavi, deposed by Islamic fundamentalists in 1979, as head of state and Mohammed Mossadeq as Prime Minister. Immediately after his election in 1951, Mossadeq presented a bill to the Majlis (Parliament) providing for the nationalisation of the Anglo-Iranian Oil Company (AIOC) which held a monopoly over the extraction of the country's oil deposits. The British government held 56 per cent of shares in the firm.[1] AIOC was aware of the possibility of a takeover and took precautions, including bribing politicians. Unfortunately for them, Mossadeq arranged a burglary at their Tehran headquarters which uncovered an up-to-date list of gifts made to a number of ministers and Majlis deputies. With proof of AIOC complicity in corruption, Mossadeq's bill was passed without opposition, and on 2nd May AIOC was taken under Iranian government control. The British were furious. Prime Minister Attlee asked the Chiefs of Staff to draft a plan for the occupation of the main AIOC refinery at Abadan. A firm response was felt necessary, not least to impress upon other Middle Eastern rulers the danger of tampering with British assets. At the Treasury, forecasts of the econ-omic effect of nationalisation were causing concern. However the plan, codenamed 'Buccaneer', was shelved when the Americans made it clear that they would not support a major military action. The prospect of difficulties at the United Nations, with Britain branded as an aggressor, was a further disincentive. The general manager of AIOC told the Cabinet that there was no harm in waiting to see what the International Court, which was considering the dispute, would eventually decide. Meanwhile AIOC organised a worldwide boycott of Iranian oil, causing serious economic problems in the country.

The autumn election of 1951 brought the Conservative party back to power. The following February AIOC suggested to them that arrangements might be made for Mossadeq's removal. Churchill agreed, although the economic rationale was no longer present: there was a surplus of crude oil on world markets and a new refinery at Aden for processing oil from Kuwait, Iraq and other British-owned fields was nearing completion. Foreign Secretary Anthony Eden was less convinced of the need for a coup. Planning started nonetheless, consuming most of the rest of 1952.

It was a turbulent year elsewhere in the Middle East. Political upheavals in Lebanon and Jordan produced new administrations. Syria, which had secured independence from the French at the end of the Second World War, became a military dictatorship. There was trouble too in Iraq, described shortly before as 'entirely within Britain's political sphere'[2] by American Secretary of State John Foster Dulles. Appalling living standards were the main cause of unrest, but troops quickly restored order and the country remained under firm British control. The biggest blow that year, however, was the overthrow and exiling of King Faroukh in Egypt, one of Britain's closest allies in the Middle East. A Revolutionary Command Council, led by General Muhammad Neguib but under the effective control of Colonel Gamal Abdel Nasser, took power.

The British network of agents in Iran was the largest of any foreign power, and included the multi-millionaire Shapoor Reporter, who later acted as the middle-man for British arms sales to the Shah. However, lack of finance forced MI6 to look across the Atlantic for help. At the end of 1951 a group of MI6 officers travelled to Washington to lobby for a joint operation.

American foreign policy was in the hands of the Dulles brothers: John Foster, the Secretary of State, and Allen, the head of the CIA. Both were obsessed with the spectre of 'international communism', and were of the opinion that Mossadeq had formed an alliance with the Soviet Union. Mossadeq was not a communist, nor even partic-ularly left-wing, although his government was supported by the Tudeh

(Iranian communist party). A further spur was that the chances of the American oil firms Gulf and Standard breaking the Anglo-Iranian monopoly had been destroyed by the state takeover. MI6's chief director, Sir John Sinclair, met the pair to lay down a framework for Operation Ajax. Day-to-day liaison over the project was entrusted to Sinclair's deputy, George Young, who had recently returned from Middle East intelligence headquarters in Cairo to take up his promotion.

The CIA agreed to the MI6 plan with alterations, chief of which was that for the purposes of the coup, the Americans would take control of the MI6 network inside Iran. The CIA was eager to show that although MI6 had helped in its establishment six years earlier, it was now the leading Western intelligence agency. Lacking an alternative source of finance, MI6 agreed. Kermit Roosevelt, grandson of ex-President Theodore Roosevelt, was appointed to control the CIA operation.

At the British end, it remained for MI6 to obtain the approval of the political leadership. Both Churchill and MI6's Foreign Office adviser, Sir George Clutton, consented. Anthony Eden was conveniently ill, and hence unable to voice his objections. An anti-Mossadeq army commander, General Fazlollah Zahedi, was selected to lead the 'revolt' against Mossadeq and provided with a large sum of money to organise a mob to follow mutineering junior officers into the streets. The British-controlled news media began anti-Mossadeq propaganda campaigns.

In the meantime, Mossadeq turned his attention to the police. Between 1942 and 1948 the Iranian force was under the command of an American, Brigader-General Norman Schwarzkopf, which left a fairly large residue of pro-American sympathy within the force. Mossadeq appointed a new police chief in April 1953, General Ashfar-Tus, who had instructions to purge the force of this group. The evening after his first day at police headquarters, he was kidnapped by MI6 agents and assassinated. Mossadeq had not sought to alienate the Americans completely: he had refrained from expelling a military mission attached to the Iranian army. Diplomatic relations with Britain, however, had been broken in October 1952. In May, he wrote to President Eisenhower asking for a loan. Eisenhower was not aware of the prospective coup, but waited a month before replying. There would be no loan, said the President, unless Mossadeq agreed to the immediate opening of talks on the future of the oilfields. The ageing premier refused, and massive demonstrations of support took place in the streets. On American advice, the army and police force remained in barracks.

While the Shah felt nationalistic abhorrence at the parasitic presence of AIOC, and in that sense welcomed and endorsed the government's takeover, he was also becoming more and more concerned with communist influence and activity which had received a fillip. Since the withdrawal of Soviet troops amid threatening gestures from the British at the end of the Second World War, a number of territorial disputes had flared up between Iran and its powerful northern neighbour which left the Shah with the strong impression that his country was a prime Soviet target. He took reassurance from the Dulles' perception of world politics which in turn reinforced his suspicion that Mossadeq, with Tudeh support, was leading Iran into the Soviet bloc.

In the midst of the turmoil over the next two months, Schwarzkopf reappeared in Tehran with a diplomatic passport. He had a quick succession of meetings with General Zahedi, another pro-Shah officer General Hassan Arfa, and several senior police officers. Mossadeq knew of Schwarzkopf's presence and had also heard of the secret meeting between Kermit Roosevelt and the Shah. Further anti-Shah riots broke out. Mossadeq had to move fast. He suspended the Majlis and announced a referendum to gauge public support for his action, also asking for special powers to deal with 'sinister elements' in the army and police. The Shah dismissed Mossadeq and appointed General Zahedi as his replacement. Mossadeq broadcast a statement over the radio refusing to obey the Shah's order. He also arrested the chief of the Shah's imperial guard. In panic, the Shah fled to Rome via Baghdad, as statues and pictures of him were destroyed throughout the city. Loy Henderson, the US ambassador, immediately authorized the release of masses of new equipment held by the military mission to support the officer revolt fuelled by CIA and MI6 cash. Crowds of haphazardly armed peasants appeared at the southern gate, having arrived from the direction of General Arfa's estate. A procession, led by the officers, filed through the city to Parliament Square. Thousands of anti-Mossadeq leaflets suddenly appeared. His supporters were nowhere in sight. Army and police units sent by Mossadeq to disperse the insurgents joined them instead. Only at Mossadeq's residence did a loyal unit fight against the crowd, killing 300 people. General Zahedi emerged from his estate and rode an American tank into the city, proclaiming a new government. He cabled the Shah to return from exile. Mossadeq was arrested, tried and sentenced to three years imprisonment. His foreign minister, Hossein Fatemi, was executed, along with thousands of Tudeh members. The Shah expressed his gratitude to the CIA, and in Britain the papers carried the headlines 'SITUATION RESTORED, AS YOU WERE IN IRAN'.[3] The total cost of the exercise was around $10 million. The problem of the oil franchise was sorted out after a year of wrangling and a special dispensation from American anti-trust laws obtained from the Justice Department. The final formula was 40 per cent of shares to AIOC, 14 per cent to Royal Dutch Shell, 8 per cent to five American firms (Standard of New Jersey, Socony-Mobil, Standard of California, the Texas Company, and Gulf Oil) and 6 per cent to Compagnie Francaise des Petroles. In addition, AIOC (which became British Petroleum) received £34,500,000 compensation from its consortium partners plus 10 cents a barrel on all exports until a sum of $510 million was reached. According to Hassan Sana, sometime co-director of SAVAK*, MI6 busied itself running the main intelligence network in the country on behalf of the Americans.[4]

When SAVAK was set up in 1957, some of its officers were trained in Britain. Others went to Israel or the United States. In exchange for information on Arab countries, claimed Sana, SAVAK was given a free hand in intelligence-gathering inside the United Kingdom. While most of its targets were politically active students, they also included Labour MPs who campaigned against the brutality of the Shah's regime. SAS personnel 'on loan' to the Iranian military trained their special forces for operations against Kurdish guerillas in the north of the country. Another SAS unit was entrusted with the protection of the GCHQ monitoring station near Mashad, close to the Soviet border; four of them were captured and executed by Fedayeen guerillas in 1972.

While co-operating over Iran, Britain and the United States differed over the future of Egypt, and their opinions diverged further after Nasser's takeover. The British had maintained a large military presence in the country since the 1870s, with bases at Cairo, Alexandria and around the Suez canal. British troops left Cairo and Alexandria during 1947 and 1948 but a planned reduction of the Suez facilities was not carried through as the British economy began to revive under the stimulus of Marshall Aid. The British had no intention of quitting the canal zone completely: they had no confidence in the ability of the Egyptians to run the canal effectively, and thus refused to take the risk of transfer for fear of disrupting the flow of traffic to the Gulf oil states and the Far East. At this time some 80,000 British troops were stationed in the area. British influence further extended to responsibility for the country's external security – a role they also held in Jordan and Iraq – and the training of the Egyptian intelligence services.

The elections of January 1950 brought Nahas Pasha to power on a reformist programme and an undertaking to put a stop to rampant governmental corruption. He immediately pulled out of the Anglo-Egyptian alliance, which provided the legal basis for British occupa-

* acronym for Iranian State Security and Intelligence Organisation, Sazman-i-Amniyat va Kishvar.

tion, and demanded immediate talks on the status of the canal. The Foreign Office, while dismissing the rejection of the treaty, agreed to negotiate. Discussions continued without agreement through 1950 and the following year, towards the end of which spasmodic assaults by communist and moslem fundamentalist guerillas started to increase in frequency and intensity. The British responded in kind, attacking the guerilla bases and finally sealing off the canal zone in December. Guerilla activity continued nonetheless, as did the British retaliation, culminating in January 1952 with an attack on the Ismailiya auxiliary police headquarters which was thought to be the guerillas' main weapons supply point. Fifty Egyptian police officers were killed during the fighting. Once the news reached Cairo, spontaneous anti-British riots erupted and British homes and commercial premises burnt down. Twelve Britons were killed during the attack on the exclusive Turf Club, the supreme symbol of the British establishment in the country, which was razed to the ground.

Nahas Pasha's drive against corruption never materialised, and the in-fighting which had dogged successive administrations became worse than ever, reducing the government to a state of almost total inertia. Disaffection among the population and, crucially, in the army increased rapidly despite the government's dismissal of all its British officials in December in response to the Suez closure. In the early hours of July 23rd, Nasser's Society of Young Officers took power in a bloodless coup. Egypt was declared a republic and King Faroukh exiled. The CIA were rumoured to have backed the takeover, although it seems strange that they should have risked offending their British allies in what would have been their first major Middle East operation. What is certain, however, is that the United States government subsequently authorised $40 million aid to Egypt and a further covert sum of $3 million to Nasser personally. The British, smarting from the disposal of Faroukh, distrusted him and remonstrated with the Americans for providing support. They also resented American moves into what they considered to be territory in their sphere of influence.

Nasser's political programme was based on an Arab nationalism not dissimilar in content to that found in Africa. He sought to restrict the powers of landowners and the bourgeoisie and destroy foreign control of the economy. Nevertheless, his Islamic doctrine precluded alignment with the Soviet Union, and in America it was felt that he would need to seek Western expertise and finance to develop the Egyptian economy. Whitehall was pleasantly surprised to find him more flexible than his predecessors on the issue of Sudan, and somewhat restrained in his attitude towards Israel. In fact, it seems that Nasser initiated a serious effort to bring about negotiations with Israel in the late summer of 1955, but he abandoned it soon afterwards in protest against Israeli attacks on Palestinians in the Gaza strip. Egypt had claimed sovereignty over the Sudan, which the British were slowly pushing towards self-administration, but Nasser seemed prepared to settle for a form of association. The issue was resolved fairly quickly with both sides agreeing to a joint administration prior to total independence by February 1956.

Nasser's major immediate problem was the canal. He established a secret commission to investigate the canal company, a little under half of whose annual toll income of $100 million went into British coffers. Negotiations began in May 1953, and took eighteen months to conclude. Guerilla groups under Nasser's control were periodically unleashed to force the pace at sticking points. At the same time the Israelis, afraid of good relations developing between Nasser and the West, sent sabotage groups across the border to attack British and American installations in Egypt. The responsibility, they hoped, would fall on Nasser. The disclosure of these operations in mid-1954 caused the fall of the government of Israel's first prime minister David Ben-Gurion.

Nasser's foreign policy centred on creating a community of Arab nations – an 'Arab Circle' – guided by the principles of the Egyptian revolution. He found support in Syria and among the large Palestinian community in Jordan, who saw an opportunity to develop a united front against Israel. Throughout the Arab states Nasser promoted 'Young Officer' groups which were modelled on his own. Egyptian support for anti-governmental groups in Jordan provoked the first serious doubts in Britain about Nasser's alignment. The American State Department, and particularly Secretary of State John Foster Dulles, began to worry when Egypt signed a commercial oil agreement with the Soviet Union in January 1954.

The future of the canal was determined in October with the signing of an Anglo-Egyptian treaty. The waterway would remain under the control of the canal company but the 80,000 British troops in the canal zone would be withdrawn by 1956. They would, however, be permitted to return in the event of war. In military terms, this was not such a great setback for the British. The advent of nuclear weapons had greatly reduced its strategic significance and the base was proving expensive to maintain. The resources saved by withdrawal were diverted to the bases in Cyprus, whose proximity to the Middle East ensured that the British retained a capacity for quick intervention in the region.

To consolidate its declining presence and influence, the British government reorganised its Middle East policy around the Baghdad Pact – the treaty mechanism had found renewed favour in both London and Washington as a device to construct regional anti-communist

blocs. In both capitals, it appears, policy-makers had forgotten
> the historic diplomatic truth that once a treaty is signed,
> the signatories inherit each other's enemies without necessarily
> being more than friends of convenience themselves. When
> alliances are put together in series, the number of enemies is
> increased to the extent that the efficacy of the structure as a
> whole is thrown into doubt[5]

Iraq, Turkey and Pakistan joined the pact with Britain in January
1955, while Iran signed in October. The United States pledged support
for its provisions, which dealt with mutual military assistance, but
did not sign. The British interpreted the American refusal as an
indication that they were prepared to leave responsibility for the
security of Western interests in British hands and themselves pursue a
more flexible policy, particularly with regard to Egypt. The British
government found this position quite acceptable, at least in the short
term. Nasser vehemently opposed the pact, mainly because of Iraqi
membership. He stepped up the already considerable anti-British
propaganda campaign, with special emphasis on Jordan, top of the
British list for potential pact membership.

Winston Churchill retired from the premiership in April 1955 at
the age of 79. His Foreign Secretary, Anthony Eden, took power.
Eden was held in high esteem at home, after his stand against Hitler
before the Second World War. Harold Macmillan, who had good
relations with the Americans, was appointed to Eden's old job. On
Macmillan's advice, Eden continued to push for Jordanian membership
of the pact. Ultimately he was unsuccessful: a delegation of British
government representatives – among them the chief of the Imperial
General Staff, Sir Gerald Templer – was greeted by anti-Western riots
in the capital, Amman. Hundreds of Britons and Americans were
forced to flee to neighbouring Lebanon. The delegation's offer of
weapons, including ten free jet interceptors, in exchange for joining
the pact was rejected. Eden blamed the Egyptians. Nevertheless, the
British continued to try and placate Nasser: with the Americans they
offered to finance in instalments the construction of the Aswan dam in
the south of the country, the centrepiece of the ruling council's plan for
economic development. However, Nasser felt that it was couched in a
form which threatened withdrawal should the two countries object to
any of his future policies. At this point the Soviets proposed a scheme
of their own which Egypt could take up if the Western plan proved
unsuitable.

Throughout 1955, Egyptian relations with the Soviet Union and
its communist allies had been gradually improving. A major arms
agreement for the supply of some $450 million of weapons was signed
with Czechoslovakia in September. The Americans had refused to

supply the types of equipment the Egyptians wanted without a mutual security treaty, which Nasser refused to accept. The Czech agreement went a long way to bringing them around to the British point of view. It certainly convinced them that their original patronage had been misplaced. Publicly, Nasser's action was portrayed as threatening stability in the region, not least by allowing the Soviet bloc a foothold in the Middle East. However, the West was similarly implicated in arms trafficking – France had been supplying tanks and advanced Mystere jets to the Israelis with British and American connivance. The Arab-Israeli conflict was ever latent, occasionally sparking into a border clash. At the time it was not the most prominent item on the Middle East agenda (for the West), more of a complicating factor. A British military intelligence report of May 1955 had expressed concern that the Israelis might not be able to restrain themselves much longer from bringing an end to a period of relatively peaceful co-existence with their Arab neighbours, especially Egypt. The arrival of communist arms gave them a pretext for the pursuit of their territorial objectives in the Sinai peninsula under the guise of a preventive war, and the Israeli military began to plan for such a campaign. Their arms requirements were fulfilled by artificially engineering a threat from Syria to the north, which like its Egyptian ally had been forging close ties with the communist bloc. A $100 million arms deal was concluded shortly after the Egyptian contract and the Soviets and Czechs were invited to offer tenders for various projects on the first Syrian oil refinery at Homs. An Israeli attack at the end of 1955 increased pressures in Syria for seeking military support from the Soviet Union. The Israelis were aware beforehand that this would happen, and that they would be able to force the Americans to increase assistance to them as a counterweight.

The British were well-placed regarding information on the Czech arms deal. MI6 had recruited Mohammed Hamdi, the commercial counsellor at the Egyptian embassy in Prague, and ran him successfully from their Vienna station until some time in mid-1956. He was uncovered after a tip-off to the Czechs by a double-agent in the Czech Intelligence Office, a London-based emigre group financed by MI6 with extensive contacts throughout the Czech communist government.

Nasser continued on the offensive over the canal. The secret commission he had set up after his takeover reported in the autumn of 1955. It showed that the canal company's claims to have completed extensive modernisation work were exaggerated and that the dividends paid to foreign shareholders were abnormally high. During December the Egyptian Ministry of Commerce asked for the company to dispose of its foreign assets, invest all its reserves in Egyptian commercial projects and to have half its board appointed in future by the government. The British government predictably dismissed these ideas as absurd.

Just before Christmas, Harold Macmillan was moved from the Foreign Office to the Treasury. His replacement was Selwyn Lloyd, a protegé of Eden's whose appointment reflected the Prime Minister's desire to maximise his control of foreign affairs. He was in increasingly desperate need of a major political success: as the British economy faltered the overseas arena looked to be the most likely source. Nasser began to appear to both him and Lloyd as another Hitler or Mussolini, a dangerous analogy which obsessed both of them. The turning point was the dismissal of Glubb Pasha, the head of the Arab Legion, the Jordanian internal security force trained and supported by the British. Glubb Pasha suffered under an unusually personalised propaganda campaign from Egypt and Syria, and the Jordanian government disposed of him against the wishes of the British. Lloyd learnt of this from Nasser personally during a visit to Egypt, which convinced him further that Nasser was responsible. Soviet overtures to Jordan were interpreted in Britain as further evidence of Nasser-inspired subversion of British Middle East interest. Nasserism had now become the most dynamic political force in the region, even achieving an impact in conservative, pro-Western Saudi Arabia which began to surreptitiously divert its American subsidies to Syria.

Although his distaste for Nasser was by now confirmed, Eden was unsure how to react. An intelligence analysis, probably from MI6 and produced around the end of 1955 after the Czech arms deal, speculated on the effects of British military intervention to defend the canal zone in the event of an Israeli attack. It warned that a strong Egyptian reaction could be expected involving the canal being closed and oil supplies to Europe cut off. Even a cold war could present Arab states with the option of threatening disruption as a political lever. At the same time, a war could work to Britain's advantage by accelerating the division appearing between Egypt and the United States, given the fundamental American commitment to Israel. It seems likely that Eden would have found this argument appealing: he was aware of the importance of aligning British and American Middle East policies, which the Foreign Office had advised him to be essential to counter communist influence. Besides, Arab states would be reluctant to curtail oil supplies and canal traffic beyond the short term because of the damage to their own economies.

Nasser was also causing trouble for the British in Iraq, their most important centre of influence in the Middle East. Kamal el-Hinawi, the Egyptian military attache, was expelled in January 1956 for plotting the assassination of the pro-British Prime Minister, Nuri es-Said, and establishing a 'National Committee of the Union of Officers and

Soldiers' with the aim of overthrowing the regime. The British revised their regional policy in March. In Selwyn Lloyd's description of it, there is the implicit objective of isolating Nasser to pave the way for his removal:

> Instead of seeking to conciliate or support Nasser, we should do our utmost to counter him and uphold our true friends. We shoud seek increased support for the Baghdad Pact and its members. We should make a further attmept to persuade the United States to join the Pact. We should seek to draw Iraq and Jordan closer together. We should try to detach Saudi Arabia from Nasser by making it clear to King Saud the nature of Nasser's ambition ... We should seek to establish in Syria a government more friendly to the West.[6]

They found an ally in the French, who were in the middle of a bloody colonial war in Algeria. Their attitude to Nasser had changed dramatically on discovering that the Algerian rebels had established their headquarters in Cairo and that the Egyptians were organising arms supplies for them. The social democratic government of Guy Mollet, who took power in January, was basically sympathetic to Israel and anticipated Egyptian military aggression. Like the British, they perceived Nasser's actions as integral to a conspiracy to destroy their Middle Eastern interests. Their relations with the United States had been bad since withdrawal from Indo-China after the humiliating defeat at Dien Bien Phu, and the granting of independence to Tunisia and Morocco was a further blow to morale. They were less concerned than the British about foreign opinion, although the British felt that a favourable, or at least neutral, attitude in the United States to any action against Nasser was essential. Given the support which the British had provided during the Korean War, this was, they thought, a reasonable expectation.

A visit to London by Krushchev and Bulganin in April 1956 clarified the Soviet position. Eden explained to them that Britain would take military action to prevent disruption of oil supplies. The Soviet leaders replied that they recognised the logic of that position, which was interpreted as a guarantee that the Soviet Union would not intervene. It was during this visit that MI6 made one of its more notorious blunders, in which the Russians discovered that a frogman had been sent to look at the cruiser's hull (see p.55). In the wake of this affair, the CIA liaison officer in London, Dan Debardeleben, warned that

> we should be even more aware of the possibility that SIS might try to salvage its reputation by coming up with some coup.[7]

Wilbur Eveland, the senior CIA officer in the Middle East during the 1950s, soon discovered that this was true. In a series of joint meetings proposed by MI6 to explain how the revised British Middle East policy would be effected, MI6 deputy director George Young took Eveland somewhat by surprise:

> Young said that Egypt, Saudi Arabia, and Syria threatened Britain's survival. Their governments would have to be subverted or overthrown. Iraq was the central point of British support and area stability; Prime Minister Nuri es-Said's position had to be strengthened as much and as quickly as possible. Turkey and Iran were considered allies, and might be of help in any British action. Since Nasser, dedicated to the destruction of Israel and now an out-and-out Soviet instrument, could not be stopped immediately, priority must be given to Syria, which was about to become a Soviet satellite. Because adverse Saudi reaction to what would be done in Syria was sure to follow, the overthrow of King Saud would have to come next. Then, before Nasser could use Soviet bombers to eradicate Israel, he would have to be eliminated. The fates of Jordan and Lebanon depended upon prompt action to overthrow Syria's government, Young warned, so no more than a month could pass before this was completed. ·
>
> Thinking that I'd entered a madhouse, I listened as George Young said that this first phase – the plan for Syria – could be implemented with Britain's own assets, with or without US approval. We could be of help, however, in containing Saudi and Egyptian reactions until, in phases two and three, King Saud and Nasser were removed.[8]

It is unlikely that the British seriously intended to put this ambitious plan into action, either by themselves or in a combined operation with the French. The object was to draw the Americans into a position where they could not mount serious opposition to the removal of Nasser because they would be compromised by being involved in covert operations at the same time. For despite their close relations, the British were uncertain about American reliability, particularly that of the Secretary of State, John Foster Dulles, whom neither Eden nor Lloyd felt able to trust.

The State Department shared Eveland's concern for British official sanity, but hoped to be able to restrain them. Dulles discussed the British plan for Syria, codenamed 'Straggle', with Selwyn Lloyd. As Young described it,

> Turkey would create border incidents; the Iraqis would stir up the desert tribes and the Parti Populaire Syrien in Lebanon would infiltrate the borders until mass confusion justified the use of invading Iraqi troops.[9]

The Americans realised that such a Western-backed action,

involving overt military intervention by Iraq, would infuriate the Saudis and push them closer to Egypt. 'No success achieved in Syria', Dulles noted, 'could possibly compensate for the loss of Saudi Arabia'.

British troops finally left the Suez canal zone shortly before the specified deadline in mid-June. A week later on the 18th Soviet foreign minister Shepilov arrived in Egypt to offer the full £1,300 million estimated cost for the Aswan dam project with repayment over sixty years at 2 per cent interest; an exceptionally generous set of terms. However, the Egyptians decided to accept the British and American loans on conditions laid down by the World Bank, possibly because of uncertainty about Soviet integrity, but more likely because they were sure that the two Western powers would withdraw their loan offer.

Their conviction was based on classified documents from meetings of the Baghdad Pact nations. The Mukhabarat – Egyptian intelligence – received the material from a highly placed Iraqi diplomat. The crucial article was a set of notes from a discussion held between the Pact's foreign ministers during March. These made it clear that the Americans had no intention of fulfilling their loan promise, under which circumstances the British would obviously act similarly.

The Egyptians' expectations were realised when Dulles and Lloyd did both refuse, arguing that the size of existing civil and military contracts with the Soviet bloc nations and China would hamper Egypt's ability to repay. Dulles went further by issuing a 'powerful diplomatic rebuff'.[10]

At the end of July King Feisal of Iraq arrived in London for a state visit. The Americans interpreted this as the occasion of a final decision on 'Straggle'. During the visit the news came through that Egyptian army units had occupied the canal zone. Military planning to retake the area with a joint Anglo-French assault began almost immediately while Eden considered various MI6 ideas to eliminate Nasser. Although a plan to kill or capture him using SAS troops was rejected,[11] assassination by pro-British army officers found approval. However, this scheme was also abandoned when Selwyn Lloyd, who had not been consulted, found out and objected strongly.

The progress of invasion planning was held up by a lack of clear political direction from Eden and Lloyd, particularly regarding what should be done once the canal zone had been reoccupied, which persisted over the next three months. In addition there were difficulties with French military staff and disagreements over timing. Even so, outside Britain and France, the declared and much-publicised intention to use force was by and large viewed as a bluff.

In fact the British were hoping that any military intervention could be preceded by several months of psychological warfare. MI6 had two major assets in the Arab News Agency (see pp.95-6) and the Sharq al-Adna radio station in Cyprus. Sharq al-Adna was established during World War II at about the same time as the news agency network described in Chapter 2. The object was to use the station to broadcast 'The Voice of Britain' but the Arab staff resigned en masse rather than send out anti-Egyptian propaganda. A troubleshooter hastily recruited from the BBC was sent out to assemble a new staff and start broadcasting ten hours a day. However,

> the only Arabs who could be cajoled into broadcasting anti-Nasser sentiments from Sharq al-Adna were a miscellaneous bunch of Palestinians whose accents were such that Egyptians unhappily mistook them for Jews.[12]

The Mukhabarat managed to obtain an enormous amount of detail about the Sharq al-Adna station, including the identities of the broadcasters and pictures of the interior, through the Greek EOKA* guerillas fighting the British authorities. Egypt supplied them with arms and money in exchange. EOKA later gave the Egyptians information on British troop movements through the island prior to the Suez invasion. The British government also discovered that Sharq al-Adna was relaying the BBC Arab service, which insisted on giving air time to critics of the government's policy. This was soon stopped, and the BBC found itself without a relay. The Foreign Office was so infuriated by the BBC's coverage of the crisis that it reduced its grant to the External Service the following year.

At the Arab News Agency's Cairo offices two British wartime intelligence hands, William Stevenson and Sefton Delmer were drafted in to write reports. Delmer doubled as a correspondent for the *Daily Express*. The agency was also the centre of a major MI6 network run by office manager James Swinburn, who had lived in Egypt for 25 years. Swinburn was to leave the country for Britain at the end of August, but was arrested shortly before his departure at a meeting with an Egyptian army contact and Charles Pittuck, the local Marconi deputy manager, who was due to take over from him. Fifteen other people, including two other Britons and four ANA staff were held as the Egyptian security service, who claimed knowledge of the network over the previous three and a half years, moved to close it down. They received the information from the Soviets, who in turn had obtained it from the MI6 double-agent George Blake.

Stevenson and Delmer were expelled along with two other journalists and two first secretaries from the British embassy, J. B. Flux and J. G. Gove. Four other Britons escaped. The British were particularly upset at the treatment of Delmer, who had been their top anti-Nazi propagandist. For British intelligence it was a humiliating defeat at

* National Organisation of Cypriot Combatants

the hands of a service which, together with the CIA, they had only recently finished helping to reorganise.

As well as the effusions from Sharq al-Adna and the Arab News Agency, there were plans for leaflet drops over Egyptian towns and overflights by 'voice aircraft', which had been used against the Mau Mau rebels in Kenya. The RAF felt the leaflet exercise to be largely futile and performed the task of dropping them only with the greatest reluctance. And there were other problems:

> The reservists who were to man the presses [for the production of leaflets] were unfamiliar with the machinery, which broke down, and the scattering device for the leaflets was found to explode not at 1,000 ft. but at Egyptian head height. When at last the 'voice aircraft' was extracted from a protesting Kenyan government, someone pinched all the loudhailing equipment during a refuelling stop at Aden.[13]

The whole effort was not helped by the fact that the man appointed Director of Psychological Warfare, Brigadier Bernard Fergusson, had no experience of the subject whatsoever.

MI6 reports from elsewhere in the Middle East gave the impression that Nasser was promoting 'Young Officer' revolutions in Syria, Iraq, Saudi Arabia and Libya, which at that time was ruled by a pro-British monarch. Their own plan for his disposal, with or without ministerial approval, was now under way. On the basis of his blood links with the Egyptian royal family, MI6 recruited Mahmoud Khalil, deputy head of Egyptian Air Force Intelligence. Khalil agreed to form a group of army officers to oust Nasser and restore the monarchy in exchange for money and intelligence material on Israel, according to a senior ex-Mossad official.[14] The planning, which began in August, appears not to have been affected by the closure of the ANA network but was put into abeyance in October when it became clear that the government had opted for overt military action.

A quick response to the canal nationalisation, in the form of armed intervention, had been expected at the beginning of August but American pressure and the slow awakening of the British military dinosaur were sufficient to forestall it. John Foster Dulles was apparently not opposed to military action in principle but thought world opinion to be a vital factor. He duly spent his time floating diplomatic solutions, such as the Suez Canal Users' Association, to allow time for this opinion to crystallise into an anti-invasion position. Manoeuvring in Western capitals and at the United Nations continued through August and September. The decision on the use of force was finally taken after the arrival of a high-level Israeli military delegation in Paris on 23rd September. Israel was clearly lobbying for support to a 'preventive war'; the French were keen on the idea, as was Eden.

Lloyd was concerned about Arab reaction but swayed in favour, most likely because of the deteriorating situation in Jordan. A pro-Nasser victory at the forthcoming election seemed inevitable, and there was continual anti-Western rioting in the capital, Amman. The three countries agreed on a joint operation: the Israelis would invade across the Sinai, and an Anglo-French force intervene ostensibly to protect the canal after delivering an ultimatum to the two sides. The timing was adjusted to coincide with the American presidential election, where reactions would be conditioned by widespread opposition to potential United States involvement in yet another European war and by candidates' fear of alienating the pivotal Jewish vote. Eden had circumvented Cabinet opposition, notably from Defence Secretary Walter Monkton, by convening an 'inner cabinet' composed of himself, Lloyd, Chancellor of the Exchequer Harold Macmillan, Anthony Head (Minister of War), Lord Home and Lord Salisbury which deliberated crisis measures.

The Jordanian elections of 21st October produced the expected result, and three days later the armed forces of Jordan, Syria and Egypt agreed to unite under an Egyptian Commander-in-Chief. This news was issued as Israeli premier David Ben-Gurion, Selwyn Lloyd and his French counterpart Christian Pineau signed a formal agreement on their forthcoming military expedition at Sevres, a small town near Paris. It seemed to reassure both the British and French that the Israelis were not exaggerating the Arab threat.

A further bonus for the invaders had come with the civil disturbances in Hungary, which had brought Red Army tanks into Budapest. With the Soviets thus preoccupied and the Americans caught up in 'Straggle' and domestic electioneering, the only major obstacle seemed to be the Egyptian armed forces.

Wilbur Eveland, the senior CIA officer on the ground in the Middle East, was responsible for implementing 'Straggle'. He arrived in Syria during October with half a million dollars earmarked for Michail Ilyan, a pro-Western politician who hoped to be Syria's new leader. After delivering the money, Eveland retired to Beirut to await the coup. On the 29th, the date set for it, news came through of an Israeli army mobilisation. Ilyan rushed to Beirut to confront Eveland and his colleagues, demanding to know how the Americans could have arranged for a coup at such a time. By that stage the Israeli army had crossed the border, swept through the Gaza strip and was pushing rapidly towards the canal. Eveland realised the Americans had been set up, and reckoned that the key factor was that Colonel Kabbani, the senior army officer working with the CIA, was in fact a British agent who had followed MI6 instructions on timing. Eveland was clearly relieved: 'Fortunately the man with whom I had been dealing listened to the radio'.[15] The coup never got off the ground. Had it done so, irrespective of the final result, the Americans would have been severely embarrassed.

Clear of any involvement in local skulduggery, the United States was able to exert maximum diplomatic leverage on the British and French to reverse their bellicose policies. After destroying the Egyptian air force on the ground, a joint force under British command successfully occupied the canal zone. The United Nations assembly condemned the invasion in the strongest terms but a far greater problem for Eden was the value of sterling, declining at an alarming rate. The Treasury made an application for emergency withdrawal from the IMF which was obstructed by the State Department. The British called a cease-fire within 48 hours of landing, and their erstwhile allies had no choice but to follow. According to a recent work on the Suez crisis, the joint planning staff at one point produced a paper predicting exactly these effects. Eden asked for the paper, read it, and immediately consigned it to the dustbin.[16]

There remains the mystery of the broken codes, about which MPs complained so bitterly after the withdrawal. The Americans, it was alleged, had been reading British military and possibly diplomatic messages and used the contents against Britain and her Suez allies. There is boundless room for speculation on this matter, and although it is probably true that the NSA had broken some British military codes, it is equally likely that the planners would have taken the possibility into account. The crucial point is that if the British and French were able to successfully disguise their intentions until after the 29th October, by which time the Americans would have been embroiled in 'Straggle', then it would not have mattered what the NSA were able to read.

Despite their military victory – in terms of attaining their objective – the British suffered a humiliating diplomatic defeat and a drastic loss of credibility. Nasser's position, both at home and internationally, was immeasurably strengthened. But while the crisis was publicly over, MI6 persevered in their efforts to remove Nasser. The plot launched the previous August under the codename 'Salamander' was reactivated. In February 1957 Mahmoud Khalil was called to a meeting in Rome with his MI6 contact. Between then and the following November, Khalil was given a total of £162,500 to finance the coup.[17] At the same time, MI6 continued to entertain the idea of killing Nasser, against the expressed direction of Selwyn Lloyd who remained as Foreign Secretary. Eden, meanwhile, had resigned and Harold Macmillan took over the premiership in January.

Wilbur Eveland describes a bizarre meeting in Beirut, where an envoy from George Young appeared, somewhat the worse for a few drinks:

> apologising neither for his lateness nor his condition, he took
> over the meeting. Teams had been fielded to assassinate Nasser,
> he informed us, and then rambled on about bloody Egyptians
> who had planned to turn the Middle East over to the 'commies'.
> His voice trailing off, he finally sank in his chair and passed
> out.[18]

'Salamander' was abruptly terminated on the 23rd December, when
Nasser announced the existence of the 'Restoration Plot' – as it came to
be known – at a rally celebrating the first anniversary of the Anglo-
French withdrawal from Suez. Khalil, it turned out, was never really
working with the British and followed the orders of his superiors
throughout.

The British began another reappraisal of their Middle East
strategy. Middle East Command was moved to the port of Aden at the
southern tip of the Arabian peninsula. Their other conclusions became
known after the trial of Percy Allen, an army staff sergeant convicted
in 1965 of selling classified defence papers to Egypt and Iraq. The
documents began by describing policy in outline: the reinforcement
of the Central Treaty Organisation (i.e. the Baghdad Pact) and the
regimes of King Idris in Libya and King Hussein in Jordan.* They
made contingency for military intervention 'in co-operation with the
United States ... in the event of internal disturbances or intervention
in the Lebanon and Sudan', at the invitation of the host government. It
is clear that British planners had begun to recognise the inevitability
of ceding the position of leading regional Western power to the United
States. Macmillan had successfully restored good relations after the
Suez rift and seemed prepared to align policy with them. Lebanon
was recognised as an American preserve and Kuwait as British
property. A British seaborne tank regiment floated around the area
waiting for trouble to break out: gunboat diplomacy had not been
discarded, it was merely required to have American approval.

The policy documents sold by Allen were probably produced
after the 1958 Ba'athist coup in Iraq. 'Ba'ath' literally means 'Arab
revival' and espouses three main political causes: Arab unity, the
removal of imperialist control of Arab states, and its replacement by
socialism. The movement originated in Syria during the early 1950s
and picked up support in Iraq, particularly among religious minorities
(despite its essentially secular nature), through the work of Syrian
exiles. It also became influential among merchant traders and in the
army. Its adherents took inspiration from the Egyptian revolution,
and the army group which overthrew King Feisal and the government
of Nuri es-Said asked Nasser for material support. Nasser refused,

* Between 1957 and 1976, King Hussein was in receipt of substantial CIA funding.

probably fearing a provocation, which did not augur well for future Egyptian-Iraqi relations. More significantly, Syria had joined Egypt in the United Arab Republic (UAR) six months before in February 1958: the Syrian and Iraqi Ba'ath movements had split over the proposed structure of an Arab federation, and the new Iraqi government immediately launched a strong political attack on the UAR. Political reforms instituted in Iraq outstripped anything which had been achieved within the UAR, while the Iraqis were suspicious of possible Egyptian hegemony over other Arab states, especially Syria. The prospects for Arab unity diminished accordingly.

The British had been unable to prevent the coup in Iraq because they had no warning of it: MI6 had committed a classic intelligence error by recruiting agents among its allies rather than anti-British elements. General Daghestani, for example, was arrested not because he was a MI6 agent – which he was – but because he was a leading figure in the government.

Elsewhere in the Middle East, 1958 was a desperate year for the Western powers. The Iraqi coup raised the spectre of an Arab bloc headed by Nasser and run from the Kremlin. The CIA, which had supported it as a means of further reducing British influence, quickly realised that they had made a serious mistake and the new Iraqi leader, General Kassem, eventually graduated onto a list of potential CIA assassination targets, along with Rafael Trujillo in the Dominican Republic and Fidel Castro.[19] Jordan and Lebanon seemed to be moving in the same direction. Uprisings in Jordan were put down by King Hussein with the help of British paratroops. In the Lebanon, MI6 organised guerilla groups with the help of the then extreme rightwing Parti Populaire Syrien. The CIA urged military action but were overruled. The situation in both countries stabilised in the short term, but the eventual rift between Egypt and Iraq removed the threat of a pan-Arab union.

The British had another opportunity to counter the spread of Nasser's political philosophy in North Yemen. The country lies in the south-west of the Arabian peninsula, with Saudi Arabia to the north and South Yemen to the south and east. The division of the two Yemens dates from the early eighteenth century, when the Sultan of the southern province of Lahej seceded from the rule of the Yemeni Imam. The boundary has remained more or less static since then, and the two countries have followed separate paths of development although the strength of a common culture and a widespread popular vision of eventual reunification has meant that political events in either part have a substantial impact in the other. While the British occupied Aden and reduced the remainder of South Yemen to an effective colony, the North was successively occupied by the Egyptians, then the Turks. At the end of the First World War the indigenous ruler, the Imam, regained control. Relations with the British were unstable but essentially unaltered over the next forty years until Imam Ahmed started to support rebel forces in the South and formed an alliance with the United Arab Republic. These moves were not born out of any strong Nasserite convictions but were necessary to undercut pro-Egyptian sentiments at home. As in Egypt, there was no organised mass opposition to the hereditary ruler; the sources of dissent were the army, in which a 'Young Officer' group had sprouted, and the merchant classes, who were disaffected by punitive taxation.

Imam Ahmed died in September 1962, and his son Mohammed al-Badr replaced him. Within a fortnight, the pro-Nasser officer group had ousted the new Imam and declared a republic. The small but influential business sector and anti-royalist tribal leaders rallied in support, and the revolution met with general approval from much of the population. The northern tribes, however, were well-armed and supported the Imam, who fled from the capital Sana'a to organise resistance. The new coalition government renamed the country the Yemen Arab Republic, which was immediately recognised by Egypt and the Soviet bloc. It is not clear whether or not Egypt actively assisted the coup; the history of the Ba'athist coup in Iraq suggests that they probably did not, but the speed with which Egyptian army detachments arrived to support the new government suggests that it was not unexpected in Cairo.

The Egyptians had three reasons for providing military support on a large scale: 20,000 of their troops were in the country by the end of 1962. The right-wing Saudi regime had moved back to its natural position after a brief flirtation with Nasser and was now adopting a more aggressive foreign policy which ran counter to Egyptian objectives. So Nasser hoped to use the YAR as a platform from which to launch political attacks on Saudi Arabia. Similarly, promoting a revolution in South Yemen would give them access to the port of Aden. Above all, the prospect of transferring control of oil reserves to sympathetic hands was most tempting. The Egyptian army felt that the YAR campaign would provide useful practice for its troops before what was seen as an inevitable war with Israel.

Both Britain and Israel, along with Saudi Arabia, had strong motives for backing the royalist side in the civil war. Britain obviously wanted to prevent a Nasserite government consolidating its hold on the YAR, while the Israelis saw an opportunity to draw a significant part of the Egyptian army away from their border and involve it in a wasteful campaign. This was the same gambit used in Southern Sudan where they assisted Anya-nya rebels to divert Sudanese forces from the Egyptian front (see pp. 159-63). All three countries supplied arms and money to the royalists but the British wanted to go further. Saudi territory, from where the royalists were operating, came under heavy attack from Egyptian aircraft during early 1963 and Egyptian ground forces were making steady progress into northern areas. The British sent a team to Saudi Arabia to train the army. The Egyptian advance came to a halt in April, and fighting died down for a few months, only to restart in the autumn.

Any overt military action by the British was inconceivable after Suez and even the lower risk of using SAS troops was too great. Conveniently, private contractors were on hand to solve the government's problem. Leading the way, not unexpectedly, was David Stirling. Early in 1964, the *Sunday Times* published documents which showed that he was involved in mercenary recruitment for the royalist forces. The great majority of them came from the SAS regiments, which co-operated fully with the project. Three years later an adjutant with the territorial 21st SAS regiment, Captain Richard Pirie, revealed that his office was passing names and military records to Stirling and the other recruiters. The most important of these others was Colonel James Johnson, who had recently left territorial service in the 21st where he rose to the position of commanding officer. Johnson was an insurance broker with the firm of Thomas Nelson and a 'name' at Lloyds; one of the people who provide capital for the operation of the London insurance market.

MI6 helped out by seconding a young RAF officer, Flight Lieutenant Anthony Boyle, to work with Johnson and Stirling. Further assistance came from the British authorities in Aden:

> For a considerable time Government House, Aden was used as a 'safe house', courtesy of the Governor's ADC. At one critical period, personnel of the Secret Intelligence Service [MI6] were co-opted to help out with radio monitoring problems.[20]

Apparently many senior officers in MI6 were unhappy about the operation, which became the 'focus of a fierce dispute within the service.'[21] The official government position was one of strict neutrality, but the rationale for their support, as explained before, was clear.

When in 1970 part of the story of the operation fell into the hands of the *Sunday Times*, Stirling got an injunction against the paper while he arranged a cover story to force them to drop it. Through a friend on the *Daily Telegraph*, he got a series of articles written which scooped the *Sunday Times*. But why did he take so much effort to cover his tracks? Was it because various intelligence agencies were involved? Stirling's response:

> It had to do with that kind of thing. Sufficient scorn was poured on it to make it impossible for the *Sunday Times* to go on with their story and they were very angry.[22]

About 100 mercenaries were organised by Stirling and Johnson. The Yemeni tribesmen's attitude towards them is not well documented. A French journalist who asked about a particular British mercenary was told:

> He is one of many British historians who are enquiring from us about contemporary events in the Yemen. [23]

The inability of the Saudis to respond to Egyptian air attacks on royalists operating inside their territory led their leaders to consider spending some of their vast oil revenues on building up the Saudi air force. Normally, American firms would have taken up the entire contract. British companies were discouraged from offering tenders since the Foreign Office viewed Saudi Arabia as an American preserve – in the same way as Kuwait was a British one. The election of a Labour government in October 1964, which was less scrupulous about observing imperialist spheres of influence, and domestic economic difficulties overrode Foreign Office apprehensions. A deal with the Saudis was concluded at the end of 1965, worth £120 million to British firms, for aircraft, missiles, a radar system and training teams. The latter, which added up to about 1,000 staff, were provided by Airwork Services* (see pp.50-1) in a contract valued at £26 million. Equally important, and perhaps more so for the British government, was that Airwork also recruited former RAF pilots as mercenaries to fly operational missions against Egyptians and republican targets along the Yemeni border. The commercial cover eventually fell apart, much to the annoyance of those who promoted it in good faith, as Anthony Sampson explains:

> The training and the maintenance of the planes proved beyond the resources of Airwork ... and eventually the British government had to set up its own organisation in Riyadh, jointly with the Saudis, to supervise the programme. What began as an apparently simple commercial sale ended up ... as a major government commitment: and the cost of providing the aircraft and services had escalated so far that the real profit was very doubtful. [24]

The British intervention was successful to the extent that it perpetuated a severe burden on Egypt resources, both financial and military. Some military analysts believe that the absence of the Yemen-based units from the Israel front during the June 1967 war tipped the balance in Israel's favour. The defeat caused a domestic crisis for Nasser, while the loss of canal revenues made him look for subsidies from Saudi Arabia, in exchange for which he agreed to withdraw all Egyptian forces from the YAR by August 1967. The

---

* The company still operates a training institute, which they describe as one of the largest in the Middle East at the port of Dhahran, opposite Bahrein.

republicans divided between the left-wing who wanted to fight on and those who favoured a truce with the royalists, most of whom thought likewise beyond a small militant element. The conciliationists prevailed after another three years of sporadic fighting between the rival groups. The new government was immediately recognised by the Saudis and by the British very soon after, which gives an accurate reflection of its political alignment.

The 1962 revolution served to inspire opponents of the British authorities in South Yemen. Only the port area around Aden was officially a colony; the rest of the country was divided into two 'Protectorates'. Because there was no substantial economic development outside the port, there was no need for any colonial administration outside it either. The nature of the port's economy was such that there was no spin-off inland: all profits were repatriated. As long as the hinterland remained politically inert, it served as a useful stabilising influence and the British were prepared to leave it alone. Any awkward tribal leaders were swiftly deposed, for example Sultan Karim in 1958.

Serious opposition to the British first appeared in June 1963 with the formation of the National Liberation Front (NLF), a loose alliance of pro-YAR tribal leaders and Adeni nationalists who organised in the northern capital of Sana'a. The front started a guerilla war in the Radfan mountains, close to the main highway which the British were using to transport supplies to the royalists fighting the YAR government. They successfully blocked it for three months until the British launched a major offensive to reclaim it. Outnumbered and outgunned, the NLF retreated, but the British were unable to defeat them. The NLF strategy was essentially the same as that which the royalists and their backers were employing against Nasser: to wear down and over-extend the British and the Federal Reserve Army (indigenous troops financed and officered by the British) and destroy the British political will. The British managed to completely alienate the mountain inhabitants fairly quickly by bombing their villages and destroying a season's crops. All types of intelligence were lacking, crucially on the organisation and aims of the NLF, which the British did not proscribe until eighteen months after the war began. SAS troops were continually ambushed because they rarely had any idea where the guerillas were. As Fred Halliday points out

> The British all along misunderstood the situation, thinking they were up against an old-style tribal resistance that could be frightened and shamed into submission.[25]

The British eventually quelled the Radfan guerillas in July 1964 with the help of 3,000 troops, but the rebellion had galvanised uprisings in other parts of the hinterland. The political torpor which upheld British rule in Aden had suddenly been undermined.

It was not long before frequent guerilla attacks, which had been occurring on and off since the mid-1950s, began in the capital in earnest. The political response from the authorities was to hold elections in October 1964, the day after the Labour party had taken power in Britain. However, as only four per cent of the 220,000 population were entitled to vote, this made little impression. The other obvious step was to try and produce a compromise between pro-British and 'moderate' nationalist leaders, which failed as there were no suitable nationalists with a strong enough political base. The British High Commissioner, Kennedy Trevaskis, was replaced with Richard Turnbull, a senior colonial administrator during the Kenyan Mau Mau rebellion, indicating that the new Labour government was prepared for a fight.

As in Radfan, intelligence in Aden was hard to come by. The entire Arab Special Branch was assassinated and the British resorted to the interrogation techniques later suffered by Irish republicans. MI6 worked from the Governor's office with a staff of one officer and two secretaries. Others were drafted in as and when needed. A colonial administrator who was in Aden during the early years of the struggle clearly remembered MI6's role:

> I was the liaison with MI6 ... I gave them the general idea of what results I wanted ... I could get someone killed ... but mainly we went to discredit people, we would find out those people who were in the pay of Colonel Nasser, receiving money from organisations in Egypt, and the rulers might kick them out of the country. This kind of operation was counter-productive if the target knew you were working against him.[26]

Those deported were sent over the border into the YAR. Initially the NLF was dependent on Egyptian finance, and the political alignment of the movement broadly Nasserite. However, as the Egyptians became disillusioned with the war in North Yemen, their support for the NLF also waned. A power struggle developed within the front between the Nasserite leadership and younger, more radical elements. Part of the leadership split off in early 1966 to join other Nasserites in the Front for the Liberation of South Yemen (FLOSY) which from that point monopolised subsequent Egyptian support in the battle against the British.

The NLF adjusted successfully to their new circumstances for by this time they had a strong political base throughout the country. The British had begun to realise that their position was untenable and announced in February 1966 that the Aden military base was to be withdrawn once 'South Arabia' achieved independence, due in 1968. In strategic terms the value of the base had been reduced as Britain moved from a global to a regional defence policy. They tried to hand over administrative, policing and other state functions to sympathetic locals although they must have known by this time that the possibility of installing a stable, pro-Western regime had all but vanished. Obsessed by the idea that every anti-British move in the Middle East was prompted by Nasser, they failed to recognise that their principal enemy was independent of Egypt and increasingly dominated by marxists. This misconception was reinforced by the Saudis, who pleaded with Harold Wilson to retain military units in the peninsula, to guard against further Egyptian subversion. The British were further encouraged by the Israeli victory in the June 1967 war, and presumably thought that the NLF would suffer as a result.

On 20 June the government announced that Britain would maintain air and naval backing for South Yemen for at least six months after independence. The same day the NLF guerillas in the Radfan mountains launched an offensive which took the British by surprise. By the end of September British troops had been pushed back into Aden; between them the NLF and FLOSY had control of the entire hinterland. Inevitably they started fighting, but the NLF finally won with the support of sections of the Federal Reserve Army. Aden itself was vacated of British troops by the end of November.

The South Yemen war was, and still is, the only occasion on which British troops have been comprehensively defeated by an insurgency. The colonial authorities showed a low understanding of their opponents' politics and were constantly hampered by a dearth of intelligence. After further manoeuvrings and divisions within the NLF regime, the country moved into a firm marxist position and adopted the name of the People's Democratic Republic of Yemen.

Since 1970, PDRY and YAR have oscillated between negotiating reunification and a savage border war between YAR troops and PDRY-backed opponents of the Sana'a regime. The Aden government has been able up until recently to regulate the amount of support to these guerillas to exert political pressure on the YAR. Transitory support from Libya also finds its way through to the guerillas. According to a recent report from the region, the YAR is now seeking external assistance:

> UK officials have confirmed that there have been talks about supply of military advisers although they say no formal request for assistance has yet been made.[27]

MI6 has been involved in a number of covert operations against the PDRY government, most recently in an alleged joint scheme with the CIA launched from Saudi Arabia. The PDRY government claims to have uncovered this plot at the end of February 1982. The Saudis deny any involvement.[28]

Proponents of the so-called 'domino theory' would not have been surprised that the emergence of a radical government in South Yemen should have coincided with an increase in guerilla activity inside the neighbouring state of Oman.

Oman houses the largest British military presence anywhere in the Middle East. As with the now defunct 'protectorates' of South Yemen, the British government has consistently tried to obscure the effectively colonial control which they have over the country. Occupied by the British in 1871 to consolidate their hold over the Indian Ocean, Oman overlooks the sea lanes along which pass the tankers carrying oil from the Gulf to the industrialised West. The country is in fact split into two: the larger part curves round the south-eastern corner of the Arabian peninsula and contains all the oilfields, while a much smaller piece of territory – some 600 square miles in size – juts out into the Straits of Hormuz. Separating the two is a strip of land about 30 miles long belonging to the friendly United Arab Emirates. The Hormuz straits are invariably described as an 'oil artery', 'jugular vein' or with other anatomical monikers to justify British control of the country in terms of national or Western survival, all the more since the Iranian revolution. However, in his mammoth study of the international arms trade, Russell Warren Howe draws attention to a CIA study 'which says that these straits are too deep to be blocked by sunken ships, and that coastal artillery would need naval and air support to close such a wide channel' and so it is unlikely that 'the Soviet navy could hope, through friendly riverine countries, to close [the straits].'[29] In fact the main object seems to be to ensure a strong platform for the export of British goods and services, and in the case of defence material and services, a virtually captive market. The Americans have made repeated efforts to break British hegemony over the country, a good example being the Buraimi oasis dispute.

The oasis lies in the ill-defined border area between Oman and Saudi Arabia. In 1949 the Saudis, backed by the American oil conglomerate ARAMCO and the United States government claimed it. ARAMCO had been prospecting around the area for some time and thought it promising. After three years of inconclusive negotiations, Saudi forces armed by ARAMCO attacked and occupied the oasis. The Sultan of Oman prepared to counter-attack but the British, who controlled the Sultan's army and feared a serious dispute with the Americans prevented it. Talks resumed in 1954 under international arbitration, but also foundered, this time after a year. The British then forced the Saudis out using the Sultan's army and the Trucial Oman Scouts, a mobile force set up by the British to deal with disturbances in Oman and the Trucial States which drew heavily on SAS techniques and resources. Foreign Secretary Harold Macmillan declared the oasis 'vital to our oil interests'. John Foster Dulles condemned the British move but accepted it as a fait accompli. The Saudis persevered and in mid-1957 incited the local Imam to form a breakaway government, little suspecting the violent British reaction that was now to follow. RAF bomb attacks and assaults by British troops and the Sultan's forces pushed the rebels back but were initially unable to defeat them. Only when two SAS squadrons were brought in from Malaya late the following year were the British able to regain control. It seems foolhardy of them to have launched such a campaign so soon after Suez, and they were fortunate not to have come under strong international pressure.

During this last campaign Macmillan, who had become Prime Minister, despatched Under-Secretary for War Julian Amery to Oman to reorganise the Omani armed forces. The system of contract mercenaries and serving British personnel on secondment which prevails in Oman today stems from an agreement signed with the Sultan after Amery's visit. The Royal Air Force was given facilities at the western town of Salalah and on the island of Masira to the east. Airwork Services Ltd were called in to help organise an air force.

The British were to have a great deal more trouble in suppressing guerillas operating in the mountainous western province of Dhofar. The well-documented savagery of Sultan Said bin Taymour's regime, coupled with the absurd proscription of items such as sunglasses, cigarettes and radios, was especially felt in Dhofar as Taymour spent much of the year at his palace at Salalah in that province. Economic development, for which there was ample opportunity in agriculture and fishing, was stifled by severe taxation. There was one hospital in the whole of the country and three primary schools.

The Dhofar Liberation Front was formed in 1962 by expatriates working in the rapidly developing Gulf states, where the oil boom had recently begun. Over the next three years it grew into the familiar heterogenous assembly of Nasserites, tribal leaders and a few leftists. In the early stages of the armed rebellion, the tribal forces were dominant. Egypt and Iraq provided some logistical support, but the DLF was largely dependent on its own resources. The conflict was rather low-key for the first year, but suddenly escalated after an unsuccessful assassination attempt on Sultan Said in April 1966. 1,000 troops from the Sultan's Armed Forces (SAF) moved into Dhofar, cutting many of the DLF's supply routes. However, the victory of the National Liberation Front in South Yemen gave the DLF a new source of arms and other equipment while the activities of the SAF and the British alienated the Dhofari population further.

Political developments described earlier affected the orientation of the DLF as much as anywhere else, and similarly produced a leftward shift. This much is reflected in the change of name which the DLF underwent in September 1968, whereupon it became the Popular Front for the Liberation of the Occupied Arab Gulf, also indicating how the horizon of the guerilla struggle had been extended beyond national boundaries. In 1974, this organisation split into the People's Front for the Liberation of Oman and the People's Front in Bahrein. For the remainder of this discussion of the Omani insurgency, the acronym PFLO will be used.

The guerillas made rapid progress through 1968 and 1969, at which point the oil deposits, first discovered in 1964, came on stream. Taymour siphoned off the money for his own personal use, most of it finding its way into American and Swiss bank accounts. He even refused to re-equip the SAF, who were thus obliged to use bolt-action Lee-Enfield rifles against the automatic weapons of the PFLO. The military situation by March 1970 was desperate for the British. The PFLO were in control of the whole of Dhofar province apart from Salalah and the nearby RAF base, which was frequently shelled. Attempts by his British advisers to persuade the old Sultan to change his policies were rebuffed, and they realised, as did Whitehall, that he would have to go. 'We need an Omani Zaid to Said's Shakhbut', said one Foreign Office official,[30] referring to the 1967 coup in Abu Dhabi — also organised by the British — in which Sheikh Shakhbut, a Said–like ruler with some even more bizarre habits, was replaced by his brother Zaid.

Said's son Qabous was his chosen successor. Qabous had been educated in the West, but on his return to Oman in 1966 was placed under virtual house arrest because his father felt threatened by him. His visitors were carefully screened to exclude those who might influence him further, but one man slipped through.

Timothy Landon was the chief intelligence officer of the SAF in Dhofar province. Landon had come to Oman in 1965 at the start of the war against the PFLO as a reconnaissance officer on secondment from the British army. After serving a two-year term he took an intelligence course and returned to Oman. He knew Qabous well from Sandhurst where they had shared a room.

Landon was able to brief Qabous on the plot which he and others were preparing. These others were Sheikh Braik bin Hamud, the son of the governor of Dhofar; a British official from the country's oil company, Petroleum Development Oman; the seconded commander of the SAF; British Consul-General David Crawford; Geoffrey Arthur, the British Political Resident in the Persian Gulf; and the new hawkish Omani Defence Secretary, Colonel Hugh Oldham. The project was delayed for several months, probably because of a forthcoming British general election: the Labour government may have been reluctant to

sanction a coup during campaigning. The Conservatives took power
at the end of June, and the date for Said's overthrow was set for July
23. On the day, a detachment of troops and officers of the SAF was
told to surround Said's palace at Salalah. They did so, believing that it
was some kind of training exercise. Sheikh Braik, Landon and a
group of soldiers including some SAS men passed through the cordon
and approached the palace gate. One of the guards at the gate was
bribed to arrange for the others to be absent. He let the party in and
led them across the courtyard. The old Sultan was prepared: he had
long suspected an attempt to dislodge him and kept rifles and light
machine-guns near every window. As the raiding party came into
view, Said and loyal guards inside the palace opened fire on them.
The bribed guard was killed outright and Sheikh Braik wounded. The
group rushed for cover, and Landon immediately radioed for air
support. British-flown aircraft from the Sultan's Air Force arrived
shortly afterwards and dropped teargas bombs, providing cover for an
advance. The raiders won the ensuing battle, during which Said was
twice wounded. After this defeat he was forced to abdicate, and after
treatment in hospital was flown to Britain. The government installed
him in the Dorchester Hotel, where he remained until his death two
years later. On taking control, Qabous announced long overdue
development programmes, to be supervised by an interim planning
committee chaired, for some reason, by Defence Secretary Hugh
Oldham. He also offered an amnesty to rebels of the PFLO (his
father's terms of surrender specified life imprisonment). The PFLO
were not impressed with the 'new agent' installed by the 'foreign
imperialists' and promised to renew their efforts against the SAF and
their British controllers.

The coup was presented by the British as a nationalist uprising
not unlike that which brought Nasser to power in Egypt; a particularly
perverse piece of propaganda given the ill-disguised rejoicing at the
Foreign Office. The British immediately started to increase their
military presence. Both the seconded and mercenary components of
the SAF rose steadily over the next three years. The mercenaries came
from two different sources: the officer group was organised by the
government, while lower ranks were recruited by private firms. The
most important of these was Airwork Services, which also supplied
military equipment, spare parts, and ground maintenance staff for the
Sultan of Oman's Air Force (made up of British planes flown by British
crews) and training facilities for Omani officers. Later on a 'British
Army Training Team' arrived, which was in fact an SAS unit with the
specific task of organising irregular forces to fight the PFLO.

Omani intelligence had been built up in the late fifties and was
run by a group of British intelligence officers under a Major Dennison.

District Intelligence Officers were attached to every important military post, although in Dhofar itself they had some difficulty with the local dialect, which is rather different from Arabic. The British also provided a psyops unit which was financially subsidised by the Omani government. The Omanis also raised a small number of civilian teams for the same purpose. Leaflet drops, radio and loudspeaker broadcasts from government positions were all used to reach guerilla-held areas. Between 1970 and 1972 the impact of the leaflets was limited by the fact that they were written by British intelligence officers in bad Arabic. They had more effect once Jordanian personnel, who came in to fight on the Government side, were composing them.

In one campaign, government forces sought to exploit the incompatibility of marxist theory and moslem teaching. Leaflets with pictures and personal details of 'Surrendered Enemy Personnel' were dropped over the PFLO. The text related how a particular defector had been duped by the communists then, revolted by their practices, had finally decided to rally to the cause of Islam and Sultan Qabous. The PFLO lost a lot of their fighters through desertions as the message struck home at the less politically-conscious.

The defectors were organised into 'firqats' or militia by the British Army Training Team (BATT). The first was non-tribal, and based on one former guerilla unit. Known as the Salahadin, it was always unstable and soon collapsed, but its members were able to join other firqats which had by then been set up. Units made up of ex-guerillas had obvious advantages over regular government forces, in terms of their knowledge of PFLO personnel, operational techniques, signals procedures and so on. From their accounts, SAS intelligence officers took three months to work out the PFLO command structure. The firqat members were paid the equivalent of £150 per month by the Omani government.

The total strength of the firqat groups grew from about 700 in 1971 to a peak of 1,000 in 1974. A senior BATT officer, Colonel Anthony Jeapes, describes an assault by a firqat force of 750, including over 100 SAS men, in October 1971.[31] Although they caused substantial difficulties for the guerillas, neither the firqats nor the regular Omani-British forces could drive the guerillas out. It was only when other countries started to lend support that the military balance swung towards the government. The Shah of Iran sent in 3,000 troops, including his specialised counter-insurgency units. As well as giving them valuable practice in the event of an internal uprising (it was not much use as later events showed) it enabled him to extend Iranian influence in the Gulf. Jordan supplied training teams and intelligence personnel; Pakistan lent 100 army officers while India gave assistance to the small Omani navy. Sudanese military staff also helped with training. The Saudis gave £6 million in aid, and with the United Arab Emirates, provided relief garrisons to free Omani troops for anti-guerilla operations. Australian and Rhodesian pilots flew with the air force. Finally Americans chipped in with a few of their 'advisers', and $150 million of CIA counter-insurgency aid channelled through the Saudi government. The main support for the PFLO came from the impoverished PDRY.

Between the beginning of 1974 to June 1975, the PFLO were reduced from controlling much of Dhofar to a number of small isolated units unable to mount more than sporadic attacks on government forces from inside the PDRY. Accurate intelligence, which had been such a problem in South Yemen, came much more easily. A great deal was obtained by medical officers attached to the SAS/Firqat units who set up clinics in areas recently captured from the PFLO, tending to the locals and their animals. Psyops staff distributed Japanese transistor radios which could pick up the radio station at Salalah, aimed at discrediting the 'vituperation and hatred vomited forth every day from Radio Aden', as Jeapes describes it.[32]

After their defeat and exile, Qabous wanted to destroy the PFLO once and for all by attacking their bases in the PDRY, and was only just persuaded against it by the Foreign Office. The victory had given him an enthusiasm for greater aggression in foreign policy, and it rather seems as if he was looking around for opportunities. His henchman Timothy Landon occupied himself organising the illegal sale of American helicopter gunships to Rhodesia during the civil war. Oman was used as a transit point, and the operation carried through without the knowledge of government ministers.[33] A further Rhodesian connection of the same period arises through Airwork: the air force camp at Seeb on the north-east coast which the company occupies was used to train Rhodesian pilots. Some of these were reported to have taken part in raids across the Mozambiquan border in September 1979 aimed at causing food shortages. In 1977 Airwork took over the bases at Salalah and, fifty miles to the north-west, at Thumrait. These were RAF bases vacated when the British decided to withdraw all their forces by April 1978. Another former RAF post on Masira Island has now been taken over by the Americans, who are spending £800 million on building facilities for their 'Rapid Deployment Force' should they need to invade the Middle East at some future date. They also have limited facilities at Seeb and near Muscat, the capital. Oman is thus the only Gulf State to have responded favourably to American representations as regards this force. In November 1981, Oman announced that it would be holding joint military exercises with Britain and the United States the following month.

Qabous and the British were both reluctant to allow the Americans a foothold in Oman, but following the Iranian revolution and the withdrawal of their troops Qabous found that his defence requirements surpassed what the British were able to provide and turned to Washington. For their part, the Americans have a far greater need than the British for a stable, pro-Western Oman as the loss of Iran affected American intelligence-gathering from the Soviet Union. Oman may be able to partially replace Iran in this sense, providing bases for U2 and SR71 reconnaissance aircraft.

Britons continue to dominate the Omani defence and security establishments which, according to the development plan for 1981-85 will absorb a massive 40.3 per cent of gross national product. Only the neighbouring United Arab Emirates and Israel have comparable budgets anywhere in the world. British firms sell weapons systems to Oman which the Minstry of Defence knows are far in excess of the country's realistic requirements.

At the time of writing all three armed services are commanded by British officers: there is speculation that an Omani may take control of the army by 1984, but Qabous accepts that the navy and air force will remain under British direction for the foreseeable future. There are many Britons in the senior ranks of the Omani police force, some of whom seem glad to have left the British judicial system behind. John Eggleston, a police officer in Northumbria for 27 years, explains:

> The British go on the facts of the case and are blind to everything else. The biggest villain unhung can get off. You are not allowed hearsay evidence, which I often thought was very unfair because it does not always give the judge the right idea.[34]

The heads of the security service – the Oman Research Department – and the foreign intelligence service are both British. The latter post is occupied by a sixty-year old ex-MI6 officer, Reginald Temple, who had experience in Singapore, Beirut, Algiers and Paris before ending his career as a divisional head at MI6 headquarters.

On one recent occasion, in March 1981, Omani intelligence was seriously at fault, as a fifty-strong SAS company discovered when they arived at Salalah to confront a non-existent local rebellion. According to the *Times*, the SAS 'were not even supposed to be in Oman this year'.[35] This is an interesting statement as it implies that the SAS had a periodic right to be in the country, for whatever reason. The death of SAS sergeant Leslie Barker in November of the same year during 'a routine training mission' – as the Ministry of Defence described it – suggests that the *Times* correspondent, Robert Fisk, was misled. Barker was neither a mercenary nor on secondment. An SAS presence outside the auspices of the Omani army has been maintained after the official departure which seems to be substantially larger than the dozen or so which was previously suspected. The British military contingent as a whole is almost certain to increase: on her last state visit to the Gulf in April 1981, Prime Minister Margaret Thatcher promised to increase the number of 'loan service personnel' – i.e. seconded personnel – in Oman.

One secondment during August 1981, General Timothy Creasey, has aroused particular interest. Creasey is an experienced counter-insurgency leader with a service record including Kenya, South Yemen, Northern Ireland (where he was in charge of army units in the province) and Oman itself, where he commanded the SAF from 1972 until 1975. It seems that his task lies, on this occasion, outside Oman. From his previous tour of duty, he is well acquainted with the Iranian armed forces, many of whom escaped to Oman after the Islamic revolution in 1979. This was also the year in which a new SAF commander was appointed: John Watts, formerly commanding officer of 22 SAS. Furthermore, over a fifth of the SAF are mercenaries from the Baluchistan region of Pakistan, which until 1958 was partly ruled from Oman. Qabous is eager, as mentioned before, to make a strong impression on the international stage. He envisages an incursion into Iran from Baluchistan, with the object of deposing the Ayatollah Khomeini and restoring the dynasty to which his late friend and ally Shah Reza Pahlavi belonged. Previously, Baluchi troops serving with the SAF entered Iran covertly to prepare the desert strip from which the abortive mission to rescue the American embassy hostages in Tehran was launched. This latest project is British-inspired, and almost certainly American-financed.

Throughout the Iran-Iraq war, Oman has consistently supported its fellow Arab state. At one stage Qabous gave permission for the Iraqi air force to launch attacks on Iranian-held islands in the Gulf. Only logistical problems prevented them from doing so and embroiling Oman, and by proxy Britain, in the war. The Foreign Office were livid, but managed to contain their anger: after thirty years of mishaps, setbacks and defeats in the Middle East, the British realise that they are lucky to have such a friendly and compliant ruler nestling snugly at the south of the Arabian peninsula. While Qabous' regime remains intact, the British have an invaluable base for covert operations in the Middle East, such as the forementioned Iran project.

American co-operation with the British, though sure to be forth-coming in that case, is at its most fragile in the Middle East. Israel, which enjoys massive American military, political and economic support, is wary of the preponderance of arabists in the Foreign Office and Arab links with senior Conservatives. Britain has been prominent in various EEC-sponsored peace initiatives in the Middle East which have consistently received a cool reception in Tel Aviv. Nonetheless, some sources maintain that MI6 assists in operations against Palestinian groups, for example the infiltration of the Rhodesian-born Diane Campbell-Lefevre into Black September. Mossad and MI6 exchange intelligence on Palestinians and common enemies such as Libya through the Kilowatt mechanism. Mossad navigators on the Boeings of Uganda Airlines flying between Stansted and Entebbe spied on Libya's military airfield at Benghazi, and the results were passed to MI6 and the CIA.

Ironically, MI6 is now understood to have a better political analysis of the Middle East than of Africa, a region where in the past it has had a great deal more success.

Notes

1.   G. de Villiers *The Imperial Shah* (1976) p.165
2.   Wilbur Eveland *Ropes of Sand* (1980) p.67
3.   Leonard Mosley *Power Play* (1977) p.177
4.   *Hibernia* (20 March 1980)
5.   Terence Robertson *Crisis* (1965) p.15
6.   Selwyn Lloyd *Suez 1956* (1978) p.60
7.   *The Middle East* (October 1981)
8.   W. Eveland *Ropes of Sand* p.169
9.   W. Eveland *Ropes of Sand* p.170
10.   T. Robertson *Crisis* p.64
11.   Chapman Pincher *Inside Story* (1978) p.90
12.   Roy Fullick and Geoffrey Powell *Suez — The Double War* (1979) p.58
13.   *Ibid*
14.   Yaacov Caroz *The Arab Secret Services* (1978) p.22
15.   *The Middle East* (October 1980)
16.   R. Fullick and G. Powell *Suez* p.187
17.   Y. Caroz *The Arab Secret Services* p.24
18.   *Guardian* (29 August 1980)
19.   Thomas Powers *The Man Who Kept The Secrets* (1979) p.163
20.   *New Statesman* (2 July 1978)
21.   *Ibid*
22.   Private interview
23.   *Le Monde* (16 May 1967) quoted in Fred Halliday *Arabia Without Sultans* (1975) p.149
24.   Anthony Sampson *The Arms Bazaar* (1977) p.163
25.   F. Halliday *Arabia Without Sultans* p.199
26.   Private interview
27.   *Middle East Economic Digest* (19 February 1982)
28.   *Ibid* (12 March 1982)
29.   Russell Warren Howe *Weapons* (1981) p.183-4
30.   F. Halliday *Arabia Without Sultans* p.288
31.   A.S. Jeapes *SAS: Operation Oman* (1980) p.133
32.   A.S. Jeapes *SAS: Operation Oman* p.34
33.   *New African* (October 1979)
34.   A. Duncan *Money Rush* (1979) p.209
35.   *Times* (30 April 1981)

Chapter 4
Covert Operations in Post-Colonial Africa

I read in the press a statement by the Secretariat of the Western European Union that a detailed survey of 'communist' activities in Africa had been carried out and that the Western powers should make preparations to 'fight communism on African soil'. Whose soil is it after all? Why should Western powers – or any other powers for that matter – fight for or against any policy on African soil? Foreign countries have no right to declare their determination to make Africa a battleground of their ideological differences.[1]

Not only did the Western powers declare this intention, they launched a massive campaign with covert operations well to the fore, in support of the policy. It began immediately after decolonisation and continues to this day; it may be held in part responsible for Africa's condition as a continent in almost perpetual turmoil. During two decades of independence, Africa has played host to a complete catalogue of covert techniques, from secret financing of political parties through clandestine mercenary wars to sponsored coups against established rulers. The British contribution, rooted in the experience of colonial administration, was among the most important and relatively successful in their terms: clearly some lessons had been learnt from the excesses of the 1950s Middle East. The CIA's entrance into the covert action arena had the effect, in crude market terms, of forcing the cost of conducting operations beyond the means of MI6, whose own resources were already stretched through economic contraction. Nevertheless, the considerable British influence in a number of key African states means that MI6 will necessarily have an important role in joint Western operations on the continent. Indeed, this pattern has already emerged.

East Africa and the Nigerian Civil War

One of these is Kenya, whose former vice-president, Oginga Odinga, is the author of the opening quotation to this chapter. As a victim of British-inspired political machination, he is in a good position to appreciate the influence that it has had on his country's course of development.

As a result of the Mau Mau uprising, most forms of African politics had been ruthlessly suppressed. The main organisation which functioned throughout was the Kenyan Federation of Labour, although its offices were frequently raided and staff harassed. Its General Secretary during this period was Tom Mboya, who became an important political leader after independence. The African population was divided along tribal lines, with the Kikuyu, the largest grouping, providing the majority of the Mau Mau rebels and the others (Luo, Kamba, Kalenjin and Masai) supporting the government. By 1956, the military operations against the rebels were confined to the Highlands and the rebellion was almost crushed. However, the Kenyan colonial government maintained the Emergency until 1960 and was able to take full advantage of its repressive powers for 4 more years; it actively encouraged the smaller tribal groups to organise into district political organisations, while denying the largely urban Kikuyu the same opportunity. Finally, it tried to make Kenyatta, formerly President of the Kenyan African Union (the largest Kikuyu party before the Emergency) and popular figurehead of African nationalism, a complete unperson.

The Emergency had an unfortunate side effect. In the internment operation after the first big Mau Mau attack, some of the country's ablest African politicians were interned. Those who weren't were forced to flee. And others were encouraged to leave the country to keep them out of trouble. The colonial government realised that if it was forced to arrest all African politicians in its security operations, it would permanently lose any goodwill towards the British that might be needed after the Emergency. One of those who fled was Peter Okoudo, a talented black Kenyan, who fled to Uganda when the KAU was banned. Instead of arresting and sending him back, the Ugandan Governor refused to deport him and gave him a job in the Ugandan Civil Service where he rose to become a permanent secretary. In another case, Tom Mboya, the prominent trade unionist and a former KAU activist, was encouraged to leave the country. In addition to a scholarship arranged through the ICFTU, Mboya was given money to study in England by the Kenyan Government, 'in order that he would not have to seek financial support from what it considered to be undesirable political quarters'. The real intention was, as James Johnson MP put it, more long-term: 'We gave him money and a scholarship at Ruskin (the Oxford University trade union college) to keep him out of mischief. We could see how good he was'.

As the Mau Mau threat receded, the colonial government came

under increasing political pressure from other African nationalists. Several national parties were formed but refused registration by the government, who wanted to retain absolute control over the form and pace of political development.

In 1957, the first African elections were held for eight seats on the Legislative Council. The successful candidates formed the African Elected Members Organisation shortly afterwards. Its first act was to reject the Lyttleton constitution, the very basis on which they had been elected, and then begin a campaign for fifteen seats in the Legislative Council. After several reformulations of the constitution, new constituencies were drawn up by a government working party composed of Kenya's two top white civil servants, the Chief Secretary and the Attorney General. Its final formula was a case of fine election rigging against the tribes (Kikuyu, Luo, Embu, Meru, Kamba and Kisii) supporting the Kenyan African National Union (KANU), the successor to the KAU. The disproportions were most starkly illustrated by the allocation of two seats to the Masai tribe and four to the Kikuyu, with respective populations of 60,000 and one million. The Luo, Kenya's other large tribe and powerbase of radical Oginga Odinga, were only given three seats, one more than the Masai.

Independence was only a distant point on the horizon, perhaps twenty years in the future. Most of the discussion was about different types of constitutions, the colonial government as always pursuing a 'multiracial' constitution which would entrench the political rights of the white settlers. The settler community was, in percentage terms, among the smallest of Britain's African colonies. In theory this should have meant that London could decolonise fairly quickly without excessive deference to their demands: the sooner the better, given the politicisation of the African population following Mau Mau. But other factors called for a cautious approach. Kenya was one of the richest East African countries, serving as a base for many British-owned companies in Africa, and it was essential that the basic economic structure should survive the transition intact. In addition, Kenya hosted the Army Command Headquarters for the east and central African regions. Previously, it had been subordinate to General Headquarters at Cairo, but was separated in 1953 following a series of failures against the Mau Mau. The Egyptian military coup of the previous year doubtless also played a part. As resistance to colonial rule grew and stretched British forces still tighter, Army Command HQ assumed paramount importance. British strategic planners, meanwhile, worked on the basis that it would become a major military installation after independence.

The colonial government lacked a vehicle for the expression of 'multiracialism' as they interpreted it. So they encouraged the leading white settler politician, Michael Blundell, to form a political party – the New Kenya Group – to fill the gap. According to historian Gary Wasserman:

> The New Kenya Group's origins lay with Europeans closely connected to the colonial government ... Tom Mboya charged that the Colonial Office had clearly given its support to the founding of the group.[2]

Blundell, before resigning as Minister of Agriculture, had spoken to Kenya's Governor, Evelyn Baring and gained his agreement. He also wrote privately to the Colonial Secretary Alan Lennox-Boyd to make his intention clear:

> It is no good developing the economy of the country, establishing great numbers of moderate and progressive African farmers who have the same interests as Europeans, if behind our backs the political situation is being eroded.

So before the new elections in 1960, Blundell's NKG sought to represent all settler opinion and swing it behind some settlement with moderate African politicians. The biggest problem for Blundell was that he was continually outflanked by the right-wing of settler opinion, which was not very interested in reaching any accommodation with African opinion. His first move was to help form a party to represent 'moderate' African opinion – the Kenyan African Democratic Union (KADU). This party was welded together from all the small tribal political associations throughout the country and the NKG played a decisive role in its formation:

> Richard Slaughter, a member of NKG and treasurer of KADU, called KADU 'the child of the New Kenya Party' ... Leslie Malville, the Executive Officer of NKP [NKG's successor] recalled doing the same work for KADU after the 1961 elections that he had done for the NKP. And he said that the central group of planners in the African party were Arap Moi, Muliwo, Ngola, Havelock, Bruce McKenzie, Blundell and R. Mcleod [the last four being NKG members] ... Richard Alexander, former Mayor of Nairobi, stressed the contribution of administrative abilities, but ... this ranged into the field of ideas, proposals and, frequently, the writing up of policy statements.[3]

For the 1960 election, the government gave as much backing as it reasonably could to KADU without appearing to favour it. Government officers addressing barazas – tribal meetings – were supposed to do no more than give information about registration for voting and the facilities for it. Despite the difficulty in distinguishing between informing and actively encouraging, there was strong evidence of officials going to some lengths to promote registration in KADU areas.

In the later election of 1963, the government provided more outright support, as the newly appointed Governor Malcolm MacDonald recalled:

> When I arrived in Nairobi I discovered that British Colonial officials (with the consent of Whitehall) were ... doing everything they discreetly could in marginal constituencies to ensure the KANU candidates would be defeated, so that as a result KADU would either form a clear majority in the new legislature or else be able to count on the support of the Kamba splinter group. In that case, Kenyatta and his KANU colleagues would either have to join a coalition administration under a KADU Prime Minister, or else go into opposition.[4]

KADU received covert government funds, channelled to the NKG through an ostensibly non-political foundation. MacDonald told us that he believed the funds were from intelligence sources. This is confirmed by a letter written by Wilfred Havelock, a key NKG member, to Michael Blundell from London the 4th May 1960:

> Yesterday I met Brigadier Hobbs (Head of Public Relations at the War Office) and as a result of our talk you will receive £1000 as soon as you have opened an account at the Ottoman Bank for our 'Progressive Association'. This is to enable us to carry on in the meantime with the issuing of pamphlets, etc. on our views. It will be necessary for you to let me know as soon as the Association is registered and the account open. It is also important that Colin Hood [a Nairobi insurance broker] should initiate the whole idea of the Progressive Association as his own with no political contamination by ourselves and without mentioning the destination of the funds entrusted to his care for the objects of the Association.

Two weeks later the NKG met KADU and the African leaders discussed their need for further funds. The main financial backer of Blundell's political career was the British brewery, Ind Coope, which has a large interest in Kenya. Several NKG members later became directors after this early association. Blundell and Lord Howick (formerly Evelyn Baring, Governor of Kenya) persuaded the brewery firm to give funds to KADU and most of these were funnelled through the foundation which was eventually set up – The Progress Foundation for Economic Development in Eastern Africa. It provided a useful means of channelling money to KADU from overseas business backers.

The Progress Foundation was not formally opened until the following year. It claimed to be a non-profit educational institution offering specialised information to investors, people investigating 'the prospects for development', and 'anyone interested in the economic' future of Eastern Africa. Its London base was in offices occupied by the E.D.

O'Brien public relations firm which handled publicity for the Katangese secessionists and North Yemeni royalists. The Foundation's first aim was to establish an Economic Development Institute,

> to undertake research, act as a host to overseas research scholars and co-ordinate studies. One of its main objectives will be to enlarge the small cadre of trained Africans at present able to participate in economic development and planning.[5]

To do this, it hoped to raise £75,000 for a three-year programme. Iain Macleod, Colonial Secretary, welcomed the Foundation in a letter written to its President, the Earl of Portsmouth, a letter no doubt used to raise funds:

> Not only will it help in dealing with the immediate economic and social problems facing Kenya: in addition because it is non-political and multi-racial, it will point towards an approach which may well be valuable in other fields

Among the sponsors were the Aga Khan, Lord Colyton, Lord Howick, Elspeth Huxley (author) and R.E.M. Mayne (a director of Coltex, another financial backer of Blundell's). More significantly, as we shall see later, it included five 'moderate' KANU members, all of whom became ministers in the post-independence government. It is assumed that these five KANU MPs were ignorant of the fact that this 'non-political' body was in fact the main conduit for funds – both from government and business – to its major rival, KADU. Perhaps it is coincidental that during precisely this period after the 1960 election the colonial government was attempting to form a coalition of KADU and 'moderate' KANU members.

Through its contacts with European politicians, KADU was also able to arrange help from the British Tory MP Sir Frederick Bennett, who acted as an unpaid political adviser to the party during the two major constitutional conferences at Lancaster House. Bennett, who has family connections with bankers Kleinwort Benson, also helped raise funds in the City for KADU. He advised the party on the thorny issue of regionalism. As KADU failed electorally, they pushed hard for a constitution giving greater autonomy to Kenya's smaller 'tribal' regions, in which endeavour they were actively advised by Freddie Bennett. At independence, Bennett was banned from Kenya after an invitation to the independence celebrations from KADU. He defended his help to KADU by saying:

> I acted as honorary and unpaid adviser to KADU when the party was in power [before independence], and again when it was the opposition party at the Lancaster House conference. In both cases I had the full approval of Her Majesty's Government.[6]

During the negotiations in London of the independence constitution at Lancaster House during 1960 and 1962, public relations played a very important part in establishing the credibility of the respective groups at the conference. KADU's PR representative in London for the March 1962 conference was Ronald Sims of Industrial Aids. Sims, formerly chief PRO at the Conservative Central Office and now owner of his own firm (included among the accounts was the Shah of Iran), was given the task of selling the regional formula for Kenya's constitution. 'We tried to build them up', he said. 'They only paid a nominal fee'. When Paul Ngei, leader of the Kamba, broke from the KANU just before the 1963 election, he found himself being sponsored by Sims and Industrial Aids. When Ngei had come to London several months previously to present himself to MPs as a possible challenger to Kenyatta, he had almost no money. Sims and company 'just offered to help' and duly made the necessary arrangements.[7]

At the 1960 polls, KADU took 11 seats on 16 per cent of the vote against KANU's 19 seats. KADU still formed the government because KANU had refused to do so until Jomo Kenyatta, who had been held in custody since the beginning of Mau Mau, was released. Macleod was described as 'almost jubilant', and as Wasserman noted:

> the British backed this up with a reception for the [KADU] delegation at which Prime Minister Macmillan was present, giving newspapers the impression of Britain's whole-hearted support for the KADU government.[8]

In November 1961, Governor Rennison openly sided with NKG and KADU at a Governor's Conference, arguing for a coalition government stage prior to internal self-government. He also committed the cardinal mistake of calling Kenyatta 'a leader unto death and darkness' and refused to countenance his release. And feeling was sufficiently strong, both in England and among the white settlers of Kenya, to make the idea unthinkable. Ex-Colonial Secretary Alan Lennox-Boyd refused to tour America on behalf of the government if Kenyatta was released. It required no great perception, however, to realise that KANU would eventually become the party of government: the voting gave ample evidence of that.

The main problem was that Rennison's paternalistic attitude to African politicians and his inflexibility over Kenyatta made it difficult to find a peaceful solution. So Rennison was removed and the next part of the British strategy was left to his deputy Griffiths-Jones. On the form of this strategy, Lord Howick wrote to Blundell in early 1962, describing discussions he had had with senior government officials. Howick viewed Tom Mboya as the man to back 'since the real danger was those who would look east', whether they be the old Kikuyu guard or those associates of Odinga supported by the Chinese. The attempt should be made, Howick suggested, to align three groups: KADU, Mboya and his followers, and other milder KANU supporters such as the Kisii and those Kamba not committed to Ngei. This might prove easier, he thought, following the evaporation of Mboya's American funds (chiefly from labour unions) and consequent weakening of his position. It was also essential that KANU should not boycott the election, since that would strengthen the 'eastward extremists': preventing this justified some expenditure and use of available agents-in-place, who could bring KADU and the westward looking part of KANU together under whatever name and in whatever relationship to Kenyatta himself.

> In the words of a British journalist who was in Kenya at the time:
>> When it became apparent that the British were going to have to give power to the Africans, acting governor Griffith-Jones became very friendly with Tom Mboya. Metaphorically, he took him up on the hill and showed him the kingdom. It was a clear attempt to wipe out Kenyatta.[9]

Blundell described Griffith-Jones as 'obsessed with the idea of splitting KANU and having Mboya emerge as national leader'.[10]. Mboya was naturally cautious and preferred Kenyatta to be made leader and use his prestige to isolate Odinga, then invite KADU to support his government. Also, according to Blundell, Mboya believed that Kenyatta could be fairly quickly jettisoned. Blundell rightly believed this to be 'quite impossible'.

Unable to get the coalition it wanted, the British government was left supporting KADU, providing much-needed economic aid to its fragile administration. In turn, to win popularity, KADU promised to release Kenyatta once a house had been built for him at Kiambu. It was, as one wit remarked, 'the slowest house ever built'.

At the final Lancaster House conference before independence, the British government, realising that there was little chance of stopping KANU, decided that its interests were best served by supporting them, and so abandoned KADU. Iain Macleod, a very wily negotiator, played the switch cleverly, using KADU's regional plans as a means of upping the ante on KANU to extract concessions and put it in a weaker position after independence. At the same time, he used news briefings to stress how moderate and responsible KANU was going to be in government. This strategy, which looked forward to the day when some KADU members would join KANU, left many on the right – white settlers and Tory MPs – stunned and confused.

As pointed out earlier, the key to taming the black nationalists and promoting the moderate elements among them was education. While some of this could be done in Africa, priority was given to basic education and further studies had to be completed elsewhere. The British government was naturally keen that on finishing their education at home, talented Africans should come to Britain where they could be more closely assessed for their suitability as future leaders. It would also remove them temporarily from the maelstrom of nationalist politics. Using unofficial channels to organise higher education was politically much safer than open government sponsorship, as it avoided the displeasure of the settler community and scrutiny from domestic politicians. Educational charities were the obvious mechanism. Such considerations gave rise to the Ariel Foundation.

Ariel was incorporated in 1960 with the stated objective of encouraging 'by practical means, understanding between countries'. One of its annual reports added that

> Ariel's contribution is particularly significant because it is independent of government and of any party, political or commercial interest. Many creative and influential people from developing countries who might have felt inhibited from accepting official hospitality have recognised Ariel's independence and have willingly participated in its projects.[11]

A cursory examination of the biographies of the trustees is sufficient to raise doubts as to the validity of the foundation's claim of 'independence'. Three of them had served political apprenticeships in the World Assembly of Youth: Charles Longbottom, then Conservative MP for York and now Chairman of the Seascope group of companies; Barney Hayhoe, a Conservative MP since 1970; and Maurice Foley, an EEC bureaucrat and Labour politician who emerged in 1971 as an intelligence link-man for operations during the Nigerian Civil War (see pp. 169-73). The fourth trustee was Denis Grennan, until recently the foundation's director. A former president of the National Union of Students, he was also peripherally involved with WAY. Subsequently, he has had considerable experience outside student affairs; as an adviser on African affairs to James Callaghan, while the latter was Foreign Secretary, Grennan visited Angola to inspect the prison conditions of British mercenaries captured by the MPLA. Shortly after Ian Smith declared UDI in Rhodesia in 1965 Grennan was seconded to the staff of President Kaunda – a personal friend – to organise an intelligence service. As the *Leveller* pointed out, it is not clear how Grennan 'acquired the expertise necessary for setting up a secret service.'[12] It is significant also that the Colonial Secretary, Iain Macleod took an active part in encouraging the establishment of Ariel. Macleod's parliamentary private secretary at the time was Charles Longbottom.

Ariel's sources of finance are difficult to track down. According to Grennan, the money used to start Ariel came from the General and Municipal Workers Union, who provided £30,000, and the Transport and General Workers Union. Both have denied having given Ariel any money. A Foreign Office source quoted in *Tribune*[13] believed that

Ariel received Foreign Office support – not specifying the nature of it – and described it as 'a discreet rather than a secret operation'. A further source with extensive working experience of African decolonisation, told the authors of Foreign Office funding adding, a little mysteriously, that he thought Ariel to be 'not totally dispassionate'. The City of London with its large supply of liquid capital, was another valuable provider. Christopher Chataway, the former athlete, was a favourite fund-raiser here.

While Ariel is reluctant to disclose the source of its money, it does give detailed accounts of its expenditure. The World Assembly of Youth, with which Ariel shared key personnel was one recipient. A little over £2,000 changed hands in 1961 for example. In Africa, which was the scene of most Ariel activity, it organised scholarships for young nationalists in Britain and exchange visits between Western and African leaders. Kaunda, Seretse Khama (Botswana) and Jomo Kenyatta took advantage of these trips. Robert and Sally Mugabe received education paid for by Ariel. Three nominees of the Zimbabwe African Peoples Union, the party led by Joshua Nkomo attended a course in basic politics and economics at the University of Sussex, again sponsored by Ariel. There is no suggestion that any of these were aware of Ariel's relationship with the British government. Ariel's contacts came from two main sources: the British Council, a government organisation existing to promote all things British throughout the world, and through ordinary diplomatic channels. As a former Ariel employee explained: 'We had a direct line to the Foreign Office. British Ambassadors would send us lists of people they wanted us to invite over. We brought over 25 per cent of them'[14]. While the contacts were in Britain personal dossiers were compiled to assess their leadership potential.

Ariel was highly successful in Kenya, where it provide substantial and varied assistance to the moderate KANU leader Tom Mboya. The Foundation commissioned a report on the country's social and economic potential which was presented to KANU. The author was Arthur Gaitskell, brother of Labour leader Hugh and an experienced colonial administrator. The report was adopted as the basis of KANU's 1963 election manifesto and Mboya was instrumental in arranging its acceptance by the party. Mboya was also involved in the Ariel project to provide scholarships for Zimbabwean nationalists.

The British government despatched Malcolm MacDonald, a high-powered diplomat with experience of tricky negotiations in Malaya, to take over as Governor in Kenya and put into effect the new British strategy. He immediately halted official support to KADU and opened lines to KANU, working through a close friend of Kenyatta. MI6, meanwhile, recruited Bruce McKenzie, an influential white settler politician who had moved over to KANU. A former fighter pilot, McKenzie sported a huge handlebar moustache and was well known as a considerable wheeler and dealer with a boisterous personality. Malcolm MacDonald told us that McKenzie had been an MI6 agent since at least 1963. It is difficult to place a date on when he was recruited but it is known that he worked with the security forces during Mau Mau interrogating suspects so it may have been during this period that he came in contact with the intelligence recruiters.

McKenzie was at one time, in Blundell's words 'my right hand man' who 'advised me constantly'. McKenzie, as the NKG's main political strategist, produced a plan to settle the problem of the white settlers' land after independence. At the first Lancaster House conference in 1960, the British government side, led by Iain Macleod and Lord Perth, suggested that it should be adopted as NKG policy. Then the NKG would be given a guarantee of government financial support, timed to achieve the maximum electoral impact.

After the election in March 1960, Bruce McKenzie broke with the NKG and KADU to join KANU. While other white settlers made the same transition his own switch can be seen to have a more Machiavellian purpose. According to Colonel David Stirling, McKenzie met Kenyatta in detention and outlined his support for him. For McKenzie's apparent boldness in switching sides, at a time when most white settlers were watching KADU, he was rewarded with the portfolio of 'shadow Minister of Agriculture' where again he promoted the plan for white land settlement. Indeed, he is widely credited as the architect of its final execution.

After independence, KANU formed the first government. There was still the problem for the British of what to do about its radical wing, led by the fiery Luo populist, Oginga Odinga. The following anecdote from Malcolm MacDonald gives some idea of how the British regarded African politicians:

> I said to the British Government 'Odinga is not a communist. He's an extreme nationalist. He receives money from the Russians and the Chinese. I'm critical of that but he won't be a stooge'. I told Odinga that I'd said this. He said 'You're absolutely right. I'm not a communist. I'm a socialist in some ways and I'm a capitalist in some ways. I'm not going to be influenced beyond a certain point by the Russians and the Chinese. When I wanted to serve certain causes, I became ambitious, so I went to the British for help. The British refused, the Americans refused. They were both giving money to my rival, Tom Mboya, I was so serious in what I wanted to do I had to get money from somewhere'.

MacDonald's advice to Kenyatta was that he should try and attract 'the best men from KADU' and it was not long before several of their most distinguished members crossed the floor. In turn, Kenyatta told MacDonald that he would break with Odinga, but he wanted Odinga to take the blame for the split.

Even before independence the KADU Government and its British advisers put considerable pressure on Odinga. A whole series of stories appeared detailing finance he had received from Eastern Europe and Ghana to split the Kenyan Labour Federation, Tom Mboya's power base. The KLF, for its part, picked up over $25,000 from the CIA-backed Foundation for International Social and Economic Education and £1,000 a month in the early sixties from the ICFTU.[15] Kenyatta, too, subsequently received indirect financing from the CIA and MI6.[16]

Shortly after independence Kenyatta let it be known that the British had refused to let him appoint Odinga as Finance Minister. Instead, he became Minister of Home Affairs, where he had to oversee the tricky process of pulling the rug out from under the regionally-biased independence constitution. He was also given the task of deporting a white police intelligence officer, Ian Henderson, a task which made him unpopular with the white settlers. Henderson subsequently turned up in Bahrein where he devised and implemented the Gulf's most elaborate and pervasive internal security system.

As his position grew weaker, Odinga accepted or was persuaded to accept Soviet help. In the spring of 1964, shortly after a mutiny in the Kenyan army (suppressed by British troops) and during a period of rapid Africanisation of the armed forces, a large number of students were sent to Eastern Europe and China for military training. By mid-1965, some 180 students were being trained in the Soviet Union, Bulgaria, East Germany, Egypt and China. All these students were sponsored by KANU as a party, now largely controlled by Odinga, and not by the Defence Ministry. Odinga also received shipments of Soviet arms which, if contemporary news reports can be believed, were flown in by unmarked aircraft and transferred into trucks belonging to Odinga's Prison Department. According to Odinga, part of this shipment, which received much press publicity, went to Kenyatta himself. Kenyatta and his advisers watched and waited. They calculated that now was not the moment to pick a fight. In February 1965, the Kenyan Asian radical Pio Pinto was assassinated. The opportunity came in April. On the 8th, troops surrounded Odinga's headquarters and seized a small cache of arms. On the 13th, it was announced that the secret training of people in Eastern Europe was 'under investigation'. The next day, the Soviet freighter, *Fizik Lebedev*, docked in Mombasa harbour with a gift of arms for Kenya.

Several days before McKenzie had advance warning of this and alerted Kenyatta, outlining his plan of action. Troops would be sent to the dockside to ensure Odinga did not receive the arms. He also contacted the head of the British Military Training Team in Kenya, Brigadier John Hardy and took him and Dr. Mungai, the Defence Minister, to see the ship. Ultimately, the equipment it carried was never deployed. Kenyatta rejected the shipment as too old, secondhand, and unfit for use in his modern army. According to the *Guardian*[17] part of it consisted of World War II T-34 Tanks, for which Kenya had 'no obvious need'. The Soviet Union ambassador issued a statement saying that the arms were 'modern types, and were just as good as any foreign arms of the same category', and besides 'full agreement was reached on the type of arms to be supplied by the Soviet Union'.[18] The question was with whom the agreement had been reached. The Russians insisted that they had been approached officially, but Western correspondents continued to cast doubt on this.

The immediate result of Kenyatta's announcement was that the shipment, along with 17 Soviet technicians who had arrived a fortnight earlier, left the country. More important, Odinga had been outmanoeuvred and lapsed into virtual disgrace, although he remained in the government until March 1965. Together, Kenyatta and McKenzie, who instigated the plot, had enormously diminished his political prestige and influence. Links with the Soviet Union continued nevertheless: in January 1966 a high-level delegation, including McKenzie, arrived in Moscow seeking trade and assistance.

After independence, McKenzie had become the most important white in the country. He was appointed Minister of Agriculture, in which capacity he helped to arrange the international coffee agreements central to the Kenyan economy. His position also served to reassure the white settlers, anxious after the final departure of the Union Jack. He also retained the active role in military and security affairs, holding responsibility for overseeing the defence treaty with Britain.

With the KANU left outmanoeuvred, the British had achieved their prime post-colonial objective. The main threat to the country's stability came, until 1982, from a steady stream of political assassinations, which has severely tested the fabric of the ruling KANU. The murder of Kenyatta's heir apparent, Tom Mboya, in July 1969 led to widespread riots and the detention of Odinga whose breakaway party, the Kenyan Peoples' Union, had been banned from fighting a forthcoming election. The government was unsure how the situation would develop, and Bruce McKenzie arrived in London shortly afterwards with Defence Minister Njoroge Mungai to arrange for British troops to be available in the event of uncontrollable disorder.

Mboya's death was a serious blow to the African operations of the Ariel Foundation. Disclosures in the American magazine *Ramparts* two years earlier concerning CIA financing of international student organisations had generated suspicion among nationalist leaders towards the activities of Western-based 'charitable' groups, and Ariel did not escape scrutiny. Its debt to Mboya was reflected in the establishment of a Tom Mboya Memorial Fund which operated from Ariel's London offices and whose committee contained two Ariel trustees, but by 1976 its African programme had all but collapsed. From a mid-1960s peak of £75,000, donations to Ariel have now fallen to a mean of £25,000 per annum, largely deriving from anonymous doners. The centrepiece of the foundation's activities remains the annual Anglo-American Conference on Africa, although in recent years a significant amount of money has been devoted to a Caribbean Study Project. Nonetheless, the history of Ariel is important because it is a device which the British may well be prepared to use again. *Private Eye* reported in 1976 renewed government interest in the likes of Ariel as 'a cover for intelligence gathering and covert support for foreign movements'.[19]

Bruce McKenzie resigned from the government in 1970, ostensibly through ill-health, although attacks on him in the Kenyan Parliament had increased in frequency and ferocity. He became a director of East African Airways, and later (after EAA's collapse) of Kenya Airways. Through his chairmanship of Cooper Moters, a firm selling Volkswagen and British Leyland vehicles in Kenya and Uganda, he supplied landrovers and other equipment – possibly armoured cars – to the Kenyan security forces. These units were trained by the British in exchange for military facilities: notably the use of Indian Ocean ports and jungle training areas near Nyeri, about 60 miles north of Nairobi. The Kenyan military frequently complain that the British are not wholly fulfilling their commitments and there is some suspicion among the population regarding a possible British intervention in the event of civil disorder.[20] Unconfirmed reports suggest that a SAS unit was flown in during disturbances in March 1975 following the assassination of MP Josiah Kariuki, an often outspoken opponent of the government. There has been no suggestion of any British role in thwarting the 1982 coup attempt.

In early 1978, McKenzie was back in Britain arranging for General Rowland Mans to come to Kenya to help to reorganise the army and modernise it in case of any clashes with Somalia. The package included the updating and reorganisation of the Kenyan intelligence services but this fell through due to lack of money to finance it from the British end. His role in the Israeli raid on Entebbe is now well-publicised. Essentially, it involved arranging refuelling and medical facilities at

Nairobi airport on the return journey.

In May of the same year, almost certainly because of his assistance in the Entebbe operation, Bruce McKenzie was killed when a bomb exploded on the plane carrying him and two business associates from the Ugandan capital Kampala to Nairobi. He had long conducted business deals with President Amin, and on this occasion was selling military or semi-military equipment. He was accompanied by a former employee of Lonrho who had since worked independently. The third passenger, Keith Savage, was selling communications equipment to Amin. In a *Sunday Times* report, responsibility for the explosion was accredited to two ex-CIA agents, Edwin Wilson and Frank Terpil, employed by Amin.[21] McKenzie's funeral was attended by the MI6 officer in Nairobi from 1968 to 1971, Frank Fenwick Steel, and a representative of the Queen. The Israeli government named a forest in Galilee after him as a mark of respect.

British interests in Kenya were not adversely affected, however. The most obvious sign of their durability was the appointment of Kenyatta's successor, Daniel Arap Moi. Originally an appointed member of Legco, he passed through one of the government-supported tribal associations into the KADU; which he left to join KANU. Apparently, Bruce McKenzie had begun to align himself with Moi and give him help and advice before his untimely death. That Amin should have been the most likely culprit is ironic, for he owed his position as Ugandan President in part to the Kenyan authorities, and possibly to McKenzie personally.

Colonised by the British at the turn of this century, modern Uganda encompasses an area traditionally ruled by the four Kingdoms of Buganda, Toro, Bunyoro and Ankole. The Baganda staunchly resisted all attempts by the British to unify the country, and by virtue of their size acquired a privileged status under the colonial constitution. The upheaval in neighbouring Kenya during the 1950s reverberated through the country and stimulated the growth of nationalist politics, which found support among non-Baganda tribes. In 1960 the two main nationalist parties merged to form the Uganda Peoples' Congress (UPC) led by Milton Obote.

The 'pearl of Africa' as Winston Churchill was wont to refer to it, achieved independence in October 1962. With a broad-based crop economy and large copper deposits, the development prospects for Uganda seemed good, provided the political struggle between nationalists and tribalists could be resolved peacefully.

At elections held the previous April to determine the form of the independence government, the UPC emerged as the largest party but without an overall majority. Obote decided on an alliance with the Kabaka Yekka (the Baganda party), conceding some of the Bagandan demands for autonomy. The Baganda leader Kabaka Mutesa later became President, with Obote as Prime Minister. Obote expected, correctly, that Baganda intransigence would eventually break down and that their territorial status could then be adjusted to conform with the rest of the country. He may have been too hasty in insisting on a referendum in 1963 in areas populated by Bunyaro but ruled by Buganda. When the vote for transfer to Bunyaro control came through, the alliance was finished, but a sufficient number of MPs had by then defected to the UPC for Obote to retain control.

Two years later the Baganda were able to retaliate. Obote was supporting rebels in the Belgian Congo (now Zaire) against the right-wing government of Moise Tshombe and the current ruler, General Mobutu. Because the army commander, Brigadier Opolot was suspected of Kabaka Yekka sympathies, Obote entrusted the support operation to Idi Amin, a former member of the King's African Rifles with a strong power base inside the Ugandan army.

The Congo rebels had little money but plenty of gold and ivory, which they exchanged with Amin for weapons. Amin then sold the gold and ivory at a considerable profit. The Kabaka Yekka MPs who raised the issue also accused Obote and a number of government ministers of being recipients from the sales. In Feburary 1966, Obote seized all executive powers turning the country into a de facto one-party state and stifling a promised inquiry into the affair. The Kabaka Yekka responded by demanding the removal of the Ugandan central government from Kampala, which was Buganda territory, and the release of Kabaka Yekka supporters arrested by the security forces. Kabaka Mutesa made a discreet approach to the British asking for military intervention to oust Obote but Obote heard of the plot and immediately took action against Mutesa. Amin was sent with an army detachment to storm the presidential palace. Although Mutesa escaped, he was unable to rally resistance against Obote and fled into exile. He died in London in 1969. Amin was rewarded by being appointed army commander in place of the dismissed Opolot.

Obote set about steering Uganda towards socialist development, with UPC backing, introducing a 'Common Man's Charter' and announcing the forthcoming nationalisation of foreign assets in Uganda. Although not as far-reaching as plans in neighbouring Tanzania, the proposals were not well received in London since Obote's targets included 80 British firms and the British started to explore schemes for Obote's replacement. Idi Amin's ambition to take eventual control of the country did not go unnoticed in Whitehall: they knew him well from his service in the King's African Rifles, during which he fought against the Mau Mau rebels. Described as 'a little short on the grey matter' though 'intensely loyal to Britain' it was hoped that once Amin had been installed, a contingent of advisors could be sent out to realign the country's economic policies with British interests. They knew also of Amin's cruel and sadistic nature, manifested during his spell in charge of a Kenyan concentration camp, where he earned the title 'The Strangler'.

The core of Amin's army support was among Southern Sudanese mercenaries which the British had brought in to staff the lower ranks; many of them belong to Amin's tribe, the Kakwa, which straddles the Sudan-Uganda border. The Southern Sudanese, like the Kurds in the Middle East, are a minority ripe for manipulation by more powerful forces in the course of regional power politics. The inhabitants of the South, numbering six million out of a total population of fifteen million, are black and predominantly Christian, while Arabs, who control central government and the armed forces are a majority in the north. Southerners view the north as oppressors unconcerned with the economic welfare of the much poorer South. Though recently the Sudanese government seemed to be on the point of bowing to Southern demands for autonomy, during the 1960s it was locked into a civil war with Anya-nya guerillas, the military wing of the Nile Liberation Movement. Until 1969 Britain, which had once ruled the Sudan supported the central government. This stopped when a Nasserite Free Officers' Movement under Colonel Jaafar Numeiri replaced the civilian caretaker government. Tired of the bickering between the traditional religious parties – the National Unionist Party and the Umma (People's) Party – Numeiri appointed a Revolutionary Command Council, including two communists, to run the country. The Sudanese Communist Party, although only 8,000 strong, had successfully spearheaded a campaign to frustrate a previous military government and ultimately forced it from power. Numeiri realised that he would have to take it as an ally to avoid a repeat.

Not surprisingly, the British withdrew their military support of arms and training teams. Russians and Egyptians rapidly replaced them. Meanwhile, the Any-nya were also receiving new external support. From September 1969, the Israelis began making weekly parachute drops of weapons and medicines, while some of their regular troops helped out on the ground with training the guerillas. At least three mercenary units were also fighting with them: one led by a Frenchman named Armande; another operating in the Ethiopian border area was organised by two British mercenaries, Ron Gregory and Rip Kirby; the third involved Rolf Steiner and Alex Gay, and worked in the Kakwa tribal region near the Ugandan border. It was a fairly insignificant affair compared with the mercenary wars in the Congo, Rhodesia and Angola, but the activities of this last group in particular had a substantial impact on East African politics, paving the

way for Amin's takeover in Uganda. The Israelis were mainly interested, at least initially, in diverting Arab forces away from the Sinai
front.

Steiner, of German extraction, learnt his military skills in the
French Foreign Legion, a well-known mercenary spawning ground.
After leaving the Legion, he obtained permission to live in French
North Africa, and quickly got mixed up with the extreme right-wing
OAS, which campaigned against the French withdrawal from Algeria.
He managed to escape conviction and moved to France, where he was
later successfully prosecuted for cheque fraud. His first experience as
a military freelance was as a secondary recruiter for the Anya-nya
following an approach from the French mercenary Roger Faulques.
70 men went out on this occasion and were, in the words of one
knowledgeable source, 'duffed up badly'. Steiner moved on to Nigeria,
fighting on the Biafran side, where he first came into contact with Alex
Gay.

Born in Scotland, Gay spent the early 1960s working as a bank
clerk after two years national service in the Royal Signals Corps.
Although he first went to Africa as a sales representative, the attractions
of military action took him to the Congo in 1965 and on to Biafra three
years later. When Steiner was expelled from Biafra after a drunken
display in front of the Biafran leader General Ojukwu (whose French
advisers were glad to see the back of him), Gay went with him to
Europe, where they started to look for work with the Sudanese.

In February 1969, Steiner met Carlo Beyer, secretary of the Catholic
relief agency Caritas International. Through Vatican contacts, Beyer
arranged for a meeting with the Verona Fathers who were looking for
channels through which to send humanitarian aid to the Southern
Sudanese. They put Steiner and Gay onto the German charity FGA*
who in turn introduced them to two Britons interested in active
support.

One of these, Beverley Barnard, was referred to during Steiner's
subsequent trial in Sudan as 'a former British diplomat' although he
has no traceable diplomatic service record. Now deceased, Barnard
was in fact responsible for co-ordinating MI6 operations against Obote
and planned his attempted assassination outside a UPC Conference in
1969. The other was Anthony Divall, described to us as an 'SIS heavy'
in West Germany who lost his job after the exposure of George Blake
as a Soviet agent (a version which Divall himself disputes). He is now
an arms dealer resident in Hamburg.

Barnard and Divall ran a one-plane airline called Southern Air-
motive shipping supplies to Uganda as a commercial exercise while,
as Gay put it, occasionally 'getting lost' over Anya-nya territory and

* Förderungsgesellschaft Afrika – Society for the support of Africa.

making drops which included weapons. The FGA hired Steiner and Gay to build an airstrip at the end of July 1969, but on discovering that Steiner had different ideas about what he ought to be doing – creating a 'real guerilla army' – fired him after he returned to Europe from a preliminary two-week study of the area.

Steiner returned to Uganda nonetheless to rejoin a Kakwa group led by General Emedio Taffeng which had split from the Anya-nya and formed the autonomous 'state of Anyidi' in their tribal homeland. In Steiner's version of events[22] he arrived in Kampala to discover that Gay had been trying to ruin his chances of work by telling Taffeng that he was a fraud and an imposter. Steiner confronted Gay and in the ensuing argument Gay revealed that Barnard was using the Southern Sudanese support operation as a cover for training an Anya-nya unit to spearhead a prospective coup against Obote. Although Amin's army power base was strong, it was not sufficient to mount a takeover; but the addition of 500 highly trained troops could make all the difference. Steiner claims that Gay was working for MI6, which Gay denies, and that his task was to prevent Steiner fouling up the plans. A colleague of Gay's on a later operation* said that Gay had been recruited by MI6 during national service.

After forging a note purportedly allowing him to retrieve Barnard's luggage from Kampala's Apollo Hotel, Steiner went through the contents and claims to have found radio codes used for transmissions with London and cyphers for written communication with the British Embassy in Uganda. Steiner says that he also found evidence of bribes to Obote's Minister of the Interior, Basil Bataringaya. Divall, by contrast, has given comprehensive denial of any British connection with the Anya-nya guerillas:

> The great Southern Sudan Conspiracy, involving Messrs. Gay, Steiner, Barnard et al and myself was in fact a non-event. There was never any gun-running, mercenary activity of combative nature or aircraft operated by Southern Airmotive. Furthermore, there was no overt or covert participation by any government excepting those of Uganda/Sudan in conjunction with the deportation/trial of Steiner.[23]

This does not explain Israeli training assistance to the guerillas or the eye-witness accounts of David Robison,[24] an American journalist who accompanied an Anya-nya unit led by Steiner on military operations.

Steiner went to the Ugandan Government and told them of the

---

* Alan Murphy met Gay in Cyprus in 1960 while working at a British Signals Intelligence base. He subsequently accompanied Gay on an abortive mission to capture Fernando Po, an island off the coast of Equatorial Guinea. This operation was set up by novelist Frederick Forsyth to obtain source material for his best-selling *Dogs of War*.

plot. For his trouble he was arrested by the Ugandan Security Service and detained without charge for three months until the end of 1970. Obote was unhappy about Steiner's activities with the Anya-nya which were jeopardising Ugandan relations with the new Sudanese government. Obote had troubles at home too with his army commander Idi Amin. He realised that Amin's support from the Anya-nya was threatening his own position. Early in 1970 the head of Israeli intelligence Zvi Zamir visited Uganda and asked permission for Israeli planes flying arms to the Anya-nya to refuel at Entebbe or Gulu and for guerilla training facilities in Uganda. Obote refused. So, behind his back they approached Akena Adoka, a cousin of Obote, who ran the paramilitary General Services Unit. They told him that all secret services make arrangements independent of their governments. Adoka turned them down nevertheless. Finally they went to Amin who as an ally of the Anya-nya proved most co-operative.

The Israelis who had some military advisors in Uganda were disturbed by Obote's growing anti-Zionism and the possibility of an alliance with Numeiri. Amin, they thought, would be a useful puppet and come to rely on a large Israeli military presence for his survival.

In October Obote created the post of Chief of the General Staff, in an effort to move Amin upstairs. Amin had a further problem: another embezzlement scandal in which he was involved was about to catch up with him and would have led to his expulsion from the army. He approached Colonel Bar-Lev, former head of the Israeli military mission in Uganda. Amin told him that he wanted to mount a coup against Obote. He knew the Israelis would be sympathetic as Obote's stance was becoming increasingly anti-Israeli. Amin told Bar-Lev that the biggest obstacle to a coup was that his loyal supporters were outside Kampala and Obote would be able to arrest and kill him before they would be able to rescue him. Bar-Lev advised Amin to bring to Kampala those soldiers who were from the same area as himself, and to make sure he had paratroops, tanks and jeeps. The strike force for the coup was made up of troops loyal to Amin and 500 Anya-nya guerillas from Barnard's camp inside Southern Sudan.

Britain's support for a coup against Obote became stronger with the controversy over British arms sales to South Africa. On this issue Obote went into a head-on clash with the British. The new Conservative government under Edward Heath had decided to sell arms to white South Africa. This reversal of previous British policy was opposed by the Commonwealth leaders, strongly led by Nyerere, Obote and Kaunda. All three threatened to leave the Commonwealth unless Heath changed his mind. With such a respected triumvirate there was the threat of embarrassing African opposition to the British position. For Heath, it became almost a test of the virility of British foreign policy in Africa. The arms issue was going to come to a head at the Commonwealth Prime Ministers' Conference in Singapore. Obote had twice said that he would not attend this conference, but had been asked to go by Kaunda and Nyerere and the Ugandan cabinet decided he should go to present a united African opposition to the South African arms sales. He left for the fateful conference on 11th January 1971 providing the coup plotters with an ideal opportunity. At the conference, when one of the leaders described Heath's policy as 'racialist', Heath retorted 'I wonder how many of you will be allowed to return to your own countries from this conference.'[25]

The coup was a complete success. The strike force, with the Anya-nya, led an assault on the Malive barracks and completely overpowered an armoured battalion loyal to Obote. The Parliament Buildings in the capital, Kampala, were surrounded. Nubians loyal to Amin seized most of the country's armouries. The Israelis were on hand to provide technical back-up, driving the tanks used and piloting the jets at a celebration fly-past. Colonel Bar-Lev was even said to have helped Amin pick his first cabinet.

The last part of the coup was engineered by Kenyan intelligence, which ever since independence has worked closely with the British. Some reports suggest that Obote may have been harbouring and perhaps providing training facilities for anti-Kenyatta guerillas, providing a further incentive for Kenyan collusion. When Obote came back from Singapore, after the coup had been announced, he flew to Nairobi. From there he intended to make a quick assessment of the situation from his hotel by telephoning contacts inside Uganda. He would then drive back to Uganda to link up with loyal troops. He arrived at the hotel with the Vice-President of Kenya, Arap Moi, who immediately put a call through to Kenyatta. But when Obote's aides tried to get through to Uganda, they were told the lines were out of order. Suspicious, Obote sent one of them into town to try from there. The phone lines to Uganda were working perfectly. When Arap Moi returned to see Obote, the hotel phones which were also claimed to be out of order were miraculously restored to full working order. When Moi left, they went dead again. A huge security cordon around the hotel made it impossible for Obote to slip unobtrusively away.

Immediately on taking power, Amin declared his support for Heath's stand on the South African arms issue. The British government recognised the regime officially before any other government, and applied enormous diplomatic pressure to get it accepted in Africa. Soon after, Uganda was granted ten million pounds in economic aid (to be administered by Britain), fifteen 'Ferret' and thirty-six Saladin armoured cars, other military equipment, and loaned a training team for the army. However, Amin resented the British refusal to supply him with jet fighters and other more sophisticated equipment for his planned invasion of Tanzania in order to acquire a port of his own.

By this time, Rolf Steiner, whose activities had almost sabotaged the plot was back in Sudan. The Ugandan authorities had handed him over despite the absence of a formal extradition treaty, and the Sudanese government planned for a high-profile trial highlighting Western interference in African affairs. Barnard and Divall moved their Southern Sudan support operation to bases in Ethiopia, while Gay returned to Europe.

In the weeks preceding the opening of the trial, Numeiri's government was almost overthrown, and was only able to re-establish itself with British help. This confirmed that the regime was slowly moving into a pro-Western position. The Steiner trial was eventually allowed to go ahead because of international press interest but after Steiner's conviction his death sentence was commuted to 20 years imprisonment and he was finally repatriated to Germany for 'humane reasons'.

Numeiri's regime had been put under pressure by the Western powers from the start. Although he did not rely on the traditional religious parties, they still retained considerable influence and were identified by the West as an obvious target for covert support. On a visit to their main stronghold on Aba Island, in the Nile, Numeiri was almost stabbed to death by an Umma Party supporter. The incident sparked off a half-hearted rebellion, fomented by the British and Americans, which Numeiri quickly crushed by bombing the island.

However, there were serious policy disagreements within the Revolutionary Command Council, to which Numeiri responded by removing the two communist members and taking more of the important decisions alone. He also banned several political organisations and introduced new laws restricting the trade union movement. With his support dwindling, Numeiri realised that he would need external assistance, which could only come from the West since his alienation of the Communist Party. There was much foot-dragging by the West, and results were slow to come from this change of attitude, as the regime was still considered too left-wing.

On 19 July 1971, Major Hashim al-Atta, one of the officers pushed off the Revolutionary Command Council, seized power. In a broadcast after the coup, he said it was aimed at 'correcting the course of the May and October revolutions' and he lifted the ban on communist-led organisations imposed by Numeiri. The new regime was headed by a seven-person Revolutionary Council, chaired by Lieutenant-Colonel Babiker el-Nur, who from London claimed that he had been in effective command of the coup.

El-Nur and another council member, Major Hamadallah, made

preparations to return to Sudan from London. El-Nur was well-known to the British since he had trained in military intelligence at Ashford. On 21st July, El-Nur told reporters that he would be returning to Khartoum that evening. There was only one flight, BOAC 045 leaving Heathrow at 21.45 GMT, which both men boarded. The first leg of the flight to Rome passed off without incident. After a 45 minute stopover the plane headed southwards out to sea passing over the heel of Italy. At about 0.50 GMT the plane passed into the Malta air traffic control area and made a routine call to Luqa airport. Luqa queried the VC-10's destination: the controller thought that Khartoum airport was closed, but was satisfied when the pilot, Roy Bowyer, explained that he had clearance.

Although Luqa's high frequency radio was effective over the whole of Libyan airspace, air traffic control regulations stipulated that planes flying to Khartoum over Libya at below 40,000 feet should come under the control of Benina, near Benghazi, for a period of 20-25 minutes. According to the BOAC version of the flight, the following events took place. At 1.28 GMT, when the plane was directly over Benghazi at 33,000 feet, Benina ordered the plane via VHF radio to land, an unusual order from flight control. Bowyer switched to his high frequency channel, leaving the co-pilot tuned to Benina, and requested clearance from Luqa to fly back towards Rome. Permission was granted. The plane began a slow 180 degree turn to reverse its course. Just as it started, clearance from Luqa was withdrawn and Benina announced that if the plane did not land then it would be shot down. The plane was only 40 miles into Libyan airspace and could easily have cleared it within 5 minutes, avoiding interception by Libyan fighters.

Instead the pilot chose to land the plane. An air steward informed the two men, who quickly disposed of their private papers. Although aware that the break in the flight would probably cost both of them their lives, Major Hamadallah could not resist a joke about having another whisky before landing. Libya is 'dry'. On arrival at Benina, both were taken off by Libyan security officials.

The second prong of the counter-coup was masterminded by two pro-Numeiri officials who were out of the country at the time of the Atta coup. Defence Minister Khalid Abbas and Mohammed Abdul Hashim, who were in Belgrade, were flown to Cairo in a private jet supplied by Lonrho. Abbas then flew to Tripoli with the Egyptian Defence Minister where the final preparations were made. The plans involved the use of the Egyptian military academy at Jebel Aulia as an operational base, with the assistance of Egyptian army officers. The Sudanese forces were led by Mohammed Ali Kergassi and other officers who had refused to join Atta. Late on the 22nd July, it was announced over Khartoum Radio that Numeiri had been restored to power. El-Nur and Hamadallah were flown back to Khartoum and executed. Numeiri launched a massive round-up of Communist Party members.

In the ensuing turmoil, the mystery surrounding the hijacking of the VC-10 was forgotten. Bowyer returned to England and went home. At a press conference given by his flight manager, John Meagher, the awkward question of why Luqa had withdrawn clearance was never answered: the Maltese said that since the plane was under 40,000 feet, it was out of their control and they were not in a position to grant or deny clearance. The press conference was, as one journalist observed, 'so diplomatic as to be embarrassing'. Malta flight control was then run by International Aeradio, whose largest shareholder was BOAC. Although all its staff were Maltese, the three top managers were British. In reply to a parliamentary question on the incident, Foreign Office minister Joseph Godber declared that

> HM Government take a most serious view of the action taken by the Libyan authorities which is clearly in complete violation of international civil aviation practice. On hearing of the matter, I immediately summoned the Libyan ambassador and told him that his Government's action had been outrageous. I protested in the strongest possible terms at an action which we condemned as inexcusable.[26]

In an extensive investigation into the incident carried out by Eric Rouleau of *Le Monde*, cracks began to appear in the BOAC version of what happened:

> Captain Bowyer maintains that the control tower in Malta refused to let him enter the air corridor which would have allowed him to fly back to Rome. This explanation is officially denied by Valetta. Captain Bowyer's docile acceptance of Libyan instructions appears all the more suspect to some people as he was in constant touch with one of the BOAC directors in London, who himself repeatedly consulted a senior member of the Foreign Office during the flight.[27]

Before this revelation, a story appeared in British gossip and satire magazine, *Private Eye*, which claimed that the men's departure was 'carefully shepherded by Foreign Office officials and at least one British intelligence agent'.[28] It also drew attention to the Maltese denial that they had withdrawn clearance and pointed out that if the pilot had flown a few thousand feet higher to 40,000 feet he would have been clear of Libyan airspace. This story was followed in its next issue by an anonymous letter, rather wittily signed 'Ex Officio', which added to the previous speculation:

> The 'at least one British Intelligence Agent' in attendance in fact numbered seven SIS agents, including one who boarded the

flight at Rome to assist Captain Bowyer should certain gentle-
men in the first class section of the aircraft become 'over agitated'
during the unscheduled descent into Benina.[29]

Never slow to spot a story, *Private Eye* followed up by asking
BOAC for the flight's passenger list:

> Sorry, said a spokesman, we cannot release the passenger list.
> We usually only do that in the case of an accident. "Wasn't the
> hijacking an accident?" In a sense, yes. "So what about the
> passenger list?" Sorry no, said BOAC. As you can imagine
> there might be circumstances where some of the passengers
> would not want it to be known that they were flying on a
> particular plane.[30]

There is, it appears, no official record of the incident. In Britain,
neither the Department of Trade nor the Civil Aviation Authority
have any reference to it; neither does the International Civil Aviation
Organisation. Shortly after the coup all Soviet bloc advisers to the
Sudanese army left the country. Two months later a £100,000 grant
was given by the British government for scholarships and the Export
Credit Guarantee Department gave 5 years credit on £10 million worth
of Sudan government orders. The export agreement followed preliminary work done by Lonrho, which was itself able to sign a lucrative
investment agreement with the Sudanese. British army officers were
put in to run the Sudanese Staff College briefly after the Soviets left
and military training links with Britain were resumed.

The credit agreement was unusual for two reasons. At the time,
total British exports to Sudan were only £12 million, so that the volume
of trade between the two would be almost doubled at a stroke. Also,
the Conservative government was not given to extending credit to
regimes which had nationalised British assets (as Numeiri had) without compensation. Lonrho was appointed sole agent for Sudanese
purchases in the UK under the agreement, as a reward for the help. It
was not the only occasion on which Foreign Office and Lonrho interests
have coincided.

Although the Foreign Office and MI6 must have been pleased
with the success of their 1971 East African schemes, even the best laid
plans can backfire, and so it is that the British government now holds
joint responsibility for installing one of the most savage regimes of
recent times.

Purges and massacres by Amin's troops began almost immediately after the takeover with units from Obote's armed forces the first
target. Amin's financial ineptitude quickly became apparent as well:
his erstwhile allies, Britain and Israel, refused to commit funds before
making feasability studies and insisted that they should be tied to
specific projects. Amin's need for ready cash, generated by the need

to guarantee the loyalty of his largely mercenary army, forced him to seek out allies who could satisfy the demand. Libya proved the most receptive and in early 1972 Amin rapidly switched allegiances, expelling his Israeli military advisers as part of the package. He became disillusioned with the British after they refused to supply him with arms to launch an invasion of Tanzania and retaliated by expelling the entire Ugandan Asian community, most of whom carried British passports and whose commercial activities were central to the Ugandan economy. He also nationalised British-owned businesses; exactly what he was installed to avoid. There are reports that the British considered plans for his removal in the autumn but confined themselves to despatching a Major Graham to Uganda in order to, in the words of one intelligence source, 'bring him to heel'.

Meanwhile official support continued: Ugandan military intelligence officers were trained at Ashford until at least the middle of 1974, after the collapse of a British-sponsored training scheme in Uganda.

Even when the barbarity of Amin's regime became internationally recognised, the British did not withdraw completely. Diplomatic relations between the two countries were broken in 1976 but communications and signals equipment found its way into Uganda up until February 1979 via the notorious 'whisky run' from Stansted airport. British firms including Pye Telecommunications and the Cambridge-based Security Systems International supplied surveillance devices to Amin's State Research Bureau. This agency is held responsible for much of the well-documented torture and maltreatment of detainees. The contracts were arranged after groundwork by MI6's Kenyan agent, Bruce McKenzie.

Amin was overthrown by a joint force of Ugandan rebels and Tanzanian troops in 1979. In the next eighteen months, events were to come full circle. Milton Obote, who had spent almost a decade in exile in Tanzania, returned to Uganda and achieved a disputed victory in elections held in December 1980; yet since then, the rampant violence which overtook Uganda during Amin's rule has continued unabated – some say on an even worse scale. Obote has rejected the socialist programme which he tried to implement during his first period in office, and now espouses a free market economy. As a result, he enjoys Western support, despite the electoral irregularities and questionable policies towards political opponents. A London-based security firm, Falconstar, trains the new Ugandan special forces while teams from the World Bank and the International Monetary Fund lay down loan conditions – in effect a complete blueprint for the savaged economy. There is little optimism in financial circles, for as one British banker confided to a journalist at a Ugandan Commercial

Bank reception, 'this country is finished. Finished.'[31]

Among Amin's military advisers during the early years of his rule was Major Ian Walsworth-Bell, a surprising fact since the Major's insistence on extracting unemployment benefit from the British Government after dismissal from his previous job caused acute embarrassment to the Foreign Office. Moreover, the benefit tribunal accepted Walsworth-Bell's contention that he had been recruited to undertake intelligence work by former Labour minister Maurice Foley.

Walsworth-Bell specialised in intelligence during his military training, taking courses in guided weapons, technical staff work and advanced intelligence as well as learning Russian. In 1956 he was seconded to the King's African Rifles in Kenya, and then went to Austrialia the following year for the British atomic trials. After a course in nuclear science and technology at the Royal Military College of Science he was posted to the British Embassy in Washington. In 1963 he joined the brewery firm Guinness, where he claims to have worked as a taster, and then moved to a job with the Zambian Youth Service, supposedly dealing with the problems of young unemployed Zambians. Nothing is known of his subsequent career until early in February 1969 when he was approached by Maurice Foley, then a junior minister at the Foreign Office with whom he was acquainted through a mutual friend, Barney Hayhoe. Foley asked him to become a member of the International Observer Team sent to Nigeria, at that time rent in two by civil war.

After obtaining independence from the British in 1960, Nigeria was ruled by elected government until the beginning of 1966. At this point a section of the army made an attempt to overthrow the government in the wake of civil disorder which followed allegations of poll-rigging at the October elections. The Nigerian army commander, Major-General Ironsi, foiled the mutineers and took power himself the next day after the Council of Ministers decided unanimously that they were unable to control the situation. A number of senior civilian politicians were killed during the attempted coup, including several northern leaders and Prime Minister Balewa, whose body was later found in a ditch. The British Premier, Harold Wilson, had been in Nigeria only days before attending a Commonwealth summit. Diplomatically, nothing could have been more embarrassing and Wilson was furious that the large MI6 station in Lagos had failed to predict the coup. He is supposed to have made efforts to restrict the agency's budget during subsequent economy drives.

Ironsi abolished the federal system of government which had prevailed since independence, replacing it with a single administration based in Lagos. Further rioting broke out, the most serious of which took place in the northern provinces where widespread killing of easterners, particularly from the Ibo tribe followed: the ringleaders of the coup were all Ibos, and the massacre was stimulated by revenge for the death of the northern leaders. In July, Ironsi was overthrown by the army chief of staff, Lieutenant-Colonel Gowon. The new government reverted to the federal constitution, but the massacre of Ibos continued unabated. Many thousands fled to the eastern provinces, while attempts to sort out the differences between regional administrations stalled.

By May 1967, some 30,000 lives had been lost in the north and the governor of the eastern region, General Ojukwu, came to the conclusion that the country's internal problems were irresolvable. On the 30th May Ojukwu declared the Independent Republic of Biafra in the eastern region under his control. Gowon dismissed Ojukwu and promised to crush the secession, prominent among his motives being Biafra's large oil deposits. The war proper began in July: for the first two months, the Biafran forces were in control of the entire eastern region and made significant advances towards the Mid-Western regional capital of Benin City, some 150 miles from Lagos. Gradually, Nigerian government units pushed them back into Biafra as arms and especially aircraft flowed in from Britain and the Soviet Union. The Biafrans opened up an air corridor from their largest airstrip at Uli, into which was ferried munitions and weapons from their international backers, who included France, South Africa and China.

As the former colonial power which had ceded independence smoothly to a unitary state, it was to be expected that the British would take Gowon's side in the war. However, there was scant pressure at first to force them out of a neutral posture. Soviet intervention was the first thing to change this view. The Kremlin judged that there was little chance of British and American support being rendered to the Biafrans, and hence Soviet backing for the Nigerian government would probably not produce the kind of proxy war which Soviet policy in the immediate post-Krushchev period sought to avoid. Exploiting the British prevarication over Nigerian arms requests could in the long term increase their political influence in the country, largely through spare parts dependency. Soviet military analysts predicted eventual victory for the Nigerians provided equipment supplies were maintained, and the Warsaw Pact states began sending arms in August 1967. The first shipments arrived while the government was on the defensive, and made a considerable difference in reversing the situation. The Nigerians were pleasantly surprised.

Power politics is driven as much by oil as by weapons, and Nigeria proved no exception. The presence of Shell/BP as the largest operator in both Biafra and the rest of Nigeria was also critical in the erosion of British neutrality (the British government then held a 49%

share in BP). The investment of these two companies totalled £250 million, with about three-fifths in Biafra. Ojukwu was concerned that the royalties due to the Nigerian government, about £7 million per annum, should go to Biafra, not only for the obvious financial benefits but also for the legitimacy which a demonstrable revenue-raising ability would confer on a Biafran government. As Nigeria's main oil terminal and only refinery (at Port Harcourt) were under Biafran control, Ojukwu was in a strong position. Shell/BP's main concern was to guarantee a continuous oil supply, which involved being as inoffensive to both sides as possible. They negotiated a deal with the Biafrans over royalties, ducking out of contractual obligations to the Nigerian government by claiming force majeure. The Nigerian government was furious and responded with a naval blockade of the Biafran coastline, followed by a succesful marine assault on the oil terminal at Bonny. The Biafrans accused British employees of complicity in its capture and arrested the regional manager, Stanley Gray, although the charge against him was never proven. The war broke out soon afterwards and oil supplies once again came under threat. With the Suez Canal closed after the Six Day War, Britain's oil needs were crucially dependent on the exceptionally pure Nigerian product.

Eager to find a quick solution to the crisis to restore the oil flow, and with one eye on the growth of Soviet influence on the Nigerians, Britain committed itself to the government side. Less important factors also contributed: some commentators stress the close personal relationship between Harold Wilson and the British High Commissioner in Nigeria, Sir David Hunt, a strong supporter of Gowon.

At the beginning of 1969, around the time of Walsworth-Bell's recruitment, Ojukwu's troops were confined to an L-shaped area centred at Owerri with one extremity at Onitsha on the Niger river to the north and the other on the Cross river to the east. This was the situation into which Walsworth-Bell was to be sent as an 'objective and impartial' observer. The team of observers to which he was attached was established by the Nigerian government to report on allegations of atrocities and maltreatment levelled at the Nigerian army. Composed of British, Canadian, Polish, Swedish and Algerian officers, it was supposed to be strictly neutral. However, as a British journalist covering the war discovered, 'their reports invariably acquitted the Nigerian army of serious breaches of the rules of war [and] some doubts were expressed in pro-Biafran quarters as to the impartiality of the Observer team.'[32] Moreover, Walsworth-Bell, who was deputy head of the British contingent, later claimed that at a meeting on 5 March 1969 with Maurice Foley and Ronald Burroughs, respectively Parliamentary Under-Secretary and Assistant Secretary in the Foreign Office, he was given an additional, undercover role of 'collecting information of military significance'. Additionally, he was instructed by Foley to advise the Nigerian Army on the quickest way to bring the war to an end. The next day, in the palatial surroundings of the Oriental Club dining room, he was briefed by the MI6 Nigerian desk officer Craig Smellie on the military information he was required to send back. To pass back this information, Foley told him to use a secret channel of communication. All messages were to be sent in double envelopes; one was to be addressed to a senior official in the Foreign Office, and inside this envelope would be placed his unofficial communications on a personal basis to Foley.

His mission started badly. No sooner had he arrived in Lagos, than he discovered that his intelligence contact at the High Commission, Major Shepherd, had left two months previously. On asking his successor whether he did the same work, he received a very unfriendly 'no'. This innocent question revealed his secret role and the news of it alarmed the High Commission staff. He had a couple of interviews with the Acting High Commissioner, who gave him a dressing-down; but he didn't take this very seriously, for as he wrote in explanation to Foley: 'For the good of the cause I took it like a lamb'. To satisfy protocol, according to Bell, he was given a further ticking-off by Foley personally in Nigeria and received a letter asking him to confine himself to his duties as an observer. However, he continued to send letters full of military intelligence back to Foley, who admitted he had received the letters from June onwards.

Major Walsworth-Bell also fed Brigadier Hassan Katsina, the Nigerian Chief of Staff, and Lt-Colonel Odulaye at Army Headquarters in Lagos with a stream of reports, comments and suggestions. The advice, given by word of mouth, amounted to a strategy and detailed tactics for ending the civil war; both the strategy and tactics offered were actually used to end the war in December of that year.

One of Bell's messages to Foley said that 'you will learn quite soon that the disposition of the three divisions is going to be altered', which Bell claimed was a direct result of advice given by him. In this letter, Bell told Foley that he had persuaded the Nigerian commanders to pull their 2nd Division back across the Niger from its bridgehead at Onitsha, disengage it, and retain it as a 'mass of manoeuvre' for 'a swift thrust into rebel territory at vital objectives'. In another memo to Foley, he said he had urged the Nigerians to take troops away from the eastern fronts and concentrate them for simultaneous thrusts from the north and south on Owerri and the vital airstrip at Uli in Biafra. Most of his advice was subsequently taken by the Nigerian Army.

At the beginning of May, Walsworth-Bell returned to London and went to see the Defence Intelligence Staff to brief them on the military situation. A couple of days later Walsworth-Bell met Foley at the

House of Commons to hand him two papers of comments and suggestions for the Nigerian armed forces. Foley asked him to send any future letters to his private address. He also gave Bell an introduction to the Nigerian High Commissioner in London, Brigadier Sam Ogundipe.

In the first class cabin of the VC – 10 back to Lagos on 18 May, Bell scrawled some notes in pencil. He was now concerned to find a more suitable cover for his work as military adviser to the Nigerian Army. As Bell outlined it to himself, 'there are three possibilities a) remain as an observer, b) join the Nigerian Army, c) take up a 'job' locally'. After carefully weighing the pros and cons, he decided he must find a local 'job'. Later in August, he approached Shell/BP in Nigeria for a job, but was turned down. Bell then applied to the Nigerian authorities and in a document supporting his application wrote, 'only one person in the UK knows about this'. That person, Bell claims, was Maurice Foley. At this point, under pressure from the Foreign Office, Walsworth-Bell was dismissed from his position as observer for 'misconduct'.

His first attempt to obtain unemployment benefit was unsuccessful but at the appeal, which he won, Rawden Temple QC commented while giving his verdict that

> At the local tribunal hearing it was plainly suggested that the claimant (Walsworth-Bell) had fabricated part of his evidence . . . I do not accept that the claimant either invented or imagines any part of his evidence[33]

Foley strongly denied to the press that he had given Walsworth-Bell a 'second and secret role' but admitted that he had received letters from him:

> He did write to me from time to time, just normal chit-chat from a friend. He would write about the country and the people and the climate. There was nothing unusual about this.[34]

But as the *Daily Telegraph* concluded 'None of Major Bell's evidence about this double role has been refuted by Mr. Foley or two other Foreign Office officials at any stage'.[35]

The Nigerian government forces, numerically superior and better equipped, should have defeated the Biafrans very much earlier – some military historians say eighteen months – than they eventually did. The reason lies in the dearth of aircraft pilots which afflicted both sides and which they solved by recruiting mercenaries. Ojukwu also called in Europeans (mainly French but also a few Britons) to train and lead Biafran commando units, and the government forces were reported to be receiving some assistance from hired advisers and military technicians. Some sources maintain that the Nigerians had taken a policy decision early in the war that they would not use mercenaries with their ground troops.

In July 1967, Major John Peters, a Briton who had succeeded the notorious 'Mad Mike' Hoare as a mercenary leader in the Congo, signed a contract with the Nigerians for the recruitment of pilots to fly DC-3s on bombing raids. Discarding his quiet life as a London estate agent, Peters was quite open about his 'list' of 600 men who were seeking mercenary employment, yet a British government spokesman said at the time that

> We'd like nothing better than to stop the recruiting but first we
> must identify the people who are involved in such operations. [36]

The author Frederick Forsyth who covered the war from the Biafran side as a BBC correspondent alleges that Peters

> was 'introduced' to his new patrons by sources not a thousand
> miles from our own government.

and moreover, the history of African mercenary wars shows that despite official statements, the British government has never made any effort to discourage mercenary recruitment when it suits its economic and strategic interests.

Airwork Services which the Biafrans on more than one occasion referred to as 'a semi-official British government agency' provided engineers and maintenance staff for the Nigerian air force. The British government denied the official connection.

The mercenary pilots on the government side numbered between a dozen and twenty and were restricted at first to American-built bombers. As the war progressed, it became clear that the Egyptians flying Soviet-supplied MiG 17 fighters were ineffective and some of the hired pilots were moved onto them. Their bomber role was the more important though and in this they badly let down their employers.

After the capture of the south-eastern town of Port Harcourt by government forces in May 1968, the Biafran's main airstrip for the rest of the war was at Uli. With the Nigerians in control of all land routes into Biafra, airlifts were the only source of supplies and the stretch of converted highway at Uli was the best equipped to deal with them and the best protected in terms of geography and air defence systems. Neither the small corps of Nigerian pilots nor the Egyptians were skilled enough to destroy the airstrip, and the latter refused to fly at night when it was in use (during the day, the outbuildings were camouflaged). Artillery attack was hampered by the Nigerian inability to get nearer than ten or fifteen miles from Uli and Gowon held back from an all-out attack in case of hitting a relief shuttle. International opinion was concerned at the plight of the Biafran civilians and Gowon was desperate not to jeopardise his fragile diplomatic support.

Only the mercenary bomber pilots could destroy Uli, and keep it from being rebuilt. This presented them with something of a problem. Paid monthly in Swiss bank accounts – as opposed to by results – their interests were not best served by destroying a target which would bring the war to an end. Some of the mercenary pilots had friends fighting on the opposite side and were reluctant to engage in operations which might prejudice their careers and safety. So

> bombing of the strip and general harassment – to allay the Nigerians' suspicions – were regarded by the Federal [government] pilots as fair game but more ruthless action which would have scared the relief and gun-running pilots off for good and closed Uli permanently was ruled out[37]

Uli became an important symbol of the Biafran resistance, holding out until the very end of the war. Ojukwu escaped from the airstrip to exile in The Ivory Coast only days before Nigerian government soldiers danced triumphantly over the same stretch of ground.

Southern Africa

At the tribunal hearing his claim for unemployment benefit following the Nigerian excursion, Ian Walsworth-Bell was asked how he became qualified for intelligence work. In reply, the major cited his 'work in Zambia'.

Formerly the British colony of Northern Rhodesia, Zambia's postwar political history mirrors to some extent that of Kenya in the struggle for independence. The first mass nationalist party was the African National Congress (ANC), formed in 1951 from political groupings in the quasi-trade union Federation of Welfare Societies (trade unions as such were banned) and led by the Methodist teacher Harry Nkumbula. Support for the ANC grew rapidly after the British government announced a federation plan for Northern and Southern Rhodesia and Nyasaland. The plan was constructed so as to concentrate regional power in more developed Southern Rhodesia: since this colony had by far the largest white settler population it was clearly devised with their interests in mind. Nkumbula and his ally Hastings Banda (now president of Malawi) campaigned vociferously but unsuccessfully against it, and the Central African Federation was formally created in September 1953 with an all-white government. The ANC's growth continued unabated until the beginning of 1955, when the authorities decided to crack down. Nkumbula and two other ANC leaders, Wittington Sikalumba and Kenneth Kaunda were arrested and charged with possession of prohibited literature. Sikalumba was acquitted but Kaunda and Nkumbula were sent to prison for two months with hard labour.

Nkumbula was badly affected by the experience and became dispirited with the battle against the Federation. On leaving jail he became friendly with Harry Franklin, a white settler politician who had served as Minister for Education and Social Services in the colonial government. To the dismay of his ANC colleagues, Nkumbula started to take political advice from Franklin, a person not known for his enlightened views on either racial discrimination or the federation issue. In 1956, Nkumbula suggested that the ANC should fight a forthcoming election in alliance with Franklin's multiracial Constitution Party, allied to David Stirling's Capricorn Africa Society. The 'Two Harrys' proposed the same scheme to their respective parties in a carefully planned manoeuvre, which was only thwarted by a sharp-witted ANC member who produced a copy of a memorandum distributed to Constitution Party members which outlined the alliance scheme. The white government had realised Nkumbula's potential usefulness by this stage, and intimated to him through Franklin that the ANC might be recognised if its more radical leaders could be shed.

These early machinations came to nothing. The Constitution Party collapsed and the ANC radicals stayed in place, refusing to entertain any form of compromise with the government.

Nkumbula had successfully antagonised large sections of the ANC: bringing Franklin to an ANC executive meeting, during which the settler politician had referred to 'barbarians', had done him no good at all, and he began to use more autocratic methods to preserve his position. In May 1957, he handed the CID at Ndola information against ANC officials regarding party financial affairs; and although he claimed he had done so to rid the party of dishonest officials, the CID's subsequent investigations in July roused much bitterness amongst both officials and the party's rank-and-file members in the copper belt. This supposed move against corruption was widely interpreted as an attempt to check his political opponents. The following year a group of disillusioned members, including Kaunda, split from the ANC to form the Zambian African National Congress. The ZANC soon took over the mantle of spearheading the campaign against Federation to which the government responded by outlawing the ZANC and interning its leaders. Announcing the ban in March 1959, Governor Benson claimed that plans had been hatched at the Pan-African Conference in Ghana (a newly independent state ruled by the radical Kwame Nkrumah) for armed rebellion in Zambia. Although both ZANC and Nkumbula's ANC were present, Nkumbula had rejected the plan and returned to Zambia early, said Benson.

Nkumbula's premature departure may in fact have been prompted by allegations made to Nkrumah by Nkumbula's erstwhile friend Hastings Banda. Quoting a source close to the governor, Banda told him that Nkumbula had secretly accepted federation. Certainly the Northern Rhodesian government did not think at this time that Nkumbula was opposed to it: they gave him discreet electoral assistance in the form of hampering opposition parties (particularly the ZANC) and helping with arrangements for obtaining the requisite number of 'Chief's Certificates' – endorsements needed from the tribal leaders.

While this form of support was valuable, Nkumbula was unable to solve the problem of disintegration which had dogged the ANC since the ZANC split. The ANC divided again, and the government again bestowed legality on the Nkumbula faction; but even they began to realise that he was finished.

The moderate trade unionist Lawrence Katilungu was picked out as a successor to Nkumbula, on the strength of his work in curbing union militancy in the all-important copper belt which then as now provided the basis for the country's export economy. Yet Katilungu was suspect in the eyes of many nationalists because of his involvement with the Capricorn Africa Society, and the authorities compounded it by appointing him to the Monkton Commission examining Federation in the hope of giving him a higher political profile.

The ZANC, whose leaders trickled out of prison during 1960, transformed itself into the United National Independence Party (UNIP). The colonial government resorted to its usual harassment tactics; banning the party, arresting and fining or imprisoning UNIP activists. This strategy was not properly implemented because of the opposition of a senior Provincial Commissioner in the copper belt who did not think that UNIP could be effectively suppressed. He also believed that it would foster a false hope in the white community that African nationalism could be contained indefinitely by government controls. The government argued that the plan gave time for Katilungu, who had withdrawn from the Monkton Commission, to return to the copper belt and re-establish himself in the artificially created political vacuum. Katilungu eventually took over the ANC in 1961, replacing the faded Nkumbula, but the organisation was almost completely moribund. They even recruited the right-wing Tory MP Sir Frederick Bennett as a political adviser (he performed a similar function for the KADU) but the British government was not impressed. Colonial Secretary Iain Macleod supervised the shift of government favour from ANC to UNIP, whose leader Kenneth Kaunda met Macleod shortly before the 1962 election. At the meeting it became clear that the British government was preparing for independence. The Ariel Foundation and the CIA-funded African-American Institute moved to set up educational and training schemes, some of them jointly sponsored.

UNIP won the election, which was held in October, and formed Zambia's first black government with qualified support from the ANC. Its first priorities were to secure independence and the dissolution of the Central African Federation, and in turn control of the copper revenues which were divided up between the mining companies and the British government. All these objectives were achieved by the end of 1964, with the issue of mineral rights coming last. The British South Africa Company, a relic from the pre-1920 era when control of Zambia was contracted out by royal charter to Cecil Rhodes, collected royalties for all minerals extracted in the territory. The company poured money into the ANC in its anxiety to retain this dubious right after independence, but to no avail.

After independence, Anglo-Zambian relations did not follow the cosy course of Anglo-Kenyan relations. The main reason was the problem of Zambia's southern neighbour, Rhodesia.

The Rhodesian government first took up an opportunity to exploit tribal and regional differences in Zambia during 1961. The traditional rulers of Barotseland, one of Zambia's largest provinces, had sought independence from the rest of the country but had been rejected by the colonial authorities. The Rhodesians then offered to arrange finance for a secessionist movement, using its influence with the Katangese leader Moise Tshombe* to get him to put up the money. This would be forthcoming if the Barotse rulers agreed to a new federation of Southern Rhodesia, the Zambian copper belt, Katanga and Barotseland. The Barotse ruler, Mwanawina, rejected the offer. Rhodesian premier Roy Welensky raised the same plan with Commonwealth Secretary Duncan Sandys. He told Sandys that he would accept the departure of Nyasaland and the eastern part of Northern Rhodesia from the Central African Federation in return for acceptance of the scheme put before the Barotse rulers. Sandys apparently took the plan seriously on his own initiative without discussing it with local colonial officials: no mention of it is made in the papers of Rowland Hudson, HMG's representative in Barotseland.

The Rhodesian-backed Barotse secessionist movement failed miserably in the 1962 election and the plan was dropped as suddenly as it was conceived. Opposition from the colonial administration proved the decisive factor: it was able to point out that central government in Northern Rhodesia (Zambia) had given £250,000 to Barotseland. This seems to be one occasion on which the Colonial and Commonwealth Offices were in disagreement, although Welensky may have been deceived by Sandys.

Rhodesia was unique among British colonies in Africa because of the size of its white settler population. Post-war immigrants, attracted

* The Katanga province of Zaire (also known as Shaba) lies to the north-west of Zambia. Part of the copper belt spreads into Katanga and there are large deposits of other minerals. Katangese leaders have made repeated efforts to secede from Zaire since independence from Belgium.

with promises of higher wages and superior status, had swelled the ranks of the privileged in the country; it was the only colony which could claim to have a white working class. As the colonial snobs used to say: 'Kenya is the officers' mess and Rhodesia is the sergeants' mess'. Its economy was built around the laws of separate development, which had ensured that Africans were denied the chance of competing with whites in almost every sector of the economy. In the early 1960s, the Rhodesian government made several attempts to change this institutional structure by repealing some of the more racist laws: like the British, they were anxious that the country should start to encourage an African elite who would be able to play some part in the country's development. These attempts were rejected by the white workers who voted for the anti-British, white supremacist Rhodesian Front, putting it into office after the December 1962 elections.

Once in power, the Rhodesian Front government rejected British efforts to arrange an independence settlement. They felt that people like Welensky had been tricked over Federation and wanted to throw off the last vestiges of control from London. They no longer trusted a government that had suddenly switched from backing a white-controlled Federation to demanding African majority rule within five years. Slowly they weeded out pro-British officials in the army and civil service. Talk of UDI – a Unilateral Declaration of Independence – among prominent Rhodesian officials became commonplace. Prime Minister Winston Field resisted pressure to make the break with Britain until he was ousted in a palace coup in April 1964 by his deputy Ian Smith. Roy Welensky attempted to rally moderate white opinion against Smith's hard line on independence and ruthless suppression of black nationalists, but his efforts were undermined by a by-election defeat at the hands of the Rhodesian Front. Smith called a general election in May 1965, and won all fifty white seats.

Having secured the support of the European population, Smith moved quickly to UDI in November 1965. White opposition was small and faction-ridden; 3,000 of them were on file at Special Branch headquarters in Salisbury and their leaders were subject to close surveillance. It never presented Smith with any serious political challenge, which was what the British government really wanted.

Despite pleas from Zambia, the British Labour government refused to send in troops to dislodge Smith. Harold Wilson, at least publicly, believed that a short burst of sanctions would erode the stability of the UDI government and bring Smith to the negotiating table. The policy was thought to be optimal in terms of Labour's prospects for the imminent 1966 elections.

Except for the drafting of a few legal orders, no contingency plans had been produced for the implementation of sanctions, although the prospect of UDI had been apparent for several years. One reason, according to a former Foreign Office official, was 'the idea prevalent in the summer of 1965 that, if the British government were too obviously working on what would happen should Mr Ian Smith unilaterally declare independence, this might incite him to do so.'[38] Clearly, the government had little faith in its own ability to devise plans in secret. MI6 took on board large numbers of contract employees for intelligence work on sanctions, while seeking political intelligence on Rhodesian Front attitudes to British diplomatic proposals. This was vital in view of the danger in which Britain's low-key reaction was putting its relations with African Commonwealth states. Chapman Pincher has argued that if Wilson had received better political intelligence he would never have made a speech claiming that sanctions would break the Rhodesian economy 'within weeks rather than months'.[39] It does not appear, however, despite such pronouncements, that it was ever the British government's intention to seriously destabilise the regime. Wilson was searching for a form of pressure which would force Smith to make concessions.

MI6's ability to collect political intelligence was hampered by the type of contacts its embassy-based staff were making. They despised the Rhodesian Fronters and only invited the less racist British-leaning opposition on to their cocktail circuit in any numbers. On one occasion, an MI6 man was closeted after dinner with several Rhodesian Front politicians; the ladies, in true British fashion, had retired to another room. One of the Rhodesians started a blistering attack on the Queen, the Wilson government and all things British. The MI6 man, an ex-Guards officer, refused to be drawn into an argument – which would have produced some intelligence – but left the room, saying testily: 'I'll not listen to any more of this. I'm going to join the ladies.'

From their liberal contacts, MI6 believed that the Smith regime could be toppled from within and this optimistic assessment was transmitted to London. For the first six months of 1966, though, there was little hard information on the Rhodesian government itself. To overcome this weakness, MI6 sent a number of agents into Rhodesia posing as visitors. One of these was Tory MP Henry Kerby. His mission was to assess the balance of forces in Smith's cabinet after the talks between the Rhodesian leader and Harold Wilson on HMS Tiger during December 1966. In May 1967, Kerby made another private visit arranged for him through Angus Graham, the Duke of Montrose and Smith's external affairs minister. With such well-placed connections, he was able to conduct his business unobserved. As he wrote later in his report: 'In a town the size of Brighton the local reporters,

TV, etc. were unaware of my presence'. Kerby successfully discovered the strength of the opposition to the Tiger proposals and how they were turned down. After a stormy meeting lasting all day, during which Smith 'was not even allowed to go home to have a shower', the cabinet rejected the proposals, and Kerby believed that any future agreement would also be vetoed by the cabinet.[40] Another of MI6's visitors was a White Russian with business connections in the area who provided similar information for an earlier period.

The second element of MI6's operation was monitoring the British government's trade blockade. At best this could only ever be half effective because the British had agreed not to blockade the Mozambiquan port of Lourenco Marques because the South Africans used it to land some of their oil supplies. Two committees were set up by central government to deal with the imposition of sanctions. At the top was a small steering committee, nominally headed by the Commonwealth Secretary, but in practice the Permanent Under-Secretary took the chair. This committee included all the PUSs from the departments concerned and, when necessary, a representative from MI6. It supervised general policy and made recommendations. Under it was a much larger committee chaired by the Minister of State at the Commonwealth Relations Office which covered day-to-day business. This in turn spawned another committee with the dual function of supervising aid to Zambia and the construction of a radio relay station in Botswana. Zambia was hardest hit by sanctions: Kaunda was comparatively scrupulous in observance of them, which forced the direction of Zambian trade and the structure of its transport system to be drastically altered.

The Botswanan relay station was ostensibly used to beam BBC broadcasts into Rhodesia. Set up in the dusty border town of Francistown, it covered sixty acres and was guarded by British troops. The station was not actually run by the BBC but by the Diplomatic Wireless Service, which operates and maintains communications equipment for British overseas missions. An experienced wartime intelligence officer who specialised in 'black' propaganda was sent out as an adviser at the station. It was also used as a listening post and linked up to GCHQ in Cheltenham. Later on, the Botswanan police supplied the guard, which was paid for by the British government.

Rhodesia's oil lifeline ran through Portuguese-controlled Mozambique. The British closed this off by putting a frigate at the mouth of the country's main oil port of Beira. The effect was not substantial. The Beira pipeline was indeed closed but oil continued to arrive in Rhodesia through Lourenco Marques and from South Africa. To check shipping in Beira, MI6 put first one, and then several people to work, watching the port through a small network of informers. The activities of these agents were the cause of considerable diplomatic friction as they caused a sharp drop in trade to Mozambique. Agents of the Portugese intelligence service, PIDE, slashed their car tyres and generally made life difficult. On the diplomatic front, Portugal made frequent complaints about them.

MI6 headquarters for the Rhodesia operation was set up in Blantyre, Malawi and another office established in Lusaka, the Zambian capital. This latter was also used to increase intelligence-gathering on the Zambian government, which the British suspected of planning to start the break-up of the Commonwealth. This probably came after Kaunda's expulsion of the British advisers who headed the Zambian intelligence apparatus since experienced African officers were lacking. Kaunda discovered that some of them were supplying information to the Rhodesians and South Africans. As he was unable to identify with certainty which were responsible, he quietly issued orders that they should all be deported together at very short notice. One of them later complained that he did not even have time to make copies of any of his material, and described Kaunda's move as a 'masterful operation'. Over the next few years a series of British subjects were arrested and proven to have been spying for Rhodesia. Anthony Flavell, a Briton working for the Rhodesian Special Branch was caught while crossing from Rhodesia into Zambia in April 1969. He said that

> he had been sent to Zambia to join the intelligence network set up five years ago with the objectives of causing political and economic chaos in Zambia

and pointed out that

> his passport was so swiftly renewed by the British mission in Salisbury that he concluded that the mission must have been given reasons for the hurry and that, therefore, Britain must be secretly helping Rhodesia against Zambia.[41]

After UDI, the embassy staff in Salisbury was reduced to a 'Residual Mission', which MI6 used for work on the ground. Among the agents recruited by intelligence officers on this staff was a prominent British journalist who provided information until he was 'PIed' – declared a prohibited immigrant. This journalist tells a story which illustrates the confusion reigning at the time. He was told to meet his first contact in the bar at the exclusive all-white Meikles Hotel in Salisbury. Normally, this would have been a good place for a discreet meeting over a drink. Unfortunately his contact was black.

It was, as one expatriate security man in a neighbouring country remembered, 'open season'. To stop this, Ian Smith made several waves of expulsions culminating in a major swoop against business executives sympathetic to Britain in 1967. Meanwhile, on top of recruiting agents, there was the low-level 'legalised spying'. A journalist would be invited to the British Mission to talk to an old contact. On arrival the contact asked 'would you mind if a new member of my staff sat in on this', at which point an MI6 officer appeared to join them.

The absolute lack of preparation is perhaps best shown by the comical Beit Bridge episode in 1966. Working on a tip-off from a well-placed businessman, two Pretoria embassy officials – William Harper and Neville Lomas – motored up to Beit Bridge, the span joining Rhodesia and South Africa, to look for oil wagons. The South African press carried reports of their excursion and they were carefully watched by South African security officials in a nearby car. In fact much of the oil from South Africa travelled along an obscure railway line which skirted Beit Bridge and passed through Mozambique.

The first major spying incident passed almost unnoticed in the British press. In early 1966 the Ministry of Information in Salisbury issued a terse statement saying that Neville French, a First Secretary in the British Mission who had already left Rhodesia 'had abused his position by taking part in espionage directed at undermining Rhodesia in economic and security matters'. French had recruited a civil servant, William Black, who supplied classified information. The Rhodesians watched him for a while and then arrested him. Black confessed and agreed to give the names of others involved in espionage in exchange for immunity from prosecution. Neville French was told to get out of the country in polite diplomatic language. The real reasons for his departure were lost in the row over Rhodesian diplomatic representation in London.

Stanley Fingland, the acting Deputy High Commissioner, was also expelled. The Rhodesian Special Branch cottoned on to him when they found him talking to Rhodesian contacts while out walking his dog. Another First Secretary, Anthony Freemantle, was expelled in the spring of 1969.

Further embarrassment followed when a junior mission official, Royden Childs, was forced to resign membership of Salisbury's city sports club after allegations of spying on members. Peter Carter, head of the mission and an ex-Metropolitan Police officer, told the press that 'the whole story is disagreeable and we would rather forget about the whole thing'. Not exactly an emphatic denial.

The embassy effort was backed by secret government funds from the UK and the use of unwitting individuals to back British government policy. In January 1966, two months after UDI, Peter Benenson, the president of Amnesty International, asked Polly Toynbee to go to Nigeria and Rhodesia to help political prisoners. When Toynbee arrived in Rhodesia, she found the Salisbury office in chaos. She had not been properly briefed and had no idea where to begin. As she later told the *Sunday Telegraph*:

> We looked at the lists of people detained or restricted, wrote to their families and sent them money. I suspect we got conned in every direction – we just didn't have the facilities for checking up on the information given.
>
> Also we were supposed to be arranging legal aid for prisoners, but we kept getting orders from London to drop particular cases – for no reason.

In the six weeks before she was expelled she reckons she must have handed out two to three thousand pounds. With apparently limitless amounts of money available she became suspicious that it was government money and challenged Benenson about it.

> At first he told me not to ask such questions. But then he admitted the money was coming from the government, and he told me it had been hard to get.

As the last Amnesty worker to leave Salisbury she was handed a pile of letters, left abandoned in a safe. She only later discovered what they were. Most were addressed to Robert Swann, the Amnesty general secretary who had been working in Rhodesia. The letters, written from what was Benenson's address in north London, were in an easily understandable code. The references to 'Harry' are to the British government, as the following extract shows:

> Feb. 2
>
> Harry has developed a sudden enthusiasm for litigation. What with North Hull ... Harry wants a fair buzz of legal activity. Harry's financial problems apparently have been solved, and he's in a generous mood.[42]

The Labour government had just won a crucial by-election and seemed anxious to go on the offensive in Rhodesia. The need for litigation was a result of its desire to mount a conclusive test of the regime's illegality through the Rhodesian courts.

Some assistance in monitoring sanctions was forthcoming from the Americans, who wanted to maintain the trading advantages which some American-owned firms had acquired through exploiting the vacuum in the market caused by the absence of Rhodesian products. As the UDI government gradually devised methods of evading sanctions, the American government gradually came under pressure to take action, particularly from tobacco consortia who had done well in the intervening period. The CIA set about working out how sanctions were being broken. Two of its most effective agents were Roger Nicholson, a financial journalist working for the *Rhodesian Herald*, and Trevor Gallaher, a lawyer and member of the Rhodesian Front executive. The exposure of Gallaher and discovery of the theft of a number of classified documents from party headquarters forced Smith to reverse the policy of tolerating CIA activities in the interests of good relations with Washington. Nicholson and Gallaher were arrested by the Rhodesian Special Branch in 1969 and charged under the Official Secrets Act. At his trial, Nicholson said he thought that he had acted in Rhodesia's best interests because he believed that the information he had provided would help correct false impressions that an 'unnamed foreign power (America) was receiving from other quarters (Britain)'. Both were paid by the CIA using Chase Manhattan bank accounts in New York. Information supplied by Gallaher, including bills of lading, was said to have resulted in the prosecution of the British firm, Platt Brothers, for sanctions violation.

At the time of the trial, the Rhodesians made strenuous efforts to use the spies as a bargaining counter with the Americans. The Rhodesians hoped to stop the planned closure of the American consulate in Salisbury in exchange for their release. The Americans agreed but were forced to renege on the deal by the British, who leaked the details surrounding the arrest of Gallaher and Nicholson, thus forcing the consulate to close. Before it did the unfortunate Irl Smith, a 'political officer' at the consulate and the CIA chief of station, found himself getting a lot of attention as the spies' contact man: 'I haven't read the story', he said when asked for a comment by a South African journalist. 'I wouldn't like to comment in detail until I have read it'. Part of Smith's job was liaising with the head of Rhodesian security and he was also seen picking up messages from Nicholson at a dead-letter drop in a Salisbury post office.

Britain supplied some of the results of its intelligence operation to the UN committee on sanctions. The main object was to cause diplomatic embarrassment to countries which could be shown to be sending goods to Rhodesia, and the main targets were France and the Soviet Union. A report from Henry Kerby showed that eleven countries broke sanctions during 1967 and that the main offender was Israel.

All of which served to divert attention away from the activities of British firms. In the scandal now known as 'Oilgate', it transpired that Shell and British Petroleum were systematically organising illegal oil supplies to Rhodesia with the assistance of Whitehall civil servants in the Ministry of Power. Another British firm, Airwork Services, was contracted to do maintenance work for the Rhodesian air force, itself staffed by some 400 Britons. Neil Forster, the managing director of Airwork's parent company, British and Commonwealth Shipping, denied at the end of 1979 any formal trading links with the Rhodesian subsidiary, but conceded the existence of 'continuing social contacts'. These 'social contacts' included informing British and commonwealth managers in Rhodesia that if they wanted any merchandise advertised

The man who 'bubbled int in Rhodesia'?

in the company's house magazine they should contact a Mr. Gower at the Salisbury office of Cayzer, Irvine (Central Africa), one of B&C's subsidiaries. This guidance was certainly given while sanctions were still in force.

Moreover, the British government did little to stop mercenary recruitment for the Rhodesian army, which inceased dramatically after the withdrawal of 3,000 South African troops from inside Rhodesia. Advertisements appeared in the popular press and in local papers circulated near army bases with headlines such as 'Join Ian's army: it's a great life' and 'Service careers in the Sun'. Richard Stannard, sometime head of army propaganda operations in Northern Ireland, left to take charge of Rhodesian propaganda. The recruiters even took on members of the paramilitary Ulster Defence Association, some of them convicted of firearms and explosives offences. Following the bad publicity caused by this, the government was forced to take some action against mercenary organisers. The anti-communist activist Roy Dovaston was stopped in the middle of a recruiting drive for Rhodesia and Angola and charged with sanctions offences in April 1977. The case fell on a technicality, and Dovaston moved to South Africa the following year. One successful prosecution was that of Gordon Ward, a former RAF corporal, in August 1978. Ward received a two-year conditional discharge after admitting that he wrote about 300 letters to ex-servicemen giving information on how to apply for posts in the Rhodesian armed forces. The addressees' names were obtained from a card-index, compiled by an organisation known as the British Mercenary Force, of which he was in effective charge.[43]

The sanctions net failed on every level. Successive British governments lacked the means to apply full and effective pressure on the UDI government: the massive British financial stakes in South Africa and the Portuguese colonies meant that they were unable to force a withdrawal of support from Smith by these countries. Equally, they lacked the will to bring sanctions violators to court, not least their own corrupt officials. As the years passed, such determination as existed withered away. By the end of the 1960s, the Sanctions Committee in London was rarely convened. The Beira patrol made its last interception in 1972 and turned its attention to monitoring FRELIMO signals in the north of Mozambique. Essentially, long-term British commercial interests were best served by white supremacy, which was only overturned after a decade of bitter guerilla war. According to Richard Crossman,[44] Wilson never considered a propaganda offensive or any other form of covert action against Smith and later governments appear to have followed the precedent. Some of the MI6 mission staff did engage in small-scale rumour-mongering, notably the story that Smith was a moderate in his own cabinet.

Wilson himself has now admitted that it was never the British government's intention to bring the Smith government down. He may have realised that it would have been comparatively difficult due to the proximity of South Africa, yet the sanctions method chosen had too many serious imperfections to ever produce the desired effect. Smith, for his part, correctly judged British strategy at almost every stage.

Prosecutions of sanctions violators were hampered by possible compromise of the intelligence sources which would have had to provide the main evidence. Between 1965 and 1972 there were seventeen convictions of which only two involved major transactions. In the words of one journalist who covered UDI:

> British intelligence was directed to trying to find out how screwdrivers and kippers were getting through. They couldn't do anything about it.[45]

Furthermore, MI6 refused to co-operate with Zambian intelligence after the expulsion of British security advisers and other Anglo-Zambian disputes (Zambian support for Biafra and, in 1971, the dismissal of all other British military advisers). With limited resources, Zambia's own investigations remained small and ineffective; goods on false bills of lading passed through Zambia to Malawi and thence to Rhodesia. Finally as the expulsion rate of officers under diplomatic cover shows, MI6 found it difficult running operations in a country where British intelligence had always relied on the local Special Branch for information.

By contrast, Rhodesian intelligence on British government intentions towards its errant colony was more than adequate. The main network was run by John Fairer-Smith, a sergeant in the Rhodesian Special Branch. He arrived in Britain in 1960 to organise infiltration of British-based opposition groups and sympathetic bodies such as Amnesty International, using a firm named Thermal Developments as cover. Between then and 1965 he attended an MI6 course on which one of the speakers was Malaya veteran Evan Davies. After UDI he turned his attention to the government and one of his agents, Norman Blackburn, managed to recruit Helen Keenan, a typist in the Cabinet Office who supplied Cabinet documents. MI5, who up until this point had tolerated Fairer-Smith's activities, decided he had gone too far and instructed the Special Branch to arrest Blackburn. In Parliament, Fairer-Smith was named as Blackburn's controller. Fairer-Smith denied the allegation. Despite pressure from MPs, nothing was done about Fairer-Smith, and he remained in Britain to set up the Argen group of security firms.

It must be assumed that Fairer-Smith has some kind of working relationship with British intelligence. Such arrangements do exist: MI5 and the Special Branch worked with Rhodesian intelligence on surveillance of Zimbabwean nationalists, particularly during the critical Lancaster House conference where Rhodesians helped with the translation of African dialects used in intercepted conversations. Two senior Rhodesian intelligence officers, Ken Flowers and Derek Robinson made frequent visits to Britain throughout UDI, which they announced to British embassy staff in Pretoria beforehand, and received escorts through customs and immigration formalities. Co-operation springs from mutual interests. Relations between British intelligence and their Zimbabwean counterparts now depend on the policies of the black government and any changes it may force upon the white-dominated intelligence system.

White-ruled Rhodesia's strongest and most reliable ally was always South Africa, whose support for Rhodesian espionage in Britain was maintained throughout UDI. The South African targets are similar to the Rhodesian: dissident emigre organisations and human rights groups. South African agents successfully penetrated the International Defence and Aid Fund run by Canon John Collins and also Christian Action, who were tipped off by the government in 1969. On the whole the South Africans were given a free run in Britain until the mid-1970s when relations underwent a severe deterioration.

This is variously attributed to the BOSS*-inspired smear campaign against Liberal politicians or a series of burglaries of premises belonging to black nationalists and anti-apartheid groups. In reaction guidelines were drawn up to restrict collaboration between British intelligence and BOSS. Peter Deeley of the *Observer* described how this was to work in practice:

> It seems that British security will not pass on any information about South Africans living in Britain ... except where the individual is suspected of criminal – as opposed to political – acts.

A further intention was to end 'South Africa's use of British freelance operatives' so that 'if the South Africans want to carry out a covert operation in Britain, they must bring their own men'.[46] There was no suggestion that they would be prevented from carrying out such operations.

The awkward state of Anglo-South African relations arises from a desire to maintain good relations with black-ruled Africa and a genuine widespread abhorrence of apartheid in Britain counterbalanced by commercial and defence interests. On the intelligence level, there is the exchange of 'hammer and sickle' material – information on communist and Soviet activities – to take into account. There seems little

* Bureau of State Security, the South African intelligence service. Later renamed Department of National Security, and now the National Intelligence Service.

W.O. Joseph Klue (Boss Brigadier in 1980s) and ANC office burglaries.

doubt that intelligence co-operation has been reduced since the time when MI5 could loan staff to the diamond-mining house De Beer Consolidated to assist with security measures against smuggling. There have been reports that, in collaboration with Swedish intelligence, MI6 staged a burglary of the South African embassy in Stockholm.

In 1977, Britain also ceased the flow of NATO information to South Africa, and in retaliation the South African government halted the return traffic, most of which derived from the Silvermine monitoring complex near the Cape of Good Hope. Silvermine claims that its project ADVOCAAT is able to provide continuous data on air and naval movements within a 3,000 mile radius. For the South Africans, the system has considerable potential if NATO countries are prepared to use the information: originally, the centre was linked to the US naval station in Puerto Rico, the Royal Navy in Whitehall and the French and Argentinian defence departments. (Its role, if any, during the South Atlantic conflict is as yet unknown.)

Until 1976, the Royal Navy maintained staff at the South African naval base at Simonstown, but simultaneous to their withdrawal, the British were privately leading the lobby for full incorporation of Silvermine into NATO's defence communications network. Signals specialists from GCHQ assisted in the installation of electronic and computer equipment at Silvermine, and the United Kingdom was represented at the official opening of the complex in the person of Vice-Admiral John Treacher (now chairman of Playboy's UK operation). The British position was opposed by Norway, which was unhappy at the apparent legitimacy which would be afforded to the South African regime by the link-up. Ultimately the Norwegian view prevailed and it was decided that Britain and other nations who wished (US, France, West Germany) could have their own links outside the NATO framework. It was this that the British severed in 1977, but in the last two years both they and the Americans, who also withdrew, have started to reconsider both Silvermine and the naval facilities at Simonstown. Further developments as far as Silvermine is concerned may depend as much on the equipment there as the prevailing military doctrines in Whitehall and the Pentagon. A former NSA employee, Winslow Peck, reported in *Counterspy*[47] that the claims made for Silvermine by the South Africans may be fraudulent, and designed to curry favour with the West.

The differences between British and South African intelligence, and indeed between the latter and the Americans (who take a less restrictive attitude) have not stood in the way of the pursuit of common economic and security interests. Their intervention in the Angolan civil war is a perfect illustration.

The largest and richest of Portugal's African colonies, Angola boasted mineral reserves of copper, manganese, diamonds and iron ore plus a large coffee crop and some oil deposits. British capital was heavily invested in the diamond-mining consortium DIAMANG and the British firm Tanganyika Concessions owned and operated the Benguela railway which bisects the country from west to east, running into Zaire with branches to Zambia. As elsewhere in Africa, nationalist consciousness rose during the 1950s, and the first nationalist party, the Movimento Popular de Libertacao de Angola (MPLA) came into being in 1956. Clandestinely organised, it managed to galvanise an uprising against the colonial government in February 1961, which was promptly crushed. The movement reorganised in exile under the leadership of Agostinho Neto, a poet turned politician said by Western commentators to lack charisma, a quality considered useful for running an independent state. The MPLA's natural constituency was in the eastern and central area of the country and it also drew support from dissident Portuguese. The main nationalist movement in the north of the country was the Union of the Peoples of Angola (UPA) whose leader, Manuel Necaca, died a few months after its inception in 1957. His position was assumed by Jose Guilmore, a tall dour figure never seen without a pair of dark glasses. A month after the abortive uprising of February 1961, the UPA organised another, unsuccessful rebellion among coffee plantation workers.

Of these two groups, the Americans favoured the UPA while the Soviets lent their support to the MPLA. It is not clear which acquired international backing first: Guilmore is supposed to have been on the CIA payroll from 1959, but it is difficult to trace the origins of Soviet interest in the MPLA.

After the failure of the March rebellion, Guilmore, who had changed his name to Holden Roberto, moved to Zaire whose President Mobutu was his brother-in-law. There he carved out a lucrative career in real estate. The UPA absorbed some of the smaller nationalist groups who had also fled to Zaire and renamed itself the Frente Nacional de Libertacao de Angola (FNLA) and proclaimed an Angolan government-in-exile. A third nationalist movement, the Uniao para a Independencia Total de Angola (UNITA) emerged following the resignation of Jonas Savimbi, the exile government's foreign minister. A large, bearded man with no recognised shortage of charisma, his power base was among the southern Ovimbundu people who frequently gathered at large rallies addressed by him. Savimbi's political career began in Switzerland, where he studied law, with the formation of a student organisation affiliated to the CIA-funded International Student Conference (ISC). At an ISC conference in Kampala in 1961, he had several long discussions with the Kenyan politician Tom

Mboya, who persuaded him to join the UPA.

Savimbi left the government-in-exile in mid-1964, but it was almost two years before he announced the formation of UNITA. In the intervening period, according to one American source, Savimbi was recruited by British intelligence.[48] Later on, UNITA established links with the Portuguese military to co-operate in the neutralisation of the MPLA. The movement remained, however, almost completely unknown until the overthrow of the Caetano dictatorship in Portugal in 1974.

The army took power under General Spinola, and after initial doubts decided on a rapid transfer to majority rule. In January 1975, the MPLA, FNLA and UNITA signed an agreement establishing a tripartite transitional government, confirming, perhaps, the CIA view that the ideological differences between the nationalist parties were not substantial. Nevertheless, the MPLA, the largest and best -organised of the three, threatened to dominate this and subsequent post-independence governments. The CIA applied at this point to the Forty Committee* for the release of $300,000 political aid for the FNLA, which was authorised, and $100,000 for UNITA, which was not: the committee was somewhat wary of the movement's residual Maoist tendencies. The FNLA grew in strength over the next three months, until it tried to oust the MPLA from the government in April. They failed and were expelled from the capital. The Soviets extended their aid to include military equipment and several hundred Cuban advisers arrived in the country. From this stage onwards foreign intervention escalated a fairly limited conflict into a full-scale war. The CIA prepared another covert aid paper, this time with a military component and costed at $6 million. Following the American withdrawal from Vietnam, a quick victory was thought essential on political grounds, as a result of which the programme was revised up to $14 million. Aid to UNITA, who were then engaged in clandestine discussions with South Africa, was included in the package, which was passed by the Forty Committee.

In July, the FNLA tried again to dislodge the MPLA through an assault on Luanda, which was repulsed. On the southern front the MPLA were in control of most of the coastal zone but were unable to take Huambo (Nova Lisboa), headquarters of the FNLA/UNITA Democratic Popular Government. Savimbi concluded an agreement with the South Africans, who with American encouragement and supplies sent in regular troops in a force known as the 'Zulu Column'. The column advanced up the coast, taking Lobito and Benguela before meeting stiff resistance at Novo Redondo. A month before the date

* A small, top-secret group chaired by Secretary of State Henry Kissinger, whose approval was required to clear major US covert action programmes.

set by the Portuguese for independence, the MPLA were bottled up in a narrow strip of territory stretching eastwards from Luanda. The MPLA then called in Cuban troops.

Britain became involved in the war around this time because American support was meeting with opposition from Congress. On top of the $14 million already earmarked, a further $18 million was authorised during 1975, but there was strong suspicion that the CIA had resorted to a favourite accounting trick of under-valuing the materials sent, so that the true figure may have been many times larger than that put before and accepted by Congress. An accountant seconded from the General Accounting Office, a separate government agency, believed that the figure for the value of arms transfers should have been at least doubled. There was a limit, though, to Congress' tolerance of arithmetical sleights, and Kissinger was forced to turn to Europe.

Washington made at least two formal approaches to the Foreign Office via the CIA's London station. They desperately wanted Britain to send rockets, which from America would have required the acquiescence of Congress. Kissinger's colleagues on the Forty Committee were also anxious to get America's Western allies more involved in Angola. With regard to the missiles, the British government delivered a firm 'No'. Anything so easily traceable would have undermined their public position of concerned neutrality; they had already made attempts to resurrect the coalition government and wished to retain the option of acting as a mediator. Behind this studied facade, however, they had for some years been giving political and financial support to UNITA.

Before the war, Savimbi had visited the British embassy in Lusaka and received a promise of support. He also came to London, where he met the then Parliamentary Under-Secretary at the Foreign Office, Joan Lester. When fighting broke out, he cashed in on the promises. Covert aid was arranged by an MI6 officer on the Lusaka embassy staff, who played a vital role in ensuring that UNITA was quickly supplied. The most useful contribution was a complete communications system from Racal Communications. This comprised seven radio stations which were set up at strategic points across the sprawling UNITA area. They were assembled by Ron Goodey, a technician on loan from Racal's Zambian subsidiary. The crates of equipment arrived at Lusaka airport addressed to UNIP, the Zambian government party, but went straight into a plane bound for Angola. British intelligence was able to arrange medical treatment for wounded UNITA officers in private London clinics.

The British also replenished the Zambian army inventories, from which UNITA obtained small arms and ammunition. The Zambian government was an open supporter of UNITA, not least because it was generally in control of the Benguela railway. After the closure of the Rhodesian border in 1973 and before the opening of the Tanzam rail link to Dar-es-Salaam, the Benguela line was the only practicable means of transporting Zambian copper out of the country.

Shipping the aid into Angola required a regular air freight service. This was provided by Pearlair, which flew a daily shuttle to Huambo with an ageing Viscount aircraft. This strange airline started life in the British colony of Hong Kong in 1972, under the auspices of a British solicitor, Martin Fairburn, and an American pilot named Kendall Everett. To the best of Fairburn's knowledge, 'the company never got off the ground, never did any business [and] never managed to take delivery of an aeroplane'. At the beginning of the war, the company's registration was shifted to the West Indian island of Grenada, where it changed its name to Pearl International Air. Enquiries at the Grenadan High Commission revealed that throughout the period of the Huambo shuttle, Pearl's company records declared that no business was being carried on. For its work during the war, Pearl received almost $150,000 from the CIA.

Another airlift was organised by the British multinational Lonrho. Its boss, 'Tiny' Rowland, was no stranger to the world of undercover diplomacy, having combined his considerable political influence with British government efforts on more than one occasion. He had already provided a Lear jet for Savimbi, which proved invaluable for making trips to increase UNITA's diplomatic support. The incentive for Rowland was the prospect of large business contracts accruing from a UNITA victory. To operate an airline, he bought a shell company named Armitage Industrial Holdings off the Slater Walker group and made his personal pilot Wilhelm Wilming a director. Its daily flight, designated G-BAZA, was used to transport arms and other supplies. Both Pearl and Armitage worked from an obscure corner of Lusaka airport, separate from ordinary commercial operations, without the troublesome interference of customs officials.

Meanwhile, inside UNITA-controlled teritory, was an ex-intelligence man on what seemed a very unlikely mission. To visiting journalists this bumbling English gentleman figure, Evan Davies, claimed to be producing an 'economic plan' for Southern Angola. If pressed, he would pull out a short typed document proposing large-scale agricultural development, but which ignored the area's vast iron ore resources.

Davies had officially quit MI5 in 1972. His varied career had included bodyguard duties for Winston Churchill, a spell in Malaya as a Special Branch officer (see chapter 2) and finally lecturing on MI6 training courses. He had a long-standing friendship with Jorge Sangumba UNITA's foreign affairs minister, which began in the late

1960s. He was very critical of UNITA's early days, dismissing them as a 'bunch of semi-maoists'. Nevertheless, he helped Sangumba to get money from a CIA-backed charity. Since Davies has proved unwilling to answer questions, and denied that his friendship with Sangumba was anything other than natural, his precise role remains unclear.

In any event, there was a lack of intelligence on the extent of Soviet and Cuban involvement, and on the size and morale of the main participants. Most of the British intelligence officers who arrived in Angola had been spotted fairly quickly, although one or two posing as journalists had a certain amount of success.

As the war in the north entered its closing stages, with no sign of any halt in the MPLA advance, the West decided on military intervention. It was felt that regular troops could not be deployed for fear of reprisal against commercial interests by black African states. The ideal force, they concluded, would be one made up of mercenaries. For MI6, this raised the possibility of infiltrating army-trained personnel into their ranks, thus solving the intelligence problem.

The CIA received the go-ahead from the British government to recruit mercenaries for the FNLA with American and Zairean money totalling around £300,000. The main recruiter was John Banks, who had served a spell with the Parachute Regiment which ended with a dishonourable discharge. Using a firm named Security Advisory Services as a front, he recruited a total of 120 mercenaries. Their departure was heavily publicised and badly organised. Of the second group of twenty, which left Heathrow in January 1976, eleven were either without passports or on bail. Nevertheless, they all boarded the aircraft. One of them, who was subsequently captured by the MPLA, explained the process at his trial. He said he showed a 'piece of paper' to an official at the airport. The official laughed but after making a telephone call allowed him through. The piece of paper was an identity card mugged up by Banks at the last minute to overcome the lack of passports.

The mercenary's defence counsel, Mr Warburton-Jones, pointed out that there had either been 'bribery at the airport' or 'unofficial complicity by the authorities'. John Banks, who was later a key Special Branch witness for the prosecution of four Irish republicans, made a sworn statment explaining what had happened at the airport which suggests the latter explanation:

> at that time I had a close relationship with the Special Branch and had told them about the recruitment. The man at the Special Branch I was in touch with was Detective Inspector Ray Tucker. That was why there was no hindrance at the airport.

Also in this group were two MI6 men. One of them, Vic Gawthrop, an overweight 51-year-old, died of a heart attack on his first patrol. The other, John Lockyer, was sent back to England with a leg wound after his jeep was blown up. One of the mercenaries later named two further MI6 agents on the expedition, Lou Elford and Barry Thorpe. According to the CIA Angolan task force leader, John Stockwell, MI6 agents were also fighting in the south with UNITA. Their efforts were to no avail. With Cuban support, the MPLA rapidly routed the FNLA and the South African column. The latter, over-extended and without supplies, was forced to fall back after the South African government decided that it could not risk a major war with the Cubans without continued American support. A documentary, compiled by South African military intelligence and scripted by Brian Crozier from the Institute for the Study of Conflict, was broadcast on South African television and derided the United States for pulling out. British aid also ended as soon as defeat appeared inevitable. Those MI6 men still left alive left the country, following their own carefully planned escape routes.

Neither the FNLA nor UNITA were completely destroyed, and UNITA in particular has caused the MPLA government considerable difficulties. The South Africans continued to support the movement which now claims armed forces of 15,000. 1,200 of the FNLA guerillas were regrouped into the South African army's '32 Battalion' with mercenary officers and instructors*. Western governments have supported such plans but have been careful to avoid direct involvement, especially in America where a statute known as the Clark amendment prohibits aid to Angolan opposition movements. A British army officer attended a series of meetings held in the last two months of 1977 in Western European capitals at which further mercenary recruitment was discussed. Among the other participants were representatives from UNITA, Mozambiquan dissident groups, the Rhodesian and South African armies and an executive from an unidentified oil company. The situation remains uncertain for the time being, but since the settlement in neighbouring Zimbabwe, the Western powers have felt less restricted and more prepared to take an aggressive position over Angola.

Further incidences of co-operation between the West and South Africa have become apparent in the Indian Ocean region. Western interest in the region is supposedly concerned with the security of tanker routes from the Gulf although there are other more potent motives: the restriction of Soviet shipping movements through the denial of port facilities, possible offshore oil deposits and, recently, the securing of bases for the American Rapid Deployment Force. Britain passed most of its policing responsibilities to the United States

* The battalion has carried out a series of incursions deep into Angolan territory from bases in Namibia.

* I was offered the job of QM of 32 Recce, as a Major based at Pretoria + the Caprivi

with the general withdrawal of military units from east of Suez, a process completed in 1976, but a number of British naval vessels are believed to have returned in 1979, at American request, to the mid-ocean island of Diego Garcia, which is British-owned but leased to the US. This indicates an increase in Western preoccupation with the Indian Ocean, and no doubt more strenuous efforts to unseat or mollify some of the region's less co-operative governments.

One of these is in the Seychelles, an archipelago whose main populated island Mahe lies 1,000 miles due east of the Kenyan port of Mombasa. Ninety per cent of the 60,000 population live on Mahe and depend on fishing and tourism for the majority of their income. Insulated from mainland Africa by the expanse of ocean, the Seychelles never experienced strong nationalist turbulence during the 1950s and local politics remained virtually moribund. The first political party, the Seychelles Democratic Party (SDP), was formed in 1963 by a 24-year-old lawyer, James Mancham, who campaigned for integration with Britain. Two years later another lawyer, Albert Rene, established the Seychelles People's United Party (SPUP) which took an exactly opposite position and worked for full independence.

These two men have since dominated the island's politics, with Mancham overcoming Rene in the three elections before independence despite switching to a pro-independence platform in 1974. His conversion was prompted by advice from the British government that integration was not acceptable to their mainland African allies and that it was likely to produce domestic difficulties in the future. Denis Grennan was seconded as Mancham's constitutional adviser and managed to persuade him that independence was the only realistic option. On a trip to London around the same time, he was visited by a man using the name 'Fox-Talbot' who announced himself as a representative of an 'anti-communist organisation' – in reality, MI6 – who promised financial support for the pro-SDP newspaper *Seychelles Weekly*.[49] Over a three-year period, some £3,000 was routed into Mancham's account via a Swiss bank.

Mancham made a number of conditions in return for his promise of a volte-face. These were mainly concerned with security. He obtained the agreement of the Foreign Office that British officials would be made available to assist the development of a paramilitary force and an intelligence service, but was told that the money would have to come from the Ministry of Overseas Development. Mancham later complained, in a letter to the *Sunday Times*, that this proposal was rejected by Judith Hart, who rightly pointed out that her ministry was solely interested in social welfare, and 'it appeared that there was nobody in a position to overrule her'.[50] Mancham then contacted 'Fox-Talbot', who put him in touch with an associate named 'John

Tolman'. Sporting a portfolio of non-existent addresses in South-ampton, Oxford and Tunbridge Wells, Tolman told Mancham that his request would be put before 'the Board'. It appears that no aid was forthcoming, since Mancham later signed an agreement with the CIA similar in content to the proposals explored with the British. In January 1976, a final constitutional conference was held in London to sort out the form of the government after independence and settled on the end of June as the time by which it should take control. Sometime in the intervening period, Mancham alleged in another letter to a London Sunday newspaper, he was visited by a CIA officer based in Nairobi. Because of the presence of an American satellite-tracking station on Mahe and unspecified 'geo-political factors', Mancham claims to have been convinced that his government would come under threat from the Soviet Union and its local 'proxies'.

> As a result, I signed a document under which the CIA would
> have helped us build an intelligence organisation ... and ...
> provide us with necessary support and finance for a para-
> military unit which could be useful in the eventuality of internal
> insurrection.[51]

The satellite station was one of a total of seven world-wide which receive data from radio-transmission satellites, and building per-mission was granted by the British on the understanding that the United States 'might accomodate them with a similar favour if the need and opportunity should arise'. Most of the island's inhabitants were, at the very least, unsure what benefits the 'big white ball' – the radome – was bringing them.[52]

The independence arrangements went according to plan, and on June 28 Mancham became president of the new republic with Albert Rene as prime minister. To his chagrin, Mancham's deal with the Americans also collapsed. Initially, press revelations about CIA fin-ancial support for King Hussein of Jordan and Jomo Kenyatta caused second thoughts in the Nairobi station, which were later compounded by the oncoming American presidential election. When Carter took over from Ford, Mancham was told he would have to wait until the attitude of the new administration towards outstanding CIA projects became clearer. Meanwhile he had built up useful South African contacts, which produced money for his pre-independence presid-ential campaign and promises of economic aid in exchange for diplomatic support, Seychellian passports for South Africans wishing to travel in black Africa, and aircraft landing facilities.

Mancham's desperate desire for international connections arose from his conviction that Rene was plotting his overthrow with the backing of Tanzania and the Soviet Union. Rene certainly resented the president's laissez-faire attitude towards the islands' social and economic problems and his declared intention of turning the Seychelles into an offshore banking haven. Mancham told his British security adviser, Douglas Mott, that Rene was plotting against him. Mott replied that his main contact inside Rene's political apparatus, Rolly Marie, was unable to confirm this. Mott suffered under the misapprehension that Marie had managed to infiltrate the SPUP, although it was well known within the party that Marie was an inspector in the Special Branch. In fact Marie was working for Rene, which accounts for Mott's lack of accurate information. Warnings from French embassy staff that a coup was imminent failed to shake Mancham's confidence in Mott and he left inadvisedly for the 1977 Commonwealth Conference in London during the first week of June.

On June 5 Mancham was preparing, with the help of Denis Grennan, a speech replying to Prime Minister Callaghan's toast of the assembled guests when news came through of Rene's coup. Mott and five other senior British officials were detained for twelve hours prior to deportation. In a post-coup statement, the new regime announced that Mancham was no longer welcome in the Seychelles. He decided nonetheless to fulfil his ceremonial duties in London. One of the deportees was Peter Walker, a Grenadier Guards officer in charge of training a 120-strong internal security force, although it is not clear who was financing this programme.

The coup was a severe embarrassment for the British government and a bitter row broke out between the Foreign Office and MI6 over the lack of warning. MI6 officials on the mainland, it was alleged, should have been aware that a group of twenty left-wing Seychellois had undergone training in Tanzania several months previously. It was this group which carried out the coup, killing a sentry at the police barracks and two other officers.

Since Rene's takeover, there have been several attempts to overthrow his government and more or less continuous plotting against it. The view in Western capitals that Rene might not prove as radical as his rhetoric was dispelled when the government started to implement a socialist programme and Tanzanian military advisers arrived on the islands. Two plots involving French mercenaries were uncovered in 1978 and 1979, while a coup by mainly South African mercenaries posing as the ancient Order of Foam Blowers drinking club was pre-empted by Seychellois security forces at the end of November 1981. Mancham, resident in London since his overthrow, claims powerful allies among governments and commerce – including the Saudi millionaire Adnan Khashoggi. The fate of the nearby Comoros Islands, where a force of 100 French mercenaries overthrew the left-wing government in May 1978 (and their leader installed himself as vice-president) weighs heavily on Rene's memory.

The British have not been heavily involved in the plotting against Rene's government: the view in Whitehall seems to be that a local uprising caused by increasing economic difficulties is due in the near future and that Mancham's best chance of regaining power lies in being prepared to step in at that time. In the short term, they are more concerned with developments in Mauritius, another former colony 1,000 miles to the south. From the granting of internal self-government in 1964 until elections held at the beginning of 1982, Mauritius was governed by the Labour Party under Sir Sewoosagur Ramgoolam, apart from two periods when it entered into coalition with the right-wing Parti Mauricien Sociale Democrate (PMSD).

In the defence policy review of 1967, British military chiefs decided to move the naval communications station at HMS Highfyer in Sri Lanka to the Mauritian town of Vacoas, where it was renamed HMS Mauritius. On obtaining independence in March 1968, the Mauritian government immediately signed a defence treaty with Britain, allowing for continued use of HMS Mauritius and – according to the British interpretation – waiving any territorial claim over Diego Garcia. In exchange, the British were to train the island's security force and guarantee to advise on external security threats. Within two years the agreement paid dividends for the former colony. A team of 400 French-descended islanders travelled to South Africa for commando training, with the aim of overthrowing the Mauritian government and replacing its anti-apartheid policy with one more favourable to South Africa. The plan was thwarted, however, because the government had been forewarned by British naval intelligence officers. The rebels were politically sympathetic to the PMSD whose leader, Gaetan Duval, had recently joined the government as Foreign Minister, but retained his post until the dissolution of the coalition at the end of 1973. This was caused by a policy disagreement over the provision of port facilities to an annual quota of Soviet fishing vessels in exchange for economic aid; Duval urged that this should be annulled and closer links established with South Africa. The British also objected, on the grounds that some of the trawlers might be equipped with electronic monitoring apparatus which could be used to intercept signals to and from HMS Mauritius. The station was eventually closed in March 1976.

In December of the same year, the first elections held since independence produced a shock. The Mouvement Militant Mauricien (MMM), which held one seat in the previous assembly from a 1970 by-election victory, took 34 of the 70 seats and became the largest single party. Only another coalition between the Labour Party and the PMSD kept it from power. Its remarkable progress produced consternation in Whitehall. Ramgoolam's majority was unstable and further elections seemed almost certain to produce a left-wing majority.

British trepidation was reflected in the appointment of a new High Commissioner* to Mauritius in January 1981: James Allan, an experienced MI6 officer who participated in the 1975 cease-fire talks with the Provisional IRA and later took over as head of the Foreign Office's Overseas Information Department. The CIA augmented its Mauritius station around the same time.

The MMM is now in power, and Mauritius has joined the non-aligned bloc of Tanzania, India, the Seychelles and the Malagasy Republic in calling for a demilitarisation of the Indian Ocean. Their main target is the Anglo-American facility at Diego Garcia, which the Reagan administration has pledged to expand. Successive Mauritian governments have attempted to raise the issue of Diego Garcia's sovereignty with the Foreign Office but have received little more than a cursory hearing. The new administration has promised more vocal agitation.

It can be expected that the British will increase resources devoted to covert action in the region, with Mauritius a high priority target. Propaganda campaigns alleging secret deals between Albert Rene and the Soviet government have been under way for several years and the MMM government can expect similar treatment. Diplomatically, the threat of destabilisation can be used to temper MMM demands.

The West's strongest ally in east Africa, Kenya, will have a vital role to play in Western plans. Rene has already accused the Kenyan government of complicity in the plots against his regime; there have been reports of discussions along those lines between one of Mancham's ministers, David Joubert, and the then Kenyan Attorney-General, Charles Njonjo, soon after his takeover. Njonjo has denied any involvement. There is growing internal dissent in Kenya and much depends on how this develops.

The difficulties in that country are symptomatic of the fragility of the stratified societies which the colonial powers had encouraged before their departure. Class rivalry and tribal rivalry form an explosive mixture, and the high incidence of military government in Africa follows from it being the only method of maintaining control. The economic fortunes of Africa are irrevocably chained to those of the industrialised north; and thus the recession in the north places further burdens on the black middle classes, on whose skill and acumen the West relies to maintain the existing structure of trade relations. The odious anomaly of South Africa has become more than just the subject of political rhetoric for black Africa as it starts to show a more aggressive attitude towards its neighbours, with the sanction of Washington and London. Deteriorating economies and the constant threat of destabilisation do not augur well for the future of the continent.

* The title of High Commissioner is used in place of ambassador in former British colonies.

Notes

1. Oginga Odinga *Not Yet Uhuru* (1967) p.295
2. Gary Wasserman *Politics of Decolonisation: Kenyan Europeans and the Land Issue, 1960-65* (1976) p.38
3. Gary Wasserman *Politics of Decolonisation* p.67
4. Malcolm MacDonald *Titans and Others* (1972) p.249
5. Progress Foundation prospectus, not dated, p.1
6. *Africa Diary* (15 November 1963)
7. R. Kisch *The Private Life of Public Arrangements* (1964) p.79
8. Gary Wasserman *Politics of Decolonisation* p.85
9. Private interview
10. Gary Wasserman *Politics of Decolonisation* p.98
11. *Ariel Foundation Annual Report* 1969 p.5
12. *Leveller* pilot issue (February 1976)
13. *Tribune* (11 April 1980)
14. Private interview
15. Dan Schechter, Michael Asmara, David Kolodney, *The CIA as an Equal Opportunity Employer*, article in *Ramparts*, not dated
16. S. R. Weissman *Two Decades of US policy in Africa: some lessons from experience*, paper delivered at the annual meeting of the African Studies Association, Boston, Massachusetts, 4 November 1976, p.24
17. Guardian (24 April 1965)
18. *Radio Moscow* (30 May 1965)
19. *Private Eye* (30 April 1976)
20. *New York Times* (7 March 1982)
21. *Sunday Times* (11 December 1980)
22. Rolf Steiner *The Last Adventurer* (1978) pp.190-3
23. Letter from Divall to authors (9 March 1982)
24. *Washington Star* (4 April 1971)
25. *Private Eye* (27 April 1979)
26. *House of Commons Hansard* (22 July 1971)
27. *Le Monde* (28 August 1971)
28. *Private Eye* (13 August 1971)
29. *Private Eye* (27 August 1971)
30. *Private Eye* (10 September 1971)
31. Quoted in Guardian (4 June 1982)
32. Jonathan Aitken *Officially Secret* (1971) p.86
33. Decision of the Commissioner, Claim for Unemployment Benefit, Case no. 11/3, 1 September 1971
34. *Daily Telegraph* (6 September 1971)
35. *Daily Telegraph* (3 September 1971)
36. *Observer* (10 December 1967)
37. John de St. Jorre *The Nigerian Civil War* (1972) p.318
38. Paul Gore-Booth *With Great Truth and Respect* (1974) p.331
39. Chapman Pincher *Inside Story* (1978) p.16
40. *Sunday Times* (13 February 1977)
41. Guardian (28 June 1969)
42. *Sunday Telegraph* (5 March 1967)
43. *Morning Star* (20 August 1976); *Times* (16 August 1978)
44. Richard Crossman *The Crossman Diaries* Volume 1 (1975) p.379
45. Private interview
46. *Observer* (7 September 1980)
47. *Counterspy* (Spring 1976) p.56-60

48.   *Covert Action Information Bulletin* No. 4 (April-May 1979) p.28
49.   Private inverview
50.   *Sunday Times* (2 March 1980)
51.   *Observer* (16 December 1979)
52.   *Report of the Committee on International Relations: Special Study Missions to Africa, November 1972 and November 1973* US Government Printing Office (1974) p.50

Chapter 5
The Empire – Where To?

The political groundwork done by the British during the last three decades in the states bounding the Indian Ocean has proved essential to the establishment of the American Rapid Deployment Force (RDF) for military intervention in the Middle East. Three of the five main bases which are being used to house facilities for the RDF – Mombasa in Kenya, the Omani island of Masirah and Diego Garcia – are situated in territories with British-created systems of government and where Britain continues to exercise substantial influence. Anything short of full co-operation from Whitehall for the RDF will reduce its flexiblity accordingly.

The RDF idea is not a new one: the emergency strike force established by the British in 1956 at Kenya's Kahawa air base was the first of the species, with the dual function of conducting security operations against rebellious nationalists and intervening in the Middle East in support of pro-Western rulers and Western commercial interests. As the cost of maintaining the force escalated towards an unrealistic limit the Ministry of Defence started to consider a joint force with the United States – as the documents sold by Percy Allen to Egyptian intelligence showed (see p. 126). The emergency strike force was eventually disbanded in 1965 following objections from the Kenyan government, and the east of Suez withdrawal which began soon afterwards meant that future initiatives for a Western intervention force lay exclusively with the Americans. The Defence Secretary, Robert McNamara, immediately took up the reins and obtained authorisation from Congress for the relevant military hardware. The Pentagon maintained an RDF-type force, variously known as the Strike Command or Readiness Command, from this time until the American defeat in Vietnam. Not surprisingly, a wholesale review of American global military strategy followed the humiliating withdrawal from South-East Asia, while the balance of political opinion shifted against interference in Third World conflicts. (Hence the difficulties in obtaining authorisation for military aid to FNLA/UNITA during the Angolan civil war.)

It was probably too much to expect this self-restraint to last more than a few years. The American military and the political right mounted sustained attacks on it, arguing that it would be exploited to the full by the Soviets and their allies. In the event it was the fundamentalist revolution in Iran, owing little to Kremlin machination, which finally reversed American policy to its original, more aggressive stance. Contracts valued at over £1,000 million in Britain alone were lost as a result of the Shah's demise. The RDF has been reintroduced with an accompanying strategic plan known as 'Tripwire' to prevent any possible repetition elsewhere in the Middle East – Saudi Arabia is thought to be a prime candidate. The problem of oil supplies has been grossly overexaggerated: the analytical journal *State Research* has made a strong case for the view that by far the most powerful element in the process of oil transfer from well to consumer is the small group of Western-owned multinational oil corporations which controls the greater part of the world's refining and distributing capacity.[1] Any lost production caused by political upheaval is invariably temporary and can be fairly easily made up from other sources: for most Middle Eastern countries oil is the main export commodity. Evidence from the period when OPEC members imposed a boycott on supplies to America in retaliation for its active support of Israel during the 1973 Arab-Israeli war shows that US oil imports fell by a little over 5 per cent and that the much-cited 'oil weapon' is a fiction.

The British military detachment for the RDF, announced by Prime Minister Thatcher at the end of 1981, will be 1,000 troops from two battalions of the Parachute Regiment. This is an essentially token gesture which affirms the diplomatic support which Britain is giving to the RDF policy, and which gives it the veneer of a multinational Western, rather than solely American force. The government also announced, in October 1982, that the British naval detachment in the Indian Ocean will be increased to counter the 'growing Soviet presence'. In the light of this, it is worth quoting the assessment of Sir John Killick, formerly the United Kingdom's permanent representative to NATO, that

> At sea, the capability of the Soviet Navy in ... the Indian Ocean, lacking effective air capability would be hopelessly vulnerable to the power and sophistication of an American carrier task force.[2]

The Arab nations, with the exception of Oman and Egypt, reacted sourly to the original American announcement, and most West European nations, concerned to maintain their relations with Arab states, have expressed doubts. However, a more important British contribution will come from intelligence-sharing as enshrined in the WASP

agreements. Signals intercepts, in particular, will be of vital importance in the assessment of whether or not, and if so how, the RDF will
be used. From this angle, Britain has no choice other than to support
American military intervention policy while the Sigint Pact still exists,
just as America was obliged to assist in the Falklands/Malvinas war.

The inconsistency of Britain having its major intelligence liaison
agreements with the United States while its most important trading
relations are with the nations of the EEC was referred to in Chapter 2.
Both the British and Americans have procedures for routing commercial
intelligence to their business sectors. Some American firms have
NSA officers attached to their staffs, while in Britain:

> Officials in virtually every department, including the Ministry
> of Agriculture, Fisheries, and Food, and the Bank of England,
> are cleared to see secret intelligence from SIS or 'sigint' from
> GCHQ. But the distribution also goes beyond Whitehall, part-
> icularly to 'certain industrial confidants' of the Department of
> Trade and Industry. These include major companies like ICI,
> BP or Rio Tinto Zinc.[3]

Meanwhile the Foreign Office occasionally instructs its overseas
missions to institute campaigns denigrating the products of other
countries. The Middle East arms market was one recent target,
following the award of several large contracts to French countries.

As regards the more important function of predicting and, if
possible, preventing political upheaval in countries with large British
investments, the Foreign Office and MI6 have failed to give sufficient
warning on a number of occasions. It is as much in the financial
interests of government as of business to correct this since it will often
have to pay out to the companies affected by a collapsed contract
under the export credit guarantee system. Prevention is a different
matter, and here Britain is hampered by a lack of resources. Covert
action solutions are frequently regarded as the most appropriate
method of restoring stability, and the WASP link-up necessarily
favours securing American support although British economic interests
are more closely allied to those of the other EEC members. Logistically,
it is easier to organise covert operations with a single agency – the CIA
– than with a group of European intelligence services. Therefore,
covert operations designed to secure markets for British companies
will only take place if they correspond simultaneously with American
interests. The Iran coup of 1953 is an early example of this dependence.
A number of errors in assessment of the stability of particular regimes
and national economies by Western governments have had serious
impacts on the international business community. The enormous
cost to Britain of orders lost following the revolution which overthrew
the Shah of Iran has been well documented. Misinterpretations of the

situations in Nicaragua and Poland further undermined commercial confidence in the effectiveness of Western governments' antennae. This led directly to the growth of firms specialising in political risk analysis – in effect, private intelligence agencies.

Most multinational companies do employ analysts of their own to make risk assessments but they have often succumbed to organis-ational pressure to produce reports conforming to the established corporate view, a phenomenon dubbed with the Orwellian term 'groupthink'.

There are about 20 firms recognised in the field at the moment. One of the best known, because of the involvement of a former British Prime Minister, is International Reporting and Information Systems (IRIS). The firm's promotional material explains its purpose:

> the founders believe that the lack of reliable and objective information about government and political activities has in-hibited the development of many opportunities for international trade and commerce. The new service will overcome many of the difficulties of the past and stimulate new, greater and wider activities in world business investment and trade.

IRIS is the creation of Anthony Stout, the Washington-based publisher of the *National Journal* and head of the Government Research Corporation, a firm which collects and disseminates information pri-marily concerning American politics and government policy. Both private organisations and official agencies subscribe to it. After the Iranian revolution, Stout was approached by a number of his clients who asked if the range of topics covered by GRC could be extended to international affairs. After a two-year feasibility study, IRIS was set up with over £5 million raised from GRC, the London merchant bankers Henry Ansbacher, the Bank of Liechtenstein, the Swedish Skandia group and the British-owned Seascope group of companies.

IRIS recruited an 'international advisory council' to monitor its output and guarantee that it is both 'reliable and objective'. Edward Heath, British Prime Minister between 1970 and 1974, chairs the council, whose other members are ex-World Bank president Robert McNamara, former French Trade Minister Jean-Francois Deniau and Roderigo Botero who was at one time the Colombian Finance Minister. Heath says that his IRIS work, for which he is being paid $100,000 per annum, will occupy him for 'only a few days a year' and it may well be that the composition of the council is geared towards enhancing IRIS prestige rather than ensuring the accuracy of its products.

Although the company is registered in Holland (for tax reasons), much of the work will be done in the United States: in particular, the computer system will be housed there to take advantage of American legislation prohibiting government interference in information-gathering activity. Composed of three linked Burroughs 780 computers, the system was designed by a former CIA consultant and modelled on that used by the agency.

As well as the advisory council, IRIS has a managing board appointed by the shareholders which supervises overall policy. The board is chaired by Charles Longbottom, head of the Seascope group and a trustee of the Ariel Foundation. IRIS itself is divided into five directorates: information and intelligence; strategic services, which is concerned with computer operations and software, and training; marketing; public relations and finally administration. Paul Boeker, a retired American diplomat, is head of the information and intelligence department. Under him are six regional departments with a total of 33 analysts working on raw material from newspapers, periodicals, television and radio broadcasts plus reports from about 100 correspondents, (mainly moonlighting political journalists).

IRIS subscribers receive a terminal linked to the IRIS computer by satellite through which they are able to call up basic reports in synopsis form about any area of interest. At an additional charge, a number of more sophisticated services are available. These include direct consultation with IRIS analysts, storage of the subscribers' own data and computer evaluations of the consequences of imaginary developments fed in by the subscriber. The basic cost is $30,000 annually, rising to $250,000 for the full range of services*.

According to the difficulty of obtaining basic information, and the extent to which it is involved in international commerce and politics, each country is assigned to one of four categories. Developed capitalist countries make up the 'easy access, great interaction' category A while most African countries and some Middle Eastern countries (Libya, Oman, Iraq, both Yemeni states) belong to the 'difficult access, limited interaction' category D.

During the two-year planning stage, Stout and his assistants identified 14 potential competitors and divided them up, also into four groups, according to methods and coverage. Business International, based in London, New York and Geneva, emerged as the main competitor. It produces newsletters and briefing papers for its clients and is extensively involved with Africa, listing some forty leading multinational companies in its 'Africa Group'. Business Environment and Risk Index (BERI) is a California-based consultancy founded in 1966 by Dr F. T. Haner, a former academic with commercial experience in both Europe and the United States.

* However, in January 1983, IRIS filed for bankruptcy with debts reported as over £1 million. Low demand was held to be the main cause: according to the *Observer* (30 January 1983) 'not a single genuine paying customer has been signed' over its first two years of life.

To cater for its 500 clients, BERI employs two separate panels of international experts, comprised of more than 170 business executives, political scientists and diplomats, who provide reports according to a specific formula, adding their own qualitative comments. In addition, there are 11 full-time research assistants who monitor legal and fiscal developments. BERI publishes a thrice yearly bulletin covering 45 countries per issue, and six longer analyses annually, all chosen on the basis of 'current business interest'. It also supplies analytical forecasts on 50 of the 'most requested' countries. BERI claims to have predicted the 1981 military coup in Turkey, the overthrow of Edward Gierek in Poland and the assassination of President Park Chung Hee in South Korea, although it made incorrect forecasts about President Mitterand's election victory and the survival of Nigerian President Shehu Shagari, whose demise BERI has been expecting since 1979.

Another serious competitor picked out by IRIS is the World Political Risk Foundation, which publishes the monthly F & S Political Risk Letter. The newsletter is divided onto three sections: a table of high-risk countries, new forecasts and a summary of political risk scores for 65 countries. About Iraq, for example, the newsletter date-lined 3rd March 1982 states that

> strongman Saddam Hussain is in trouble and Iraq's political stability is in serious jeopardy, primarily because of difficulties in the war with Iran ... rumours of disaffection abound and anti-Saddam plots are uncovered more often.

It concludes, however, that a new regime controlled by Ba'ath leaders 'would not be likely to radically alter policies towards international business'.

In Britain, a company better known for its unusual insurance services has recently moved into risk analysis. Control Risks is the market leader in kidnap and ransom insurance, a phenomenon which has grown from negligible proportions to a multi-million pound business since 1970. The company was the brainchild of Julian Radcliffe, a London insurance broker, who became a director after the wholesale resignation of the board of Control Risks' previous incarnation, the A1 Insurance Agency. After two years of inactivity, Control Risks began trading from offices in the City of London. The directors were Radcliffe himself, another insurance broker, and a 'security consultant' named David Walker, a former army officer who had served with the SAS and as a security specialist at British embassies in Latin America. The company now operates from offices in Victoria in London with a staff of 60 and an annual turnover of approximately £1 million. The board has now acquired three other ex-SAS officers, including the managing director, Arish Turle; also the former Metropolitan Police Commissioner Sir Robert Mark, and General Sir Frank

King, latterly chief of the British Army of the Rhine and previously army commander in Northern Ireland. Other directors include Peter Goss, who after a long career in the army Intelligence Corps worked for Diversified Corporate Services (see p. 50) and in the Cabinet Office, and Major-General Richard Clutterbuck, the counter-insurgency theorist and sometime member of the council of the Institute for the Study of Conflict (see pp. 98-99). Two of Control Risks' staff come from the ISC: the former research director Peter Janke and Richard Sims, who was the Institute's librarian.[4]

The growth of these firms has spawned an analysts' club, the Association of Political Risk Analysts, which has 300 members while Georgetown University in Washington is running a course on the subject given by a former CIA officer. In 1981 the prestigious Wharton School of Business at the University of Pennsylvania organised the 'First International Political Risk Management Seminar'. For $700 each some 100 corporate executives and academics assembled to discuss how to deal with governments which interfere with multinational business. Speakers advised corporations to gain maximum 'control' of the host government and to obtain insurance from the US government before making an investment and then listed the various devices for maximising profits and keeping the interference of the host government to a minimum. The importance of local intelligence-gathering was pointed out to the audience although a note of caution was introduced regarding the use of local employees: despite being the most valuable source of routine information, they are often reluctant to supply information which could lead to the company withdrawing from the country. Hence warnings of political upheaval, for example, are likely to be missed.

The private organisations described above are in an entirely different category to the companies described in Chapter 1. While the latter represent, broadly speaking, an adjunct of the official intelligence establishment, the risk analysts have materialised in the wake of corporate disillusionment with the state's inability to provide the necessary support for their commercial operations. For many business executives, it is another piece of evidence to support their view that the nation-state is a redundant form of social organisation. Back in 1967, Business International told its subscribers in a research report that

> the nation-state is becoming obsolete: tomorrow it will in any meaningful sense be dead – and so will the corporation that remains essentially national.[5]

Thus risk analysts function, in a sense, in direct competition with traditional national intelligence agencies. Inadvertently, they have also become something of a security hazard: in their attempts to drum up business, details of intelligence methods brought by staff from their previous employers – the state intelligence agencies – have been used in promotional material. The facilities available to clients give some indication of how, for example, efforts to transfer analytical procedures to computer systems have progressed. The CIA has tried to restrict the private agencies by extending regulations covering the use of information learnt within the agency to former as well as serving employees, although it well knows that these are unenforceable. The agency has also adopted different training programmes for its officers to instil new methods of crisis monitoring. It is suggested that they rate the significance of events on a scale from 1 to 20, using coloured chips for easy recognition of trends, making charts and superimposing different time periods and, finally, using computers to store and recall information quickly.

An important question for the future is whether private enterprise will try to develop a signals intelligence capability. It is reasonable to assume that some corporations will try and reduce research and development costs and gain market advantages by resort to industrial sigint aimed at their competitors, in particular by tapping the vast computer networks used in modern global business transactions. Inevitably the range of targets will grow from there. At the same time, mass consumer electronics is providing private individuals with the means to transmit and receive coded communications.

From these two areas the sigint monopoly of the WASP agencies has come under a strong challenge, and they have responded vigorously:

> NSA and its partners are fighting a furious battle to control the blossoming public interest in cryptography. They have attempted to stop publication of scientific papers by independent researchers; they have tried to interfere in the allocation of grants.[6]

GCHQ would fare badly from an expansion of cryptography in Western countries outside their own 'monastic order'. The number of readable targets would suffer a sharp decline while 'blossoming public interest' is liable to encompass the agency's own work. A number of significant discoveries in the past few years have produced some of the details, which taken as a whole indicate that GCHQ functions largely as the British subsidiary of the NSA.

Corporate use of covert action methods is already well-recognised: the efforts of ITT and other American-based multinationals in subverting the Chilean government of Salvador Allende in 1973 provide the most notorious example. Turning to this side of the Atlantic, it has been shown that Lonrho assisted in a number of covert operations in Africa. Recession produces two contradictory effects with respect to this kind of corporate skulduggery: curtailing it through lack of resources while stimulating it as the desire to maintain and improve trading positions grows, irrespective of the structure of the market. Since the British government's ability to produce covert action solutions is conditional on American involvement, British companies are more likely to take the initiative themselves. Whether they can assemble a group of sufficiently skilled operatives is a different matter: 24 SAS may have a role here.

During the 1970s, British intelligence was confronted with escalating problems inside the United Kingdom. National security appeared to be under the severest threat since the Battle of Britain. The prospect that Whitehall's regulation net curtains might soon conceal members of the Socialist Workers' Party and the Irish Republican Army rather than the appropriate batch of mandarins run off the Oxbridge production line was canvassed among the more blimpish ruling circles with some seriousness. And despite various overseas operations, some of which have appeared in preceding chapters, most MI6 resources were devoted to the United Kingdom during this period. The *Sunday Times* political editor, Hugo Young, quoting an 'impeccable authority', states that 'through most of the 1970s a colossal distortion was permitted in MI6's work … in these years, MI6 became preponderantly an internal security arm.[7] Although Young proffers other explanations, some of this is undoubtedly attributable to operations in Northern Ireland. The province is strictly speaking the preserve of MI5, but for a variety of political and strategic reasons, MI6 has been drafted in.

During World War II, MI6 had about 30 officers in Dublin watching the German embassy's efforts to use the IRA to mount attacks in the north. After Hitler's defeat it was preoccupied with developments in the global arena and paid scant regard to happenings across the Irish Sea. The three-year IRA border campaign which ended in 1962 was dealt with by MI5, who sent several officers over to reorganise intelligence storage. The IRA had not, on that occasion, developed sufficient political support to wage an effective guerilla war.

The situation at the end of the 1960s was very different. The failure of Northern Ireland's devolved government to respond to catholic demands for an end to discrimination against them in jobs and housing, followed by attacks on catholic areas by protestant paramilitaries and the police 'B Specials' – to which the IRA, such as it existed, was unable to respond – produced a more militant attitude among catholics and a large growth in IRA strength. The solution for most northern catholics was, as it has been for centuries throughout Ireland, the ending of British rule and this to be followed by unification of the north and south. Since that time, the republican military campaign has been fought primarily by the Provisional IRA.

The division of the IRA into the Official and Provisional wings came about after the movement had rearmed sufficiently to repel further protestant attacks. The faction which evolved into the Officials believed that once this position was reached, and the IRA was capable of performing a civil defence role in the catholic ghettoes, there was no need to extend the armed struggle further. The Provisionals, by contrast, saw the politicisation of catholics born out of the civil rights movement as an opportunity to launch concerted resistance to British rule. The Officials were once the larger tendency, and to this day have always held access to larger arms stocks than the Provisionals. The Provisional armoury is, however, a great deal more sophisticated and many of the Officials' weapons have no doubt decayed through lack of use.

The Provisionals couched their struggle in terms of a national liberation movement: the sectarian division was interpreted as a colonial form of divide and rule. The colonial analogy has been recognised by such establishment figures as Robert Mark, sometime commissioner of the Metropolitan Police. Of Northern Ireland he has written that

> only its association with the United Kingdom and its represen-
> tation at Westminister prevented it from being seen in realistic
> terms as in no different a relationship to Great Britain than
> Cyprus, Aden or any other of the countless colonial territories
> from the great days of the empire.[8]

Mark made the comment on the basis of his membership of the Hunt Commission inquiry into the Royal Ulster Constabulary (RUC) after its violent excesses against civil rights protestors. By this stage it had been recognised that the RUC were incapable of any form of policing in republican areas and the task was handed over in its entirety to the army. Oliver Wright* was recalled from his ambassador's post in Copenhagen to take charge of intelligence co-ordination, which at that time was virtually non-existent. D Squadron of 22 SAS was sent in to root out the sources of paramilitary weapons. Two MI5 officers arrived in the province to help the army sort out their intelligence apparatus: prior to 1969, military intelligence in the province consisted of half a dozen officers mainly engaged in vetting for military and civil service posts. Army intelligence staff were 'strictly forbidden to give information to the RUC',[9] although the following year the director of military intelligence established a joint working party with the RUC Special Branch to draw up a list of people who might be usefully interned. The main object was to find out who the lower-ranking Provisionals were: two sources close to the leadership were

* He took up the post of ambassador to the United States in September 1982.

able to supply broad strategic outlines but targets and combat personnel were a mystery. Most of the work involved picking out faces from thousands of photographs taken by the army at meetings, funerals and demonstrations, and matching them up against RUC files. A list of 500 was drawn up. The army command was unsure of the value of internment, but a particularly active spell in the IRA campaign forced them to accept it, in the absence of a viable alternative. On the 23rd July 1971, 1,800 troops with police support raided houses in Belfast and nine other towns.

The effect of internment was substantial but not conclusive. Part of the problem lay with the poor state of RUC Special Branch intelligence. Some of the prospective internees had died years before, others were well past retirement age, yet others had left the country. Typical of the changes the army made to improve intelligence quality was a wholesale revision of the telephone tapping system. The RUC had intercepted calls on a small scale for years but the apparatus in use was relatively archaic: calls were recorded manually, which meant a disproportionate amount of labour for the number of calls handled; and 24 hours notice was required for the placing of a tap. Most important of all, it simply did not have the capacity to monitor all the calls the army thought necessary. Liaising with the Post Office, the army took over the top floor of Churchill House, the Belfast telephone area headquarters. An elaborate system of monitor consoles, switching gear for allocating taps, and banks of multi-tracked tape recorders was installed. Meanwhile, a three-man Post Office team wired up selected lines to tapping relays, positioning the taps to minimise the likelihood of removal by other engineers. All Belfast exchanges were found to have large numbers of taps: at one point, the Balmoral exchange, which serves the Andersonstown area of Belfast was so overloaded with tapping circuits that potential subscribers had to be refused phones.

The key to the army's ability to tap so many phones is a method of locking into chosen lines within seconds. The landline intercept operation, as it was known, reached a peak in 1974, since when it has declined and control probably handed back to the RUC. The tapping programme was deemed a failure, due to overkill and the difficulty of purging IRA sympathisers from the Post Office. At least 150 lines were subject to continuous tapping: targets included politicians and journalists as well as paramilitary suspects.

Covert operations began once it became clear that internment had failed to suppress the IRA. 1971 saw the replacement of Oliver Wright with Howard Smith, later ambassador to the Soviet Union and head of MI5, as intelligence co-ordinator, and the establishment of a psychological warfare unit at the army's Lisburn headquarters. Described as the 'Information Policy Cell', its official function was to 'advise the General Officer Commanding on the public aspects of operations and to prepare public information programmes'. Lieutenant-Colonel James Barden, then head of the unit, told journalists that 'there was nothing sinister in this'.[10] The army established a number of community projects and 'bisectarian' youth clubs; organised dances, hiking trips, sports facilities and a meals-on-wheels service for elderly residents of Derry.   Neural's first tour.

Many of the correspondents who covered the Falklands/Malvinas campaign noted that the army were far more responsive to their demands than were their naval counterparts. There is no doubt that the army's experience in Northern Ireland was responsible for the difference in service attitudes towards the press: most naval officers retain an ill-disguised contempt for the journalistic profession. Military commanders in the province and senior Whitehall officials realised the importance of continuous coverage of the army's role for the British audience. Their solution was

> a basic policy of openness with the press, making every facility available to them, providing information, allowing them to come on patrols and operations, and encouraging individual soldiers to explain their job to the press – the army recognised that on TV the private soldier is sometimes more credible than the GOC.[11]

For many journalists, the army was the only source of information, but some developed contacts elsewhere and those who strayed from the official line – that the army was a buffer between two warring communities – found themselves under pressure. Often this took a subtle form: Simon Hoggart of the *Guardian* has explained how journalists could be reined in by a drip of good stories from army press officers, thereby diverting them from sources in less desirable quarters. The technique affords an additional advantage in providing outlets for disinformation. The reverse flow is equally useful to army intelligence: civilian personnel working for the army's press department are encouraged to cultivate reporters and glean information from them.

The Information Policy Cell was also responsible for the development of black propaganda, another integral part of counter-insurgency operations. An early example appeared in an ITN news bulletin during 1972, which alleged that the IRA had used three eight-year-old girls to plant a massive bomb in a pram outside Belfast's Victoria Hospital. The army press office later admitted that the story was untrue, but ITN carried no denial. The same week, reports describing how IRA men had raped several girls at gunpoint appeared in the *Sun* and the *Evening News*. In this case, the army was sufficiently perverse to get the RUC to issue a statement denying the story – on the grounds that it might be seen as an illustration of IRA potency (according to the details, four of the girls became pregnant). The army's senior press officer was Colin Wallace, who although he held the post of civil servant in the Ministry of Defence was also an officer in the Ulster Defence Regiment, the paramilitary force controlled by the army which was to assume the functions of the B Specials. Before his dismissal in 1975 – for supplying classified documents to *Times* journalist Robert Fisk – he was a key figure in the army's black propaganda work. Wallace is now serving a ten-year prison sentence for the manslaughter of a Sussex antique dealer.

The decision to use black propaganda techniques was the first indication that the British assessment of the situation had altered from its initial position. A temporary breakdown in law and order had, it turned out, evolved into an onslaught against the foundations of British rule in the province. The army's expectation of a brief peace-keeping operation was replaced, with trepidation if not reluctance, by the realisation that they were required to fight a counter-insurgency campaign against citizens of the United Kingdom (albeit unwilling ones). The pretence of a buffer role collapsed with the upsurge of loyalist violence during 1970 and 1971. That the army were unable to react to it was in part due to an almost complete absence of RUC intelligence on loyalist paramilitaries. This failure was noted by the republican population, which drew the appropriate political conclusions.

The second indication of this important policy shift also came during 1971. For the first time, an SAS detachment was deployed in an offensive rather than passive intelligence-gathering role. Moved secretly into Belfast, the SAS troops were attached to the so-called 'Duck Squads'. The name was coined after the first night on which the squads were used. It rained heavily, and the drenched soldiers were followed through the streets by children shouting 'Quack Quack'. Nevertheless, their purpose was lethal. Squad members, faces blackened, waited in concealed positions for anyone carrying a gun or explosives. They could then shoot on sight. There is some evidence that a SAS unit was detailed to cause explosions in order to discredit the IRA around this time. David Seaman, who claimed to be a member of the unit, made the allegation at a Dublin press conference in 1972. His claims were given little publicity in Britain and he was later found dead in a ditch with a bullet through his head. His assassins were never found.

It has also been claimed that SAS troops were involved in the 'Bloody Sunday' incident of January 1972, when 13 unarmed demonstrators were shot dead in Derry by soldiers from the Parachute Regiment. The SAS men were apparently under instruction to shoot at the paratroopers from the roof of a nearby post office, giving them an excuse to fire on the crowd. A number of other accounts have maintained that the incident was planned, although common to all is the lack of a satisfactory motive other than gratuitous anti-republican violence. It is difficult to imagine that even the most bovine army officer could have countenanced an action of such astonishing political inanity. The IRA response was predictable and bloody. The Official wing contributed to a massive campaign of bombing and shootings, which by March had convinced the British government that there was no way in which the devolved Northern Ireland assembly at Stormont Castle could possibly maintain an effective administration. The Stormont parliament was dissolved and London assumed executive and legislative powers over the province.

For the army, the campaign served as an unwelcome reminder that internment had failed tactically – as well as having adverse political effects – and that a major revision of their intelligence-gathering system was required. At the same time, regular army units were unable to patrol in urban republican areas. During 1972, military intelligence underwent a large expansion and army chiefs started to look for a unit which could combine the functions of intelligence-gathering and aggressive patrolling inside republican enclaves.

These were the conditions under which the Military Reconnaissance Force was created. SAS-trained and with a sizable contingent from that regiment, the MRF numbered about forty soldiers armed with Browning 9mm pistols and Sterling sub-machine guns. They were divided into units of around 15, assigned to a particular area, and worked in squads of two to four travelling in a single unmarked vehicle. The army has admitted that on at least three occasions prior to November 1972 the MRF shot civilians. A member of the unit was tried and acquitted of attempted murder in June 1973 after a shooting incident in the staunchly republican Andersonstown district of Belfast. Provisionals who had been 'turned' were used as MRF agents for short periods, making tours of republican areas in specially adapted surveillance vehicles pinpointing safe houses and arms caches.

The MRF's most celebrated intelligence-gathering exercise was the Four Square Laundry, a cut-price dry cleaning service housed above an evangelical bookshop in the Twinbrook area of Belfast. The operators of Four Square drove their van around picking up laundry and local gossip. The clothing was sent to a special unit where it was analysed for traces of explosives and gunpowder. The operation provided a number of arrests. The IRA eventually learnt the function of the laundry and launched a machine-gun attack on the van at the beginning of 1972, killing the driver.

After the 1973 trial of two of its members, the MRF was reorganised into the <u>Special Duties Team</u>, but with little change in its methods or purpose. For instance, *Republican News* claimed that a group of women who for three years sold cosmetics door-to-door belonged to an army intelligence unit. Together with SAS intelligence units they mounted undercover patrols and staffed border surveillance posts.

The second important change made to the British intelligence establishment in the six counties during 1972 was a revised brief for MI6. The agency's work in Ireland before this time was confined to political operations in the Republic: it is understood to have set up the arms deal which led to the trial of Irish government ministers Charles Haughey and Neil Blaney. Although acquitted, they were forced to resign, with the consequent weakening of the republican element in the cabinet. MI6 had now been given a more prominent role in the struggle against the IRA. Three operations from this period have come to light.

The best-known, perhaps, is the saga of the tragi-comic Littlejohn brothers, Kenneth and Keith. Accusations of incompetence levelled by MI6 against army intelligence rebounded embarrassingly onto the agency on this occasion. In 1970, Kenneth Littlejohn was in Ireland, a fugitive from the British police, who believed that he would be able to help with enquiries into a £38,000 robbery for which his brother-in-law, Brian Perks, was gaoled for six years. Littlejohn had a criminal background of robbery which dated back to his military service with the Parachute Regiment, who discharged him 'ignominiously' in 1959 for stealing a cash box. He made a living in Ireland from a Dublin-based clothing firm established under his pseudonym of Kenneth Austen. Home for Littlejohn was County Kerry, where he achieved a reputation as something of a jet-setter. The clothing firm ran into difficulties fairly quickly, and Littlejohn moved to County Louth, near the Irish border. There 'Austen' developed useful links with the republican movement. He learnt a great deal about the types of weapons in IRA use and their sources. Debt-ridden and faced with a summons from the Dublin High Court, he decided to put his knowledge to use. In November 1971, Brian Perks' conviction was quashed by the appeal court, on the grounds that the original trial judge did not give Perks a full hearing. The case against Littlejohn collapsed. On the 21st November, he flew into London.

Kenneth's younger brother, Keith had spent most of 1967 in Borstal, also for robbery. While there he got to know Lady Pamela Onslow, a voluntary prison visitor. They had kept in regular contact after Keith's release, which Kenneth saw as the best opportunity for making contact with the British government. Keith told Lady Onslow that his brother possessed information on the IRA which he wanted to pass on. Lady Onslow contacted the Defence Minister, Lord

Carrington, a personal friend. Carrington authorised his army minister, Geoffrey Johnson-Smith, to meet the Littlejohns at Lady Onslow's house in Kensington. On the evening of the 21st, the meeting took place. Kenneth Littlejohn told the Minister, during a three hour conversation, that the Officials had obtained AK49 assault rifles and planned to assassinate John Taylor, Ulster's hard-line Minister for Home Affairs.

Johnson-Smith was impressed by Littlejohn, and offered to put him in touch with the Special Branch. Littlejohn refused, saying that he was 'not anxious to renew his acquaintance with the police'.[12] The Minister agreed to bring the matter up with the 'appropriate authorities'. The next day Littlejohn went to a flat in Cavell St., in London's East End, where he met an MI6 officer who introduced himself as Douglas Smythe, better known as John Wyman. Littlejohn repeated what he had said to Johnson-Smith. Wyman said he would get back to him.

Littlejohn's offer was finally taken up in February 1972 when an attempt was made to kill John Taylor as he was leaving an office in Armagh. One of those who Littlejohn alleged was responsible, Joe McCann, a battalion commander in Belfast, was shot dead a few days later by an army patrol. Littlejohn's brief was to infiltrate and inform on the Officials, particularly in the Republic, and more importantly to act as an agent provocateur, organising and conducting bank robberies and bomb attacks in the Republic for which the Officials would be held responsible. MI6 were hoping that this would force the Irish government to introduce stronger legislation against the IRA, many of whose members had fled to the south when internment began. Additionally, the bomb attacks would undermine the Officials' political support in the south.

As a spy, Littlejohn was largely ineffective. Much of the information he supplied to Wyman, whom he met regularly, was inaccurate. The Gardai watched in bemusement as Littlejohn cavorted around the country. Individual officers have since stated that they were told to leave both the brothers alone. Between February and October 1972, Littlejohn claims to have been involved in twelve bank robberies. One of these, in June 1972 in the northern market town of Newry, netted £70,000. RUC detectives questioned the Littlejohns about the raid, following a tip-off from a local solicitor whose suspicion was aroused after he had received a large deposit in £10 notes on a house in Louth. No charges were brought. Kenneth Littlejohn claims knowledge of at least four other robberies which were cleared by British intelligence, but in which he took no part. He has also said that he was required to kill IRA leaders, from both factions. One of these was Seamus Costello, an Official who later became one of the founders of the Irish Republican Socialist Party; another was Sean Garland, who he was told was also an Official; the third, Sean MacStiofain, director of Provisional intelligence. MacStiofain was at that time on the IRA delegation led by Daithi O'Conaill which was engaged in secret discussions with British officials at which a fifteen-point plan for Irish unification was floated. According to Littlejohn, MI6 'were convinced that if it had not been for him the whole problem could have been solved'.[13] The list of those to be killed was given to Littlejohn by his controller, Wyman. Two petrol bomb attacks, on police stations at Louth and Castlebellingham, both in the Republic, are cited as further examples of Littlejohn's work.

The career of the Littlejohns as British agents came to an end after a raid on the Allied Irish Bank in Grafton St., Dublin. On the morning of the 12th October 1972, a group of men, consisting of the Littlejohns and some disenchanted Officials, arrived at the home of the manager, Noel Curran. His family was held at gunpoint while Curran drove the Littlejohns to Grafton St. to open the vaults. The staff were bundled into these as they arrived and locked in after £67,000 had been removed. Kenneth Littlejohn left his fingerprints all over the building, and neither man made any effort to hide his face: they were subsequently identified by no less than fourteen members of the staff. Keith then drove Kenneth's car to Dublin airport, managed to wipe all the prints off, but left an electricity bill inside with Kenneth's address on it. The brothers then travelled to London via Belfast and Scotland, and met up with Kenneth's wife and his former business partner, Robert Stockman. They planned to buy a restaurant in Torquay with the proceeds of the Dublin robbery, but their dream was short-lived. On the morning of October 19th, Littlejohn had his last meeting with Wyman in Trafalgar Square. Shortly afterwards armed police burst into Stockman's home, arresting him, Kenneth and Kenneth's wife. Leading the raid was Inspector John Parker, who had flown into London once the Gardai had accumulated evidence of the Littlejohns' involvment. Officers from Scotland Yard's Flying Squad made up the arresting group. The intelligence services were unaware of what had taken place until Kenneth Littlejohn asked Parker to phone an Inspector Sinclair at the Special Branch. Wyman had told Littlejohn that in the event of any difficulties with police, a call to Sinclair, who ran the Branch's Irish desk, would suffice to clear the ground. Parker rang Sinclair, informing him of Kenneth Littlejohn's arrest (Keith was picked up the same day at his home in Torquay). 'So what?' replied Sinclair.

MI6 realised that there was nothing they could do to prevent proceedings against Littlejohn without a lot of unseemly publicity. The change of heart on the part of the Gardai resulted from the disillusionment within a section of the force who were taking the blame for failing to curb IRA activity, while they knew all the time that British agents were responsible. MI6 were caught. Disrupting or undermining the extradition procedure would incur the wrath of the Gardai and diminish the chances of future security co-operation, while failing to help Littlejohn would lead to an unwelcome spotlight on themselves. They decided to risk the latter course, hoping perhaps that the story from his lips would be fairly implausible, and besides, there was still a moderate chance of preventing him from saying anything. On the 21st December, the Littlejohns' solicitor, Peter Hughman, wrote to the Ministry of Defence laying out his clients' claim to have been working for MI6. On January 3rd, Irish and British officials met to discuss the case. The British fully admitted that the Littlejohns were their agents. The following day Hughman obtained a reply from the Ministry confirming that the meeting with Johnson-Smith had taken place. Extradition proceedings resumed on January 10th. Counsel for the Attorney-General moved that the rest of the case be held in camera, which the presiding magistrate accepted. The remainder of the hearing was held behind closed doors; when it ended after a fortnight, extradition orders were granted for the two brothers and Stockman. An appeal to the Lord Chief Justice, Lord Widgery, failed and the three were extradited to Dublin in March 1973. The charges against Stockman were dropped on arrival, but the Littlejohns were committed to trial for the Allied Irish robbery in the juryless Special Criminal Court. Only witnesses who would tend to disprove their part in the robbery were deemed admissable; any who might testify that although the brothers were present they were acting on instructions from the British authorities were barred from taking the stand. The brothers were duly convicted and received severe sentences: 20 years for Kenneth and 15 for Keith. (The Irish parole system is rather less liberal than the British.)

Kenneth enjoyed a brief spell of freedom when he escaped from Dublin's Mountjoy prison during 1974. From his refuge in Amsterdam, he gave interviews to the BBC *Panorama* programme and to the London magazine *Time Out*, which had followed the story closely. Both brothers were eventually released prematurely in September 1981 on humanitarian grounds.

While the Littlejohns were fighting extradition in London, their erstwhile controller, John Wyman, was in trouble in Dublin. On the 19th December 1972, Wyman was arrested with Patrick Crinnion, a sergeant in the Gardai's Special Branch then working in section C3, which deals with terrorism and subversion. Two days later, both men were charged under the Irish Official Secrets Act of 1963: Crinnion with obtaining and communicating official information between

August 1 and December 19, 1972, and Wyman with knowingly receiving it. A second British intelligence officer, named as Andrew James Johnstone, was sought but never found; and another Garda was also believed to have been recruited by the British. At the time of Crinnion's arrest at Dublin's Burlington Hotel, ten documents were found secreted under the carpet of his car. All originated from the files held by the Gardai on the IRA. The fact that such information had reached Whitehall became clear at a meeting between Edward Heath and Jack Lynch during 1972, at which Lynch was reportedly "'astounded' at the depth and accuracy of Mr. Heath's knowledge of IRA activities in the Republic".[14]

Wyman and Crinnion were remanded in custody until January 12. Wyman faced two charges and Crinnion four. At the next hearing, counsel for the Irish Attorney-General said that further charges against Wyman were under consideration, and asked for a further adjournment. During the next court session, most of which was held in secret, Wyman's background came under scrutiny in the press. He had given his address as 3 Swan Walk, a block of flats in the Chelsea district of London. He did not in fact live there but was acquainted with the two sisters who did. His occupation was given as private investigator; his employers, Bateman Investigations of Long Hanborough, Oxfordshire – a firm run by <u>Brian Bateman,</u> a former police detective who retired as head of Oxford CID. Bateman Investigations paid Wyman's defence costs and arranged for a leading copyright lawyer and thriller writer, Michael Gilbert, to travel to Dublin to arrange legal assistance for him. The *Sunday Times* summarised the enigma surrounding this peculiar set of circumstances:

> We have not discovered why Bateman Investigations should have been employing Wyman – a man about whom nothing but a Chelsea address is known – in Dublin; nor why a lawyer with a lucrative copyright practice should have arrived to help him.[15]

On February 13, Wyman and Crinnion appeared in court once again. The documents which had been found in Crinnion's car, and which formed the main part of the evidence against both men, were not brought to the court because they were deemed too sensitive, even though the session was held *in camera* with the most rigorous security. As a result, the original six charges were dropped. Four supplementary charges remained against Wyman and his agent. Again they were remanded in custody, this time until February 26. On the 27th both men were found guilty of the charge of attempting to obtain or communicate official information, which carries a maximum sentence of six months. The national security aspect had been dropped with the main charges a fortnight before. Wyman and Crinnion were both sentenced to three months imprisonment, but having already served two on remand, were immediately released.

Speculation immediately arose that the British and Irish governments had arranged an exchange: the Littlejohns for Wyman and Crinnion. The following August, Jack Lynch's former Attorney-General, Colm Condon, furiously pronounced the thesis 'a disreputable lie', saying that Lynch had only been informed of the purely legal aspects of the Littlejohn case, and not of its sensitive political nature. This was a disingenuous statement, and unfortunately for Lynch was contradicted later in the day by the Government Information Service, which issued a press release indicating that Lynch had been told of the Littlejohn's espionage activities soon after the meeting between British and Irish officials on January 3rd. Lynch's memory had failed him, as sometimes happens with government ministers.

Despite the public embarrassment of their security authorities, the British government achieved its main objective: the passage of strong anti-terrorist legislation through the Dail. Two conveniently timed car bombs, which exploded in Dublin the night before the vote, produced an overnight switch of policy in the opposition Fine Gael and Labour parties, whose votes in favour carried the measures through the Dail.

When Littlejohn escaped from Mountjoy prison in 1974, MI6 sent another of their agents, Leslie Aspin, to find him and persuade him to give himself up. Aspin managed to locate Littlejohn but failed to persuade him, and returned to London alone. Aspin's handler, 'Homer', was not pleased and his career as an MI6 agent came to a temporary close. Aspin had been a smuggler transporting goods into Britain from the Middle East. In 1970 he was arrested at Heathrow airport by Special Branch officers on instruction from MI6. After a four-hour interview, during which Aspin says he was shown photographs of himself talking to contacts, he was allowed to leave, having been told 'how much good I could do my country'.

> A couple of days later I was visited by a man who gave me a 'queen and country' lecture, appealing to my patriotism.
>
> Mind you, he also told me it would be a great pity if my friends in the Middle East knew I had been talking with security men.[16]

Aspin took the point ... Several meetings with 'Homer' and deputy 'Frank Abbott' took place at London's Cumberland Hotel. As a result of these Aspin was sent back to the Middle East to develop contacts which could later be used to organise arms deals with the IRA. He also provided information on the activities of Palestinian guerilla groups, particularly Black September. His first success was to learn of the *Claudia* arms shipment from Libya for the Provisionals. Aspin contacted 'Homer', and an air and sea watch was mounted to chart the progress of the *Claudia* from Tripoli to the Irish Republic.

When the boat reached Irish territorial waters, Irish security officers seized the boat, but only after most of its cargo had been jettisoned. MI6 were impressed by 'Homer' and instructed him to set up a deal between the IRA and Middle Eastern sources. 'Homer' told Aspin to contact Kenneth Littlejohn in Newry. For the supplier, Aspin found a Libyan diplomat in Malta willing to provide arms. After a series of trips between Malta, Amsterdam and Dublin, Aspin arranged the shipment of six Soviet rocket launchers and seven tons of automatic weapons. The *Sea Fox* picked up the consignment from Malta and set off for its final destination of Killala Bay off Ireland's west coast, where it was planned to drag the cases into the nets of fishing boats waiting in the bay. Through 'Homer', the Irish security forces were informed, and a patrol boat prepared to intercept the *Sea Fox* before the exchange was made. The patrol boat missed the incoming vessel, and by the time it was found, the greater part of the consignment was in the possession of the fishing boats. As before, Aspin was not affected by this mishap: he was paid by both MI6 and in a commission from the Libyan dealer.

Aspin's last job relating to Ireland, as mentioned, was to ferret out Kenneth Littlejohn. Two years later he turned up as an assistant to John Banks in the mercenary recruitment scheme for Angola. His intelligence contacts had clearly not deserted him.

Aspin claims to have located Littlejohn in Amsterdam at a bar named 'The Pink Elephant' during March 1974. Curiously enough, the premises above the bar were, at some time in the same year, occupied by James McCann, an arms dealer who regularly supplied the Provisionals, and who was the target of an apparently separate MI6 operation.[17] Their agent was Howard Marks, a drug dealer and friend of McCann's. Marks graduated from Balliol College, Oxford in 1967 and after a cursory effort at postgraduate work at the University of Sussex returned to Oxford to run a boutique called Annabelinda's. He also became heavily involved in drug smuggling and through contacts in the business got to know McCann. This association had not escaped the notice of British intelligence. According to an account published in the *New Statesman* in 1979,[18] Marks was recruited following a visit from an MI6 officer and former Balliol contemporary, Hamilton McMillan, who told him to co-operate or be handed over to the Customs authorities. There is some evidence that his recruitment pre-dated this incident, which took place in 1972, by perhaps a year or so. In this second version of the story the recruitment method was identical, but it has not been possible to confirm the details.

Marks was under instruction to gather information about McCann, and MI6 also asked him to set up branches of Annabelinda's in Zurich and Amsterdam for use as fronts. Marks started to strengthen his friendship with McCann, staying at his home just ouside Dublin and holidaying with him in Ibiza.

In September 1973, the American end of the drugs ring Marks worked with was broken. It was shipping hashish from Europe to America – a novel idea at that time – and carrying marijuana on the return journey. The plants and resins were hidden inside musical and electronic equipment belonging to a non-existent rock group. The following month, McCann's girlfriend was arrested in Hamburg and questioned in depth about McCann. McCann began to suspect Marks as an informant. Shortly afterwards he was ambushed by a group of heavily-armed men, which he has since claimed was an assassination attempt by MI6. McCann survived the attack but before he could trace Marks, the dealer had been arrested, apparently by coincidence, by Dutch police. Two British customs officers flew to Amsterdam to interview Marks, after which he voluntarily agreed to return to Britain, although he was not threatened with extradition. He was charged with drug smuggling and remanded in Brixton prison. Shortly afterwards he was released on £50,000 bail and went back to Oxford, due to face trial in May 1974.

On April 19th a man called at Marks's home. Marks left with him, jumped bail and travelled to Italy. It is still unclear with whom he departed. A trial would certainly have been embarrassing for MI6, in view of the recent Littlejohn affair and the death of Kenneth Lennon (a Special Branch informer). Marks was known to be working on the defence that his actions were necessary to his function as an intelligence agent. However, Marks's girlfriend, Rosemary Lewis, told the *Daily Mail* that 'Howard was under pressure from the American drug racket. I am convinced they are behind his disappearance'.[19] Another report states that the visitor announced himself as from 'Customs and Excise'. Whoever was behind his flight, it was most timely for MI6.

Marks's parents visited him in Italy during September. He told them he had been abducted, but refused to say by whom, claiming that he was still under a threat. He explained to them how MI6 had blackmailed him into working for them, and said that one of his tasks was to find out which banks the money used to finance arms deals was being kept in. McCann, meanwhile, had surfaced in Dublin, where he gave an interview to the *Sunday Independent* in which he described a special unit composed of MI6, Customs and Special Branch officers set up to combat arms smuggling. He said that the unit operated from Tintagel House in London, close to the River Thames, and busied itself setting up front companies for arms deals to see who used them. He also claimed that Marks was a double-agent, working for the IRA.

During the police investigation into Marks's disappearance, MI6 confirmed that he had been working for them. Superintendent Fairweather of Thames Valley police, who was in charge of the enquiry, was summoned to the offices of Bernard Shelton, the MI5 legal adviser, who told him McMillan had requested Marks to obtain information on the Provisional IRA.

Marks was not rearrested until 1980, although he had been able to come back to Britain and move freely around the country. Only when he became involved in drug smuggling once again did Customs decide that they should act in spite of possible embarrassment to MI6. The story had already broken by then in the form of an article in the *New Statesman*.[20] A programme based on the same material was scheduled for London Weekend Television but came off at the last moment after Programme Controller Michael Grade took legal advice. The Independent Broadcasting Authority would have banned it anyway on instruction from MI5. LWT apparently knew 'only one twentieth of the whole story',[21] in the words of an IBA spokesman. Part of what is still submerged relates to Marks's alleged involvement with intelligence work for the Mexican government, directed against the Cuban exiles who run much of the arms and heroin trade in the Carribean basin. The 'one twentieth' which LWT did know was largely based on Superintendent Fairweather's report of the police inquiry. Fairweather committed suicide in December 1981: no reasons were presented at the inquest, contrary to normal practice. The most popular theory is that he was under investigation for having leaked copies of his own report to the press. Special Branch officers are known to have been making enquiries into the leakage of the report, copies of which are now widely available, around this time.

Marks was picked up in the Suffolk town of Lakenham and committed for trial charged with the importation of 15 tons of Colombian cannabis. The trial jury acquitted him, the result of inconsistencies in the prosecution evidence, but found him guilty of an additional charge of possessing a false passport. (He had at least half a dozen.) A new charge relating to the original transatlantic smuggling operation was filed against him, for which he was found guilty and sentenced to three years imprisonment. Having already served 18 months in custody on remand, he has, at the time of writing, almost certainly been released.

The Littlejohn fiasco and the attendant publicity led to the removal of many of MI6's field officers in both parts of Ireland, who are believed to have numbered up to 20, and also of the senior MI6 men in Lisburn and Belfast, who were replaced by MI5. 1974 was also a year of momentous political developments. On the UK mainland, the Heath government self-destructed in the face of miners' strikes, landing Harold Wilson back in Downing Street. In Northern Ireland,

MAY 1975
Craig.
Smellie
replaced
by Ian Cameron.

sections of the loyalist leadership launched an immense attack on the power-sharing executive which had assumed some of the functions of Stormont – security was under direct control from London. An all-out strike by the loyalist Ulster Workers' Council (UWC) began in the middle of May 1974, with the objective of bringing an end to power-sharing. The army and MI5 were quietly pleased by the executive's disintegration, as an intelligence officer told David McKittrick of the *Irish Times*:

> we could tell from the start that the UWC strike could develop into something serious ... our assessment was that while we could run the power-stations at ordinary times, we could not have coped with major faults, or with sabotage. For those reasons we advised Rees [Secretary of State for Northern Ireland] not to move against the strikers. But some of us also hoped that the strike would make progress and Wilson and Rees would be defeated. We thought that if the Protestants won, Wilson would be discredited. And we hoped that if power-sharing failed, then the United Kingdom population would say Ulster had had its last chance politically, and would advocate an all-out effort for military victory.[22]

Although the strike was successful, the Wilson administration remained intact. Its next move was to renew contacts with the republican movement. The Provisionals were split in their response to the UWC strike; an editorial in *Republican News* welcomed the action, but it reflected only the opinions of right-wingers who saw the possibility of accommodation with the loyalists. The editorial line switched back in subsequent issues. MI5 and the army both believed that the IRA could be destroyed – the *Irish Times* informant claimed that military intelligence had a wall chart of the entire Belfast brigade – and only needed the green light from London. Several Belfast commanders had been arrested in quick succession and the IRA realised that it was in serious trouble. London evidently decided that these were the best circumstances in which to conduct negotiations with the IRA, for the government felt that extracting concessions from them was essential for a lasting peace. The British team, which included Sir Frank Cooper, Permanent Under-Secretary at the Ministry of Defence and James Allan from MI6, arranged a truce with the Provisionals, which was to be monitored through a network of incident centres.

While armed hostilities ceased temporarily, the propaganda war continued. A new committee chaired by Michael Cudlipp was set up in 1974 to take charge of black propaganda operations. Staffed by representatives of the Northern Ireland Office, RUC, and the army, including Jeremy Railton, head of the Information Policy Unit, its targets included both republican and loyalist paramilitary leaders.

Lurid details of their personal lives, allegations of embezzlement and involvement in sectarian assassinations were fabricated and fed to selected journalists.

Further additions were made to the British intelligence establishment in the province. At the beginning of 1975, some 40 to 50 SAS *1974.* were attached to military intelligence, which used the cease-fire to improve its knowledge of IRA units outside Belfast as well as monitoring Provisional attitudes towards the cease-fire. Politically, the government made little headway in this period and the cease-fire collapsed at the end of 1975 amid mutual recrimination, although it had outlived its tactical use to both sides. The IRA, rested and regrouped, resumed its attacks on military and economic targets at the end of 1975. The government declared that no future negotiations would take place with the IRA, and announced a new policy described as 'Ulsterisation' or 'normalisation'. This was a belated use of a strategy well-known to counter-insurgency theorists: the deployment of indigenously-raised security forces to undercut the nationalist political position. The fact that both the RUC and the Ulster Defence Regiment were, and remain, over 90 per cent staffed by protestants was unlikely to reassure republicans, but removing the IRA's ability to make a clear identification of the army as the main enemy was seen as a valuable political gambit. Reorganisation of the RUC had begun in 1974, with 'normalisation' then a possibility if circumstances allowed. Over the next two years the RUC was moulded into a 6,000 strong paramilitary force equipped with high-velocity weapons and riot control gear, and including the United Kingdom's largest Special Patrol Group and second largest Special Branch (after that of the Metropolitan Police). The government then decided that the first stages of transition from army to RUC policing could begin, the RUC gradually supplanting the army in the forefront of the war against the IRA. Internment, so politically damaging to the government, was phased out, and with it the 'political status' afforded to paramilitary prisoners and detainees. A new formula was devised for taking paramilitary suspects out of circulation, constructed around a revised legal process. The key element was the 'Diplock Court' after the judge of the same name. The most important feature of this type of court is that there is no jury, and the evidence is assessed by a panel of judges. Significantly, they are able to convict only on the basis of statements (made by defendants while in RUC custody). The easiest way – and often the only one – of securing convictions, then, was to ensure that suspects could be routinely induced to sign statements.

Military psychologists have long believed that the most effective method of breaking a prisoner's resistance to interrogation is by self-inflicted pain: hence the technique of making prisoners stand, legs apart, leaning on a wall supported only by their fingertips for long periods. Hooding, sleep deprivation, large variations of cell temperature and subjection to continuous 'white noise' quicken the process of breakdown. The responsibility for interrogations using these methods was assigned to the RUC's four Regional Crime Squads in 1976, whose 89 officers received instruction in the techniques from military intelligence officers.

In the first years of its use, the policy was highly successful. By the middle of 1977, over 2,000 convicted Provisionals were in prison. The army's initial opposition to 'normalisation' faded, and it came to accept its role of support to the RUC and intelligence-gathering. The number of SAS men in the province had by now been increased to 160 and a new army commander appointed: General Timothy Creasey, one of the growing corps of senior army officers with experience of counter-insurgency. Creasey led the Omani armed forces for three years in the successful campaign against the PFLO (see p.141). Secretary of State Roy Mason, who had replaced Rees, publicly announced the success of 'normalisation'. Although no doubt pleased by the apparent triumph, there must have been mixed feelings down at Century House: MI6 had been all but expelled from the province by Mason, and remained outside it until 1979.

Again the IRA was in a state of crisis, but this time there was no chance of obtaining a breathing-space to regroup. It became clear to Provisional commanders that a fundamental structural revision was essential to avoid a real threat of annihilation. The task for British intelligence was made simpler than it need have been by the nature of Provisional organisation, which used a formal army structure of brigades, battalions and companies. Moreover, each Provisional unit was assigned to a particular area, making it easier to fit suspects to particular attacks. The Provisionals felt that the system did have political advantages, chiefly the close contact it allowed them with the republican community. In particular, their ability to police certain republican enclaves was an important demonstration of their legitimacy in these areas. The solution, in essence, was to divide the functions of policing and conducting the war between different sections of the organisation. The IRA was reorganised on a regional basis, with volunteers from each brigade (Belfast, Derry, Border etc.) working in autonomous 'active service units' of no more than half a dozen members. Different phases of each operation – obtaining vehicles, moving weapons, and so on – are carried out by different units, which have no designated fixed area within the brigade region. This type of structure, which is more like that used by other guerilla organisations, had been employed on a small scale in 1973 but now became the norm for the organisation. Policing and community contact became the responsibility of a new body described as the Civil and Military Administration, which worked closely with the republican political organisation Sinn Fein, sharing the tasks of community control, political mobilisation and propaganda.

Around the same time, it became apparent that the northern-based republican movement had undergone a decisive political shift, with the political and military apparatus coming under the control of secular, radical elements, displacing the pre-eminent catholic strain in the movement. (Such a process is not uncommon among guerilla organisations, as the political development of the Cuban guerillas led by Fidel Castro and the South Yemeni National Liberation Front shows.) Over the next two or three years a similar transformation occurred inside Sinn Fein, with the result that the republican movement as a whole now rejects the legitimacy of the Dublin government, which it describes as 'quisling', and is firmly committed to opposing it politically. It seems likely, moreover, that long-term Provisional military strategy allows for armed opposition to the Irish state. For while the main political parties in the Republic, especially the Fianna Fail party led by Charles Haughey, have publicly supported reunification, they are equally committed to the capitalist economic development of the country. The priority for the IRA, however, remains the expulsion of British rule from the six counties.

Further innovations and refinements to the intelligence machinery continued while changes to the IRA organisation took place. Probably the most important was the introduction of computers to assist the army. There has been some confusion – generated deliberately, it seems – over the precise capabilities of the system installed at the army's Lisburn headquarters. What is certain is that computers are used to analyse vehicle movements. Part of the army's task is staffing road checkpoints at the entrances to large towns and frontier posts, where soldiers are able to call up details on a car and its occupants by radio from indexes held at Lisburn. 12 of the most-used border crossing points are equipped with terminal link-ups.

Towards the end of 1978, evidence of the ill-treatment in custody on which the RUC relied for extracting confessions had accumulated beyond the level at which it could be dismissed as republican propaganda. An Amnesty International study confirmed that the allegations were supported in fact. The government set up an enquiry under Judge Bennett, whose report broadly supported Amnesty's conclusions and recommended the monitoring of interrogations by closed-circuit television. The security forces were badly upset by the exposures, as illustrated by the smear campaign against a former RUC doctor who had made numerous examinations of paramilitary suspects detained by the police and described typical injuries to the press. The 'normalisation' policy was crucially dependent on these interrogation techniques, and when it was no longer possible to use them, the policy disintegrated.

The army began to lobby for a return to the pre-1976 situation where they were in overall charge of security, as a result of which their relations with the RUC deteriorated to their lowest point since the beginning of the decade. Roy Mason's optimistic pronouncements of 1977 were quietly forgotten as the prospect of outright victory over the IRA dwindled. A Defence Intelligence Staff report obtained by the IRA in early 1979, and published in part during May of that year, conceded that

> the Provisional leadership is deeply committed to a long campaign of attrition. The Provisional IRA has the dedication and sinews of war to raise violence intermittently to at least the level of early 1978, certainly for the forseeable future.

The document, entitled 'Northern Ireland Future Terrorist Trends' and classified as 'secret', discussed likely trends in the tactics and weaponry of the IRA up to the end of 1983.[23] It made a cursory mention of the Irish National Liberation Army (INLA), the guerilla organisation politically allied to the Irish Republican Socialist Party formed by Seamus Costello and Bernadette MacAliskey. An operational agreement between the IRA and INLA, which was eventually arranged, was seen as particularly dangerous.

Politically, the most interesting feature of the document was its despairing assessment of potential developments. There was little chance, in the DIS's view, of removing the raison d'etre of either the IRA or the INLA:

> Even if 'peace' is restored, the motivation for politically inspired violence will remain. Arms will be readily available and there will be many who are willing and able to use them. Any peace will be superficial and brittle.

The army's senior staff were clearly resigned to a long period of attempting to contain republican military activity as best they could, an attitude which was noted by the IRA:

> The Brits are very, very good at undercover work. This is what they're into now. Nevertheless we are totally satisfied that we know why our active service units are caught. While the British are good we always know where they operate and why they operate. Because the population is hostile to them they tell us about them. They're not that effective but they're a hindrance and they probably perceive their role as that.[24]

Provisional leaders admit nonetheless that approximately five out of six operations are postponed or cancelled as a result of British surveillance. Security force morale, already poor following the demise of 'normalisation' was further lowered by a series of attacks by the IRA and INLA which achieved immense political damage. In March 1979, the IRA killed the British ambassador to the Netherlands, and the INLA planted a bomb underneath the car of Tory Northern Ireland spokesman Airey Neave, which exploded just outside the House of Commons car park. The death of Neave was a severe personal blow to Mrs Thatcher: he was a close personal friend, and was expected to join her cabinet after the May general election, probably as 'minister without portfolio' with responsibility for the intelligence complex. The election campaign itself, as on preceding occasions, pointedly ignored the issue of Northern Ireland, reflecting the 'bipartisan' policy prevailing at Westminster. Although the background to it is somewhat different, the policy compares unfavourably with the colonial and other secret wars fought by Britain with the tacit approval of both major parties and beyond the reach of public debate. Almost four months after the Conservative victory, the IRA assassinated the Queen's cousin, Earl Mountbatten, with a bomb inside a lobster pot in his habitual holiday fishing area off the west coast of Donegal. On the same day eighteen soldiers were killed near the Armagh village of Warrenpoint by two IRA culvert mines.

Selective internment was widely expected as the response to these two attacks. Instead the government announced the appointment of Sir Maurice Oldfield as security co-ordinator. The ageing spy-master was wheeled out of All Souls' College, Oxford, where he was writing a book on international affairs, to take up the post – which the government gave the impression of having recently created. It had in fact been in existence since 1970, but a major change was made to the brief before Oldfield took over: previous appointees were confined to 'tasking' – delineating collection areas for different services – and arbitration in inter-service disputes. Each agency submitted its own reports. Thatcher was apparently appalled by the disparity between reports, whose net value was virtually zero. So Oldfield was instructed to take charge of all intelligence production from Northern Ireland. Although he retired after six months suffering from mental fatigue, the structure he originated was inherited and maintained by his successor, Brooks Richards. Oldfield's appointment itself had nothing to do with Warrenpoint and Mountbatten.

According to details published in the Dublin-based *Sunday Tribune*,[25] Oldfield established an intelligence directorate known with quaint bureaucratic anonymity as 'The Department', and moved in a lot of MI6's old Ireland hands, including the Littlejohns' controller, John Wyman. The senior 'Department' officer in Northern Ireland is from MI6 and works under the direction of the Security Co-ordinator from London. He chairs a committee composed of representatives of

MI6, MI5, military intelligence, the SAS, the RUC Special Branch and the Bronze section of the RUC Special Patrol Group which has plain-clothes patrol duties. The committee has a support staff of 20 drawn from the RUC, army and the Northern Ireland Office.

The committee organises tasking on a day-to-day basis for the army through a DIS colonel, and for the RUC Special Branch through a lieutenant-colonel on the staff of the Intelligence Corps. This latter officer, codenamed Echo Five, is also responsible for yet another intelligence squad named the Special Military Intelligence Unit, to which Robert Nairac, an SAS captain executed by the IRA in 1977, belonged. The unit's precise function is obscure. 'The Department' supervises the work of MI5 and MI6 in Ireland: significantly, it has assumed control of MI6's Dublin station.

Outside of the UK and Ireland, the largest slice of the directorate's work is in the United States, where the 20 million strong Irish-American community has long been a source of finance and support for the IRA. Money from America is believed to provide about 20 per cent of the Provisionals' annual income of between £1 million and £1.5 million. Among political lobbies associated with a particular country, the Irish is second only to the Jewish in effectiveness. Again the 1978 DIS report did not anticipate any change in this situation. The lobby's impact has been softened to some extent by the close attentions of the Federal Bureau of Investigation. MI6 appears to be equally concerned by the influence of prominent establishment politicians with Irish constituencies or political bases who make criticisms of British government policy. Among these are Senator Edward Kennedy, Hugh Carey (Governor of New York) and Thomas 'Tip' O'Neill, the Speaker of the House of Representatives. They are not so troublesome for the British as they were, having made note of the political shift within the Provisionals.

As far as weapons are concerned, it may be that some US-based supporters assist with arms shipments, but there are numerous American arms dealers who would sell weapons to anybody. The IRA has a reputation for prompt payment.

The British government's attitude towards the Irish-American lobby is that its views are based on ignorance and the blind acceptance of republican propaganda. They have, therefore, concluded that counter-propaganda is the best way of tackling it. An interesting recent example was *Northern Ireland Chronicle*, a 50-minute documentary film under production during 1981. It was made by the Central Office of Information – a government department providing publicity materials and services to other government departments – for the Foreign and Commonwealth Office, with the American market as the main target. The FCO has isolated twenty 'points of issue' on which to base its campaigns: these will deal with 'some of the more commonly raised questions about Northern Ireland', in the words of the introduction to the draft script. It continues by saying that,

> in the final film it is expected that most if not all of these points with be dealt with, in a manner which reflects the guidelines set down by the FCO.

The end product shows that the tenets of propaganda operations which directed the massive IRD campaigns of the 1950s are still adhered to in Whitehall; primarily, careful selection and ordering of facts to give a misleading impression. The commentary of the film explains Diplock courts as follows:

> although, as in a Magistrate's Court, there is no jury ... the basic principles of British justice have been maintained: the defendent is tried publicly in an open court, is represented by a lawyer, and has an automatic right of appeal.

The key issue of conviction on the basis of unsupported statements is completely avoided. Furthermore, the analogy with Magistrate's courts is spurious since Diplock Courts hear charges, such as murder and weapons offences, which in Britain would automatically be referred to a jury court.

The proscriptions made against certain protestant paramilitary groups – 'the UVF*, the Ulster Freedom Fighters and the Red Hand Commandos ... like the IRA are illegal' – is used in the film to give an illustration of the even-handedness of the security authorities. It does not explain why the Ulster Defence Association, referred to earlier in the documentary as a protestant paramilitary organisation (it is also the largest) has not been proscribed. On a more bizarre note, the Easter-Rising is described 'as the great Republican myth'.

Returning to 'The Department', it retains the function of minimising friction between different intelligence services. Reports that the RUC is planning to deploy an SAS-type unit will, if true, not make its task any easier. Yet despite the myriad agencies, technologies and methods in use, the latest tactic for dealing with paramilitaries seems to have been borrowed from the Italian security forces, who have used it with great success against the Brigate Rosse: for while 1982 may be 'Information Technology Year' elsewhere, in the urban ghettoes of Northern Ireland it is the 'Year of the Supergrass'.

In the past, members of paramilitary organisations have been 'turned' within their group and used in other ways, by the MRF for instance, but getting them to give evidence against large numbers of their former associates has not been tried before. The incentive for 'supergrasses' is immunity from prosecution, money, a new identity and a new home, either abroad or in one of Britain's new towns. The

* Ulster Volunteer Force.

problem of juries refusing to believe 'supergrass' evidence does not affect Diplock courts, but some prospective 'supergrasses' have withdrawn their evidence, claiming that statements were extracted under duress. The policy has other purposes beyond simply bringing large numbers of paramilitaries before the courts. The appearance of a former colleague as a 'supergrass' has a demoralising effect on remaining members of the organisation, raising doubts about their own roles and heightening suspicions towards their fellows. For the state, there are obvious propaganda dividends from parading disillusioned paramilitaries and also from the effect it has in diverting attention from its own activities. At the time of writing, a number of important cases are outstanding and their degree of success will naturally determine future 'supergrass' policy.

The current security force strategy remains one of disruption; the objective a tolerably low level of paramilitary violence, with the recognition that certain areas cannot be policed. The IRA, for their part, realise that there is a negligible chance of driving the British out of the north but that they do have the ability to make the administration of the province an immense economic burden. It is impossible to give figures for the additional cost of maintaining security forces resulting from IRA and INLA activity but it is certainly in hundreds of millions of pounds. The economic cost in destruction and frightening off of potential investors is similarly large and inestimable.

A model counter-insurgency campaign has never been possible in Northern Ireland because of the difficulty of devising the relevant political formulae which must be coupled with the security measures in order to suppress and undermine the basis of republican support. The IRA, which is not, strictly speaking, conducting an insurgency recognises a maximum possible level of support of about 40 per cent of the population. It does not even try to woo loyalist opinion any more. The IRA is at a stage where it can predict, with reasonable accuracy, the change in support for them following particular military actions. The participation of Sinn Fein on an abstentionist basis in the elections for a new northern assembly should provide similar data for assessing a range of possible political initiatives.

A standard form of political action, in the Bissell sense of the term, is covert funding of political parties and one obvious candidate is the catholic, middle class dominated Social Democratic and Labour Party. There is not even the suspicion that it has ever received clandestine help from London, attributable probably to the difficulty of finding a suitable channel. The party has close and long-established links with the political parties in the Republic, which obviates any need to turn to London should it need assistance.

On the protestant side, it is likely that loyalist leaders will become more pliable as the northern economy deteriorates and the traditional loyalist industries – shipbuilding, aircraft and transport – collapse. The margin of cheaper labour and a guaranteed market share for British firms in the province provided the primary economic motives for maintaining British rule, but these advantages have been offset by the cost of Westminster's special subventions. Economic quesions have not been prominent over the last decade, but now form a central feature of a new policy which has emerged from London, the effect of which has been to internationalise the problems of Ireland.

When Ireland joined the EEC in 1973, at the same time as Britain, the supply of cheap labour made it a natural location for multinational companies, notably American, to use as an export platform for the European market, taking advantage of the removal of tariff barriers. The absence of any significant manufacturing base made this task relatively simple, but did produce problems. The Irish transport and telecommunications systems were inadequate to cope with the capital influx while the enthusiasm of the Irish government to increase it still further led it to make over-generous fiscal concessions: removing taxes on export products and providing 50% non-repayable grants for factory establishment. Although on paper the Irish economy was among the healthiest in the West, the cracks began to show through with the onset of recession. Ireland now has a larger per capita debt than Poland. With the economies of Britain, Northern Ireland and the Irish Republic in parlous condition, some scheme involving capital from the United States and the healthier parts of Europe became essential to redress the imbalances in the Irish economy. Additionally, corporations in both parts of Ireland saw better co-ordination of northern and southern economic activity as potentially a substantial source of mutual benefit.

A prerequisite to the latter was improved cross-border security co-operation. In 1980, the Irish government established a Border Task Force to mount patrols and observation posts in the same way as had been practised in the north for years. It also authorised a considerable increase in overflight facilities for British military aircraft into Irish airspace. The Gardai has devoted more resources to tracking down IRA arms dumps and training camps. Meanwhile the Dail has introduced legislation allowing for prosecution of suspects in the south for crimes committed in the UK. The complaints of the DIS at the end of 1978 that the Irish government did not have much heart for the pursuit of terrorists are no longer justified. This is not to say that Irish intelligence has ceased its habit of spreading disinformation to deceive Whitehall and the northern security forces, when appropriate.

The EEC has been a useful forum for discussion between British, Irish and other European officials on economic matters, and with the

British and West German governments leading the way, this has slowly extended to cover political co-operation and certain aspects of European security. Despite being outside NATO (the only EEC member in this position) Ireland was routinely represented at informal discussions on these topics and engages fully in European initiatives in this area. Ireland is a signatory, for example, to the European Convention on Terrorism, which defines categories of offences for which there is no right to political asylum. The Irish police computer is linked up to the massive West German security computer complex at Wiesbaden. The Irish government has so far resisted attempts to formalise the existing system of consultation and discussion on the grounds that it compromises the nation's official position of military neutrality. Politically, Ireland is firmly in the Western camp, with both foreign and domestic policies aligned to those of the NATO countries. There is a body of right-wing opinion in Ireland which argues that military neutrality is inconsistent with the country's political position, and besides, the nature of modern warfare is such that it would be impossible to maintain it anyway. While Fianna Fail and Fine Gael may not be persuaded by these arguments, they are aware that NATO membership holds out the best chance of securing aid to regenerate the economy. On the other hand, they realise that it poses a considerable electoral problem. Recent Irish governments have been composed around fragile coalitions and slim majorities and the sole prospect of breaking traditional voting patterns which sustain this situation lies with an election fought on a major, previously submerged issue – such as military neutrality. Any premature attempt to usher the country into NATO could consign the offending party to a long period of opposition. Yet the convergence of the two parties on the increasingly important issue of the economy has led to talk of a possible Fianna Fail/Fine Gael coalition. This would of course remove the electoral obstacle, as would another recently cited alternative: a military coup.

A paper given to a London conference on defence and security issues in November 1981[26] listed three main items on NATO's Irish shopping list: UHF radio communications into the Atlantic, forward bases, and radar cover (also into the Atlantic). All of these, the paper argues, arise from the change in NATO strategy which took place in the late 1970s. The concept of mutual annihilation was discarded in favour of a thesis which holds that a limited nuclear war could be fought and won in Europe. An essential American contribution, under these circumstances, would be the rapid reinforcement of NATO's European-based ground troops by American units flown over from the other side of the Atlantic. This process would be made a great deal easier if NATO had access to any of the three things listed above.

Taking them in order, many of the aircraft crossing the Atlantic will only be equipped with UHF radio, which works through line-of-sight signals and is thus limited in range by the earth's curvature. Radio relay stations on the west coast of Ireland would allow UHF reception several hundred miles further out into the Atlantic. Forward air bases would be used to house refuelling tankers and perhaps interceptors to counter a possible Soviet air attack on Britain from the eastern Atlantic. Radar bases in Ireland have been proposed with a similar scenario in mind. Briefly, this scenario is that Soviet bombers from the Kola peninsula in north-west Russia take off, flying to the north of Scandinavia, and veer south-westwards through the Scotland/Iceland gap, dropping to low level to avoid radar detection. From 2-300 miles off Britain they would then be able to attack ground targets with nuclear missiles. This threat does not exist at present: the range of the main Soviet strike bomber, the Tupolev-26 'Backfire', is insufficient to launch such an attack without air refuelling, through which it would become highly vulnerable to interceptor attack. However, a more powerful successor to 'Backfire' is believed to have reached the test stage. Advance Warning and Control (AWAC) aircraft would be stationed over the Atlantic, both to detect Soviet aircraft taking the 'back door' route and to act as radio relays for the transport fleet, but they might come under missile attack from Soviet submarines. Land-based radio and radar in Ireland would provide valuable back-up.

There is no doubt that NATO would like facilities in Ireland, but there is some debate about what Ireland might get in return. The loyalist conspiracy theory maintains that the Irish government and NATO are arranging a deal involving Irish unification in exchange for accession to NATO. The Canadian-born loyalist politician Kennedy Lindsay forecasts a military environment similar to that described above and concludes that the British and American governments are engaged in a covert operation 'to entice a donkey in the form of the Irish Republic out of its neutrality by dangling in front of it the carrot of Irish unification'.[27] The theory has many prominent adherents, including the Official Unionist leader James Molyneaux, who also believes that 'paramilitary groups in Northern Ireland, including the IRA, are being manipulated in a complicated international conspiracy to bring the Republic of Ireland into a Western defence alliance.'.[28] It is true that Taoiseach Haughey told the Dail in March 1981 that Ireland's 'long-held policy of neutrality' could be altered if a political solution could be found for the north, but he did not specify unification. There are compelling economic reasons why no Irish government should wish to court unification: the Westminister subvention of over £1,000 million per annum which prevents the economy from collapsing completely is far beyond Dublin's means, even with EEC grants. Together with certain apprehensions about the political consequences, this should more than counterpoise any republican aspirations among Irish politicians.

The three central issues of unification, NATO and the economy of Ireland as a whole are now firmly interlocked. The major economic initiative in Ireland is a growing tableau of cross-border projects: a north-south pipeline to pump gas from the Kinsale field near Cork to the north, due on stream in 1983; the reconnection of the electricity link and plans for joint schemes in the fishing and tourism industries. The tone of the details which have emerged from the Anglo-Irish talks begun in 1980 suggests that economic fusion could act as a precursor to political unity, but this is by no means definite.

The EEC is the obvious source of finance for economic development in Ireland, and it has been recognised by the Americans as a conduit for the economic aid which they hope to use to enhance their political leverage in Ireland. The influential American journal *Foreign Policy* notes that

> the EEC's special fund for depressed areas offers a fortuitous international mechanism through which American help can be channelled. Its use would avoid the politically difficult task of seeking congressional appropriations for either England or Ireland. There is ample precedent for America's participation in a consortium with organisations such as the EEC. Similar programmes through the World Bank or the United Nations development programme have often been preferred methods of involvement in overseas projects. [29]

So far, the long awaited overhaul of Ireland's telecommunications system gives the best indication of how the economic and strategic development of Ireland within the Western bloc is likely to proceed. A major part of the United Kingdom's civil and military communications is handled by the 'Backbone' microwave network. Microwave is better able than low frequency signals (UHF or VHF, for example) to carry large amounts of information at high speed. Microwave networks use aerials mounted on towers at intervals of up to 50 miles to transmit signals. 'Backbone' carries inter-city telephone traffic, television programmes, military communications, and transmits data from UKADGE* coastal radar stations to military air control centres at West Drayton and High Wycombe. The network has an additional function which has not been positively identified but is probably connected with Sigint. The branch of the network which serves south-west Scotland extends across the North Channel to a relay in the Belfast suburb of Ballygomartin, which is in turn linked to the

* United Kingdom Air Defence Ground Environment

UKADGE station at Bishop's Court, near Downpatrick. It has been known for some time that British Telecom, which operates 'Backbone', leases a microwave channel from the Irish Department of Posts and Telegraphs (IDPT/P & T) for reserve use in the event of any difficulties with the Belfast-Stranraer route. In this reserve route, signals from the north travel to another relay near Belfast at Standing Stones Hill, south-west to Forkhill, Co. Armagh and on to Dame Court, Dublin via Ardee and Enfield, Co. Meath. From there they cross the Irish Sea to Holyhead and rejoin 'Backbone'. The P & T says it is obliged to provide a reserve route following a directive from the International Telecommunications Union, and that it has no control over what British Telecom decides to transmit down it, even if the signals come from the NATO radar station.

There is no immediate cause to doubt this explanation for the Belfast-Dublin-Holyhead link, but it has no validity with respect to another microwave route which the P & T has been operating since the middle of 1981. Construction began on a large communications facility at Mount Gabriel in western Co. Cork during 1976. This site is linked to a station at Three Rock Mountain in Co. Dublin through Mullighanish (Co. Kerry), Cork, Youghal, Dungarvan, Waterford, Wexford, Enniscorthy, and Arklow. The Irish government has confirmed that Mount Gabriel is a radar station, and that its signals are relayed to Holyhead (and 'Backbone') from Three Rock Mountain.[30] They refused, however, to disclose the source of finance for the construction of the network.

Ireland now has a functioning microwave system covering the east and south of the country. In 1979, the P & T embarked on a five-year plan to expand it up the western coastline, bringing in the towns of Galway and Sligo and reaching up to Letterkenny. It is highly probable that Letterkenny will link up with a new station in Derry which connects with Belfast via Draperstown, also under construction. By the mid-1980s, the network will carry RTE programmes, telephone calls and other telecommunications, including NATO radar traffic, and be completely integrated into 'Backbone'. Some information has emerged regarding the funding of the five-year plan, which is costed at £800 million at 1978 prices: the main foreign contributors are the EEC, through development funds, the World Bank, and the French government, which has provided a loan conditional on the purchase of French telephone switching equipment.

The obvious conclusion is that the NATO countries are financing Ireland's new telecommunications infrastructure, on the condition that the P & T makes provisions within it which are compatible with their military requirements. The evidence is circumstantial, but this is the most plausible explanation of why the Irish government is allowing NATO radar stations to be based on Irish soil and make use of the Irish microwave network. The improved communications should serve to attract foreign business to Ireland. The problem for the Irish government is that the bulk of Irish opinion is still wedded to the heritage of neutrality. Nor has the whole of the political establishment abandoned it either. The tactic which the pro-NATO sector appears to have adopted is the same as that which brought the vast American military and intelligence apparatus to Britain: to introduce it quietly, suppressing public debate beyond a series of carefully controlled leaks leading to the eventual presentation of a fait accompli.

Kennedy Lindsay makes the interesting observation, confirmed elsewhere, that the Irish mass media has been penetrated by British or American intelligence.[31] He suspects that the object is a propaganda campaign to destabilise Fianna Fail, which he describes as 'hard-line' and 'neutralist'. Since Fianna Fail leadership is privy to the details of communications development and has not opposed them, there does not seem to be much point in such a campaign. The forthcoming task of persuading Irish sceptics of the gravity of the Soviet menace and the current one of reminding the nation of the threat to stability posed by the IRA form a more pressing brief for any MI6/CIA plants.

The original 'Irish question', born of the 1922 partition, has become superseded by questions of economics and military strategy. Economic integration between north and south and full political alignment of Ireland and the UK within the NATO bloc would remove part of the rationale for maintaining the border. The pace of unification then depends on relaxing the stranglehold of the Catholic Church on Irish society to a level palatable to northern loyalists. The depth of opposition in the Republic to the legalisation of abortion, for example, gives some indication of the gulf which must be closed. Nonetheless, some loyalists, like the late Roy Bradford have caught on to the idea:

> If you could have individual liberties, education, taxation, the climate in which business operates, mobility of labour, mobility of investment, common pattern of voting rights – if all of these were standardised ... it wouldn't make an awful lot of difference whether you were living in Southern Ireland or England, Northern Ireland or Scotland. There's a long-term aim to create that kind of uniform pattern throughout the island, I believe.[32]

And Provisional Sinn Fein also seem to have recognised it:

> what we may well see is a changing around of the scenery, but basically the position of domination, imperialism and exploitation in Ireland will remain, and the Irish people would not become supreme in their own country, would not secure the decision-making process in their own country and would not

be able to determine their own future.[33]

The policy outlined by Bradford is, by all indications, that which the NATO governments, led by Britain on this occasion, are now pursuing. The main opponents are, in the north, Provisional Sinn Fein and the IRA, and in the south, the Catholic Church and the left-wing Workers' Party*: an unlikely yet formidable combination. There is still plenty of work for the 'Department'. The war against the IRA is more or less stalemated and the security forces should be able to keep it that way if they can avoid making too many mistakes like shooting unarmed civilians. British intelligence also has considerable experience of containing nationalist and leftist political groupings. The financial chicanery of the Vatican bank in relation to the collapsed financial empire of Roberto Calvi shows that the Catholic Church is not invulnerable. A major change of British government policy, even with a change of party, is highly improbable. The programme of economic stimulation and integration, NATO membership and, later on, unification, could yet be realised.

Recalling Hugo Young's comment about the internal bias of MI6's work during the 1970s, the theme of the article in which it appeared was the possibility of serious civil disorder in Britain arising from mass unemployment. Two main reasons were given for government optimism on this score: the safety valve of the black economy, towards which the Thatcher administration takes a most liberal attitude, and the low level of 'subversive' activity, believed necessary to spark off organised violent opposition – the piece was written before the urban rioting of 1981, notably in Liverpool 8 and the Brixton area of London. The immediate cause was oppressive policing, the origin of which is at least partly due to social conditions. There have been several recurrences since then, mainly in Liverpool, accompanied by a distinct lack of press coverage. Both areas are assuming certain characteristics of the ghettoes of Belfast and Derry, but there is as yet no tangible threat to the authority of central government. The figure of three million out of work passed by with a volume of protest which can hardly be said to have reached a crescendo, and it is not impossible that the Conservative party may win a further term of office.

The centrepiece of British foreign policy remains the straddling act between Europe and America. Thatcher and her supporters share a common vision with the Reagan administration of an end to welfare capitalism and a return to unbridled free enterprise. As John Nott told Terry Coleman of the *Guardian*, 'I'm a nineteenth century liberal. So is Mrs. Thatcher. That's what this government is all about'.[34]

The Thatcher/Reagan philosophy is one manifestation of a global

* The political descendents of the Officials, whose electoral advance in 1982 saw them hold the balance of power for a while in the Dail.

trend of nostalgia. Britain's influence within the EEC is essential to prevent what the Americans suspect to be the community's emergence as a rival economic bloc, possibly leading to its uncoupling from the Western alliance (there have been veiled accusations of latent neutralism from Washington) and pursuit of entirely separate world-wide trading arrangements. The current system of international trade is of immense advantage to the United States: many transactions not involving the US are done in dollars, oil purchases from the Middle East, for example, which leads to a continual demand for the currency. When the American economy first showed significant signs of stagnation, the government printed more dollars. Because of the international demand, these did not stay in the domestic economy to cause inflation but were exported with the inflationary increment, enabling the United States to maintain its levels of overseas investment and military spending. The European Monetary System, which fixes the values of European currencies relative to each other within small percentage limits, was specifically created to combat this. Britain did not join, apparently because British governments like to think of the pound as an international currency and London as an important financial centre. It also pleased the Americans, which may be incidental. The roots of an international trade war may be identified here. The Middle East is the most likely setting for the preliminary sparring:

> The EEC must sell the Arabs as much in manufactured goods and services as it buys in oil: at the moment it has a growing deficit with the Middle East and, if it fails to staunch this haemorrage, it will not be able to finance its trade with the rest of the world. The Europeans have, in short, to drive the Americans out of the Middle Eastern markets, whatever the cost,

as David Clark explains it.[35] Britain is partially exempt from the oil problem for the time being by its own oil deposits.

These economic factors fit with the attitudes of European governments towards the Rapid Deployment Force which were assessed earlier in this chapter from a more political standpoint. As far as policy is concerned, Britain is very much closer to the US than the other EEC nations are.

Policy towards, or against the Soviet bloc would at first sight be the best prospect for a sustained joint Western approach. The row over the Soviet gas pipeline to Western Europe has thrown this into disarray, although this quarrel has a distinctly transitory feel about it. The Western alliance has survived worse; Suez, for example. Anticommunist operations should continue much as before.

Crystal-gazing is a dubious art at the best of times. In a sphere of life where deception is an essential tool and facts are only valid and meaningful in the presence of others of compatible content, it can border on the ridiculous. James Angleton, sometime head of CIA counter-intelligence, used the phrase 'a wilderness of mirrors' to describe the obliquity of Soviet foreign policy. It seems no less applicable to any broad conclusion to the events described here. Angleton's conviction of a 'super-mole', a mega-Philby, within the CIA came close to destroying the organisation. The intelligence trade lends itself readily to conspiracy, but also it co-exists, necessarily, in reasonable harmony with diplomacy, strategy and commerce. On these worldwide pillars it depends, much as books depend on readers.

Notes

1. *State Research* No. 2
2. Sir John Killick 'Southern Africa in Turmoil' article in *NATO's Fifteen Nations* (August-September 1981)
3. *New Statesman* (19 November 1982)
4. *The Middle East* (July 1982); Companies House microfiche.
5. Quoted in Richard Barnet and Ronald Muller *Global Reach* (1975) p.19
6. *New Statesman* (2 February 1979)
7. *Sunday Times* (14 February 1980)
8. Robert Mark *In the Office of Constable*
9. *Irish Times* (22 April 1980)
10. *Guardian* (28 October 1976)
11. David Charteris 'Intelligence and Psychological Warfare in Northern Ireland' article in *RUSI Journal* (September 1977) p.25
12. *Sunday Times* (12 August 1973)
13. *Daily Express* (19 September 1981)
14. *Guardian* (1 March 1973)
15. *Sunday Times* (11 February 1973)
16. *Sunday People* (29 September 1974)
17. Aspin autobiography; various press reports
18. *New Statesman* (13 July 1979)
19. *Daily Mail* (3 May 1974)
20. *New Statesman* (13 July 1979)
21. *Magill* (July 1980)
22. *Irish Times* (24 April 1980)
23. Brigadier J. M. Glover *Northern Ireland Future Terrorist Trends* Defence Intelligence Staff (15 December 1978)
24. *Magill* (September 1980)
25. *Sunday Tribune* (5 April 1981)
26. 'NATO Requirements in Ireland' paper given to *Researching State Structures Conference* University College London (7-8 November 1981)
27. Kennedy Lindsay *The British Intelligence Services In Action* (1980) p.249
28. *Guardian* (23 March 1982)
29. *Foreign Policy* No. 37 (Winter 1979/80) quoted in *NATO and the Third World War* (1982) p.61
30. *In Dublin* (6 August 1982)
31. Kennedy Lindsay *The British Intelligence Services In Action* p.242
32. Interview on BBC *Panorama* programme (30 March 1981) quoted in *NATO and the Third World War* p.58
33. Ruairi O'Bradaigh interview in *Iris* (April 1981)
34. *Guardian* (13 September 1982)
35. *Leveller* (13 November 1981)

List of Abbreviations

ANC	African National Congress
ASIS	Australian Secret Intelligence Service
BBC	British Broadcasting Corporation
CAS	Capricorn Africa Society
CIA	Central Intelligence Agency (USA)
CID	Criminal Investigation Department
CPRS	Central Policy Review Staff
DIS	Defence Intelligence Staff
EEC	European Economic Community
FBIS	Foreign Broadcasting Information Service (USA)
FNLA	National Front for the Liberation of Angola
FRELIMO	Front for the Liberation of Mozambique
GCHQ	Government Communications Headquarters
GRU	Soviet Military Intelligence
ICFTU	International Confederation of Free Trade Unions
INLA	Irish National Liberation Army
IRA	Irish Republican Army
IRD	Information Research Department
ISC	Institute for the Study of Conflict/International Student Conference
JIC	Joint Intelligence Committee
KAU	Kenyan African Union
KANU	Kenyan African National Union
KADU	Kenyan African Democratic Union
KGB	Soviet Intelligence
MCP	Malayan Communist Party
MIO	Military Intelligence Officer
MLC	Member of the Legislative Council (Kenya)
MPLA	Popular Movement for the Liberation of Angola
MSS	Malayan Security Service
NATO	North Atlantic Treaty Organisation
NIO	Northern Ireland Office
NSA	National Security Agency (USA)
NKG	New Kenya Group
NKP	New Kenya Party
NUP	National Union Party (Sudan)

OAU	Organisation of African Unity
OID	Overseas Information Department
PFLO	Popular Front for the Liberation of Oman
PUS	Permanent Under-Secretary
RUC	Royal Ulster Constabulary
SAF	Sultan's Armed Forces (Oman)
SAS	Special Air Services
Sigint	Signals Intelligence
TAVR	Territorial Army Volunteer Reserve
UDI	Unilateral Declaration of Independence
UDR	Ulster Defence Regiment
UNIP	United National Independence Party (Zambia)
UWC	Ulster Workers' Council
UNITA	National Union for the Total Independence of Angola
WASP	White Anglo-Saxon Protestant
WAY	World Assembly of Youth
ZANC	Zambia African National Congress
ZIPRA	
ZANLA	

Bibliography

Agee, P. and Wolf, L. (editors) *Dirtywork: The CIA in Western Europe* Lyle Stuart, New Jersey, 1978

Aitken, Jonathan *Officially Secret* Weidenfeld and Nicholson, London, 1971

Allfree, P. S. *Warlords of Oman* Robert Hale, London 1967

Bailey, M. *Oilgate* Coronet, London, 1979

Barber, N. *The War of the Running Dogs* Collins, London 1971

Barnes, Trevor, article in *The Historical Journal* London, Vol. 24, 1981

Barnet, R. and Muller, R. *Global Reach* Jonathan Cape, London 1975

Blackstock, P. and Schaf, R. L. *Intelligence, Espionage, Counterespionage and Covert Operations: A Guide to Information Sources* Gale Research Company, Detroit, 1978

Blundell, Sir Michael *So Rough A Wind* Weidenfeld and Nicholson, London, 1964

Bulloch, J. *MI5* Barker, London, 1963

Bunyan, T. *The Political Police in Britain* Quartet, London 1977

Burchett, W. and Roebuck, D. *The Whores of War* Penguin, Harmandsworth, 1976

Burkholder-Smith, Joseph *Cold War Warrior* G. P. Putnams, New York, 1976

Caroz, Y. *The Arab Secret Services* Corgi, London, 1978

Charity Commissioners' Annual Reports, London, 1978-80

CIA: The Pike Report Spokesman, London, 1977

Copeland, M. *The Real Spy World* Sphere, London, 1978

Cronje, S., Cronje, G. and Ling, M. *Lonrho* Penguin, Harmandsworth, 1976

Crossman, R. *The Diaries of a Cabinet Minister* Hamilton and Cape, London, 1975

Crossman, R. *New Fabian Essays* J. M. Dent, London, 1970

Deacon, R. *A History of the British Secret Service* Muller, London, 1976

Deacon, R. *The Silent War* David and Charles, London, 1978

Dempster, C. and Tomkins, R. *Fire Power* Corgi, London, 1978

De St Jorre, J. *The Nigerian Civil War* Hodder and Stoughton, London, 1972

De Villiers, G. *The Imperial Shah* Weidenfeld and Nicholson, London, 1976

Diplomatic Service List, HMSO, London, various dates

Dumoga, J. *Africa Between East and West* Bodley Head, London, 1969

Duncan, A. *Money Rush* Hutchinson, London, 1979

Eveland, W. C. *Ropes of Sand* Norton, London, 1980

Frankel, J., *British Foreign Policy 1945-73* Oxford University Press, London, 1975

Frost, Richard *Race Against Time* Rex Collings, London, 1978

Fullick, R. and Powell, G. *Suez – The Double War* Hamish Hamilton, London, 1979

Gehlen, R. *The Gehlen Memoirs* Collins, London, 1972

Geraghty, T. *Who Dares Wins: The Story of the Special Air Service 1950-80* Arms and Armour Press, London, 1980

Lord Gladwyn, *The Memoirs of Lord Gladwyn* Weidenfeld and Nicholson, London, 1972

Glover, Brigadier J. M. 'Northern Ireland: Future Terrorist Trends' Defence Intelligence Staff paper, 15 December 1978

Good, R. *UDI* Faber and Faber, London, 1973

Gore-Booth, Paul *With Great Truth And Respect* Constable, London, 1974

Grosser, A. *The Western Alliance* MacMillan, London, 1980

Hagen, L. *Secret War for Europe* Panther, London, 1969

Hale, J. *Radio Power* Paul Elek, London, 1975

Hall, R. *The Secret State* Cassell Australia, Melbourne, 1978

Halliday, F. *Arabia Without Sultans* Penguin, Harmandsworth, 1974

Harper, S. *Last Sunset: What Happened on Aden* Collins, London, 1978

Haswell, J. *British Military Intelligence* Weidenfeld and Nicholson, London, 1973

House of Commons Hansard, London

Howe, Russell Warren, *Weapons* Abacus, London, 1981

Ignatyev, O. *Secret Weapon In Africa* Progress Publishers, Moscow, 1977

Information Research Department *The Soviet Presence in the Indian Ocean* London, 1974

Insight *Ulster* Penguin, Harmandsworth, 1972

International Defence and Aid Fund *BOSS: The First Five Years* London, 1971

Jeapes, A. S. *SAS: Operation Oman* William Kimber, London, 1980

Jeffries, Sir Charles *The Colonial Office* Allen and Unwin, London, 1956

Kanogo, Tabitha 'Politics of Collaboration or Domination: A Case Study of the Capricorn Africa Society' *Kenya Historical Review* Vol. 2, No. 2, 1974

Kellner, P. and Lord Crowther-Hunt *The Civil Servants* MacDonald Futura, London, 1980

Killick, Sir John 'Southern Africa in Turmoil' article in *NATO's Fifteen Nations*, August-September 1981

Kisch, R. *The Private Life of Public Arrangements* MacGibbon and Kee, London, 1964

Kitson, F. *Low Intensity Operations* Faber and Faber, London, 1971

Lakin, F. H., 'Psychological Warfare Research in Malaya 1952-5' UK Ministry of Defence Army Operational Research Establishment paper given 11th Annual US Army Human Factors Research and Development Conference, October 1965

Lee, J. M. *African Armies and Civil Order* Chatto and Windus, London, 1969

Lewis, D. *Sexpionage* Heinrich Hanau, London, 1976

Lindsay, K. *The British Intelligence Sevices in Action* Dunrod, Dundalk, 1980

Lloyd, S. *Suez 1956* Hodder and Stoughton, London 1978

MacDermott, G. *The New Diplomacy* Plume Press, London, 1973

MacDonald, Malcolm *Titans and Others* William Collins, London, 1972

Maclean, D. *British Foreign Policy since Suez* Hodder and Stoughton, London, 1970

Majdalany, Fred, *State of Emergency — The Full Story of Mau Mau* Longmans, London, 1962

McGuffin, J. *The Guinea Pigs* Penguin, Harmandsworth, 1974

Mark, Robert *In the Office of Constable* Collins, London, 1978

Marks, J. and Marchetti, V. *The CIA and the Cult of Intelligence* Knopf, New York, 1974

Martin, D. *General Amin* Sphere, London, 1978

Miller, H. *Jungle War in Malaya: The Campaign against Communism 1948-60* Barker, London, 1972

Moorhouse, G. *The Diplomats: The Foreign Office Today* Jonathan Cape, London 1977

Mosley, L. *Power Play* Weidenfeld and Nicholson, London, 1977

NATO and the Third World War Little a, London, 1982

Newman, B. *Spy and Counterspy* Robert Hale, London, 1970

Odinga, Oginga *Not Yet Uhuru* Heinemann, London, 1967

Page, B., Leitch, D. and Knightley, P. *Philby, The Spy who Betrayed a Generation* Penguin, Harmandsworth, 1969

Paine, L. *Britain's Intelligence Service* Robert Hale, London, 1979

Philby, K. *My Silent War* Granada, London, 1969

Pincher, C. *Inside Story* Sidgwick and Jackson, London, 1978

Powers, Thomas *The Man Who Kept the Secrets* Pocket Books, United States, 1979

Prados John, *The Soviet Estimate: US Intelligence and Russian Military Strength* Dial Press, New York, 1982

Progress Foundation prospectus, London, not dated

Ray, E., Schaap, W., Van Metter, K. and Wolf, L. *Dirtywork 2: The CIA in Africa*, Lyle Stuart, New Jersey, 1979

Researching State Structures Conference 'NATO Requirements in Ireland' (paper), University College London, 7-8 November 1981

Robertson, T. *Crisis* Hutchinson, London, 1965

Sampson, A. *The Arms Bazaar*, Hodder and Stoughton, London, 1977

Searle, P. and McConville, M. *Philby, the Long Road to Moscow* Hamish Hamilton, London, 1973

Smiley, David *Arabian Assignment* Leo Cooper, London, 1975

Smith, J. B. *Cold War Warrior* G. P. Putnams, New York, 1976

Special Committee on Relaxation of Trade Barriers Report (18 December 1943)

Steiner, R. *The Last Adventurer: from Biafra to Sudan* Weidenfeld and Nicholson, London, 1978

Stockwell, J. *In Search of Enemies* W. W. Norton, New York, 1978

United States Congress *Report of the Committee on International Relations: Special Study Missions to Africa, November 1972 and November 1973* US Government Printing Office, Washington, 1974

United States Congress *Senate Select Committee to study Governmental Activities with respect to Intelligence* US Government Printing Office, Washington, 1976

United States Defence Intelligence School Bibliography of Intelligence Literature 6th Edition, Washington D. C., 1979

Wallace, W. *The Foreign Policy Process in Britain* Royal Institute of International Affairs, London, 1975

Warner, P. *The Special Air Service* William Kimber, London, 1971

Wasserman, G. *Politics of Decolonisation: Kenyan Europeans and the Land Issue 1960-65* Cambridge University Press, 1976

Watson, P. *War on the Mind* Hutchinson, London, 1978

Weissman, S. R. 'Two decades of US policy in Africa: some lessons from experience', paper delivered at annual meeting of African Studies Association, Boston, Massachusetts, 4 November 1976

Wise, D. and Ross, T. B. *The Espionage Establishment* Bantam Books, New York, 1968

Wise, D. and Ross, T. B. *The Invisible Government* Vintage Books, New York, 1974

Woodhouse, C. M. *Something Ventured* Granada, London, 1982

Wynne, G. *Contact on Gorky Street* Atheneum, New York, 1968

Young, K. *Rhodesia and Independence: a Study in British Colonial Policy* J. M. Dent, London, 1969

Unpublished Items

British Youth Council, Archives

Fletcher, Richard 'The Free Flow of News' unpublished paper, 1979

Rathbone, Richard, papers collected by

Rhodes House Archives

Newspapers and Magazines

Africa Confidential (London)
Africa Diary (Nairobi)
Africa Now (London)
China News Summary (Hong Kong)
Covert Action Information Bulletin (Washington DC)
Daily Express (London)
Daily Telegraph (London)
Daily Mail (London)
First Principles (Washington DC)
In Dublin (Dublin)
Iris (Dublin)
Irish Times (Dublin)
Izvestiya (Moscow)
Le Monde (Paris)
Leveller (London)
Magill (Dublin)
Guardian (London)
Middle East Economic Digest (London)
Morning Star (London)
New African (London)
New Statesman (London)
New York Times (New York)
Observer (London)
Republican News/An Phoblacht (Dublin, Belfast)
RUSI Journal (London)
Private Eye (London)
State Research (London)
Sunday Telegraph (London)
Sunday Times (London)
Sunday Tribune (Dublin)
The Middle East (London)
Times (London)

APPENDIX

The appendix is a list, compiled by the authors, of certain civil servants who have held official posts overseas since 1945. The majority are or were attached to the Foreign and Commonwealth Office, and accompanying each is a brief official biography. The list is divided into four parts, the first three of which are:

1) those named in published sources as having been involved in intelligence or covert action operations at least at some stage in their career.

2) those listed in official directories as engaged in the same.

3) those who by virtue of their official biographies can be deduced to be former or serving intelligence officers.

The entries in these three sections are all members or ex-members of MI6, GCHQ, the Information Research Department or, serving as an overseas security advisor or liaison officer, of MI5. We have not included the names of military attaches stationed in overseas missions because all are assigned to the Defence Intelligence Staff and, therefore, are all intelligence officers.

The fourth section is a list of embassy personnel who, over the years, have been accused by host governments of engaging in intelligence activities. This has been followed by deportation or barring of re-entry. Of course it is possible that in some cases the local counter-intelligence agency has mistaken an ordinary diplomat for a spy. However, in all cases the action will be regarded as significant by other countries to which the diplomat is or might otherwise have been sent and therefore has importance in itself.

The list illustrates, in the main, typical postings of intelligence officers. The reason for the number of apparent diplomats is simple enough: as explained in the text, the majority of intelligence officers working overseas are installed in embassies – under 'light' cover. While the list does not give a fair reflection of the proportions of 'light' and 'deep' cover personnel, the presence of so many 'diplomats' does, we hope, draw attention to one of our principal arguments, that intelligence and covert action are integral to the conduct of British foreign policy. More specifically, we hope that the list is useful as a research source for historians, journalists and political activists concerned with this subject. Finally, it is also our intention to extend and complement the work of the Washington-based periodical *Covert Action Information Bulletin* which has done similar and more voluminous analysis in relation to the CIA since 1978.

When reading the biographies, the reader should bear in mind the following points:

1) Since 1945, the bureaucratic structures of British overseas missions and the corresponding home departments have undergone a number of changes. On January 1st, 1965 the Foreign Service, Commonwealth Service and the Trade Commission Service were disbanded and replaced in toto by the Diplomatic Service. The Colonial Office and Commonwealth Relations Office were merged on 1st August 1966 to form the Commonwealth Office, which joined with the Foreign Office on 1st October 1968 to produce the Foreign and Commonwealth Office.

2) The positions given in the biographies (2nd Secretary, Counsellor etc.) are not wholly artificial, and give some idea of seniority in each case. Where no position is given, it can be assumed that there has been no change from when the last promotion was made.

3) In a few cases, the ranks 'Grade 9' and 'Grade 10' have been used. Grade 9 corresponds to a Vice-Consul or 3rd Secretary while Grade 10 is generally a clerical grade such as might be held by an archivist.

Sources

Who's Who	A. & C. Black (Publishers) Ltd. London 1940-82
The Diplomatic Service List 1966-82 (and its predecessors)	Her Majesty's Stationery Office, London
Philby Disclosures	On 2 October 1971, in the Soviet newspaper *Izvestiya*, the double-agent Kim Philby named a number of British intelligence officers.
Wynne Trial	At the trial of British intelligence agent Greville Wynne in Moscow in 1963 the prosecution named a number of British intelligence officers

Keesings Contemporary Archives

Other sources where stated

Published Sources

ALLAN, James Nicholas b. 22/5/32 MI6
1951-3	Army
1956	Assistant Principal, Commonwealth Relations Office
1958	3rd later 2nd Secretary Pretoria/Cape Town MI6 Station Officer
1959	Private Secretary to Parliamentary Under-Secretary
1961	1st Secretary, Freetown
1964	Nicosia
1964	Commonwealth Relations Office, later FCO
1969	Peking
1971	Luxembourg
1973	Counsellor, seconded to Northern Ireland Office*
1976	FCO
1978	Head of OID
1981	High Commissioner, Mauritius

* *MI6 Chief of Station. Involved in 1975 truce with Provisional IRA*
Source: *Irish Times*, 4 February 1980

ASTLEY-RICHARDS, Roy MI6
May 1972	Joined security firm Diversified Corporate Services Ltd (DCS) as a 'special consultant'
1977	Left DCS

Source: *New Statesman* 22 February 1980

BENTON, Kenneth Carter b. 4/3/09 MI6
1937	Joined Foreign Office
1937-8	Assistant, Passport Control Office, Vienna
1938	Vice-Consul, Riga
1940	Foreign Office
1941	3rd later 2nd Secretary, Madrid*
1944	2nd later 1st Secretary, Rome
1948	Foreign Office
1950	Rome
1953	Madrid
1956	Foreign Office
1962	Lima
1965	Foreign Office
1966	Counsellor, Foreign Office
1968	Retired
1974-5	Chairperson, Crime Writers' Association
	Wrote *Conflict Studies No. 2* 'Peru's revolution from Above', Institute for the Study of Conflict

* *Cover for head of counter-espionage*
Source: Deacon, R. *The British Connection*, Hamish Hamilton, London, (1979), p.179

BRIMELOW, Sir Thomas Barron (1971) GCMG (1975) KCMG (1968) CMG (1959) OBE (1954) b. 25/10/15 MI6
1938	Probationed Vice-Consul Danzig
1939	Served in Consulate, Riga
1940	Served in Consulate-General, New York
1942	3rd Secretary and Vice Consul, Moscow
1945	Foreign Office
1948	1st Secretary (Commercial) and Head of Chancery, Havana
1951	1st Secretary and Head of the Russian Secretariat, Moscow

1954	Commercial Counsellor, Ankara
1956	Head of Northern Department, Foreign Office
1960	Counsellor, Washington
1963	Minister, Moscow
1966	Ambassador, Warsaw
1969	Deputy Under-Secretary of State (Europe), FCO
1973	Permanent Under-Secretary of State, FCO and Head of Diplomatic Service
1975	Retired
1977-8	Member European Parliament
1978-	Chairperson, Occupational Pensions Board

Source: G. Moorhouse *The Diplomats: The Foreign Office Today*, Jonathan Cape, London, (1977), p.127

CHALMERS, Ian Pender, OBE (1980) b. 30/1/39 MI6

1963	Foreign Office
1966	2nd Secretary, Beirut
1968	FCO
1970	1st Secretary, Warsaw
1972	FCO
1976	Paris
1980-	FCO

Source: Philby Disclosures

CLUBE, James Roderick, OBE (1972) b. 3/7/20 MI6

1947	Berlin
1949	Hong Kong
1952	Foreign Office
1955	Vienna
1958	Foreign Office
1961	2nd Secretary (Commercial), Havana
1964	1st Secretary, Foreign Office
1967	Beirut
1970	1st Secretary (Economic Affairs), Baghdad*
1971	FCO
1980	Retired

* *Deported, 1971*
Sources: Keesings Contemporary Archives, 1971, column 25041; Philby Disclosures

COHEN, Kenneth CB (1954) CMG (1946) b. 15/3/00

1918	Special Entry Royal Navy Cadet
1926	HMS *Iron Duke*, Torpedo duties
1932	Royal Navy Staff College
1935	Lieutenant-Commander

1939	HMS *President*
1940	Commander
c.1945	Attached to Foreign Office acting Personnel Director, MI6
1953-66	European adviser to United Steel Companies
1963-75	Counsellor, Royal Institute of International Affairs
1967-72	Chairperson, Franco-British Society
1972-	President, Franco-British Society; President, European League for Economic Co-operation

Source: Andrew Boyle, *The Climate of Treason*, Hodder and Stoughton, London, (1980), p.278

COOK, Don GCHQ
1980　　GCHQ chief, Hong Kong
Source: *New Statesman* 23 May 1980

ELLIOTT, John Nicholas Rede b. 15/11/16 MI6
Served in World War 2 with HM Forces (temporary Major, Intelligence Corps); tours of duty after war with MI6 in Berne, Vienna and Beirut, also in Central Africa. Confronted double-agent Kim Philby in Beirut in 1963 with his Soviet connection, after which Philby fled to the Soviet Union. After leaving MI6 became a director of Lonrho.
Source: *Guardian* 26 January 1980

FIGURES, Colin Frederick CMG (1978) OBE (1969) b. 1/7/25 MI6

1943-8	HM Forces
1951	Foreign Office
1953	Control Commission, Germany
1956	3rd later 2nd Secretary, Amman
1958	Foreign Office
1959	2nd Secretary (Commercial), Warsaw
1962	FCO
1966	1st Secretary and Head of visa section, Vienna
1969	FCO (Counsellor 1975)
1982	Chief of MI6

Source: *Sunday Times* 7 November 1982

FRANKS, Sir Arthur Temple CMG (1967) KCMG (1979) b. 13/7/20 MI6

1940-6	Special Operations Executive
1949	Entered Foreign Office
1952	British Middle East Office

1953	2nd Secretary Tehran, involved in Iranian coup
1956	Foreign Office
1962	1st Secretary Bonn, MI6 Chief of Station
1966	1st Secretary later Counsellor FCO (MI6 Divisional Head)
1978	Chief of MI6
1982	Retired

Source: *State Research* No. 8 October/November 1978

FRENCH, Neville Arthur Irwin CMG (1976) MUO (1968) b. 28/4/20 MI6

1939-45	Fleet Auxiliary and Special Duties, Ministry of War Transport
1948	Colonial Administration Service
1949	District Commissioner
1961	Principal Assistant Secretary (External Affairs)Prime Minister's Office, Dar-es-Salaam
1963	Central African Office
1964	Commonwealth Relations Office
1964	1st Secretary (Political), Salisbury
1966	1st Secretary and Head of Chancery, Rio de Janeiro
1970	Assistant Head, Western, Organisations Department, FCO
1972	Counsellor and Charge d'Affaires, Havana
1975	Governor and Commander-in-Chief, Falkland Islands
1977	Deputy High Commissioner, Madras
1980	Retired

Source: Radio Salisbury 25 March 1966

FULTON, S. J. MI6

1955-7	MI6 Chief of Far Eastern Operations; (cover) 1st Secretary, Singapore

No further details available
Source: Smith, J. B., *Cold War Warrior*, G. P. Putnam and Sons, New York, (1976), p.165

GANE, Barrie Charles OBE (1978) b. 19/9/35 MI6

1955-7	Her Majesty's Forces
1960	Joined Foreign Office
1961	3rd Secretary, Vientiane
1963	Seconded to staff of Governor of Sarawak
1963	2nd Secretary, Kuching
1966	FCO
1967	2nd Secretary (Commercial), Warsaw
1967	1st Secretary, Kampala
1970	FCO
1977-	1st Secretary on loan to Headquarters of British Forces, Hong Kong; MI6 Chief of Station

Source: *New Statesman* 12 December 1980

HARPER, William Harold b. 6/9/18 MI6

1936	Clerical Officer, Agriculture Ministry
1939-47	Royal Air Force
1950	Transferred to Foreign Office
1951	Moscow
1952	Paris
1953	Foreign Office
1956	Jerusalem
1957	Vice-Consul, Jerusalem
1961	Consul, Helsinki
1964	2nd Secretary (Commercial), Pretoria
1967	2nd Secretary later 1st Secretary, Blantyre
1969	Consul, Aden
1972	1st Secretary, FCO
1977	Retired

Source: *Guardian* 6 September 1978

HORLING, Michael MI6
Career MI6 Officer
Deputy Chief under Oldfield
Source: *Time Out* 16th April 1976

JOHNSTONE, Andrew James b. 20/9/33 MI6

1956	Joined Foreign Office
1959	Served with police as Assistant Political Officer, Aden
1960	Assistant Political Officer, Dubai
1963	2nd Secretary, Damascus
1965	Foreign Office
1967	1st Secretary, Rawalpindi
1971	1st Secretary (Commercial) and Consul, Pnomh Penh
1971	1st Secretary, FCO
1971-3	Dublin
1973	Implicated in the Wyman Affair and recalled to England

No further information available
* Source: *Guardian*, September 1973

JONSEN, Cyril b. 13/1/35
1952   Foreign Office
1953   HM Forces
1955   Bangkok
1957   Singapore
1959   Kabul
1962   Madrid
1963   Foreign Office
1965   Diplomatic Service
        Administration
1966   Prague*
1969   Kuching
1972   2nd Secretary, Dakar
1974   FCO
1978-   Nairobi
* *Accused by Czech government of having
organised an intelligence network in the
country*
Source: *New York Times* 24 January 1977

JOY, Peter OBE (1969) b. 16/1/26 IRD/
MI6
1944-7 Royal Air Force
1952   Foreign Office
1959   1st Secretary, Ankara
1962   1st Secretary (Information),
        New Delhi
1965   Foreign Office
1968   1st Secretary (Information),
        Beirut
1973   Counsellor FCO
1975-7 Assistant IRD
1979   Counsellor, Kuala Lumpur
1980   FCO
Source: Philby Disclosures

KING, Roger MI6
1963   Named in Wynne trial
1972   Retired from FCO
1972   'International Security
        Consultant'
1978   Hired by Iberian Airways to
        advise on security at Spanish
        Airports*
* Source: *Daily Mail* 25 May 1978

LOMAS, Neville Wears b. 12/5/29 MI6
1945-54 Board of Trade
1948-50 HM Forces
1954   Port of Spain
1958   Assistant Trade Commissioner,
        Melbourne
1961   2nd Secretary (Commercial),
        Pretoria*
1967   Bombay

1968   1st Secretary (Commercial),
        Calcutta
1970   Athens
1974   Baghdad
1977   1st Secretary, FCO
1980   Retired
* 1966 Monitoring rail traffic to Rhodesia
   from Mozambique and South Africa
Source: *Guardian* 6 September 1978

LONGRIGG, John Stephen CMG (1973)
OBE (1964) b. 1/10/23 MI6
1939-45 Lieutenant Rifle Brigade
1948   Foreign Office
1948   Paris
1951   3rd Secretary, Baghdad
1953   Foreign Office
1955   Berlin
1957   Cabinet Office
1958   Foreign Office
1960   Dakar
1962   1st Secretary, Pretoria
1964   Washington
1965   Foreign Office
1967   1st Secretary, Bahrain
1969   Counsellor, FCO
1974   Seconded to Headquarters
        British Forces, Hong Kong;
        MI6 Chief of Station
1976   Counsellor FCO, MI6 Divis-
        ional Head
1979   MI6 Deputy Chief
1982   Retired
Source: *New Statesman* 29 May 1981

LUNN, Peter Northcote CMG (1957) OBE
(1951) b. 15/11/14 MI6
1940   Royal Artillery
1947   Foreign Office
1948   Vienna
1950   2nd Secretary, Berne
1954   West Berlin
1956   Foreign Office
1957   1st Secretary, Bonn
1962   Beirut
1968   1st Secretary, FCO
1972   Retired
Sources: Philby Disclosures
         Named by George Blake as hav-
         ing initiated one of the most
         important telephone tapping
         operations for British Intel-
         ligence. *Daily Telegraph*
         17 February 1970.

McMILLAN, Norman Hamilton
b. 28/10/46 MI6
1968   FCO
1970   3rd later 2nd Secretary, Vienna
1972   2nd later 1st Secretary, FCO*
1977-   1st Secretary, Rome
* 1972 *Recruited Howard Marks to work for MI6*
Source: *New Statesman* 13 September 1979

MURLEY, John Trethargen b. 22/8/28 MI6
1955   Foreign Office
1976-80   Counsellor, Washington, MI6
            liaison officer with the CIA
Source: *New Statesman* 29 May 1981

NELSON, Terry GCHQ
1980   Government Communications
            Officer – in charge of Little Sai
            Wan Monitoring Station,
            Hong Kong
Source: *New Statesman* 12 December 1980

PECK, Sir Edward Heywood GCMG
(1974) KCMG (1966) CMG (1957)
b. 5/10/15 MI6
1938   Vice Consul, Barcelona
1939   Foreign Office
1940   Sofia
            Intelligence Officer, Ankara;
            (cover) 3rd Secretary
1944   Acting Consul, Andana
1945   Iskenderun
            Consul, Salonika
1946   UK delegation to UN Special
            Commission on the Balkans
1947   Foreign Office
1950   Seconded as 1st Secretary to
            High Commissioner's Office,
            Delhi
1952   Foreign Office
1953   Appointed Counsellor
1955   MI6 Chief of Station, Berlin;
            (cover) Deputy Commander,
            British Sector, Berlin
1958   On staff of Commissioner-
            General for South East Asia
1961   Assistant Under-Secretary of
            State, Foreign Office
1966   High Commissioner in Kenya
1968   Deputy Under-Secretary of
            State, FCO
1968   Chairperson of DIC
1970   British Permanent Represent-
            ative to North Atlantic Council
1975   Retired

1976-   Honorary Visiting Fellow in
            Defence Studies, Aberdeen
            University
1977-   Council Member, Institute for
            the Study of Conflict
Source: Cookridge, E. H. *The Third Man*,
            Arthur Barker, London, (1968),
            p.143-4

PATTERSON, Geoffrey T.D. MI5
1952-3   MI5 Liaison Officer, Washing-
            ton; (cover) 1st Secretary
No further details available
Source: Searle, P. and McConville, M.
            Philby: The Long Road To Moscow,
            Hamish Hamilton, London,
            (1973), p.214

NEWMAN, Prudence Anne b. 27/3/33
MI6
1952   Foreign Office
1956   Vienna
1959   Panama
1961   Foreign Office
1964   1st Secretary, Algiers
1965   Diplomatic Service
            Administration
1967   2nd Secretary and Vice Consul,
            Beirut
1969   Resigned
Source: Philby Disclosures

PRICE, David Lynn b. 14/5/39 IRD
1960s   IRD, Poland and Arab Gulf
            desks
1962   Foreign Service
1963   Djakarta and Paris
1969   Researcher, Forum World
            Features
1970   Researcher, Institute for the
            Study of Conflict
1978-   Consultant and political analyst
            on Middle Eastern affairs
            Editor, *Arab Oil*, Kuwait
Source: *Leveller*, No. 13, March 1978

RAMSAY, Margaret Mildred b. 12/7/36
MI6
1959-61   President, Scottish Union of
            Students
1962   Associate Secretary, Inter-
            national Student Conference,
            Leiden, Holland
1965-7   Secretary, Fund for Inter-
            national Student Co-operation
1969   2nd Secretary, FCO

1970	Stockholm
1973	1st Secretary, FCO
1981	1st Secretary (Chancery), Helsinki

Source: *Leveller* pilot issue, February 1976

ROLO, Cyril Felix OBE (1959) b. 13/2/18 MI6

1940	HM Forces
1946	Foreign Office
1947	Allied Commission for Austria, Vienna
1948	2nd Secretary, Rome
1950	Berlin
1952	Foreign Office
1957	1st Secretary, Vienna
1962	Foreign Office
1971	Retired

Source: *Guardian* 23 February 1981

ROWLEY, Frederick Allan CMG (1978) OBE (1959) MC (1945) b. 27/7/22 MI6

1939	HM Forces
1948	Foreign Office
1949	Vice-Consul, Addis Ababa
1950	Foreign Office
1953	2nd Secretary, Rangoon
1955	Office of the Commissioner-General, Singapore
1957	Foreign Office
1960	Seconded to Australian Department of Defence, Melbourne
1963	Foreign Office
1965	'Resigned'
1967	'Re-joined' Counsellor (Foreign Affairs), Kuala Lumpur
1971	FCO
1972	Under-Secretary, seconded to Northern Ireland Office
1973	Counsellor, FCO Divisional Head, MI6
1976	Deputy Chief, MI6
1979	Retired

Source: *New Statesman* 29/5/81

SINDALL, Adrian John b. 1937 MI6

1956	Foreign Office
1958	Middle East Centre for Arab Studies
1960	Baghdad
1962	Rabat
1965	2nd Secretary, Rabat
1967	Foreign Office
1968	1st Secretary, FCO

1970	Beirut
1972	1st Secretary and Head of Chancery, Lima
1976	FCO
1979-	Counsellor, Amman

Source: Philby Disclosures

my boss!

SMELLIE, Craig Connell b. 15/2/23 MI6

1941-6	HM Forces
1955	Vice-Consul, Alexandria
1956	2nd Secretary, Baghdad
1957	Foreign Office
1959	Rome
1961	1st Secretary, Khartoum
1966	Tripoli
1969	FCO
1973	Seconded to Northern Ireland Office
1975	Athens
1977-8	FCO

Source: *Irish Times* (22 April 1980)

SMITH, Sir Howard Frank Trayton KCMG (1976) CMG (1966) b. 15/10/19 MI5

1939	Foreign Office
1947	2nd Secretary, Oslo
1950	2nd later 1st Secretary (Information), Washington
1953	1st Secretary and Consul, Caracas
1956	Foreign Office
1961	Counsellor, Moscow
1964	Head of Northern Department, Foreign Office
1968	Ambassador to Czechoslovakia
1971	UK Representative in Northern Ireland*
1972	Seconded to Cabinet Office as Deputy Secretary
1976	Ambassador to Soviet Union
1979	Director-General, MI5*
1981	Retired

* *Cover post for security co-ordination in the province*

Source: *New Statesman* 8 February 1980; *Observer* 9 September 1979

TEMPLE, Reginald Robert b. 12/2/22 MI6

1940-6	His Majesty's Forces
1947	Stockbroking
1951	Foreign Office
1952	Office of HM Commissioner-General for South-East Asia, Singapore

1956	Foreign Office
1958	2nd Secretary, Beirut
1962	Foreign Office
1964	1st Secretary, Algiers
1966	FCO
1967	1st Secretary, Paris
1969	1st Secretary later Counsellor, FCO
1979	Retired
1979	Oman Government Service

Source: Philby Disclosures

YOUNG, George Kennedy CB (1960)
CMG (1955) MBE (1945)
b. 8/4/11 MI6

1936	Editorial Staff, Glasgow Herald
1938	British United Press
1939	Commissioned, Kings Own Scottish Borderers
1941	Despatches East Africa
1943	Specially employed list, Italy and Western Europe
1946	Berlin correspondent British United Press
1946	Joined Foreign Service
1949	Economic Relations Department, Foreign Office
1951	British Middle East Office
1953	'attached' Ministry of Defence, specialised in 'economic and defence' intelligence Involved in Iranian coup
1960	Under-Secretary
1961	Retired
1961-76	Joined Kleinwort Benson Ltd
1969	President Nuclear Fuel Finance S.A.
1976	Retired

'former deputy director of the Secret Service'

Source: *Daily Express* 14 June 1974

Directory Listed

ALLOT, Elizabeth Rosemary OBE (1972)
b. 2/7/18 IRD

1945	Allied Commission for Austria
1948	Foreign Office
1962	1st Secretary
1970s	South America desk, IRD
1978	Retired

BARCLAY, Christopher Francis Robert
b. 8/6/19 CMG (1967) IRD

1940	HM Forces
1944	Middle East Centre for Arab Studies, Jerusalem
1945	Political Officer, Northern Iraq
1946	Assistant Information Officer, Baghdad
1946	Foreign Office 2nd Secretary, Cairo
1950	1st Secretary, Foreign Office
1953	Bonn
1956	Foreign Office
1960	Regional Information Officer, Beirut
1961	Assistant, IRD
1962	Counsellor and Head of IRD
1967	Head of Personnel Department (Training and General), FCO
1969	Assistant Secretary, Civil Service Department
1973	Assistant Secretary, Department of the Environment
1976-80	Secretary, Government Hospitality Fund
1976-	Council member, City University
1980-	Warden, Saddler's Company

BARKER, Thomas Christopher
b. 28/6/28 IRD

1947-8	Army
1952	Foreign Office
1953	3rd Secretary, Paris
1955	2nd Secretary, Baghdad
1958	Foreign Office
1962	1st Secretary, Head of Chancery and Consul, Mexico City
1967	FCO
1969	Counsellor and Head of Chancery, Caracas
1971	FCO
1972	Head of IRD
1976	Seconded as Under-Secretary, Northern Ireland Office, Belfast
1976	Retired
1980-	Curator, Scottish National War Memorial

BONSALL, Sir Arthur (Wilfred) KCMG
(1977) CBE (1957) b. 25/6/17 GCHQ

1940	Air Ministry
1942	Transferred to Foreign Office
1962	Imperial Defence College
1973	Director GCHQ
1978	Retired

BRASH, Robert b. 30/5/24 IRD

1943-6	HM Forces
1949	Foreign Office
1950	IRD
1951	3rd Secretary, Jakarta
1955	Foreign Office
1956	1st Secretary, Foreign Office
1958	Consul, Jerusalem
1961	1st Secretary, Bonn
1964	Head of Chancery, Bucharest
1966	FCO
1968	Counsellor and Head of East-West Contacts Department
1970	Canadian National Defence College
1971	Counsellor and Consul-General, Saigon
1974	Counsellor, Vienna
1978	Consul-General, Düsseldorf
1981	Ambassador, Jakarta

BROWN, Denys Downing CMG (1966) b. 16/12/18 IRD

1939	HM Forces
1946	Entered Foreign Office
1947	2nd Secretary, Warsaw
1948	Foreign Office
1949	Private Secretary to Permanent Under-Secretary of State for German Section
1951	Foreign Office
1952-3	IRD
1955	Consul, Ismailia
1956	Foreign Office
1958	1st Secretary and Head of Chancery, Belgrade
1962	Head of Chancery and Counsellor, Belgrade
1963	Head of General Department, Foreign Office
1967	Counsellor and Head of Chancery, Stockholm
1970	Minister (Economic) Bonn
1971	Retired
1971-80	Executive Director, Peninsular and Oriental Steam Navigation Company

BURROUGH, John Outhit Harold CB (1957) CBE (1963) b. 31/1/16 GCHQ

1934	Royal Navy College, Dartmouth, Midshipman
1936	Sub-Lieutenant
1938	Lieutenant
1944	Lieutenant-Commander
1946	Foreign Office (GCHQ)
1964	Imperial Defence College
1965	Counsellor, Washington
1967	Under Secretary, FCO (GCHQ)
1976	Retired
1976	Director, Racal Communications Systems Ltd

BUTCHER, Peter Roderick b. 6/8/47 IRD

1974	FCO
1975	IRD East Africa Desk
1978	Research Department
1979-	2nd Secretary (Technical Co-operation), Lima

BUTLER, Keith Stephenson CMG (1977) b. 3/9/17 IRD

1939	HM Forces
1947	Foreign correspondent, *Sunday Times* /Kemsley Newspapers
1950	Foreign Office
1951	IRD
1952	1st Secretary (Information), Ankara
1956	1st Secretary and Head of Chancery, Caracas
1959	Foreign Office
1962	Canadian National Defence College
1963	1st Secretary (Information), Paris
1965	Regional Information Officer, Montreal
1968	Consul-General, Seville
1969	Bordeaux
1974	Naples
1977	Retired
1978-	Appeal Director for various charities

CLIVE, Nigel David CMG (1967) OBE (1959) MC TD b. 13/7/17 IRD

1939	HM Forces
1946	Foreign Office 2nd Secretary, Athens
1948	Vice-Consul, Jerusalem Foreign Office
1950	2nd Secretary, Baghdad
1953	Foreign Office
1958	1st Secretary, Tunis
1962	Algiers
1964	Foreign Office
1966	Counsellor
1968	Head of IRD
1970	Advisor to Secretary-General of Organisation for Economic Co-operation and Development
1981	Editorial consultant, Institute for the Study of Conflict

CONQUEST, George Robert Acworth
OBE (1955) b. 15/7/17 IRD

1946	Foreign Office
1949	IRD
1956	Resigned from Foreign Office
	Fellow, London School of
	Economics
1959-60	Fellow, University of Buffalo
1962	Literary Editor, *The Spectator*
1964-5	Fellow, Columbia University
1976-7	Fellow, Woodrow Wilson
	International Centre
1977-	Fellow, Hoover Institution
	Editorial Board, *Soviet Analyst*

CROOK, Kenneth Roy CMG (1978)
b. 30/7/20 IRD

1937	Board of Trade
1939	Ministry of War Transport
1941	Royal Navy
1946	Board of Trade
1949	Commonwealth Relations
	Office
1951	2nd Secretary, Canberra
1954	Commonwealth Relations
	Office
1956	1st Secretary
1959	Commonwealth Relations
	Office
1962	Deputy High Commissioner,
	Peshawar, West Pakistan
1964	Dacca, East Pakistan
1967	Counsellor, FCO
1969	Head of IRD
1971	Governor, Cayman Islands
1974	Canadian National Defence
	College
1975	Head of Science and
	Technology Department, FCO
1976	Ambassador to Afghanistan
1979	Retired

DONNELLY, Joseph Brian b. 24/4/45
GCHQ

1970	GCHQ
1973	2nd Secretary, FCO
1975	1st Secretary, UK Mission to
	the United Nations, New York
1979-	1st Secretary and Head of
	Chancery, Singapore

DRINKALL, John Kenneth CMG (1973)
b. 1/1/22 IRD

1942	Indian Army
1947	Foreign Service
1948	3rd Secretary, Nanking
1949	Vice-Consul, Tamsul

1951	Acting Consul
1951	Foreign Office
1953	1st Secretary, Brasilia
1957	Foreign Office
1960	Brasilia
1962	Foreign Office
1963	Assistant, IRD
1964	Counsellor
1965	Nicosia
1967	Brussels
1970	FCO
1971	Canadian National Defence
	College
1972	Ambassador, Kabul
1976	High Commissioner in
	Jamaica and Ambassador
	(non-resident) to Haiti
1981	Retired

EVANS, Wayne b. 29/8/53 GCHQ

1969	GCHQ
1971	FCO Grade 10
1974	Paris
1977	Archivist, Maseru
1979	FCO

HOOPER, Sir Leonard James KCMG
(1967) CMG (1962) CBE (1951)
b. 23/7/14 GCHQ

1938	Air Ministry
1942	Transferred to Foreign Office
1953	Imperial Defence College
1965	Director GCHQ
1974	Co-ordinator of Intelligence
	and Security in the Cabinet
	Office
1978	Retired

HORN, Alan Bowes CVO (1971)
b. 6/6/17 IRD

1940	Army
1946	Joined Foreign Service
1948	Vice-Consul, Marseilles
1949	1st Secretary, Tel Aviv
1951	1st Secretary, Foreign Office
1952	IRD
1953	Deputy Head of British
	Information Service, New
	York
1957	1st Secretary, Helsinki
1960	Foreign Office
1963	Ambassador to Malagasy
	Republic
1967	Counsellor, Warsaw
1970	Consul-General, Istanbul
1973	Retired

HUTSON, John Whiteford OBE (1966)
b. 21/10/27 IRD

1949	His Majesty's Forces
1951	Foreign Office
1953	3rd Secretary, Prague
1955	Foreign Office
1956	2nd Secretary, Berlin
1959	Saigon
1961	1st Secretary, Saigon
1963	Consul (Commercial), San Francisco
1967	1st Secretary and Head of Chancery, Sofia
1969	FCO
1970	Counsellor
1971	Assistant IRD
1971	Counsellor (Commercial) Baghdad
1972	Inspector, Diplomatic Service
1974	Head of Communications Operations Department, FCO
1976	Counsellor (Commercial), Moscow
1979-	Consul-General, Frankfurt

IMBERT-TERRY, Alison Jean
b. 6/2/52 IRD

| 1975 | IRD |

No further information available

JACKSON, John Edward CMG (1977)
b. 24/6/25 IRD

1943	Royal Navy Volunteer Reserve (Sub-Lieutenant)
1947	Joined Foreign Service
1947	Foreign Office
1949	3rd Secretary, Paris
1952	2nd Secretary, Foreign Office
1956	Bonn
1957	1st Secretary
1959	Guatemala City
1963	Foreign Office
1964-5	Assistant IRD
1968	Counsellor
1969	NATO Defence College, Rome
1969	Counsellor (Political Adviser) British Military Government, Berlin
1973	Head of Defence Department FCO
1975	Ambassador to Cuba
1980-	UK delegation leader, negotiations on Mutual and Balanced Force Reductions, Vienna

JONES, Sir Eric Malcolm KCMG (1957)
CB (1953) CBE (1946) b. 24/4/07 GCHQ

1925	Textile Merchant and Agent
1940	RAF Volunteer Reserve
1946	Civil Servant
1952	Director, GCHQ
1960	Resigned
1966-77	Director, Simon Engineering Ltd.

LESLIE, Lewis Derek Malcolm b. 9/4/24
GCHQ

1942	HM Forces
1947	Foreign Office
1958	Ankara
1959	Foreign Office
1960	Rome
1962	Foreign Office
1965	3rd Secretary, Moscow
1966	Foreign Office
1968	Singapore
1970	FCO
1973	Signals Officer, British Government Relay Station, Darwin
1975	FCO
1977	Retired

LOEHNIS, Sir Clive KCMG (1962) CMG
(1950) b. 24/8/02 GCHQ

1920	Midshipman, Royal Navy
1924	Lieutenant
1928	Qualified in Signals Duties
1932	Lieutenant-Commander
1935	Retired
1938	Re-employed in Signals Division, Admiralty
1942	Commander on retired list
1942	Naval Intelligence Division
1945	Demobilised and entered Foreign Office
1952	Deputy Director, GCHQ
1960-64	Director, GCHQ
1967-70	Chairperson, Civil Service Selection Board

McMINNIES, John Gordon OBE (1965)
b. 1/10/19 IRD

1938	Reporter *Western Mail*
1939	Reuters
1940	HM Forces
1946	2nd Secretary (Information), Athens
1949	Warsaw
1950	Vice Consul, Bologna
1952	Foreign Office

1953	Malayan Government Information Services
1955	Foreign Office
1957	1st Secretary, Nicosia
1959	Foreign Office
1961	Nairobi
1965	Delhi
1966	FCO
1972	Assistant IRD
1976	Deputy Head IRD
1977	Retired

MOON, Sir Peter James Scott KCVO (1979) CMG (1979) b. 1/4/28 IRD

1952	Home Office
1954	Commonwealth Relations Office
1956	2nd Secretary, Cape Town/ Pretoria
1958	Principal, Commonwealth Relations Office
1960	1st Secretary, Colombo
1963	Private Secretary to Secretary of State for Commonwealth Relations
1965	1st Secretary, United Kingdom Mission to United Nations
1969	Counsellor, FCO
1970	Assistant, IRD
1970	Private Secretary to Prime Minister
1972	NATO Defence College
1972	Seconded to NATO International Staff, Brussels
1975	Counsellor, Cairo
1978-	High Commissioner, Tanzania and Ambassador to Madagascar

MORGAN, Douglas Alan b. 8/7/32 GCHQ

1949	RAF
1957	Foreign Office
1970	Islamabad
1972	FCO
1974	Deputy Manager and Engineering Supervisor, British Government Relay Station, Darwin
1975	FCO
1976	Singapore
1980-	FCO

MURRAY, Sir (Francis) Ralph (Hay) KCMG (1962) CMG (1950) CB (1957) b. 3/3/08 IRD

1934	British Broadcasting Corporation
1939	Foreign Office
1945	Allied Commission for Austria
1946	Special Commissioner's Staff South East Asia
1947	Foreign Office
1949	Head of IRD
1951	Counsellor, Madrid
1954	Minister, Cairo
1957	Assistant Under-Secretary of State, Foreign Office
1961	Deputy Under-Secretary of State, Foreign Office
1962	Ambassador to Greece
1967	Resigned
1967-73	A Governor of the British Broadcasting Corporation
Latterly	Chairperson, McAlpine Sea Tank Ltd; SAFT (UK) Ltd; CSM Parliamentary Consultants Ltd

O'CONNOR-HOWE, Josephine Mary b. 25/3/24 IRD

1942	Inter-Allied Information Committee later United Nations Information Office
1945	Joined Foreign Office
1945	The Hague
1946-50	International News Service and freelance journalist
1952	Foreign Office
1962	1st Secretary, Foreign Office
1974	Counsellor, FCO
1975	Deputy Head, IRD
1976-7	Assistant, IRD
1979	Resigned
1979-	Magazine Administrator, *Reader's Digest*

PARROTT, Sir Cecil Cuthbert OBE (1947) CMG (1953) KCMG (1964) b. 29/1/09 IRD

1939	Ministry of Information, Assistant Press Attache, Oslo
1940	Assistant Press Attache, Stockholm
1945	Press Attache, Prague
1948	Transferred to Foreign Office
1949	Assistant, IRD
1950	Head of UN (Political) Department, Foreign Office
1952	Counsellor, Brussels
1954	Minister, Moscow
1957	Director of Research, Librarian and Keeper of the Papers, Foreign Office
1960	Ambassador to Czechoslovakia Accused of organising

espionage network with *Times* journalist Richard Davy*

1966   Retired

1966-76   University of Lancaster, Professorial posts in Russian, Central and South-East European Studies

* Source: *New York Times* 24 January 1977

PECK, Sir John Howard KCMG (1971) CMG (1956) b. 16/2/13 IRD

1937   Assistant Private Secretary to 1st Lord of Admiralty

1939   Assistant Private Secretary to Minister for Co-ordination of Defence

1940   Assistant Private Secretary to the Prime Minister

1946   Transferred to Foreign Office

1946   Served in the United Nations Department

1947   The Hague

1951   Counsellor and Assistant, IRD

1952   Head of IRD

1954   Counsellor (Defence Liaison) and Head of Political Division, British Middle East Office

1956   Director General of British Information Services, New York

1959   United Kingdom Representative to the Council of Europe and Consul-General, Strasbourg

1962   Ambassador to Senegal and Mauritania

1966   Assistant Under-Secretary of State, FCO

1970   Ambassador to Republic of Ireland

1973   Retired

REDDAWAY, George Frank Norman MBE (1946) CBE (1965) b. 2/5/18 IRD

1939-45   HM Forces

1944   Camberley Staff College

1946   Joined Foreign Service

1947   Private Secretary to Parliamentary Under-Secretary of State

1949   2nd later 1st Secretary, Rome

1952   1st Secretary, Ottawa

1955   Foreign Office

1956   Assistant, IRD

1960   Imperial Defence College

1961   Counsellor, Beirut

1965   Counsellor, Office of the Political Advisor to the Commander-in-Chief, Far East, Singapore

1967   Counsellor (Commercial), Khartoum

1970   Assistant Under Secretary of State, FCO

1974   Ambassador to Poland

1978   Retired

1978-   Chairperson, English International; Director, Catalytic International; Secretary, Farmington Trust; Trustee, Thomson Foundation

1979-   Director, Overseas Marketing Corporation

1980-   Trustee, Trinity Trust

RUNACRES, Eric Arthur b. 22/8/16 IRD

1939   Royal Engineers

1946   J. and P. Coats Ltd.

1948   Foreign Office

1949   Services Liaison Department (Foreign Office representation on Joint Intelligence and Joint Planning staffs. Liaison with Ministry of Defence and Chiefs of Staff)

1950   IRD

1951   1st Secretary, Cairo

1954   Resigned

1954-71   British Productivity Council

1960-66   Vice-Chairperson, Organisation of Economic Co-operation and Development; Committee on National Productivity Centres

1973-77   Executive Director, Commonwealth Agriculture Bureau

1978-   Consultant, Industrial Facts and Forecasting Ltd

SIMPSON, Kenneth John CMG (1961) b. 5/2/14 IRD

1937   Vice-Consul, Addis Ababa

1938   Alexandria

1939   Tehran and Kermanshah

1945   Consul, Tehran with rank of 3rd Secretary

1947   1st Secretary, Madras

1950   Foreign Office

1956   Consul-General, Hanoi

1958   Head of General Department Foreign Office

1961   Consul-General, Stuttgart

1963	Counsellor, Bonn
1965	Inspector, Diplomatic Service
1966	Counsellor, FCO
1969	Assistant, IRD
1971	Retired

SNODGRASS, John Michael Owen CMG (1981) b. 12/8/28 IRD

1951	Assistant, IRD
1953	3rd Secretary (Commercial), Rome
1956	Foreign Office
1960	1st Secretary (Information), Beirut
1964	1st Secretary
1967	FCO
1970	Counsellor, FCO
1970	Consul-General, Jerusalem
1974	Counsellor and Head of Chancery, Pretoria
1977	Head of Pacific Dependent Territories Department
1979	Head of South Pacific Department
1980	Ambassador to Zaire and to Burundi (non-resident)

SOMERVILLE, John Arthur Fownes CB (1977) CBE (1964) b. 5/12/17 GCHQ

1936	Midshipman, Royal Naval College, Dartmouth
1938	Sub-Lieutenant
1940	Lieutenant
1945	Lieutenant-Commander
1950	GCHQ
1969-77	Under-Secretary (GCHQ), FCO

SOUTHERN, Miss Edith Joyce OBE (1970) b. 27/4/14 IRD

1940	Ministry of Information
1946	Foreign Office
1958	1st Secretary
1971	Assistant, IRD
1973	Retired

STEER, James McLeod b. 31/1/27 GCHQ

1945	HM Forces
1948	Department of Civil Aviation, Australia
1950	Air Department, New Zealand Foreign Office
1960	Accra
1961	Foreign Office
1963	Lisbon
1966	Foreign Office
1968	Pnomh Penh
1972	Beirut

1974	FCO
1977	Station Officer, British Government Relay Station, Darwin
1980-	FCO

TILL, Peter Edward b. 17/1/28 IRD

1946	HM Forces
1955	HM Overseas Civil Service; retired as Chief Inspector of Police
1963	Foreign Office
1969-	1st Secretary, FCO
1975	On staff of IRD

TOVEY, Sir Brian John Maynard KCMG (1980) b. 15/4/26 GCHQ

1945	Service with Royal Navy and subsequently Army (Intelligence Corps and Royal Army Educational Corps)
1948	School of Oriental and African Studies
1950	Junior Assistant, GCHQ
1957	Principal
1967	Assistant Secretary
1975	Under-Secretary
1978-	Deputy Secretary and Director

TUCKER, Herbert Harold b. 4/12/25 IRD

1944-51	*Western Morning News, Sheffield Telegraph, Nottingham Journal, Daily Telegraph*
1948-49	Economic Information Unit, Treasury
1951	Foreign Office
1958	Counsellor, Foreign Office
1972	Assistant, IRD
1974	Deputy Head, IRD
1974	Counsellor (Information) and Director British Information Services, Canberra
1979	Consul-General, Vancouver

WAKEFIELD, Derek John b. 21/1/22 GCHQ

1939	The Commonwealth School, Air Ministry
1942	Lieutenant, Royal Pioneer Corps
1947	The Commonwealth School, Air Ministry
1952	GCHQ
1973-	Governor Barnwood House Trust, Gloucester
1978-	Under-Secretary, GCHQ

WATSON, John Hugh Adam CMG
(1958) b. 10/8/14 IRD

1937	Foreign Office
1939	British Legation, Bucharest
1940	Cairo
1944	Moscow
1947	Foreign Office
1950	Assistant, IRD
1950	Washington
1956	Head of African Department, Foreign Office
1959	Consul-General Dakar
1960-1	Ambassador to the Federation of Mali
1960	Ambassador to Senegal, Mauritania and Togo
1963	Ambassador to Cuba
1966	Under-Secretary, FCO
1968	Diplomatic Adviser, British Leyland Motor Corporation
1973	Visiting Fellow, Australian National University
1974-	Director General, International Association for Cultural Freedom
1978	Visiting Professor, University of Virginia

WHISTANCE, Bertrand Harry
b. 22/12/22 GCHQ

1942	HM Forces
1947	Foreign Office
1958	Athens
1960	Foreign Office
1961	Delhi
1963	Foreign Office
1964	Beirut
1966	Foreign Office
1967	Kuwait
1968	FCO
1969	Bangkok
1970	Singapore
1971	FCO
1974	1st Secretary, Singapore
1977	Manager, British Government Relay Station, Darwin
1979-	Principal Signals Officer, FCO

WHITNEY, Raymond William OBE
(1968) b. 28/11/30 IRD

1951	Northamptonshire Regiment, serving in Trieste, Korea, Hong Kong and Germany
1960	Seconded to Australian Army Headquarters
1964	Resigned
1964	Joined Foreign Service; First Secretary, Commonwealth Relations Office
1966	1st Secretary and Head of Political Section, Peking
1969	Head of Chancery, Buenos Aires
1972	Assistant Head, East African Department FCO
1973	Deputy High Commissioner and Economic Counsellor, Dacca
1976	Head of IRD
1977	Head of Overseas Information Department
1978	Resigned
1978	Elected Conservative Member of Parliament, Wycombe

WRIGHT, John Henry CBE (1964)
b. 6/12/10 GCHQ

1934	Vice-Consul, Genoa
1937	Addis Ababa
1939	Havana
1943	2nd Secretary later 1st Secretary, Quito
1948	Foreign Office
1950	1st Secretary (Commercial), Helsinki
1953	Santiago
1958	Counsellor, Shanghai
1960	Foreign Office
1961	Consul-General, Rotterdam
1963	Ambassador, Honduras
1970	GCHQ
1977	Retired

WRIGHT, Sir John Oliver DSC (1944)
CMG (1964) KCMG (1974) GCVO (1978)
b. 6/3/21 IRD

1941	Royal Navy Volunteer Reserve
1945	Joined Foreign Service
1946	Vice-Consul, New York
1948	3rd Secretary, Bucharest
1950	2nd Secretary, Singapore
1952	Foreign Office
1954	1st Secretary, Berlin
1957	Pretoria
1959	Imperial Defence College
1960	Assistant, IRD
	Assistant Private Secretary to Secretary of State for Foreign Affairs
1963	Counsellor and Private Secretary

1964	Private Secretary to the Prime Minister
1966	Ambassador to Denmark
1969	Seconded to Home Office as UK representative to the Northern Ireland Government
1970	Chief Clerk, Diplomatic Service
1972	Deputy Under-Secretary of State, FCO
1975	Ambassador to Federal Republic of Germany
1981	Retired
1981-	Director, Siemens Ltd.

ZETTER, Israel Sydney
b. 11/11/17 GCHQ

1940	HM Forces
1947	Foreign Office
1959	Singapore
1961	Foreign Office
1963	Singapore
1965	Foreign Office
1969	St. Helena
1971	FCO
1973	Manager, British Government Relay Station, Darwin
1975	Principal Signals Officer, FCO
1977	Retired

Controversial

ALLEN, Douglas George b. 26/6/30 MI6

1948	Foreign Office
1949-51	HM Forces
1954	The Hague
1957	2nd Secretary, La Paz
1961	Assistant Private Secretary to Lord Privy Seal (1961-3) and to Minister without Portfolio
1966	1st Secretary, Panama
1969	FCO
1972	Counsellor, seconded to Northern Ireland Office
1974	Paris
1978	Inspector, Diplomatic Service
1980	On loan to the Office of the Parliamentary Commissioner for Administration (Ombudsman)

BOWMAN, John Hood b. 24/7/13 MI6

1937	HM Forces
1948	Foreign Office
1949	Control Commission, Germany
1954	Foreign Office
1956	1st Secretary, Buenos Aires
1958	Helsinki
1960	Foreign Office
1963	1st Secretary (External Affairs), Salisbury
1965	1st Secretary, Foreign Office
1968	Resigned

BROWNE, Nicholas Walker b. 17/12/47 MI6

1969	3rd Secretary, FCO
1971	3rd Secretary, Tehran
1975	2nd later 1st Secretary, FCO
1976	On loan to Cabinet Office
1980-	1st Secretary and Head of Chancery, Salisbury

CLIFT, Richard Dennis b. 18/5/33 MI6

1957	Foreign Office
1958	3rd Secretary, Peking
1961	2nd Secretary, Berne
1962	UK delegation to NATO, Paris
1964	Foreign Office
1969	1st Secretary and Head of Chancery, Kuala Lumpur
1971	FCO
1974	Counsellor, Peking
1976	Sabbatical at Canadian Defence College
1977	Seconded to Northern Ireland Office as Assistant Secretary
1979	Head of Hong Kong and General Department, FCO

CORNWELL David John Moore
b. 19/10/31 MI6

1950-1	Military Intelligence, HM Forces
1956-8	Teacher, Eton
1960	Joined Foreign Office
1961	2nd Secretary, Bonn
1961-	Spy novelist, writing under pseudonym John le Carre
1962	2nd Secretary (Commercial), Bonn
1963	Consul, Hamburg
1964	Resigned

EASTON, Sir James Alfred KCMG (1956)
CB (1952) CBE (1945) b. 11/2/08 MI6

1926	Royal Air Force
1929-32	Served North-West Frontier, India
1935	Egypt
1937	Canada
1940	Armaments adviser to Department of National Defence
1941	Group Captain
1943	Air Commodore Director in Air Staff Branch, Air Ministry and then Royal Air Force Delegation, Washington
1945-58	Assistant Chief, MI6
1958	Consul-General, Detroit
1968	Retired Resident consultant on trade development of the Great Lakes area, USA
1975-	Associate member, Overseas Advisory Associates Inc., Detroit

HARE, Hon. Alan Victor b. 14/3/19 MI6

1939-45	Army
1947-61	Foreign Office
1961	Industrial and Trade Fairs
1963	Joined *Financial Times*
1971-8	Managing Director, Financial Times Ltd
1975-8	Press Council
1975	Chief Executive, Financial Times Ltd; Director, Economist Newspapers Ltd; Pearson Longman Ltd
1978-	Chairman, Financial Times Ltd

HARRISON, John Audley CB (1976)
b. 13/5/17 MI5

1939	HM Forces
1946	'attached, War Office'
1958-9	Security and Intelligence Adviser, Colonial Office
1969	Departmental Director, Ministry of Defence
1976	Retired

HEATHCOTE, Mark Simon Robert
b. 1/3/41 MI6

1971	2nd later 1st Secretary, FCO
1974	On loan to Northern Ireland Office
1975	Language student
1976	1st Secretary (Information),

	Athens
1979	FCO
1980-2	Buenos Aires

HERBERT Christopher Alfred CB (1973)
b. 15/6/13 MI5

1937	Indian Civil Service
1947	Eastern Manager, May and Baker (India) Ltd
1950-77	Ministry of Defence
1956	Assistant Security Intelligence Adviser, Colonial Office
1971	Under-Secretary, Ministry of Defence
1977	Retired

JENKINS, Stanley Kenneth b. 25/11/20
MI6

1942-6	Royal Artillery and Royal Engineers
1949	President, National Union of Students
1951	Foreign Office
1953	2nd Secretary, Singapore
1955	Seconded Colonial Office, Kuala Lumpur
1957	Foreign Office
1959	1st Secretary, Rangoon
1964	Foreign Office
1967	Nicosia
1969	1st Secretary later Counsellor, FCO
1978	Retired

MOORE, Michael John OBE (1981) MBE
(Mil.) b. 18/2/36 MI6

1954-6	Army
1966	Foreign Office
1967	2nd Secretary, Dubai
1968	1st Secretary, FCO
1969	Middle East Centre for Arab Studies
1971	Kuwait
1972	Jeddah
1976	FCO
1978-	Beirut

Source: *The Middle East* September 1981

MORTON, John Percival CMG (1965)
OBE (1946) b. 15/5/11 MI5

1937	Indian Police, Punjab
1947	Principal, War Office Seconded to Air Ministry as Civil Assistant, Staff of Air Officer Commanding, Royal Air Force, Iraq
1949	Seconded as Counsellor to the

Office of the Commissioner –
General, South-East Asia
Deputy Director, MI5
1952   Seconded as Director of
Intelligence, Government of
Malaya
1954   Assistant Secretary, War
Office
1959   Imperial Defence College
1961-5 Secretary of State's Advisory
Staff, Colonial Office –
Security Intelligence Adviser
1968   Assistant Under-Secretary of
State Ministry of Defence
1971   Retired
1972-8 Advisory missions for FCO to
Jordan, Pakistan, Mauritius
and East Caribbean
1973   Advisory mission for Ministry
of Defence to Northern Ireland
1972-5 Consultant, The De La Rue Co.
Ltd
1973-80 Panel Chairperson, Civil
Service Commission Selection
Board
1978-9 Aviation Industry Security
Training Steering Group

O'BRYAN, Tear Hubert Louis OBE
(1970) b. 9/12/18 MI6
1940   HM Forces
1947   Foreign Office
1950   Control Commission for
Germany
1952   3rd Secretary, Moscow
1954   Foreign Office
1956   2nd later 1st Secretary,
Stockholm
1960   Aden
1962   Foreign Office
1963   Manila
1965   Singapore
1967   Foreign Office
1967   Bahrain (Political Residency)
1972-7 Berne
No further information available

PARK, Daphne Margaret Sybil Desiree
b. 1/9/21 MI6
1943   HM Forces
1946   Allied Commission for Austria
1948   Foreign Office
1952   United Kingdom delegation to
North Atlantic Treaty
Organisation
1954   2nd Secretary, Moscow

1956   Foreign Office
1959   Consul and 1st Secretary,
Leopoldville
1961   Foreign Office
1964   Lusaka
1967   FCO
1969   Consul-General, Hanoi
1971   Honorary Resident Fellow,
University of Kent, on
sabbatical leave from FCO
Counsellor, FCO
1972-3 Charge d'Affaires (ad Interim)
Ulan Bator
1979   Retired
1980-   Principal, Somerville College,
Oxford

SACKUR, Christopher John b. 8/2/33 MI6
1951-3 HM Forces
1957   Foreign Office
1958   Berlin
1960   Foreign Office
1961   2nd Secretary, Leopoldville
1963   Salisbury
1964   2nd Secretary later 1st
Secretary, Foreign Office
1967   Nearly hired by London
Sunday Times as a Foreign
Correspondent – this would
have been a cover job
1969   Resigned from FCO
1970s   Works for Spencer Stuart
Associates
1973   Visited South Africa on behalf
of the Study Project on External
Investment in South Africa
and Namibia

SAVAGE, Thomas William b. 21/11/37
MI6
1964-6 President, National Union of
Students
1968   FCO
1970   2nd Secretary, Dar-es-Salaam
1973-   1st Secretary, FCO

SHAKESPEARE, John William
Richmond MVO (1968) MI6
1949-50 2nd Lieutenant, Irish Guards
1953-4 Lecturer in English, Ecole
Nationale Superieure, Paris
1955   Editorial Staff, *Times
Educational Supplement*
1956   Editorial Staff, *Times*
1959   Private Secretary to Paris
Ambassador

1961	Foreign Office
1963	1st Secretary, Pnomh Penh
1964	Office of the Political Adviser to the Commander-in-Chief Far East, Singapore
1966	1st Secretary (Information), Rio de Janeiro
1969	FCO
1973	Counsellor and Consul-General, Buenos Aires
1976	Charge d'Affaires, Buenos Aires
1977	Head of Mexico and Carribean Department, FCO
1979-	Counsellor and Head of Chancery, Lisbon

SHIPMAN, John Gervase Trafford
b. 7/7/39 MI6

1963	Assistant Advisor, HM Overseas Civil Service Aden Protectorate
1968	2nd later 1st Secretary, FCO
1970	1st Secretary, Muscat
1973	FCO
1977	Jeddah
1981-	FCO

STEELE Frank Fenwick OBE (1969)
b. 11/2/23 MI6

1943-7	HM Forces
1951	Foreign Office Vice-Consul, Basra
1953	British Middle East Office, Cairo
	3rd later 2nd Secretary, Tripoli
1956	Foreign Office
1958	Beirut
1961	1st Secretary, Foreign Office

1965	Amman
1968	Nairobi
1971	Counsellor and Deputy UK representative, Northern Ireland
1973	FCO
1975	Retired adviser to Kleinwort Benson
1978-	Director, Arab-British Chamber of Commerce
1979-	Director, Cluff Oil Ltd
1981-	Chairperson, Network Television Ltd

WHEELER, Lieutenant-Colonel
Geoffrey Eddleston CBE (1948) CIE
(1943) b. 22/6/97 MI6

1915	Commissioned Queen's Regiment, served in France
1917	Transferred to Indian Army
1918	Sixth Gurkha Rifles; various intelligence appointments in Turkey, Malta, Palestine
1926	Military Attache, Meshed
1928	Intelligence duties, Iraq
1931	Seventh Rajput Regiment
1936	General Staff Army Headquarters, India
1941	Director, Publications Division, Government of India
1946	Counsellor British Embassy, Tehran
1950s	'A Civil Service post in London'
1951	Press Secretary, Tehran
1953	Director, Central Asian Research Centre
1968	Retired

Deportations

BANHAM, Michael Kent b. 20/9/44

1963	Foreign Office
1967	Rawalpindi
1970	Archivist, Quito
1974	FCO
1976	3rd Secretary and Vice-Consul, Tripoli*
1980	Nairobi

* *Deported 1980*
  Source: *Daily Telegraph* 3 June 1980

CHAMPNESS, Christopher Andrew
George b. 8/5/41

1963	Paymaster General's Office
1964	Foreign Office

1965	Diplomatic Service Administration
1966	Middle East Centre for Arab Studies
1967	Ankara
1969	Sao Paolo
1971	Vice-Consul
1974	FCO
1975	2nd Secretary Polytechnic of Central London
1978	2nd Secretary (Commercial/ Economic), Baghdad*

No further details available
* *Deported 1978*
  Source: *Times* 28 July 1978

CHILDS, Royden Arthur b. 30/2/36
1968   Clerical Branch (Grade 10),
        Salisbury
1970   FCO
No further details available
Source: *Guardian*, 17 February 1969

COWELL, Gervase b. 4/8/26
1951   Foreign Office
1952   Political Division, Control
        Commission Germany
1955   Foreign Office
1958   2nd Secretary, Amman
1960   Foreign Office
1962   2nd Secretary, Moscow
1963   Declared persona non grata
        after Wynne trial
1963   Foreign Office
1964   1st Secretary, Bonn
1966   FCO
1972   Paris
1976   FCO
1978-   Tel Aviv

FEAN, Thomas Vincent b. 20/11/52
1975   FCO
1977   Middle East Centre for Arab
        Studies
1978   3rd Secretary, Baghdad*
1979-   2nd Secretary, Damascus
* *Deported 1978*
  Source: *Times* 28 July 1978

FEAST, Gordon b. 22/5/30
1946   Foreign Office
1948   HM Forces
1950   Foreign Office
1952   UK delegation to NATO and
        Organisation for European
        Economic Co-operation, Paris
1955   Baghdad
1957   Vice-Consul, Stuttgart
1959   2nd Secretary (Commercial),
        Tel Aviv
1964   Foreign Office
1967   1st Secretary, Delhi
1970   FCO
1971   1st Secretary (Commercial),
        Sofia*
1972   1st Secretary (Information),
        Stockholm
1975   On loan to Department of
        Trade
1977   Assistant Head of Trade
        Relations and Export
        Department, FCO

1980   1st Secretary and Head of
        Chancery, Accra
1981-   1st Secretary (Commercial),
        Vienna
* Deported 1972
  Source: *Times* 10 January 1972

FINGLAND, Stanley James Gunn CMG
(1966) b. 19/12/19
1936   Home Civil Service
1939   Royal Corps of Signals
1948   Commonwealth Relations
        Office
1948   2nd Secretary, Delhi
1950   1st Secretary, Bombay
1953-6 Canberra
1958   Adviser on Commonwealth
        and External Affairs to
        Governor-General, Nigeria
1960   Counsellor, Lagos
1961   Adviser on Commonwealth
        and External Affairs to
        Governor-General, West
        Indies
1962   Adviser on Commonwealth
        and External Affairs to
        Governor-General, Trinidad
        and Tobago
1962   Deputy High Commissioner,
        Port of Spain
1964   Deputy High Commissioner,
        Salisbury*
1966   High Commissioner,
        Freetown
1969   Assistant Under-Secretary of
        State, FCO
1972   Ambassador, Havana
1975   High Commissioner, Kenya
1979   Retired
* *Expelled 1966*
  Source: *Daily Telegraph* 23 March 1966

FORMSTONE, Harold B.
1970-1 2nd Secretary (Commercial),
        Moscow; later Department of
        Trade and Industry
        *Barred from re-entry into Soviet
        Union, 1971*
Source: *Sunday Times* 10 October 1971

FREEMANTLE, Anthony Stewart
b. 15/8/35
1954-6 Royal Air Force
1961   Foreign Office
1962   3rd Secretary, Mogadishu
        Foreign Office

1964	Vice-Consul, Basra
1965	Middle East Centre for Arab Studies
1966	2nd Secretary, FCO
1967	1st Secretary, Residual Mission, Salisbury*
1969	FCO
1970	Resigned

* Declared persona non grata, 1969
Source: *Guardian* 29 January 1969

GORDON, John Keith b. 6/7/40

1966	3rd later 2nd Secretary, Foreign Office
1968	Budapest
1970	2nd later 1st Secretary, FCO
1971	On loan to Civil Service College
1973	FCO
	UK Mission to United Nations, Geneva
1975	1st Secretary, Head of Chancery and Consul, Yaounde (also Charge d'Affaires at Libreville and Bangui
1977	FCO
1980	1st Secretary and Cultural Attache, Moscow*

* Expelled August 1981
Source: *Times* (24 August 1981)

GOVE, J. G.

1955-6	1st Secretary and Head of Visa Section, Cairo
1956	Expelled

No further details available
Source: Caroz Y. *Arab Secret Services* (1978) p.25-6

HOLMES, Alan b. 27/2/40

1958	Ministry of Housing and Local Government
1964	Foreign Office
1966	Archivist, Kabul
1968	Clerical Branch Grade 10, Paris
1970	FCO
1971	Administrative Attache, Moscow*
1971	Geneva
1973	FCO
1975	Middle East Centre for Arab Studies
1976	3rd Secretary (Commercial) later 2nd Secretary (Commercial), Tripoli
1980-	2nd Secretary, Jeddah

* Expelled, 1971
Source: Keesings, 1971, column 24887

HONE, Michael Stuart MBE (1978) b. 19/5/36

1951	HM Forces
1961	Commonwealth Relations Office
1962	Kingston (grade 9)
1964	Commonwealth Relations Office
1965	Nairobi
1967	Lisbon
1970	Bridgetown
1972	FCO
1976	Beirut
1978	Vice-Consul, Baghdad*
1979	2nd Secretary, FCO
1980	On loan to the Department of Trade and Industry

* Expelled July 1978
Source: *Times* (28 July 1978)

HUTCHINGS, Ray

1971	Russian Secretariat Member, Moscow
	Debarred from re-Entry into the Soviet Union, has left Diplomatic Service

Source: Keesings 1971 column 24887

JACKSON, Patrick

1970-1	2nd Secretary (Cultural), Moscow

Expelled, 1971
Source: Keesings Contemporary Archives 1971, column 24689
No further information available

LEWIS, Ann Walford b. 2/5/40

1966	FCO
1968	Research Assistant Grade 3
1970	2nd Secretary, Moscow*
1971	FCO
1972	Helsinki
1974	FCO
1974	Principal Research Officer
1979-	On loan to Cabinet Office

* Expelled, 1971
Source: Keesings 1971, column 24887

LONGMIRE, Robert Argent b. 1/10/23

1942-5	HM Forces
1950-2	Moscow
1954	Foreign Office
1958	2nd Secretary, Moscow
1961	Foreign Office
1963	Seconded as Director of Research, South-East Asia Treaty Organisation
1965	Foreign Office

| 1968 | 1st Secretary and Head of Secretariat, Moscow* |
| 1971 | 1st Secretary, FCO Principal Research Officer (Grade 5) |

* *Debarred from entry into the Soviet Union*
  Source: Keesings column 24887 1971

MILLER, David b. 26/3/37
1964	Foreign Office
1966	Moscow
1968	FCO, Research Assistant Grade 3
1971	2nd Secretary, Moscow*
1971	FCO
1972	British Military Government, Berlin
1974	United Kingdom delegation to Conference on Security and Co-operation in Europe (Geneva 1974)
1978-	1st Secretary and Head of Chancery, Belgrade

* *Expelled 1971*
  Source: Keesings 1971 column 24887

MORGAN, Colin b. 7/11/57
1977	FCO
1978	Middle East Centre for Arab Studies
1979	Vice Consul, Tripoli*
1981-	3rd Secretary (Commercial) Jeddah

* *Deported 1980*
  Source: *Daily Telegraph* 3 June 1980

NICHOLSON, Martin Buchanan
b. 12/8/37
1964	Foreign Office
1965	Moscow
1968	Foreign Office Research Assistant Grade 2
1969	Foreign Office Conference Interpreter/Research Officer
1971	1st Secretary and Head of Embassy Secretariat, Moscow*
1971	FCO
1972	1st Secretary, Prague
1975	FCO
1978	1st Secretary to UK delegation, negotiations on Mutual and Balance Force Reductions, Vienna

* *Deported 1971*
  Source: Keesings 1971 column 24689

ROGAN, Peter b. 17/7/34
1954	Board of Trade
1963	Port of Spain
1967	Passport Officer, Dacca
1970	FCO
1973	2nd Secretary, Lagos
1974	Ibadan
1977	1st Secretary (Commercial), Baghdad*
1978	Consul (Commercial), Vancouver
1980-	1st Secretary, FCO

* *Deported 1978*
  Source: *Times* 28 July 1978

ROLLESTON, George Lancelot St Leger
MBE (1969) b. 8/5/39
1958-69	HM Forces
1969	2nd Secretary, FCO
1971	1st Secretary, Baghdad*
1972	Sana'a
1976	FCO
1978	Sana'a
1981-	Jeddah

* *Expelled 1971*
  Source: Keesings Contemporary Archives 1972 column 25041

ROWSELL, Ivor Ninian Henry b. 29/12/15
Pre-1960	Army
1960	Mogadishu
1962	Moscow*
1963	Foreign Office
1967	Blantyre
1970	FCO
1971	Kampala
1974	FCO
1975	Retired at grade 10

Named during Wynne Trial (1963)
* *Recalled July 1963 after unsuccessful KGB blackmail attempt*
  Source: Keesings 1963 column 19489

SPARROW, Dr Bryan b. 8/6/33
1951	Foreign Office
	HM Forces
1953	Foreign Office
1954	Special leave to attend university
1957	Foreign Office
1958	Belgrade
1961	2nd Secretary, Foreign Office
1964	Moscow
1967	Tunis
1968	1st Secretary (Commercial) and Consul, Casablanca

1970   1st Secretary, FCO
1971   Debarred from re-entry into
        Soviet Union*
1972   Kinshasa
1976   Prague
1978   Counsellor (Commercial),
        Belgrade
1981-   Ambassador and Consul-
        General, Yaounde
* Source: Keesings 1971 column 24887

TAIT, Michael Logan MVO (1972)
b. 27/9/36
1961   Foreign Office and Middle East
        Centre for Arab Studies
1963   Bahrein
        Assistant Political Agent,
        Dubai
1966   2nd later 1st Secretary, FCO
1968   Private Secretary to Minister of
        State
1970   1st Secretary, Belgrade
1972   Amman
1975   FCO
1978   Counsellor and Head of
        Chancery, Baghdad*
1978   FCO
1980-   Conference on Security and
        Co-operation in Europe,
        review meeting, Madrid
 *Deported 1978
  Source: *Times* 28 July 1978

WESCOMBE, Peter b. 4/1/32
1947-57 HM Forces
1960   Foreign Office
1964   Beirut
1966   Jakarta
1967   Foreign Office
1969   Singapore
1971   FCO
1976   Attache, Baghdad*
1978   FCO
1979   3rd Secretary, Mogadishu
* *Deported 1978*
  Source: *Times* 28 August 1978

INDEX